INFLATED

Second Edition

INFLATED

Money, Debt, and
the American Dream

Second Edition

R. Christopher Whalen

WILEY

For general information on our other products and services or for technical support, please contact our Customer Care Department within the United States at (800) 762-2974, outside the United States at (317) 572-3993 or fax (317) 572-4002.

Wiley also publishes its books in a variety of electronic formats. Some content that appears in print may not be available in electronic formats. For more information about Wiley products, visit our web site at www.wiley.com.

Library of Congress Cataloging-in-Publication Data is Available:

ISBN 9781394285716 (Cloth)
ISBN 9781394285723 (ePub)
ISBN 9781394285730 (ePDF)

Cover Design: Paul McCarthy
Cover Image: © Getty Images | Ali Majdfar

SKY10100157_031325

I do not think it is an exaggeration to say that it is wholly impossible for a central bank subject to political control, or even exposed to serious political pressure, to regulate the quantity of money in a way conducive to a smoothly functioning market order. A good money, like good law, must operate without regard to the effect that decisions of the issuer will have on known groups or individuals. A benevolent dictator might conceivably disregard these effects; no democratic government dependent on a number of special interests can possibly do so.

—F.A. Hayek
Denationalization of Money
Institute of Economic Affairs (1978)

Contents

Preface

hat is the American dream? The historian and Pulitzer Prize–
winning author of *The Epic of America*, James Truslow Adams,
was the first to define the ideal:

> The American Dream is "that dream of a land in which life
> should be better and richer and fuller for everyone, with oppor-
> tunity for each according to ability or achievement. It is a difficult
> dream for the European upper classes to interpret adequately, and
> too many of us ourselves have grown weary and mistrustful of
> it. It is not a dream of motor cars and high wages merely, but a
> dream of social order in which each man and each woman shall
> be able to attain to the fullest stature of which they are innately
> capable, and be recognized by others for what they are, regardless
> of the fortuitous circumstances of birth or position."[1]

Adams's observation was as much a reflection on the nation's
past as it was asking about its future. He published *Epic of America* in
1931, during the early days of the Great Depression. His world view
was more egalitarian and libertarian than the corporate perspective
that today governs much of American life. Adams expressed hope for a

world that was not merely defined by commercial standards but comprised of a society where individuals were free to pursue their own definitions of liberty and success.

In the twentieth century, the concept of the American dream can be said to trace its roots back to the promise of "Life, Liberty and the pursuit of Happiness," the most famous line in the Declaration of Independence. Simply stated, when immigrants came to this country centuries ago, they expected to be able to achieve a level of personal freedom and material security substantially better than that available in other nations. Today, Americans as well as the thousands of immigrants who come to the United States each year still have that same promise in mind, even if the reality has greatly changed.

A big part of achieving success and security in America is earning money, defined in 1776 as gold coins. In 1776, everything in Western finance that was not money, that is gold, was a form of debt. Yet the national debate over paper versus gold as money was part of the history of America: George Selgin of CATO Institute put the history of gold in perspective:

> There is a tendency to treat U.S. monetary history as divided between a gold standard past and a fiat dollar present. For some the dividing line marks the baleful abandonment of a venerable pillar of sound money; for others it marks the long-overdue de-consecration of an antediluvian relic. In truth, the "money question"—which is to say, the question concerning the proper meaning of a "standard" U.S. dollar—was hotly contested throughout most of U.S. history. Partly for this reason a gold standard that was both official and functioning was in effect only for a period comprising less than a quarter of the full span of the U.S. history, surrounded by longer periods during which the dollar was either a bimetallic (gold or silver) or a fiat unit. A review of the history of the gold standard in the U.S. must therefore consist of an account both of how the standard came into being, despite not having been present at the country's inception, and of how it eventually came to an end.[2]

The role of money in society is important. Americans as a whole view themselves as reasonably prudent and sober people when it comes to matters of money, though the choices we make at the ballot box and in Washington seem to be at odds with that self-image. As a nation we seem to feel entitled to a national agenda and standard of living that is beyond our current means, a tendency that goes back to the earliest days of the United States. In 2024 as this revised edition was prepared, the administration of President Joseph Biden was borrowing 25 percent of federal spending. We pass laws that promise our people "price stability" to protect the value of wages and savings, but pursue policies and practices that require steady inflation of the currency. This book examines this remarkable dichotomy by reviewing our nation's past from a political and financial perspective.

Events such as the Gold Rush of the 1840s, the Civil War, the period before the creation of the Federal Reserve System, Depression and two World Wars, and the appearance of crypto currencies in the twenty-first century, are scrutinized in the context of the changing monetary aspirations of a nation. Whether taming the frontier in the 1800s, fighting the Civil War, or bailing out private banks and corporations in the twenty-first century, successive American governments turned debt and inflation into virtues in order to make ends meet, a choice not unlike that made by other nations of the world. Americans took the tendency to borrow from the future to an extreme and in the process made it a core ethic of our society. In pursuing the American dream today without limitation, we make our tomorrows ever less certain.

The generations of Americans that have come since World War II and the subsequent half century of Cold War believe that we are somehow exempted from the laws of gravity as regards finance and economics. We speak of our "special" role in the global economy even as we repeat the mistakes of Greece, Rome, and the British Empire who ultimately faltered due to currency debasement and inflation.

The same popular delusions about inflation and debt that have affected societies such as Weimar Republic, in Germany or Argentina are also present in America today. Modern Monetary Theory, which essentially says that government can create and spend endlessly, seemed attractive in the 2020s when interest rates touched the zero lower bound. But the first rule of any successful fiat system must be no fiscal deficit. Leverage is already baked into the currency. Layers of leverage, the thesis of *Inflated*, are often dangerous.

By highlighting the work of some of the great researchers of the past two centuries in the context of today's political economy, we tell the unique American story of money and debt from the perspective of an investment banker and financial historian who has worked with banks, mortgage lenders, and financial markets for four decades. And by describing the use of the printing press and credit as enduring features of the American dream, the story of a nation that is just two-and-one-half centuries old, we will hopefully illuminate these matters and thereby encourage a broader national discussion about the future of America and our role in the world economy.

Introduction

I n my experience, books are written after a dedicated and serious person has an "Aha!" moment. I witnessed that moment with Christopher Whalen in 2009 while we were together in a canoe looking for a hungry smallmouth bass. Our guide slowly paddled us down Tomah Stream, a tranquil tributary of the St. Croix River, which defines the border between Canada and the United States known as Down East.

We were fishing together on the private land of the Passamaquoddy Indian Township Reservation in Washington County, Maine, with our longtime guide Ray Sockabasin. Grand Lake Stream has been the destination of Americans seeking to enjoy the outdoors for hundreds of years. Upon passing the Massachusetts bar exam in 1867, Supreme Court Justice Oliver Wendell Holmes set off from Boston with his friend Charles P. Horton for a salmon fishing trip to Grand Lake Stream.

Tomah Stream

All morning, we had been discussing the issues around the monetary and banking history of the United States. Christopher's wealth of knowledge on the subject fueled our debate. This was the time of the Great Financial Crisis of 2007–2009 and its aftermath. It was the time of an extraordinary experiment in American central banking history. Only during World War II had the Federal Reserve maintained such an extended low-interest-rate policy. But in the 1940s, the patriotic Fed assisted the nation in fighting a war by keeping interest rates very low and also stable for years, while wartime inflation reached double digits and the debt/GDP ratio topped 100 percent. This time the culprit was the Great Financial Crisis. Chris and I recalled how it took six postwar years to unwind the wartime policy. The Treasury-Fed Accord was born in 1951 under Chairman Thomas McCabe, and the Fed era of William McChesney Martin commenced soon thereafter.

My fishing friend Christopher is first and foremost a scholar and a historian. We are sympatico in our pursuit of the details within history so that history's lessons may be articulated. As a writer and researcher,

Chris goes after the details with zest, in scrupulous pursuit. We both hope that reciting history may help guide those who contend with policymaking in the present day. That is what this second edition of his original, 15-year-old book is about, but with an added chapter covering the 2008–2024 period.

This second edition is a necessary update. The weaving into a mosaic of all that has happened in 15 years requires building on the first edition of the book. We realized this importance of history as we floated on Tomah Stream and again now since the last decade and a half has added monetary and banking history that has no precedent.

There are many examples to cite, and this book attempts to capture the most important elements. My thought in writing an introduction is to plant a seed for the reader with some recent and some ancient history.

Ask yourself about your own recollections of the Great Financial Crisis. The Lehman moment may come immediately to mind, and then the sequence of interventions involving Citigroup, AIG, and Bear Stearns may be quickly recalled. But does anyone remember that the first primary dealer to fail and be merged was Countrywide? The system of primary dealers created by the Fed after World War II was decimated by the Great Financial Crisis.

Does anyone think about the fact that all votes by the Board of Governors of the Federal Reserve were 5-0 when the Fed invoked its power for emergency actions? Does anyone contemplate that the reason they were five to zero is that the law at the time required five votes, not four, to use that emergency interventionist authority?

Does anyone recall that there were two vacancies on the board during the entire Great Financial Crisis (GFC) because of politics, as the two political parties took turns holding up each other's appointments to the central bank board of the United States?

In some ways it seems like nothing in the political spectrum has changed. I can only imagine the confidential conversations when one of the five said to Chairman Bernanke, "I cannot vote with you, Ben; it will be giving away too much." Oh, to have been a fly on that wall!

In March 2023 we had three bank failures in a row, starting with Silicon Valley Bank (SVB). The three banks combined totaled more than Washington Mutual, which previously held the record for failure size. There was no Lehman moment. There was no contagion to melt down the entire banking system. There was no Depression-era plummeting of the economy following the SVB event. Were lessons learned from the Great Financial Crisis? And are there more lessons to be observed in the future?

The most intense discussion involves debt, federal and other. Most market agents focus on the federal debt and how it has grown in relation to GDP. Let's look at the total debt of all types. Christopher is interested in the addiction to debt usage and the distortions from that debt. The ratio of total debt to GDP peaked in 2008 during the GFC. It has fallen slightly since, but can the U.S. economy outrun the debt?

Those are the 15 years that included the GFC and post-GFC recovery, an inflation flare, a 3–4-year Covid shock, zero interest rates, and many special Fed programs designed to avoid a banking system meltdown or contagion. And then there was the Fed's abrupt policy change to raising interest rates. There were large Trump deficits. They were followed by large Biden deficits. And the 2024 election year rounds out the list of challenges with the return of President Trump for a second term. That political influence really started in 2023. It included a debt-ceiling threat of default, no federal budget mechanism, and a series of political failures with short-term and temporary continuing budget resolutions.

If we dig deeper, we see that the composition of the total debt has changed. Debt burden issues have improved for households. Corporate debt has been manageable. Even mortgage debt, while pressured by the Fed's balance sheet shrinkage of mortgage-backed securities, is in better shape than it was during the GFC period. So, the increase in the federal debt to GDP ratio is essentially offset by the decrease in the nonfederal debt-to-GDP ratio. The total ratio remains about the same.

If total debt to GDP is unchanged or slightly lower, and it's the shift in composition that is the concern, then financial-market impacts should be observable if we look for them. Sure enough, they are there. The cost of credit insurance on the federal debt is rising. We can measure this by examining the market-based pricing of credit default swaps (CDS) on U.S. government debt. Meanwhile, corporate credit spreads have been narrowing.

So, is the federal debt load crowding out the private sector? This is much harder to observe. We may discuss it as a concept, but we have difficulty finding measures to estimate whether it is and by how much. Crowding out? Maybe, maybe not.

When Christopher wrote the first edition, Bitcoin was an unknown. The tokens existed, but in obscurity. Now crypto is a multi-trillion-dollar asset class. Some folks believe it's money. Others say it will replace reserves. Still others claim the U.S. dollar and all fiat currencies are doomed. These are strong words. Christopher captures two centuries of American history to guide us on our crypto learning curve, but reminds us that the paper money created by Abraham Lincoln to finance the Civil War was the first crypto currency.

Here, let me reach back to a much earlier time to augment our learning.

Consider the first coin, minted about 2,600 years ago by the Lydians. It was in gold, and thus began the use of state-issued money and the hegemony of rich King Croesus—history shows us that money is power. Croesus eventually fell to the Persians, and the Persians lost to the Greeks—they had silver mines. The drachma replaced other coinages and developed into the world's reserve currency of that era. The Greeks never debased their coin, even during the Peloponnesian War. And the Athenian "owl" was accepted throughout the Mediterranean long after regional hegemony began transferring from Greece to Rome. Those few city–states that did debase money ended as losers. So did Rome after the "Golden Age," when the debasing of currency was serially repeated. And we know what happened to Rome when it started to decline.

Are there lessons for today? Christopher Whalen warns us about them, but reminds us that repeating past mistakes is human nature. That is what makes this book in its second edition form so timely. Chris's and my time fishing on Tomah Stream was years ago and before Covid. Recently, as we were wrapping up a discussion about the world of money and banking and central banking today, I said, "Chris, you must write the second edition of your book."

And here it is. Aha!

David Kotok
November 2024

Chapter 1

Free Banking and Private Money

I n his December 1776 pamphlet *The Crisis*, Thomas Paine famously said, "These are the times that try men's souls." He then proceeded to lay out a detailed assessment of America's military challenges in fighting the British. But after the fighting was over, America faced the task of creating a new, independent state separate from British trade and especially independent from the banks of the City of London. The story of creating new money and debt in early America is the chronicle of how a fragment of the British empire broke off in the late 1700s and supplanted and surpassed Great Britain in economic terms by the end of World War II. Britain for centuries was the dominant economic system in the world, yet in just 250 years America grew to lead the global economy.

The English pound was not the first great global currency, nor will the dollar likely be the last. Mankind has been through cycles of inflation and deflation more than once, going back to before Greek and Roman times. The story of money in each society is a description of the ebb and flow of these states in economic as well as political terms. The latest version of this repeating narrative features a still very young country called America, which used money and the promise of it to build a global economic empire based upon the dollar.

When the 13 colonies reluctantly declared independence from Great Britain in 1776, the young nation had no independent banking system and no common currency, although most colonists knew the political and financial traditions of Europe. The Articles of Confederation adopted in 1777 did not even give the central government the ability to levy taxes to retire war debt. European banks and governments met America's capital needs via loans and gold coins. Pawnbrokers were the predominant source of credit for individuals, and businesses obtained commercial credit from banks, mostly foreign. Foreign coins and some colonial paper money were in circulation, yet barter was the most common means of payment used by Americans from the start of the nation's existence through the Civil War.[1]

Sidney Homer and Richard Sylla wrote in the classic work *A History of Interest Rates*:

The American colonies were outposts of an old civilization. Their physical environment was primitive, but their political and financial traditions were not. Therefore, the history of colonial credit and interest rates is not a history of innovation but rather a history of adaptation.[2]

One early adaptation of the states was to issue paper debt to pay bills. Going back to the revolution and the inception of the republic, America's leaders have always been reluctant to raise taxes. After the adoption of the Articles of Confederation, tax collection was loosely enforced and the increase in paper currency drove inflation higher in the last decades of the 1700s. Issuing IOUs was easier than collecting taxes, although the tax was paid via currency inflation.

Upon winning independence, the colonies formed states and issued colonial currency. Bonds were issued, when possible, with individuals and even the government of France subscribing in the earliest days of the young nation. The Bank of North America was established in Philadelphia by the Continental Congress in 1782 and became the first chartered bank in the United States. Creating a new bank under the control of the American government was an effort to gain some independence from private banks and also foreign nations.

David McCullough's Pulitzer Prize–winning biography *John Adams* presents several scenes where the ambassador of the new American government goes literally hat in hand to the capitals of Europe seeking foreign currency loans. The tireless Adams was able to secure huge sums that sustained the colonial war effort. But as Adams knew too well, his family and other Americans suffered horribly due to inflation and privation in those early years.

"Rampant inflation, shortages of nearly every necessity made the day-to-day struggle at home increasingly difficult," McCullough relates. "'A dollar was not worth what a quarter had been,' Abigail [Adams] reported. 'Our money will soon be as useless as blank paper.'"[3] This need was acute since the U.S. government lacked the power to tax or the means to collect it. Nor would the American people tolerate higher taxes, because of the unhappy experience with Britain. The leaders of the American revolution led a political revolt against unfair taxation; thus they were not in a position to then raise taxes.

Adams was no apologist for debt, but he believed that having a national debt was a good thing because it created relationships with other nations that helped the nation survive and grow. In his correspondence with Thomas Jefferson, Adams showed the sharp contrast between on the one hand wanting to create a constituency among financial powers for America's national debt while on the other hand expressing his opposition to having private bankers and banks.

The Mississippi Bubble, a financial scheme in eighteenth-century France that led to a speculative frenzy and market collapse, lent a new meaning to the term "bubble." The term denoted deception. Speculators were known as "bubblers" and to be cheated was to get bubbled, Harold James reveals in *Seven Crashes: The Economic Crises That Shaped Globalization*.[4]

Owing somewhat to the shortcomings of banks and bankers, Adams advocated creating a single, publicly owned national bank to serve the needs of the country, with branches in the individual states. He wanted to prohibit the states from chartering banks and to have one single, national institution. Ron Chernow wrote in his 2004 biography *Alexander Hamilton* that Adams viewed banking "as a confidence trick by which the rich exploited the poor." He quoted Adams similarly saying that "every bank in America is an enormous tax upon the people for the profit of individuals."

Adams wanted one state bank with branches around the nation, but no private banks at all.[5] He differed significantly from Alexander Hamilton on these issues, even though like Hamilton, Adams was interested in strengthening the country's finances. Hamilton, a New York lawyer who became the first Treasury secretary and a future leader of the United States, was a great advocate of private banks and debt. He believed that finance was the key both to political power and economic growth. Author Joe Costello summed up Hamilton's significance:

Hamilton understood the control of money as a fundamental component of the rule of the modern state. At the time or now for that matter, he was one of a very few to understand the role debt played as the foundation of modern money. As the first Secretary of the Treasury, in a report to President Washington, Hamilton astutely noted "government debt had a 'capacity for prompt convertibility' to currency, potentially rendering transfers 'equivalent to a payment in coin.'" In part, the constitution was established to make good the debt incurred during the revolution. Just as importantly, Hamilton understood the new federal government incurring greater debt would help unite and develop the infant nation.[6]

The charter of the Bank of North America lapsed in 1790 and two years later, the State of New York chartered The Bank of New York, which is the corporate predecessor of the company now known as Bank of New York/Mellon. Supported by New York's powerful merchants, the bank was first organized in 1784 and was led by Hamilton.

So important was the Bank of New York to the local economy that much of the region's commercial activity was financed by this single institution for decades even as other institutions were chartered. The formation of the bank was not just a financial event, but a very significant political milestone as well that greatly elevated the power of New York.[7] There was no real money nor any payment system in existence for the country. Commerce had been financed by English and other foreign banks up until the Revolutionary War. Now the United States had to create a new financial system to replace these trade relationships, a process that would take more than a century.

The demise of the Bank of North America at the end of the 1700s came as a political battle raged over whether the federal government should assume the debts incurred by the states and cities during the war against Britain. The final agreement from southerners to support the assumption of state debts was tied to the compromise over moving the location of the capital city from New York to Philadelphia temporarily and eventually to an entirely new capital on the Potomac River to be called Washington. But this Compromise of 1790 engineered by Jefferson and Hamilton did not deal with the issue of a national bank.

The Bank of the United States

President George Washington chartered the First Bank of the United States in 1791. This was the government's attempt at creating a permanent central bank of issue for the infant nation. Madison and Jefferson opposed the bank, but Adams ironically led a sizable majority in the Congress that favored the measure.

The First Bank of the United States had just a 20-year charter. While it was a bold and novel innovation, the bank only provided credit to established merchants. During the presidency of Thomas Jefferson, the agrarian and other interests not served by the Bank successfully pushed for the establishment of state-chartered institutions to serve the need for credit of a very rapidly growing nation. State-chartered banks also created alternative sources of political power in the states. Yet the First Bank's charter was not renewed due to intense attacks by the advocates of Jeffersonian cheap money principles. Taking the lesson of King George III and his taxes, local interests rightly feared that a "central bank" would be dominated by the central government. Even or, worse, it could be dominated by the bankers and merchants in Philadelphia, New York, and New England.[8]

In 1811, the First Bank of the United States was resurrected as a private entity by the New York merchants who controlled it and chartered anew by the State of New York. Today the successor to that corporation is known as Citibank N.A., the lead bank unit of Citigroup Inc. Now two of the largest banks in the new nation were located in New York. This point was not lost on representatives of the other states in the union and especially the Jeffersonian faction in the Congress, who represented agrarian interests dependent upon New York banks for trade credit.

The decision not to renew the First Bank of the United States left the country to fight the War of 1812 against Britain with no means to finance the military struggle, much less the general operations of the federal government. Then Treasury Secretary Albert Gallatin, who was no advocate of public debt, made careful plans to borrow up to $20 million via the First Bank to finance the war. Instead, Gallatin was forced to seek loans from abroad after the First Bank was dissolved.

Along with Hamilton, Gallatin was one of America's first great financial geniuses, and a talented bond salesman as well. He is memorialized in a large statue by James Earle Fraser that stands in front of the Treasury building in Washington. Gallatin founded New York University and also served as commissioner for the Treaty of Ghent, as well as minister to both France and Great Britain. Because America's position with the nations of Europe was that of debtor and former colonial possession, Gallatin's financial expertise was invaluable. His role recalled the invocation of Hamilton and also of Adams of the virtue of increasing the number of nations willing to hold the American government's debt.

As the nation reeled from the financial disaster of the War of 1812, a heated debate continued in the Congress regarding the need for a common currency and a new central bank. Notes issued by New York banks, for example, could not be used at face value to settle debts in other states. The scarcity of adequate medium of exchange that had existed since colonial times often made it difficult for creditors to secure payment from customers, even if the customer wished to pay!

By 1814, the federal government itself was unable to pay its bills and was on the brink of financial collapse. Treasury Secretary Alexander Dallas (1814–1816) was forced to suspend payments on the national debt in New England due to a lack of hard currency. By law, all Treasury debts had to be paid in gold or silver. Following the capture of Washington by the British in that year and the default on the national debt, the United States was on the verge of financial and political dissolution.[9]

The creation of the Second Bank of the United States was the American government's next attempt at establishing a central bank, an effort that came only after significant political debate and negotiation.

Many Republicans fought the resurrection of the Bank of the United States, fearing that its size and ability to do business across state lines would give it unchecked political power. There was also a strong suspicion by representatives of southern states that the Second Bank would be controlled by New York business and financial interests. But after the destruction of the Federalist Party following the War of 1812, the Republican majority in the Congress eventually chartered the Second Bank of the United States, albeit with very limited powers.

The first time the measure to create the Second Bank came up before the Senate in February 1811, it was defeated by the tiebreaking vote of Vice President George Clinton of New York, who cast the deciding vote in his role as presiding officer of the Senate. He justified his action because the "tendency to consolidation" reflected by the proposal for a national bank seemed "a just and serious cause for alarm."[10] The subsequent proposal to charter the Second Bank was not passed by the Congress until 1815, but was vetoed by President James Madison. A year later, the bill passed and President Madison signed it into a law.

The late Senator Robert Byrd, the West Virginia Democrat who was one of the longest serving members of the body, wrote in his 1991 history of the Senate that the early debates regarding a central bank "were far from over and would surface again within the coming decades to alter significantly American political history." Byrd also noted that coincident with the authorization for the Second Bank, the Congress for the first time dared to provide themselves with an annual salary. Previously, members of the Congress had been paid $6 per day or about $900 per year. Wartime inflation had greatly reduced the purchasing power of this per diem compensation, so the Congress voted itself a $1,500 per year annual salary. The decision was a political disaster and led to the defeat of two-thirds of the members of the House in the following election.[11]

Many Republicans who supported the Second Bank considered themselves heirs to the libertarian legacy of Thomas Jefferson. When they finally supported the proposal, however, they followed the plan of Alexander Hamilton of New York and other supporters of a strong central government. These same Republicans, who effectively held a one-party lock on the Congress during that time, opposed funding for interstate roads, canals, and even railroads to help the economy. Yet the fact was that the United States was changing as fast as it was growing and, with that change, lost many of its libertarian attributes. Susan Dunn, professor of humanities at Williams College, wrote:

> Jefferson and Madison's Republican Party championed the enterprising middling people who lived by manual labor. But the year before he died, Jefferson felt lost in a nation that seemed overrun by business, banking, religious revivalism, "monkish ignorance," and anti-intellectualism . . . The Founders' revolutionary words about equality, life, liberty, and the pursuit of happiness, along with their bold actions, had unleashed a democratic tide—one so strong that within a few decades many of them found themselves disillusioned strangers living in an egalitarian, commercial society, a society they had unwittingly inspired but not anticipated.[12]

After the creation of the Second Bank of the United States, the American economy grew rapidly and more private banks were created. The largely powerless federal government offered virtually no support to this growth. The Congress preferred to leave this task instead to the cities and states, which, naturally enough, turned to borrowing rather than taxation to finance economic expansion. By 1840, the total debt of the states amounted to some $200 million, a vast sum by contemporary standards given that total U.S. gross domestic product, or GDP, was just $1.5 billion. Much of this debt was issued by banks chartered by the states and was held by foreigners.[13]

Though the Founders made provision under the Commerce Clause of the Constitution for trade between the states free of tariff, there was no provision for a common currency or banking system to tie together the nation or even the individual states. A similar problem is evident today in the European Union, which has a common currency, the euro, but no real economic integration or unified banking system. State-chartered banks issued various forms of notes to the public in return for some future promise to pay in hard money—that is, gold or silver. The major difference between the private money of the

1700s and modern crypto tokens is that the former promised payment in a tangible asset—gold. The latter explicitly promises nothing save a speculative flutter on price appreciation.

In America before the Civil War, there was no common means of exchange nor any backstop for banks, which from time to time needed emergency infusions of funds. Panics occurred when public unease about particular financial institutions caused deposit runs that could grow into a general financial crisis affecting regions or even the entire country. Crises of just this sort would become the hallmark of the U.S. economy for the next century.

In 1809, for instance, the Farmer's Exchange Bank in Gloucester, Rhode Island, failed—one of the first significant bank failures in the United States. There was no Federal Deposit Insurance Corporation to organize the orderly liquidation of the bank. This task fell to state and local authorities. The demise of the Farmer's Exchange Bank illustrated the types of financial failures and bank panics that troubled the United States for decades to come.

Financial-pioneer-turned-confidence-man Andrew Dexter, Jr., writes Jane Kamensky, "challenged the notions of his Puritan ancestors by embarking on a wild career in real estate speculation, all financed by the string of banks he commandeered and the millions of dollars they freely printed. Upon this paper pyramid he built the tallest building in the United States, the Exchange Coffee House, a seven-story colossus in downtown Boston. But in early 1809, just as the exchange was ready for unveiling, the scheme collapsed. In Boston, the exchange stood as an opulent but largely vacant building, a symbol of monumental ambition and failure."[14]

A democratic society and a free market economy cannot exist without both great aspiration and equally great defeat. However, in the American experience, financial fraud and the tendency of politicians to use debt and paper money, rather than taxes raised with the active knowledge and consent of the voters, are common elements from colonial times right through to the present day. The collective failure of the Subprime Debt Crisis of 2008 is a larger reprise of the types of mini crises that occurred in the United States centuries before this period, calamities that were limited by the relatively primitive state of communication and transportation.

State Debt Defaults

By the mid-1830s, the United States was in the midst of an economic boom characterized by inflation and growing speculation in public land sales. Many of the projects for roads or canals were badly needed but were often poorly conceived. American states employed borrowing to finance needed improvements in order to avoid increasing taxes, and even used sales of public land to reduce debt.

States along the Atlantic coast, where the economy was more developed and other sources of revenue such as tariffs were available, generally avoided costly property taxes, while less developed inland states could not sustain their governments with low property taxes and ran into financial trouble. The low or no property tax regimes in many western states are a legacy from the colonial period. This unequal development became even more acute because the areas needing investment and growing rapidly were precisely the western states and territories that were starved for cash, not so much for investment but simply as a means of exchange.[15]

In some western states, the need for money was met in a primitive way by discovering and extracting gold and silver from the ground to be minted into coins. During the 1830s, speculation in land also flourished, with state-chartered banks providing the financing to fuel the rising land values. This investment bubble had the effect of making the states look fiscally sound because of rising land prices. Some inland states even suspended property taxes due to supposed "profits" on bank shares. But the illusion of wealth and public revenue faded with the Crisis of 1837, the fourth and most stunning depression in the United States up to that time and the first financial crisis that was truly national in scope.[16]

Between 1841 and 1842, Florida, Mississippi, Arkansas, Michigan, Indiana, Illinois, Maryland, Pennsylvania, and Louisiana ran into serious fiscal problems and defaulted on interest payments. The first four states ultimately repudiated $13 million in debts, while others delayed and rescheduled their debts, in some cases years later. Alabama, Ohio, New York, and Tennessee narrowly avoided default during this period.[17] Because many states used state-chartered banks as vehicles for borrowing, the public naturally became alarmed when the states ran into financial problems.

In the early 1800s, paper money issued by private, state-chartered banks generally traded at a steep discount to the face value when converted into precious metal. This was especially true for banks outside of the state or local market where it was presented for payment. The notes used at that time generally promised to pay the bearer of the note a certain amount of physical gold or silver upon demand. The experience of banks failing to honor that promise was all too common for Americans in that period. Mark Twain described the experience of Roxy in *The Tragedy of Pudd'nhead Wilson*: "The bank had gone to smash and carried her four hundred dollars with it."

The skepticism about state-chartered banks was one reason that payments by and to state and federal agencies were done only in metal coins, not paper. Most contracts of the day likewise specified metal as consideration. In the early 1800s there was no telephone, no internet or even telegraph, and no local clearinghouse for banks to validate the authenticity of paper money. People in America and around the world preferred the security and certainty of gold and silver coins to paper money, even when the banks issuing the paper were backed by sovereign states.

The negative view of paper money was part of a broader suspicion of bankers and the economically powerful that flowed through most of American society. Fleeing the religious and economic oppression of European society, Americans came to the New World for a fresh start and also an opportunity to live free of the stratified economic system of Europe. Even in the eighteenth-century opportunities for advancement were few. Having money that was independent of political authority granted individuals a level of financial freedom that was a key part of the American ideal.

When the states began to falter financially, however, the cohesion of the entire nation was threatened. Americans still identified themselves with a home state or town rather than as citizens of the United States. The political fact of union among the states had still not quite been settled because of the issue of slavery, but the overall fragility of the state-run financial system contributed to the mounting political pressures on the nation.

As many states fell into default on their obligations during the 1840s, repudiation of debt by state-chartered banks was hotly debated. In Arkansas, for example, Governor Archibald Yell explicitly urged debt repudiation in his 1842 message to the state legislature, which created various state-chartered banks as vehicles for funding state expenditures via borrowing. As a result of the debt defaults and political uproar that followed, Arkansas adopted a constitutional amendment in 1846 to liquidate all state-chartered banks and prohibit the creation of any new banks in that state.[18]

In Pennsylvania, starting in the mid-1830s the Commonwealth chartered the United States Bank of Pennsylvania to cover fiscal short-falls with debt. By 1839, the bank defaulted on its obligations several times. In a troubling presage to America's fiscal deficit in the 2020s, the response from the state legislature was to authorize more borrow-ing. The present-day problems of federal deficits are not a new phe-nomenon. In fact, Pennsylvania delayed making any meaningful fiscal reforms until the mid-1840s, by which time it was in default on its obligations.

In payment on the Commonwealth's $40 million in debt, its citizens were forced to take scrip bearing 6 percent interest because the state was broke.[19] Pennsylvania began to issue its own currency when it could not borrow or would not tax in sufficient amounts, a phe-nomenon that has reappeared in the United States in the twenty-first century. As the states, most notably California, New York, and Illinois, struggled under mountains of debt, unfunded pension obligations, and other expenses, issuing scrip again become a popular alternative to tax increases.

In the years before the Civil War, American states carried a well-deserved reputation in Europe for not repaying loans, although the U.S. government managed to service the federal debt in good order. From $75 million in debt in 1791 to a peak of $100 million after the War of 1812, the Treasury paid down the federal debt to a mere $63 million in 1849. The U.S. government only paid down its debt once in the 1830s and then only by the accident of having Andrew Jackson as president. In general, fiscal restraint at the federal level was the rule in the first century of the nation's existence. Since the federal government was not really involved in financing the economic growth of the nation, the remarkable stability of the federal debt contrasts with the spendthrift behavior of the states, counties and cities.

Figure 1.1 shows the total federal debt of the United States from 1791 through 1849.

States such as Louisiana defaulted on loans, evaded debts, and delayed settlement with creditors until the twentieth century. Many foreign investors had believed, incorrectly, that the success of New York and other Atlantic states in building profitable canals and other commercial infrastructure would be repeated in the western and southern states and territories. But in fact, looking at both the federal and state debts before the Civil War, the United States was a heavily indebted, rapidly developing country with neither organized financial markets nor even a common currency, and with a dysfunctional central government.

When the overheated economy and related financial crisis first started to boil over, many European banks refused to lend further to the U.S. government or the various states, putting intense pressure on the small nation's liquidity and political unity. In states such as Michigan and Indiana, the number of banks dwindled as first private institutions and eventually the state-chartered banks were wound

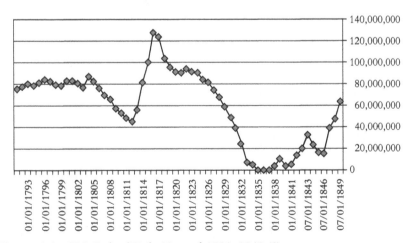

Figure 1.1   U.S. Federal Debt/Annual 1791–1849 ($).
SOURCE: U.S. Treasury.

up and closed. Willis Dunbar and George May noted in *Michigan: A History of the Wolverine State*:

> The speculation in Michigan land values of the early thirties, for example, was fantastic. The enormous note issues of the banks were obviously out of proportion to their resources. And the internal improvement programs adopted by the states were far beyond their ability to finance. The nation was importing, primarily from Great Britain, much more than it was exporting, and piling up a steadily mounting debt to British exporters and manufacturers. A day of reckoning was inevitable.[20]

The failure to make progress on the more basic issue of a national currency made the situation in the American financial markets inherently unstable. This structural deficiency, combined with the political ascendancy of Andrew Jackson and the proponents of the Jeffersonian, anti-Federalist view of banks and currency, set the stage for not merely a crisis at the end of the 1830s, but for a catastrophe. When the disaster finally occurred, it was one of the worst economic and financial meltdowns seen in Western society up to that time.

The Age of Andrew Jackson

Much of the economic instability experienced by the country in the late 1830s owed itself to one factor: the rise a decade before of Andrew Jackson. The arrival in Washington of this Indian fighter and hero of the War of 1812, known as "Old Hickory," signaled the end of the political dominance of Virginia in American politics. Jackson lost his first bid for the presidency to John Quincy Adams of Massachusetts in the election of 1824, even though the Tennessee native won a larger proportion of the popular vote and also the plurality of votes in the Electoral College. But Jackson still lost the election.

Senator Henry Clay, a Whig from Kentucky and long-time enemy of Jackson, threw his support to Adams when the election went to the U.S. House of Representatives. Henry Clay's dirty political deal ensured the election of Adams but also made the election of Jackson in

1828 certain. Clay was appointed secretary of state by President Adams as the quid pro quo for his support in the House. Although Clay sought the presidency on four occasions, he repeatedly underestimated the popular support for Jackson, the man who defeated the British at New Orleans in spectacular fashion—albeit several weeks after the United States and Britain agreed to peace. News traveled slowly in those days.

Jackson's succession to the presidency in 1828 followed an unremarkable political career, but was notable as the first time that a southerner swept into power in Washington on a wave of popular support. Jackson was the first modern chief executive because his victory marked the earliest instance where an American president was chosen by the popular vote rather than by the nation's Founders and their descendants.

The 1828 presidential campaign was a vicious affair, as might be expected when an established order is ended. Jackson was opposed by most of the nation's newspapers, bankers, businessmen, and manufacturers, especially in the Northeast, but still won 56 percent of the popular vote in 1828. Comparisons between President Jackson and Donald Trump's surprise victory over Hillary Clinton in the 2016 race and the defeat of Kamala Harris in 2024 are not unreasonable. Thus began the Jacksonian Age.[21]

Andrew Jackson's presidency was in political terms one of the most difficult in American history. Northern and southern interests competed with new western states for political advantage, even to the point of secession from the Union. Against this contentious political backdrop, Jackson and Congress fought bitterly over many issues, but none of more consequence for the economy and the U.S. financial system than the renewal of the Second Bank of the United States.

With its charter set to expire in 1836, Jackson proposed that a new government bank be set up as an arm of the Treasury. The Whigs led by Henry Clay decided to reauthorize the Second Bank early and were able to get the measure passed by both houses of Congress during the summer of 1832, but the legislation was vetoed by President Jackson on July 10, 1832.

President Jackson's objections to the Second Bank is one of the great libertarian statements against big government and the power of private interests in American history. It also predicted many of the problems caused by the creation of the Federal Reserve System 80 years later. The final paragraph of the Jackson veto message reads:

> Experience should teach us wisdom. Most of the difficulties our Government now encounters and most of the dangers which impend over our Union have sprung from an abandonment of the legitimate objects of Government by our national legislation, and the adoption of such principles as are embodied in this act. Many of our rich men have not been content with equal protection and equal benefits, but have besought us to make them richer by act of Congress. By attempting to gratify their desires we have in the results of our legislation arrayed section against section, interest against interest, and man against man, in a fearful commotion which threatens to shake the foundations of our Union. It is time to pause in our career to review our principles, and if possible, revive that devoted patriotism and spirit of compromise which distinguished the sages of the Revolution and the fathers of our Union. If we cannot at once, in justice to interests vested under improvident legislation, make our Government what it ought to be, we can at least take a stand against all new grants of monopolies and exclusive privileges, against any prostitution of our Government to the advancement of the few at the expense of the many, and in favor of compromise and gradual reform in our code of laws and system of political economy.[22]

Jackson objected to the bank as being unconstitutional, aristocratic, and, most important, because it failed to establish a sound and uniform national currency. Even then, the supporters of a central bank were numerous and outspoken. Ralph C.H. Catterall, the great historian of the Second Bank, said of Jackson's veto:

> Jackson and his supporters committed an offense against the nation when they destroyed the bank. The magnitude and enormity of that offense can only be faintly realized, but one is certainly justified in saying that few greater enormities are chargeable to politicians than the destruction of the Bank of the United States.[23]

But Claude G. Bowers, a historian sympathetic to Jackson, defended his action and alluded to many of the problems with the Federal Reserve a century later:

Even among the ultra-conservatives of business, the feeling was germinating that Jackson was not far wrong in the conclusion that a moneyed institution possessing the power to precipitate panics to influence governmental action, was dangerous to the peace, prosperity, and liberty of the people.[24]

The debate over the bank and the nature of money played a significant role in the 1832 landslide reelection victory of Jackson against the party formerly known as the Whigs, and later called the National Republican Party under Henry Clay. The Senate censured Jackson for his efforts to remove government funds on deposit with the Second Bank, yet Jackson was adamant that the bank had to go. He was willing to let his political fate be governed by that one issue. In September 1831, President Jackson told Treasury Secretary Louis McLane that he did not intend to pull down the bank merely to set up a new one.[25]

Despite Jackson's strong view on the matter, he could not disregard many voices, even in his own cabinet, who supported renewing the charter of the Second Bank. Jackson remained strong in his conviction that the central bank was a monster that was unconstitutional and concentrated power "in the hands of so few persons irresponsible to the electorate," wrote Marquis James. The great biographer of Jackson continued: "Nor was this all. With deep and moving conviction, the Jacksonian message gave expression to a social philosophy calculated to achieve a better way of life for the common man."[26]

Personal political battles contributed to the economic problems of the nation. For example, Nicholas Biddle, the head of the Second Bank and a foe of Jackson, fought the president to the last. When Jackson gave notice that the Treasury would no longer deposit its cash in the Second Bank, Biddle started to withdraw funds deposited with state banks around the country in an effort to discredit Jackson. Biddle presented notes drawn upon state banks and demanded payment in gold, a move that had the effect of draining liquidity from those communities and generating enormous anger at Biddle and the Treasury. Great antagonism was generated by Biddle's attempt to hurt the U.S. economy and wound President Jackson politically. Almost a century later, when the U.S. Congress debated the creation of the Federal Reserve System, the state bankers still referred to the actions of Nicholas Biddle and the Second Bank as a reason for opposing the legislation.

Both Clay and Biddle miscalculated badly. Jackson won reelection in 1832 with 76 percent of the vote, the largest margin since George Washington and James Madison. The pro-Jackson forces likewise prevailed in the midterm contest—even as Biddle did his best to "bring the country to its knees and with it, Andrew Jackson."[27] The political battle over the Second Bank distracted the country at a very crucial juncture. The United States went nearly three-quarters of a century without a central bank of issue for its currency until Congress established the Federal Reserve in 1913. The immediate impact, however, was the most severe economic crisis the nation had seen since its beginnings.

The Second Bank closed its doors in March 1836, leaving the United States without a common currency. What credit the bank had provided to the economy was withdrawn. Only the state-chartered banks were available to support the economy. But as with most public issues, the national Congress was largely indifferent to the needs of the nation, preferring instead to defend regional and states' rights from threats, real and imagined.

The defeat of the Second Bank of the United States was not the end of Jackson's reactionary agenda. He refused to allow the resources of the federal government to be used for financing the construction of roads and canals, and instead retired the national debt and distributed the surplus accumulated in the Treasury. By attacking the Second Bank and at the same time pursuing a very conservative fiscal policy, Jackson created the circumstances for the Great Panic of 1837.

Since there was no central bank, the withdrawal of public debt by the Treasury amounted to a deflationary reduction in the nation's money supply. In addition, the retirement of the federal government's debt encouraged states and their banks to issue paper currency in large amounts, which fueled land purchases and speculation. Coming in the midst of a growing speculative bubble based on land purchases, the Jacksonian fiscal measures helped to reduce liquidity in banks and worsen the lack of credit in an already cash-strapped society. Yet even with what amounted to a tight money policy from Washington over eight years of Jackson's presidency, the speculation that gripped the nation during the early part of the 1830s was just coming to a boil when Jackson left office.

As one of his last official acts, Jackson issued the Specie Circular, another hard money and antidebt initiative, which required that purchases of government land be paid for in coin or specie rather than bank paper. By requiring that payments for taxes, duties, and/or the purchase of federal land be made in gold coins, the Treasury was in practical terms draining reserves from the banking system and causing it to shrink. This compounded the fact that the Second Bank of the United States under Biddle had been calling in its loans. This third fiscal action by Jackson, following the closure of the Second Bank and the retirement of the government's debt, was implemented by his successor, President Martin Van Buren, and further exacerbated the liquidity crisis in the United States.

By the middle of 1837, unemployment was widespread and thousands of companies and banks had failed as the national money supply contracted. This economic recession was due in part to events in Washington and, more important, to a growing antipathy toward banks and paper money among the public. Bad paper money was literally shunned by the mass population, and the issuance of bonds likewise dried up. By the start of the 1840s, only official U.S.-minted coins and other types of specie were in broad circulation. Americans avoided privately issued paper notes and other forms of debt.[28] Most Americans in the 1840s lived with no access to cash or credit, except as provided by commercial exchanges with other people.

The Panic of 1837

As Jackson traveled home to Nashville in the spring of 1837, he observed that bank notes were trading at a steep discount to their face value and farmers were paying 30 percent for credit—all the results of his earlier executive orders. Some bankers, traders, and particularly land speculators clamored for President Van Buren to "strike down the iniquitous Specie Circular" requiring that hard money be used in the purchase of federal land or payment of federal taxes. But Jackson wrote to Van Buren:

My dear sir, the Treasury order is popular with the people everywhere I have passed. But all the speculators, and those largely indebted, want more paper. The more it depreciates the easier they can pay their debts . . . Check the paper mania and the republic is safe and your administration must end in triumph.[29]

Unfortunately for President Van Buren, Jackson's devotion to hard money was at odds with the needs of a growing nation. With the drain of currency caused by Jackson's Treasury order, and the resultant increased stress on the economy, a lack of confidence in the state banks grew. The resulting financial crisis in 1837 caused many bank failures over a period of several years. This panic was followed by a sharp economic contraction around the world that would last until 1841. To no surprise, President Van Buren was defeated in the next general election.

One of the more significant and mischievous contributions that President Van Buren made to the country's financial development was the creation of an independent Department of the Treasury. In 1837, in a special message to Congress, President Van Buren proposed that the finances of the federal government be formally "divorced" from those of the state-chartered banks. This proposal caused considerable political controversy. The Congress passed The Independent Treasury Act of 1840 and then repealed it in 1841. In 1846 Congress adopted the same proposal again. The official goal of the legislation was to ensure the independence of the banks in the country and also to support the value of the currency. Neither of these goals were met.

In practical terms, the Treasury became a "bank of issue" and a *de facto* central bank, refusing to accept notes issued by private banks and issuing its own notes in competition with the state banks. The creation of the Independent Treasury drained reserves from the banking system and effectively reduced the supply of money available to Americans for commerce. By segregating the gold reserves of the government in the Treasury's own vaults and not keeping these funds on deposit with private banks, the Independent Treasury served to exacerbate the structural deficiencies in the U.S. economy for decades afterward. In the years up through the Civil War and thereafter, the fiscal operations of the Treasury were an important and, indeed, the dominant factor in the ebb and flow of the supply of money.

By the 1840s, hundreds of banks existed in America. All of them were printing private bank notes and making loans based solely on their own resources, mostly gold and foreign currency held as reserves. With the demise of the Second Bank of the United States in 1836, only state-chartered banks existed. The United States remained dependent upon limited minting of specie, foreign currency, and barter as means of exchange. During this period, known as the Free Banking Era, rules regarding bonding and capital could be stringent. Many new banks were formed and failed, but the free banking era was also one of the great periods of expansion in the U.S. economy. The Federal Reserve Bank of San Francisco described the period:

State Bank notes of various sizes, shapes, and designs were in circulation. Some of them were relatively safe and exchanged for par value and others were relatively worthless as speculators and counterfeiters flourished. By 1860, an estimated 8,000 different state banks were circulating "wildcat" or "broken" bank notes in denominations from one cent to $20,000. The nickname "wildcat" referred to banks in mountainous and other remote regions that were said to be more accessible to wildcats than customers, making it difficult for people to redeem these notes. The "broken" bank notes took their name from the frequency with which some of the banks failed, or went broke.[30]

In reaction to the demise of the Second Bank of the United States, New York became the first state to adopt an insurance plan for bank obligations. Between 1829 and 1866, five other states adopted similar deposit insurance schemes in an attempt to stabilize their banking systems. These modest early attempts at enhancing bank safety and soundness were ineffective in controlling the emission of paper currency and forestalling periodic liquidity crises.

The Congress authorized a Third Bank of the United States in 1841, but President John Tyler vetoed the measure, leading to rioting outside the White House by members of his own Whig Party.[31] The idea of a central bank issuing paper money was popular in Washington and among the business circles that exerted influence in the lobbies of the Capitol. Tyler, who succeeded to the presidency upon the death of William Henry Harrison, vetoed the legislation creating a Third Bank of the United States twice during his term on states' rights grounds.

The defeat of the Third Bank of the United States marked yet another political defeat for the Republican leader Henry Clay. As before, Clay personally championed the idea of a central bank and, once again, he lost. With the death of Harrison, a retired general and respected member of the Whig Party, Clay believed that a new central bank was assured. But populist opposition to the idea of a central bank, or even any banks at all, was too strong. President Tyler instead used the bank issue to assert his political independence from Clay and the Whig leaders in Congress.

When Tyler's Whig cabinet resigned over the veto of the bank legislation, Tyler was left with only the venerable Daniel Webster as secretary of state. Webster knew the political and economic issues in the debate over a central bank as well as any member of the Senate. He opposed the First Bank in 1814, but then helped John C. Calhoun fashion a compromise that eventually passed by the Congress. Years later, acting in his capacity as a lawyer, Webster represented the Second Bank before the Supreme Court in *McCulloch v. Maryland*. In that landmark case, the high court upheld the implied power of Congress to charter a federal bank and rejected the right of states to tax federal agencies. The ruling in *McCulloch v. Maryland* also recognized the implied powers clause of the Constitution, an evil event that greatly expanded the power of the Congress generally and especially regarding money and debt.

"A disordered currency is one of the greatest political evils," Webster is reported to have said in one of the more significant arguments ever made by an American for sound money. He continued:

A sound currency is an essential and indispensable security for the fruits of industry and honest enterprise. Every man of property or industry, every man who desires to preserve what he honestly possesses, or to obtain what he can honestly earn, has a direct interest in maintaining a safe circulating medium; such a medium shall be a real and substantial representative of property, not liable to vibrate with opinions, not subject to be blown up or blown down by the breath of speculation, but made stable and secure by its immediate relation to that which the whole world regards as permanent value.[32]

Tyler and Webster appointed a new cabinet comprised of southerners and devoid of any Clay supporters, whose political era essentially ended with this last battle in the nineteenth century over a central bank.

As we discuss in the next chapter, Washington remained largely oblivious to the financial problems facing the nation's economy until the Civil War. Tyler's advocacy for states' rights also meant a strong resistance against using federal revenue to bail out the states from their debts. Clay was particularly keen on giving the new, heavily indebted western states the right to revenue from public land sales, a measure Tyler refused to support. Even though Martin van Buren was defeated in 1840, the influence of Jackson and the public's strong distrust of banks generally gave President Tyler the will to oppose a measure strongly supported by his Whig Party. When Tyler left office in 1845, the government received taxes and paid interest in gold, but the rest of the economy was fueled by the rapid growth in paper currency that was issued by state banks and, to one degree or another, convertible into gold or silver.

The Gold Rush

The debt crises in the various states of the mid-1840s would quickly be forgotten in 1848 when gold was discovered in California. Within months of the discovery, tens of thousands of people were headed west, over land across the Great American desert, by sea around Cape Horn, or through the jungles of Panama and Nicaragua. The tiny port of San Francisco exploded almost overnight into a boom town of some 25,000 inhabitants and continued to grow to bursting and beyond with the vast influx of humanity from all corners of the globe. By 1870, the population of San Francisco reached nearly 150,000, but this statistic only begins to describe the huge movement of people and resources from the Eastern United States to the other side of the continent. So great was the influx of humanity into California that the territory was organized into a state, held a constitutional convention, and petitioned Congress for statehood in less than two years. California was admitted to the Union as a free state via the Compromise of 1850, the fastest process of accession to statehood of any U.S. state.

The production of gold from the mines of California served to stimulate economic activity in the United States and around the world, resulting in increased imports from Great Britain and other nations, and a steady increase in prices. The influx of new supplies of gold increased the money supply which, by definition, was still governed by the amount of gold in circulation. But a great deal of gold would eventually leave the United States for destinations such as Britain and other countries to pay for imported goods. More important, the Gold Rush pushed wages and prices higher, even after the initial surge of migration from 1848 to 1852 slowed. Long after the allure of the Gold Rush faded, wages and prices in distant California remained higher than in the rest of the United States.[33]

But despite the idealized view of the Gold Rush, the fact was that most of the 49ers who traveled to California did not become rich. Making the trip to California to pan for gold was akin to playing the lottery, which meant that the vast majority of participants were losers in financial and human terms. A significant portion of the participants in the Gold Rush died attempting to reach California or due to violence in the gold fields. Those who ventured north to the Yukon in pursuit of gold faced even steeper odds, as described so beautifully by Jack London in books such as *Call of the Wild* and *White Fang*.

The more enduring impact of the Gold Rush was to create an alternative to the Puritan, conservative notion of hard work and saving that characterized the early days of the United States. The "American dream" of instant wealth achieved quickly via opportunism and speculation arose in its place. The rise of crypto currencies in the twenty-first century also illustrates this American tendency. More than simply a description of the social and economic changes that occurred in California as a result of the discovery of gold, the Gold Rush and eventually the American dream became synonymous with the ability to get a fresh start in life and, with hard work and most important, good luck, earn enormous wealth.

From the 49ers in the 1850s to oil prospectors half a century later to movie producers and technology start-up companies in the twentieth century, the get-rich-quick image of the American dream became an important fixture in the nation's psyche that would color public attitudes toward money, debt, and the role of government. The American dream was not merely about helping all Americans meet their wants and needs, but to meet them immediately. As H.W. Brands wrote in his classic work, *The Age of Gold*:

> "We are on the brink of the age of gold," Horace Greeley had said in 1848. The reforming editor wrote better than he knew. The discovery [of gold] at Coloma commenced a revolution that rumbled across the oceans and continents to the ends of the earth, and echoed down the decades to the dawn of the third millennium. The revolution manifested itself demographically, in drawing hundreds of thousands of people to California; politically, in propelling America along the path to the Civil War; economically, in spurring the construction of the transcontinental railroad. But beyond everything else, the Gold Rush established a new template for the American dream. America had always been the land of promise, but never had the promise been so decidedly—so gloriously—material. The new dream held out the hope that anyone could have what everyone wants: respite from toil, security in old age, a better life for one's children.[34]

Chapter 2

Lincoln Funds Civil War with Inflation

President Abraham Lincoln is the moral savior of the United States for ending slavery. To pay for the war, he made enormous changes in the basic relationship between the federal government and money. These changes greatly diminished individual property rights and increased the power of Washington over the private economy. Lincoln relied on the issuance of nonconvertible paper currency to support the military effort, in today's terms like forcing people to accept buttons or miscellaneous crypto currencies in payment.

In his book *The Second American Revolution and Other Essays: 1976–1982*, Gore Vidal describes Lincoln "at heart . . . a fatalist, a materialist" who "knew when to wait; when to act."[1] Lincoln used interest bearing paper money or "greenbacks" to finance the Civil War and, more significant, passed laws mandating the acceptance of paper currency as "legal tender" for all debts. Yet when Salmon Chase asked Congress to pass the legislation in order to maintain government bond prices and procure supplies for the army, the law provided that import duties and interest on the public debt would be paid in gold. Paper money was seen as inferior.

Prior to Lincoln's revolution, most Americans expected to be able to exchange paper money for gold or silver coins upon demand. But the lack of currency was so great, that merchants and others supported the use of paper money. In the 1860s, *The Economist* editor Walter Bagehot coined the phrase "John Bull can stand many things, but he cannot stand two per cent," which reflected the fact that banks had to promise high interest rates on paper to attract gold deposits. The Civil War and the extraordinary measures taken by Lincoln to finance the military conflict came at the expense of individual economic rights. Author Kevin Phillips observed:

The loose, possibly unraveling U.S. Confederation of early 1861 and the emerging nation-state of 1865 were almost different countries. Memoirs of the postwar period describe a sea change. And the massive transformation that would last through the 1890s was beginning.[2]

When the Civil War began in April 1861, the American money supply consisted of all the physical gold and silver money then in circulation, domestic and foreign coin, and the paper notes issued by state-chartered banks. Lincoln's approach to financing the war was carried out by Secretary of the Treasury Salmon Chase. Timothy Canova wrote in an essay published by the *Chapman Law Review*:

Academic interest in Lincoln has mostly focused on the darker side of wartime presidential powers, such as the suspension of civil liberties and overstepping lines of constitutional authority. Far less attention has been given to Lincoln as the activist executive who set a new standard for mobilizing public finance in a crisis, pursuant to express Congressional authority under the Legal Tender Acts, presidential authority at its zenith . . . Lincoln is remembered for overcoming enormous political and military challenges. Often overlooked, however, is the economic and financial chaos he confronted upon taking office. In the weeks prior to Lincoln's inauguration, the nation was swept by fear, the hoarding of gold, and a panic perhaps more dangerous than other classic Keynesian liquidity traps in March 1933 and September 2008, since there was no central bank in 1861 with the authority to issue currency and inject liquidity into the financial system to try to break a downward spiral by restraining the psychology of hoarding.[3]

True to Gresham's Law, Americans chose to keep hard money in the form of gold and silver coins and shunned paper money issued by the state-chartered banks around the country. Even in the mid-1800s much of American economic life was still conducted via barter and exchange. Paper notes issued by banks and even the U.S. government were always suspect compared to tangible, tradable commodities and precious metals. When Lincoln took office, about one-third of the U.S. money supply was metal and about two-thirds was comprised of paper notes and checks redeemable for specie at the bank of issue. In the 1800s, not surprisingly, notes issued by foreign banks and governments often held higher esteem among Americans than the paper money issued by local banks and state governments.

The traditional prejudice against debt caused the average American and members of both political parties to have grave misgivings about treating paper money as being equivalent to precious metals or other commodities. Despite their pretensions of conservative beliefs and claims to the anti-Federalist heritage of Jefferson and Madison, Republicans since the Civil War have been at least as friendly to inflation, debt, and central banks as their Democratic rivals.

Author and journalist William Greider, for example, liked to style himself as a "greenbacker" because of his view that a little inflation is good for the common man. But Greider agreed that sound money is ultimately the best protection for working people. "I'm not against having a functioning central bank," Greider said in a May 2010 interview. "[W]hat I'm against is setting it outside our democratic accountability and the usual principles of whom government must answer to. The Fed is supposed to answer to the people."

The Lincoln Legacy

The transformation in the distinction between the tangible world of precious metals and other tangible commodities, and paper money and debt, is perhaps the most important aspect of Lincoln's presidency in economic terms. Lincoln freed millions of Americans from physical slavery and indentured servitude with the Emancipation Proclamation, a crusade so large that it drew support from around the world. He also set the United States down the road to political control over the nature of money much like the nations and kingdoms of Europe.

Even after Lincoln's death, both Republicans and Democrats championed paper money as the political possibilities created by debt and inflation proved irresistible. The cost of the Civil War was measured not just in the blood of the fallen, but also in the growth of the power of the executive branch into areas where the Constitution is deliberately silent. The political battle over the constitutionality of President Lincoln's currency laws and the more general issue of the government's issuance of debt, marked the defeat of the strict-constructionist, anti-Federalist tendency in American politics. The locally focused, agrarian movement associated in American history with Thomas Jefferson and Andrew Jackson was overwhelmed by the rise of the nationalist and commercial Republican tendency centered in New England and Pennsylvania.

The distinction between the government borrowing and actually controlling the issuance of money is important to our narrative of the American dream. Once the two functions, controlling the amount of currency in circulation and the government's fiscal operations, are housed under the same roof, inflation and a decrease in the value of money are inevitable. American history confirms that it is always easier to borrow than to raise taxes—until borrowing is no longer possible.

The economic and political impact of the early period under the Articles of Confederation strongly influenced the framers of the Constitution to limit the ability of the U.S. government to issue debt. The occasion of the Civil War and the character of Abraham Lincoln, however, combined to provide the authoritarian formulation necessary to disregard the deliberate silence of the Constitution on this point. Lincoln not only disregarded established custom and tradition regarding money, he also established a precedent for Congress to use debt and the emission of paper currency to finance government and thereby avoid raising taxes.

Lincoln's enactment of the legal tender laws provided the political foundation for the creation of the Federal Reserve System and the gradual nationalization of money and private banking in the United States. Lincoln and later President Grant imposed legal tender laws on Americans after the Civil War by subverting the Supreme Court, setting a pattern of duplicity by the executive branch that remains today.

By giving the federal government control over the issuance of "money," which was now legally defined as a piece of paper, an expedient war leader doomed future generations of Americans to live with inflation and falling real living standards. When émigrés from Europe came to America seeking freedom, it was not just religious liberty or freedom from physical bondage, but also freedom from the tendency of monarchs to compel subjects to use the king's money.

Historian Murray Rothbard wrote in *A History of Money and Banking in the United States before the Twentieth Century*:

> The Civil War, in short, ended the separation of the federal government from banking, and brought the two institutions together in an increasingly close and permanent symbiosis. In that way, the Republican Party, which inherited the Whig admiration for paper money and governmental control and sponsorship of inflationary banking, was able to implant the soft-money tradition permanently in the American System.[4]

The Civil War led to a vast increase in federal spending, from just $66 million in total federal outlays in 1861 to $1.3 billion four years later, at a time when federal tax revenues were falling. Tariffs were the primary source of revenue for the federal government, leading voters to call for "tariffs for revenue only" and not for the unreasonable protection of domestic industries. But with the Civil War, Washington no longer had access to tariffs on southern exports like cotton, yet another reason for the North to resist southern attempts to leave the Union. Northern states had insisted on the right to leave the Union and confirmed the same at the Hartford Convention in 1815, but Lincoln had the abolition of slavery as the ultimate justification for the war.

By the time Lincoln took office, the United States was one of the last nations in the world not to have already outlawed slavery, including Brazil and the Spanish Empire.[5] The importation of slaves was outlawed in the United States by act of Congress in March 1807, but the laws were not enforced. American participation in the slave trade slackened between 1825 and 1830, but activity revived thereafter and reached a peak around 1860. Lincoln was the first American president actively to insist on enforcement of the existing laws against slave importation, even before the Emancipation Proclamation. As soon as the southerners in Congress withdrew from Washington, Lincoln began to suppress the slave trade.[6]

Financing the War

Since the public was already aware that war was coming and was likewise suspicious of paper issued by private banks, hoarding of hard money was rampant. Credit was also tight because many banks and companies in the North were ambivalent about the war and were willing to see the secession of the southern states so long as commercial and financial ties were not disturbed. The Cotton Whigs of Boston and the Republican bankers of New York all held substantial stakes in southern industry and in the continuance of southern slavery. Many northern Republicans did not support Lincoln's election. One-third of all shipping traffic originating from New York was with southern ports. For many in New York and surrounding states, following Lincoln's election the wish was for the Confederate states to be allowed to depart in peace.[7]

Upon winning the presidency in 1860, Lincoln faced a desperate situation. The federal government was out of money and literally surrounded by unfriendly troops and states on all sides of the city of Washington. Lincoln entered Washington in secret prior to the March 1861 inauguration ceremony. As he took office, there was great uncertainty whether states to the north of Washington such as Maryland and Ohio would remain in the Union.

Lincoln also worried that Great Britain might recognize the Confederacy and provide military support to the South. The Confederate attack on Fort Sumter in Charleston harbor in April 1861 forced the issue and gave Lincoln the political momentum needed to win approval from Congress for financing the conflict. But while Washington was filled with Union troops by the middle of 1861, these conscripts were ill-trained and called up only for a short-term commitment, leaving open the question of the defense of the capital later that year.

Lincoln called Congress into session in July 1861 after he issued an emergency message regarding the war in which he provided the justification for the conflict: "Must a Government, of necessity, be too strong for the liberties of its own people, or too weak to maintain its own existence?" With this question, Lincoln began the last major civil war in the English-speaking world.

Lincoln also set the template for the next century of American history with respect to the politics of money. Congress authorized an army of 400,000 men and an expenditure of $400 million. The summer of 1861 was also when Congress enacted the first income tax: 3 percent of all annual incomes over $800. New import tariffs were imposed, as were taxes on spirits, beer and wine, and tobacco.[8] But these levies did not begin to cover the cost of the war, and Congress did not specify how the Treasury would finance the expenditure.

As a politician, Lincoln dared not raise taxes as the Civil War began, so he first tried to borrow the money from the New York banks. Ironically, he depended upon a political rival, Treasury Secretary Salmon Chase, to get the job done. A senator from Ohio and political climber of the first rank, Chase was an "archetypal Republican. He was a pious abolitionist, hero of bankers, and endlessly plotted to seize power from Lincoln. Chase was forever ungrateful for his appointments as secretary of the Treasury and Chief Justice of the Supreme Court."[9]

The Independent Treasury law enacted by the Congress in the 1840s strictly limited the interaction between private banks and the federal government. Chase attempted to float a government bond issue for $150 million, but when the banks refused to pay for the debt in specie, the project was modified. The sum of $150 million represented virtually all of the hard currency reserves of the New York banks in gold and silver coin. A good portion of all money in use in the United States in 1860 was in foreign coins. The situation was made more problematic because Chase felt that he must keep in the Treasury's vaults an amount of gold coin equal to the loans made to the government by the private banks.[10]

When a smaller amount of government bonds was purchased by some banks, the specie paid was spent by the government and quickly disappeared from circulation, thwarting attempts to increase the stock of money available to the economy. This was the first in a series of failed attempts by Secretary Chase to manipulate the financial markets by issuing Treasury bonds in exchange for gold coins, one of the earliest examples of the utter failure of market intervention to achieve any tangible result—except increased inflation.

By the end of 1861, first private banks and eventually the Treasury suspended payments of gold and silver coin on debts in general, an event that many students of American monetary history consider one of the blackest periods of the Lincoln administration.[11] The Treasury continued its obligation to pay interest and principal on public debt in gold for a time after private banks suspended redemptions, but by the end of 1861 all specie payments were suspended.

The default by the Treasury sent panic racing throughout the country as hoarding of gold grew even more acute. The suspension of redemption of notes, like most debt defaults, caused the value of greenbacks to plummet. Of note, greenbacks were convertible into Treasury debt. This conversion feature was little used and was repealed by the Congress a year later, but the fact that Congress included it at all illustrates the common understanding that all paper "notes" were a form of debt.

A second $150 million in greenbacks were issued in July 1862 and another $150 million in the early part of 1863, reaching a peak of just over $400 million by 1864 or $15 billion in 2025 dollars. The reaction to this emission of unconvertible paper money was to drive down the free market value of greenbacks to below half of face value. Secretary Chase attempted to blame the drop in the value of the paper dollar on "gold speculators," but the true reason was the lack of public support for paper money. By June 1864 the value of greenback notes in gold was below 50 cents despite various schemes to arrest the decline, including prohibition on gold trading.[12]

Though the North was prevailing on the battlefield, the Republic was taking a beating in financial terms. Creditors in foreign countries clamored for payment in specie, while inside the United States most coins disappeared from circulation, including even copper pennies! The greenback was held in such low regard by the public that any sort of metal money or even notes issued by foreign countries were seen as preferable to Lincoln's paper dollars, which were actually Treasury debt.

In many history books, the passage of the Legal Tender Act of 1862 is portrayed as a modernizing step to give the nation a stable currency.

In fact, the assertion of a legal tender monopoly by the federal government marked a bold expansion of Washington's power over all aspects of life, from the means of exchange to the store of value for wealth and savings.

The Free Banking era officially ended with the passage of the National Currency Act in 1863 and the National Bank Act in 1865, but only after three decades of currency crises, securities fraud, and bank failures. With the adoption of a single national currency and the creation of a two-tiered state and federal chartering system for banks, the die was cast for the evolution of these two separate types of banking business models well into the twentieth century and beyond. State-chartered banks could no longer issue their own currency, but they could gather deposits and issue debt, a fact that would continue to be the source of great instability in the U.S. financial system.

This early model for a national currency did not solve the basic issues when it came to liquidity for banks, however, whether they were national or state-chartered. Because the national currency remained based on a private banking system with no effective rules for soundness or liquidity, the U.S. economy went from boom to bust for decades. In a national political and economic framework where Washington was still, as the framers intended, lacking in financial resources and the political will to cause great trouble, the shortcomings of the banking system were overlooked.

National banks were given a monopoly on issuing paper currency, known as "greenbacks" for the color. And these new national banks were required to purchase a certain amount of government bonds to back their paper currency. Chase was able to push the National Bank Act through both houses of Congress in 1863 by narrow margins and effectively solved the immediate problem of financing the war effort. Secretary Chase also created a new mechanism for financing the federal government that became the engine for future inflation.

Since the government had already created a national currency with the passage of the Currency Act of 1863, the United States had no real need for national banks other than to act as vehicles for financing the Civil War. This arrangement was very congenial to the bankers, however, since it allowed them not only to make loans based upon the reserves of government debt held in their vaults, but also to gather interest on the government bonds. Thus, if a new national bank had $300,000 in capital, $100,000 would be invested in government debt and the remaining $200,000 could be deployed in loans. The National Bank Act also allowed the new banks to issue $90,000 in greenbacks, which could also be loaned. As a result, national banks could essentially earn double interest on their $100,000 in government bonds and generate double-digit returns at a time when the average yield on loans was 6 percent.[13] In financing the war to end slavery, Salmon Chase created a bankers' lobby for inflation.

Salmon Chase and Jay Cooke

Chase's considerable political ambition would eventually take him to the Supreme Court, but not before he made a shambles of the finances of the U.S. Treasury. A political figure who served as governor of Ohio and lost the Republican nomination in 1860, Chase gained the post of Treasury secretary via the support of financial operator Jay Cooke.

A fellow Ohioan and like Chase a strong advocate of paper money, Cooke is remembered for fueling some of the more ambitious financial frauds in an era replete with such schemes. He knew the "true worth and character" of money to an extent that was unusual for his time. Cooke speculated with great success on the Mexican War and the annexation of Texas in 1845, in part because he already knew how Washington would dispose of the state's debts. "Large sums were realized," Cooke admitted, "by those who were directly and indirectly interested in obtaining the legislation for the final settlement" of the bondholder claims against the Republic of Texas.[14]

Cooke's early knowledge of and appreciation for the tactics used to speculate on the value of debt and paper currency gave him novel strategies that allowed him to amass vast wealth in a relatively short period. Whereas most Americans still thought of work as involving some form of honest physical or mental labor, Cooke took the art of enlightened speculation and financial fraud to new levels. None were as grand and sweeping as his main focus after 1862, namely selling U.S. government bonds.

Prior to the Lincoln administration, Cooke was involved with selling bonds for canal and railroad promotion schemes. Yet the victory by Lincoln and some vigorous lobbying by the Cooke family landed Chase in Washington as the Treasury secretary and opened new vistas of accumulation and gain. It took only slightly more effort for Cooke to be appointed exclusive agent for the sale of government debt, a position that enabled the financier to collect commissions on the sale of some $2 billion in government bonds ($38 billion in 2025 dollars) between 1862 and 1864.[15]

Cooke was a self-promoter as well as a skilled salesman. "Like Moses and Washington and Lincoln and Grant," Cooke wrote in his 1894 memoir, "I have been—I firmly believe—God's chosen instrument especially in the financial work of saving the Union."[16]

In the pamphlet *How Our National Debt May Be a National Blessing*[17] published by his firm, Cooke described the many reasons why debt is not a problem. First and foremost, it was the interest on the debt, and not the principal amount, that was the burden. Cooke described himself on the cover as "General Subscription Agent for the Government Loans," making clear his official status. In the subtitle of the booklet, Cooke summarized nicely the arguments used by the proponents of paper money and debt to win public support:

> The Debt is Public Wealth, Political Union,
> Protection of Industry, Secure Basis for
> National Currency, The Orphans' and
> Widows' Savings Fund

Of interest, while the pamphlet made a number of familiar excuses as to why the debt was not a problem, it also made an explicit reference to tariffs and the protectionist benefits of debt. In the 1860s, there was a tendency among the pro-greenback population to see debt and a declining dollar as an effective barrier to unfair foreign competition, one of the legacies of the oppressive trade ties with Great Britain and Europe. Americans were very sensitive to being put at a disadvantage by foreign trade. Mixing protectionism with easy money was a popular formula in some parts of the United States. The tone and content of Cooke's 16-page pamphlet nicely summarized the popular opinion toward public debt in the 1860s and thereafter. Americans loved currency inflation.

Despite his reputation as a leader in the antislavery movement and as a U.S. senator, Chase was eventually forced out of the Treasury. His complete failure to maintain parity in the value of the greenbacks with gold ended his career. Inflation in terms of an index of wholesale prices during the Civil War went from 100 in 1861 to 210 in 1865, or a 22 percent annual rate of increase. States, including California and Oregon, refused even to accept greenbacks during the war for payment of taxes.

After Chase resigned from the Treasury in 1864, Lincoln appointed the popular Republican as chief justice of the Supreme Court. Cooke continued to sell government bonds for Chase's successor at the Treasury, Secretary William P. Fessenden, and managed to place hundreds of millions worth of "short-term loans bearing exceptional interest rates that were well subscribed to by the American people."[18]

The inflation brought about by the massive issuance of greenbacks under Chase would be short lived. At the end of the Civil War, it took $28 in paper to buy a $10 gold piece. By 1879 the $10 greenback note slowly rose back to parity with gold coins. William Hixson notes in his book *Triumph of the Bankers*: "The decline and recovery in value of the paper money created by sound banks was the same as the decline and recovery in value of the paper money created by government."[19] Thus the war was financed and U.S. expansion accelerated by inflation. A cheap, short-term expedient and much less divisive alternative than taxes.

At the end of the Civil War, the general assumption was that Washington would reduce the supply of paper money allowed during the conflict and resume the use of specie for all payments. The total supply of currency in circulation had doubled from 1860 to 1867, mostly by printing greenbacks and withdrawing gold coins from circulation. But the advocates of cheap money, many of whom had benefitted from the stiff inflation during the Civil War, "opposed any action that would reduce the amount of currency in order to bring the greenbacks back to the level of gold."[20] Both the federal government and the railroads came out of the war years with large debts, so the attraction of keeping the greenbacks in circulation and retaining the "legal tender" status of paper money was enormous. Wealthy financial moguls such as Jay Cooke and the owners of banks and railroads worked hard to promote the use of paper money and debt to maintain and expand their own fundraising activities.

While many Americans opposed paper money as the means of exchange, the ebb and flow in the sheer demand for money and other factors, such as the Gold Rush in the West and the rapid pace of economic growth, increased the need for all forms of currency, paper and specie. Salmon Chase reportedly disapproved of the legal tender notes in principle because they could be printed in unlimited quantities and were therefore inflationary. Chase was also said to have recognized the necessity of issuing paper money in a time of emergency. Later, however, sitting as chief justice of the Supreme Court, he declared the paper notes unconstitutional.[21]

During and after the Civil War, the political and legal battle raged regarding the legality of the federal government issuing greenbacks and whether such emergency currency could be used, for example, for the payment of state taxes. Murray Rothbard notes that in a large number of state court decisions on the issue of whether paper money was legal tender and thus sufficient to pay all debts, the Republican justices upheld the constitutionality of the greenbacks, but Democrats generally held that fiat money was unconstitutional. The question eventually reached the Supreme Court in *Hepburn v. Griswold*, where the court voted by a 5-3 margin to strike down the use of greenbacks.

This decision angered the administration of President Ulysses Grant, as well as the banks, the railroads and other heavily indebted corporations, who naturally preferred to settle their obligations in paper rather than gold. When a pair of vacancies came up on the Supreme Court, President Grant nominated two railroad lawyers, William Strong of Pennsylvania and Joseph P. Bradley of New Jersey. In May 1871, a 5-4 majority reversed the Court's position and in *Knox v. Lee* upheld the legality of fiat money and the legal tender laws. Largely at the behest of a heavily indebted government and its allies among the owners and managers of the insolvent railroads, the issue of fiat currency was settled in American law.[22]

Fisk and Gould Profit by Inflation

After the Civil War, politics prevailed and resumption of free exchange of gold for paper dollars was delayed for two decades. This provided plentiful monetary fuel for one of the greatest periods of economic growth, speculation, and financial larceny in U.S. history. Led by characters such as Daniel Drew, Jim Fisk, and Jay Gould, the expansion of the American railroads and the related speculation on Wall Street as to the financing for these endeavors created huge opportunities for gain and loss by investors, both in the United States and in Europe.

Jim Fisk, for example, made his first fortune as a Civil War profiteer and then in fraud. He swindled no less than Commodore Cornelius Vanderbilt to the tune of $8 million and in the process also stole control of the Erie Railroad via a partnership with another Civil War–era profiteer named Jay Gould. Fisk went on to create a vast operation in New York City involving Wall Street speculation, real estate, saloons, brothels, and opera houses, and many other businesses that served as fronts for his criminal activities. These predecessors of today's financial buccaneers in the world of crypto currencies built fortunes upon foundations of debt and paper currency.

At some point around 1869 the already wealthy speculator Gould, who was a partner of Fisk in the Erie Railroad, took notice of the fluctuation between the price of gold and greenbacks. The period of the Civil War and Reconstruction was one of opportunity, particularly for the new class of speculators and criminals attuned to the possibilities created by the federal government and Washington politicians on the one hand and government debt and paper currency on the other.

Under the administration of Lincoln and his third Treasury secretary, Hugh McCullough, Washington adopted an active policy against speculators. The Treasury responded with market sales of specie if any speculators attempted to "corner" the market in gold. However, upon the assumption of the presidency by Ulysses Grant and the appointment of George Boutwell to the Treasury, the policy changed. Boutwell let it be known that he had a distaste for interfering with the functioning of the markets. A career bureaucrat and former member of Congress, Boutwell ran the Internal Revenue Service, established the first organized means of manufacturing paper currency, and enabled one of the financial great market scams in the history of the United States.

The modern-day fraud conducted via unregulated securities and derivatives in the twenty-first century pales in comparison to the audacity of the individuals who operated in the financial markets of the 1860s. The legal tender laws and the creation of paper money, as well as the massive issuance of debt and related expenditures during the Civil War, created a powerful new market linkage between paper money and gold. This relationship naturally appealed to Jay Gould.

Gould was born Jason Gould in 1836 in Roxbury, New York, the son of John Burr Gould and Mary Moore Gould. According to W.A. Swanberg, Gould was named after "the fabled prince who won the Golden Fleece."[23] He did know how to make money and acted through bold and often brazen speculations, and not infrequently with the credit of others, to build one of the great empires of the Reconstruction period. The widespread use of paper currency and the general atmosphere of anything goes that prevailed after the Civil War provided the perfect stage upon which Gould and his contemporaries on Wall Street would operate.[24]

In the spring of 1869, Gould purchased $7 million in gold using greenbacks. Fisk, seeing great risk of government intervention, was not as yet willing to participate in the operation. At the exchange ratio between greenbacks and gold of 1.3 to 1, his purchase of $7 million worth of gold cost about $9.1 million in paper money. From that point on, Gould obviously had an interest in the price of gold rising versus the value of paper money. In a display of extraordinary public-mindedness, he began to express worry about the plight of working people and farmers who did not have access to sufficient currency. Soon a theme that said *a rise in the price of gold would benefit the whole nation* was read and heard widely in various media organs controlled by Gould and his political ally and protector, Boss Tweed, the political kingpin of New York's Tammany Hall organization.[25]

Fisk and Gould together were already among the most influential and feared financial operators of their time. The duo, operating in alliance with Boss Tweed, was seen as "a combination more powerful than any that has been controlled by mere private citizens in America," according to Henry Adams. Though Gould was known for his boldness particularly when it came to "open market operations," his gold speculation was another notch more problematic because of the political risk. There was only about $15 million in gold in circulation in the New York market at that time, and Gould was intent upon cornering the market and forcing prices up by literally taking gold out of circulation.

Because the federal government had a reserve of nearly $100 million, Gould needed to make certain that the Treasury would not sell gold to relieve stress on the market as had been the practice under Lincoln. Gould bought his way to power and wealth with little concern for the law, but in this case he proposed nothing less than to dictate government policy on gold via a direct understanding with President Grant.

At first Fisk was suspicious of Gould's plan and refused to participate, even though the previous year the two men had managed a magnificent operation with the Erie Railroad that brought them international notoriety and millions in profit. Gould worked relentlessly to win President Grant, Jim Fisk, and anyone else to the cause of higher prices for gold and a weaker value for greenbacks. Through the summer and into the fall of 1869, Gould—and eventually Fisk—purchased more and more gold, believing that their machinations in Washington, including winning the complicity of Grant's family into the market manipulation, would support their plan to corner the gold market. Gould and Fisk even lured President Grant into taking a ferryboat ride up the Hudson River for the express purpose of lobbying him on the issue of the price of gold, but the cautious Grant refused to cooperate.

In early September, Grant's wife wrote to her sister-in-law Jenny Corbin, whose husband was used by Gould disastrously as the fixer to attempt to influence Grant. Upon learning of her husband's unhappiness with Corbin's activities, Mrs. Grant wrote to her sister warning that "the President is very much distressed by your speculations and you must close them as quickly as you can."[26] This revelation made both Fisk and Gould understand that their political stratagems were a failure, but nonetheless the duo persisted in their brazen scheme.

In September 1869, Fisk made one last attempt to ramp the market higher by using funds he obtained from the Tenth National Bank, an institution that he and Gould controlled. As the posted price of gold displayed in the Gold Room in lower Manhattan rose past $150 greenbacks for $100 worth of gold, Fisk and his confederates bid prices up even higher. Panic ran through the market and caused financial ruin for many gold bears, who were short the metal at lower prices. On

September 22, 1869, Fisk and his surrogates made it clear via public statements that President Grant himself supported their cause and would not sell gold from the Treasury's stock.

To no one's surprise, Gould was secretly selling gold at a profit during this last stage of the market corner. While Fisk bore the financial burden of supporting the market and the brunt of the public attention as a result, Gould quietly disposed of his gold horde. Talk that Grant was involved with Fisk and Gould was picked up by the media, creating a national scandal for President Grant, perhaps the most damaging of his already soiled presidency. The entire nation began to focus its attention on President Grant and a couple of market speculators who were threatening the economy. Markets around the United States fell as uncertainty and fear froze investors in place—even as gold prices crept steadily higher. The price of gold in greenbacks peaked at $160 per $100 worth of gold coins just before noon that day. Then came word from Washington that the Treasury would sell $4 million in gold on the following Monday. Prices for gold, stocks, and pretty much everything else collapsed. And Jay Gould sold all the way down, taking full advantage of the market crisis that became known as Black Friday.

Although Gould was the mastermind of the gold market operation, the flamboyant Fisk took most of the blame. He was forced to go into hiding to escape angry investors. Fisk and Gould defaulted on many contracts to buy gold and used corrupt connections with Boss Tweed and others to avoid collection in the New York courts. Gould made over $11 million buying and selling the metal, largely the result of his flexible strategy, a vast sum in today's inflated dollar. Since 1869, the dollar has lost 96 percent of its value, making Gould's $11 million windfall worth over $300 million in 2025 dollars. The Gold Room was closed as the nation's economy reeled from this shameless market speculation. But both Gould and Fisk reckoned their profits in paper greenbacks.[27]

The Panic of 1873

The gold market crisis of 1869 orchestrated by Gould and Jim Fisk illustrated that paper money was a powerful new tool for speculation in gold. Paper money was essentially another form of debt leveraged against the national banks, which in turn supported the state banks and the real economy's need for liquidity. Gold remained the unit of account and store of value, but greenbacks were now accepted as a means of exchange by a growing portion of the population. Some observers believe that the crisis in the gold markets was the precursor to the financial and economic crisis four years later known as the Panic of 1873, which plunged the United States and the Western world into years of political and economic turmoil.

An important component of the crisis of 1869 and subsequent crises was debt made available by banks to finance purchases of gold and securities. Leverage in the form of bank loans was increasingly available, especially if one controlled a bank. More important was the pyramidal structure created atop the Treasury by the national banks. Larger "reserve city" banks and, in turn, community banks, were able to expand their balance sheets dramatically, providing finance for the real economy and speculative activities alike. But when the markets failed, there was no government backstop to absorb the impact on banks or the economy.

Rothbard notes in his *History of Money and Banking in the United States* that the whole nation was able to leverage the resources of a few New York City banks, which provided funding to the larger reserve city banks around the country. These larger banks in turn provided liquidity to community banks.[28] However, the continued fear of inflation and the vast amount of fraud associated with bank deposits, stocks, railroad bonds, and various other paper financial instruments, left the U.S. economy vulnerable to shifts in public mood.

The end of the dominance of the railroads as speculative vehicles in the U.S. economy was partly a function of the completion of the transcontinental rail link, but also due to the volatility and crisis that gripped the financial markets for debt issued by the rail lines. In 1873, not quite four years after the gold market crisis of 1869, the inherent instability of a fiat money system based upon national banks again resurfaced with the Great Panic of that year.

The crisis of 1873 was caused by the collapse of Jay Cooke's financial empire, which by that time included a bank in New York and investment sales offices around the United States that financed the construction of the railroads. The insolvency of Cooke's Northern

Pacific Railroad venture set the stage for a financial crisis that began in the Northeast and spread to the rest of the United States and around the world.

After starting his career selling bonds and raising money for the U.S. government during the Mexican War, Cooke became wealthy enough to capitalize on his connections in Washington, which extended back to before the Civil War. Cooke had formed a banking company in 1861, Jay Cooke & Co., and used this as the primary vehicle for the role as bond sales agent for the U.S. Treasury. Cooke's boldness and bravado in promoting American debt as secure and patriotic investments helped to finance the operations of the U.S. government.

By 1873, Cooke's luck ran out along with his ability to sell debt, exposing the inherent insolvency of his Northern Pacific scheme. Cooke's particular excesses, though, were part of a broader problem. The U.S. economy was growing at a very rapid pace in that period. Financial and human fatigue were ingredients in the economic reversal that soon developed. Whatever specific factors drove the economic correction that began in September 1873, the result was the failure of a quarter of all the railroads in the country, the bankruptcy of thousands of private businesses, and double-digit unemployment in the United States and Europe.

The virtuous circle of the big New York banks providing liquidity to smaller reserve city and community banks was reversed with horrible consequences. Banks were drained of gold reserves and the public was left without access to cash or credit of any description. Banks, stockbrokers, and businesses failed in droves, stock prices collapsed, consumer and commodity prices declined, and unemployment increased nationwide in a deflationary wave of economic instability that lasted for more than two decades.

Despite the market contagion, Cooke, an intimate friend of President Ulysses Grant, was able to tap bailouts from the Treasury to save part of his far-flung enterprise from eventual ruin. Cooke had other businesses, including Jay Cooke, McCullough & Co. in London, which acted as agent for the Treasury in the United Kingdom and was actually owed money by both Cooke & Co and the U.S. government when the crisis began. In 1871, Cooke's firm was appointed fiscal agent for the Treasury regarding all naval expenditures. Over the next few months, the Treasury advanced hundreds of thousands of dollars to Jay Cooke, McCullough & Co. and thereby helped the speculators and his compatriots avoid the worst of the economic depression.[29]

The bailout of Jay Cooke, McCullough & Co. was a historical precursor for many bailouts, large and small, by Washington for private financial companies. At a primitive level, the rescue of Jay Cooke's financial situation was not so different from the political bailouts of Citicorp in the 1980s as the result of foreign lending or Goldman Sachs and other dealers with the collapse of American International Group in 2008. But 1873 marked the first and in many ways the worst general economic crisis in modern U.S. history, one that persisted for many years thereafter. When it came to September 17, 1873, Matthew Josephson wrote in *The Robber Barons*, "[t]he seven years of plenty after the war must now make way for the seven years of dearth in a land literally 'flowing with milk and honey.'"[30]

Despite, and to some extent because of, the existence of national banks and a common fiat paper currency, major banking panics would occur in the United States in 1873, 1884, 1890, 1893, and 1907. Canadian banks of that time had the flexibility to issue additional banknotes when currency demand increased. In the United States, no such facility existed for national banks and, indeed, was forbidden by law. The ethic of hard money among the American public was still too strong to allow the flexibility permitted to banks in Canada. When U.S. bank deposits went out of favor with the public and, more important, with the nation's foreign creditors, bank balance sheets shrank along with the money supply of the entire nation.

Gold Convertibility Restored

The period of great economic growth and financial excess from the Civil War to the creation of the Federal Reserve System in 1913 was arguably as "pure" a private national banking model as ever existed in the United States. One of the ironies of the period following the Panic of 1873 was that the United States eventually restored the convertibility of the fiat dollar in gold. America had gone off the gold standard during the Civil War and nonconvertibility remained until 1879. The decision to return to convertibility was actually made by President Grant in 1875, who ordered that the convertibility of the dollar would resume four years later. At the time, the paper currency was trading at about a 20 percent discount to gold, meaning that it took $120 in greenbacks to purchase $100 worth of gold.[31]

The period following the restoration of gold convertibility in 1879 was remarkable for a number of reasons. First, the nation's economy grew strongly, but with remarkably little inflation and indeed, sometimes too much deflation. Although producer prices fell from the conclusion of the Civil War through the end of the 1880s, wages actually rose in real terms. Capital investment flows into the U.S. economy also were strong. Interest rates continued to fall through the 1870s and 1880s, resulting in strong incentives for saving and investment. There would continue to be periodic financial crises involving banks and the financial markets in the United States, but the real economy actually enjoyed a boom period that increased the wealth of the average American.[32]

The low level of inflation during this period was reflected by the fact that prices for gold and silver remained relatively stable, although the latter would soon suffer from increased supply and decreased demand. After the end of the Civil War, in anticipation of the resumption of gold convertibility of paper dollars, Congress actually dropped silver from the list of monetary metals for use by the Treasury in minting coins. There was great public outcry, but the fact was that silver coins were out of favor as a medium of exchange. A ratio of 16 to 1 had existed between the price of silver and gold going back nearly a century, but increased supply in the United States and a drop in demand around the world in nations such as India and the United Kingdom caused the ratio between gold and silver to slip to almost 30 to 1 by the 1870s.[33]

With silver prices falling, the metal was not seen as a particularly robust store of value, but the attraction of free silver coinage for some proponents remained very powerful. There were large deposits of the metal in the western United States and the farmers and ranchers of those states often owed money for purchases of land. Some silver advocates, as the pro-silver advocates were known, sought to provide a more plentiful means of exchange to stimulate the economy. Other proponents of silver saw a resumption in government use of the metal for making coins as a natural solution to the decline in market demand, especially since prices for the silver continued to be under pressure. But three years later, silver coins were stripped of their status as legal tender, a move that again caused an uproar from people with stakes in the silver mines of the West. The proponents of free coinage of silver in the Senate, who were known at the time as the "Bonanza Kings," sought to have the Treasury resume purchases of the metal at the old price ratio of 16 to 1 versus gold, even though the market price for silver was half that level.

Silver and Tariffs

As Congress slowly came around to the restoration of gold convertibility of dollars, a great political debate developed about the restoration of silver coins as legal tender. Western silver interests made a straightforward argument for government intervention to stop the slide in the price of silver relative to gold. The idea of returning silver coins to the money supply also appealed to farmers who believed that increasing the money supply would boost economic activity and thus prices for their goods, while reducing the real cost of servicing their debts.

"A whole generation of Americans was embroiled from the 1870s to the 1890s in the argument over silver," Richard Hofstadter wrote in "The Paranoid Style in American Politics."[34] In the 1880s, the public clamored for an increase in the money supply. Dozens of proposals were floated in the Congress in the next several years either to require government purchases of silver, increase the money supply, or both. Senator John Sherman (R-OH), the brother of General William Tecumseh Sherman of Civil War fame and a strong supporter of a return to the gold standard, introduced a bill in the Congress in January 1874 to increase the money supply.

Sherman's proposal to purchase silver had the effect of increasing the money supply via the issuance of greenbacks, which were used to make the purchases. The resulting expansion in the supply of paper dollars was less than was demanded by the inflationist, free silver proponents, but a larger amount than was acceptable to those in favor of resuming the gold standard. Known as the "Inflation Bill," the

Sherman legislation was debated for nearly four months. The measure eventually passed the Republican-controlled Congress, but on April 22, 1874, President Grant vetoed the legislation. This move would "make the stand of the Republican Party official" when it came to aligning itself with business interests rather than the working class, according to Grant biographer William Mcfeely.[35]

From the time of the Grant veto of the Inflation Bill forward, the Republicans for a time became known as the party of sound money and business interests, and the Democrats as advocates of inflation and the working man. So passionate was the national debate over silver that the Republican Party divided over the question for years to come up to the present time. The debate over the free coinage of silver and the national money supply eventually was a factor in the undoing of the Republican Party's control over Washington.

In 1888, President Grover Cleveland attempted to use the growing Treasury surplus and a reduction in the tariff as an issue to gain reelection, but he underestimated the attraction of protectionism—a theme that modern American politicians led by President Donald Trump rediscovered in the twenty-first century. The incumbent Cleveland won a slim majority in the popular vote, but when the votes were cast in the Electoral College, Cleveland lost by 233 to 168 to Benjamin Harrison from Ohio. This was an early example of the election-winning power of the Republican political machine. By 1890 the Treasury amassed a surplus of nearly $150 million in gold, a symbolic affront to farmers and populists who proclaimed the federal government to be "an octopus" that was strangling the economy. In that same year, a young lawyer from Nebraska, William Jennings Bryan, won his first term in the House of Representatives.

With the Republicans again in control of both houses of Congress and President Harrison in the White House, one of the more important items on the political agenda was raising the tariff. Known as the McKinley tariff after Rep. William McKinley (R-OH), the legislation only raised the national tariff slightly, but the political debate slowed the process to a crawl.

The Democrats initially opposed the bill but eventually decided to allow the measure to pass and go to the Senate in the hope of using the tariff issue in the 1892 election. President Harrison, passed the

McKinley tariff, raising the average duty on imported goods to 50 percent. Forty years before the passage of Smoot Hawley in 1930 and long before the start of the Great Depression, tariffs on imports were already very high in the United States.

Republican proponents of the Tariff Act said it was necessary to maintain the high standard of living of the American workingman, "but as the employers were fighting (hard) against the trade unions, and were willing to import the new immigrant labor to reduce wages, this could not be taken quite seriously," wrote James Truslow Adams in *Epic of America*.[36] Republicans also presented higher tariffs as a way to protect farmers and the new states in the western United States from foreign competition—and found a ready audience for that viewpoint. The McKinley tariff bill was signed into law in October 1890.

The political price extracted by the silver advocates for supporting the passage of the McKinley tariff was that Republicans would back legislation to increase purchases of silver and a resumption of free coinage of the metal. In addition to the tariff legislation, the Republicans, led by Henry Cabot Lodge in the House, pushed for new voting rights laws to protect black voters and Republican candidates in the South. Southern Democrats opposed the measures to protect black voting rights and dubbed the legislation the "Force Bill." They claimed that the Republicans were prepared to use federal troops to enforce the political franchise of freed slaves in the South.

When Republicans brought the Force Bill to the floor of the Senate in December 1890, the leader of the silverites, Senator William Stewart of Nevada, seized his opportunity. In January 1891, Stewart used a procedural motion on the floor of the Senate to substitute legislation for the free coinage of silver for the Lodge voting rights legislation, and the pro-silver forces in both parties sustained his maneuver. The free coinage of silver and, importantly, inflation of the currency, was more popular politically than protecting voting rights in the South.

In the winter of 1891, the American economy was again sinking into depression, with unemployment and business failures spreading around the country. A solution via increased issuance of paper currency was seen by politicians in both parties as the answer. Even Senator Sherman, who long guarded against allowing the silver advocates to push their inflationist agenda, was forced to concede that the political pressure behind free coinage of silver was irresistible. A majority of Republicans believed that the combination of the new tariff legislation and a pro-silver bill would protect them at the polls in 1890.[37]

The compromise legislation crafted by Sherman in July 1890 repealed the Bland-Allison act and called for the Treasury to purchase four million ounces of silver per month, essentially equal to the amount of silver produced in the United States during that time. The Treasury paid for these purchases with paper dollars, and this had the effect of rapidly increasing the money supply. The increase in the supply of paper currency caused by the Sherman Silver Purchase Act placed a considerable drain on the government's gold reserves.

Many Americans immediately exchanged the paper money for silver in order to buy gold coins. Even though demand for paper currency continued to rise, the preference for either gold or paper money over silver was pronounced and silver prices continued to fall. Imports of gold into the United States surged since the demand for the metal increased with the supply of greenbacks as the Treasury continued its required purchases of silver.

The fascination with silver was much like the craze surrounding crypto currencies in the twenty-first century but had an even more irrational quality. Treasury purchases of silver rose to 50 million troy ounces annually, but world production of silver rose from 63 million ounces per year in 1873 to over 150 million ounces in 1892. The market volumes expanded to meet the Treasury's needs, and the price continued to fall. And silver advocates were unrelenting in their clamor for further government support.

Representative Edwin A. Conger of Iowa, who was chairman of the House Committee on Coinage, Weights, and Measures and supported limited coinage of silver, called the lobbying effort by the pro-silver forces prior to the passage of the Sherman Silver Purchase Act "the most persistent, courageous and audacious lobby upon this question I have ever seen since my term of service began here."[38]

Despite the passage of the National Bank Act several decades before, political meddling by Washington in the structure and composition of the U.S. money supply resulted in nine different types of money being placed into circulation by the 1890s. The legal mandates placed upon the Treasury to redeem paper money with gold or silver, and to purchase and/or coin silver, became completely unmanageable and were depleting the once-large official reserves of gold. So great was the drain of gold from the Treasury and the increase in the money supply, as we discuss in the next chapter, that within three years of the passage of the Sherman Silver Purchase Act, the law was repealed.

The money supply of the United States grew dramatically during these final years of the nineteenth century, yet public confidence in banks, financial markets, the U.S. currency, and the economy was at a new low. America would see more political discord and economic upheaval than at any time since the Civil War—and most of it caused by the debate over the nature of money.

The many changes occurring in American economic life drove the intensity of the national debate over currency. The end of the conquest of the American frontier, the consolidation of industries such as steel, oil, and railroads, and the rise of the great fortunes of the Robber Barons, caused many Americans growing unease. This was a situation not unlike the one confronting America today. Urban unemployment, hard times on the farm, wage and price inflation in the growing cities, and a general sense that the endless vistas and opportunities of early America were not so infinite, affected the national mood.

The economic depression in 1882–1884 did a great deal of damage in confidence in the limitless possibilities for economic betterment. The role of wealth in American politics, then as today, made many of our citizens wonder whether the promise of the American dream could or would really be fulfilled for the vast majority of people. Historian Harold Faulkner noted that "the late eighteen eighties had brought hard times to the farmer, the workingman, and to many businessmen as well, and with hard times, doubts and disillusionment; in the nineties came open revolt, a challenge to old beliefs, a repudiation of old shibboleths, a fragmentation of old parties. There was almost everywhere a feeling that somehow the promise of American life was not being fulfilled."[39]

The American political class in the late 1800s responded to popular angst regarding the economy by imposing tariffs on imported goods. In the nineteenth century, tariffs were one of the chief sources of revenue for the federal government. Republicans were the traditional proponents of tariffs to protect domestic industries. Democrats generally were opposed. By the last decade of the 1800s, the Treasury was already running a considerable surplus because of the protective tariff enacted by Congress during the economic crisis of 1882–1884, so there was little need for additional revenue. Indeed, the Treasury's accumulation of gold after the repeal of the Sherman Silver Purchase Act may have been a deflationary factor in the decade prior to 1900. The high tariffs of the 1880s is an important point to remember when later we consider the Great Depression and the enactment of the Smoot-Hawley tariff legislation in the 1930s.

Chapter 3

Robber Barons and the Gilded Age

With the creation of a monetary system based upon national banks during the Civil War, the assumption was that the U.S. economy would become more stable. In fact, the opposite was the case. The tendency of Americans to prefer gold over paper money was unchanged from pre–Civil War days. The instability of U.S. banks, whether national or state-chartered, and the unreliability of paper money and investments, made Americans more cautious and also encouraged speculation between paper and metal. The inhabitants of Wall Street earned and lost great fortunes by using paper assets of various types to manipulate the markets and thereby deprive the public of their savings.

The rise of the investment trust also occurred during the 1890s. Trusts were a very important development in the history of American finance, especially when it comes to the story of money and debt. The investment trust was a canard behind which the Robber Barons concealed manipulations in stocks and bonds, and flaunted antitrust laws through hidden control stakes in many companies. For the individual, the investment trust was a way to emulate the investment strategy of the Robber Barons, at least in theory. Yet a century later, trusts and other "innovations" would be used to fuel bubbles in technology stocks and real estate based upon funding provided by individual investors.

The assets of choice for the Robber Barons of the Gilded Age were railroads, coal, and oil companies, but any industry could and would be the target of an enterprising investment trust operator. The similarity between the trusts in the early nineteenth century and today's world of structured finance lies in the use of debt and other instruments to finance the vehicles and a near-total lack of disclosure. By the 1920s, when these schemes were widely distributed to individual investors, there were literally hundreds of such trusts.

The speculative character of the U.S. financial markets was made more extreme due to the near-total absence of commercial rules imposed by the government. The Treasury operated as another participant in a completely private marketplace. "Anything goes" and "caveat emptor" were the operative norms. The state and local courts were left to provide legal regulation of banking and finance. Stocks and bonds were sold from private banks, parlors, saloons, and the backs of wagons—much like Wall Street today. Securities dealing was reckoned to be speculative and thus socially suspect.

The biblical, pejorative view of the "money changers," to borrow the title of the 1926 book by Upton Sinclair, still held sway with many Americans, especially those who supported silver as the means for national salvation. The evangelical silver believers of the nineteenth century are the analog for crypto currency advocates today. But at least silver added something to the aggregate wealth of the nation.

The pro-business tendency of the Republican Party, which dominated the politics of the nation during much of this period, encouraged and enabled a level of speculation that would result in several serious economic depressions. Only after a string of financial collapses from the 1880s through to October 1929 would the United States see regulation as a counterbalance to unrestrained private competition.

The final decades of the nineteenth century following the Civil War were described aptly by Mark Twain and Charles Dudley Warner in their sardonic book *The Gilded Age: A Tale of Today*. The book told the story of politicians, soiled doves, and other characters who were caught up in the get-rich-quick environment of the period. Twain used the comparison between Washington and the hinterland to great effect in his classic tale. The comparison of Twain's Gilded Age and the stock and real estate bubbles seen in the United States a century or more later confirms the repetitive nature of man's behavior when it comes to money. Twain described his work in typically facetious style:

This book was not written for private circulation among friends; it was not written to cheer or instruct a diseased relative of the author's; it was not thrown off during intervals of wearing labor to amuse the idle hour. It was not written for any of these reasons, and therefore is submitted without the usual apologies. It will be seen that it deals entirely with a state of society; the chief embarrassment of the writers in this realm of the imagination has been the want of illustrative examples. In a State where there is no fever of speculation, no inflamed desire for sudden wealth, where the poor are all simple-minded and contented, and the rich are all honest and generous, where society is in a condition of primitive purity and politics is the occupation of only the capable and the patriotic, there are necessarily no materials for such a history as we have constructed out of an ideal commonwealth.[1]

Twain's description of American political life and especially Washington in *The Gilded Age* summarized a period of great economic growth and equally prodigious political corruption; a period of enormous partisanship and also significant social reform. Steven Mintz of the University of Houston observed that "It is easy to caricature the Gilded Age as an era of corruption, conspicuous consumption, and unfettered capitalism. But it is more useful to think of this as modern America's formative period, when an agrarian society of small producers was transformed into an urban society dominated by industrial corporations."[2]

Private banks issued the majority of the nation's currency but also operated with almost complete impunity, with little or no interference from Washington or the states. The owners of the New York banks sat at the apex of the financial and political world of nineteenth-century America, but other cities such as Chicago and Detroit were also growing in wealth. Institutions controlled by J.P. Morgan and other Robber

Barons grew in political influence and power. There was no national bank or federal regulatory structure to counterbalance their economic ascendance. The banks helped to finance trade and collect taxes and duties on behalf of the government. The cash balances of the "independent" U.S. Treasury were deposited with these same large banks.

J.P. Morgan, who as Matthew Josephson wrote, "won respect by force of arms as well as business acumen," assumed the role of *de facto* central banker along with the likes of John D. Rockefeller, who was to the oil industry what Morgan was to banking.[3] Together with William Rockefeller and partners, John Rockefeller created Standard Oil. It was the largest oil refining business in the world and the first great American trust. The founding partners of Standard Oil financed the initial capital for their oil trust through the large New York banks. In 1877, John Rockefeller founded his own bank, the Chase National Bank, whose successor operates today as JPMorgan.

The market dynamic among and between paper money, gold, and silver remained one of the most important economic and political issues facing the country. The nature of money was seen as a far more important issue than a discussion of banks or anything else that people today might associate with finance. Sound money was scarce—at least in the public mind, and this made money a hot political issue. "Money is gold and nothing else," observed J.P. Morgan in 1912, meaning nothing else is money. Everything else is credit. This was a popular view with many Americans, who wished to see a return to full gold convertibility, but it had the effect of constraining economic activity and causing deflation.

Milton Friedman and Anna Schwartz, in their classic work *A Monetary History of the United States*, found that between 1892 and 1897, the nation's money supply was stable to down slightly, but that the final years of the decade saw "a dramatic reversal of economic conditions."[4] The practical reality felt by Americans as a result of Washington's thrift between 1892 and 1897 was a scarcity of any type of money. This led many Progressives to believe that the issue of money, and especially the end of using silver in coins, was connected to falling prices for farm products and a general economic malaise during much of this period.

The irony of the position of the proponents of silver and currency inflation is that as early as 1900, some 90 percent of all commercial transactions in the country were affected via the transfer of credits from one bank to the next. The key issue for reforming the U.S. financial system seemingly was to provide adequate reserves for banks, not to facilitate the issuance of greenbacks or metal coins for physical transactions. However, the political popularity of the silver movement overwhelmed such practical considerations. The more silver the Treasury bought, the less gold remained in circulation.

Republicans Embrace Silver and Inflation

The passage of the Sherman Silver Purchase Act in the summer of 1890 not only failed to stabilize the price of silver, but also drained the Treasury of gold at a more rapid pace as Americans sought to exchange their paper currency for gold. The law roughly doubled the Treasury's purchases of silver. Payment was made for the silver through a new issue of paper currency, which was redeemable in either gold or silver at the discretion of the Treasury. The United States was on the road to a dual gold-silver monetary standard, but also confirmed the Republican Party as an advocate for *soft money* and high tariffs.

Whatever enduring commitment the Republican Party had to sound money when President Grant vetoed the Inflation Bill a decade before was swept away in the name of political expediency. The economic times in the 1890s were increasingly volatile and so were the politics, benefiting challengers and making elections risky for incumbents. Focusing on the rising public support for inflation was good politics for members of either major party. The inflationary tendencies of the U.S. government were further confirmed in that same year, when the Treasury changed its long-standing practice of requiring payment of import duties in gold. Greenbacks largely replaced gold coins in the payment of customs receipts from that time forward.[5]

The increasing popularity of inflation among the American people and the growing tendency of the federal government in Washington to accommodate it did not go unnoticed around the world. Like America's citizens, foreigners reacted with alarm to the shift from gold to silver as a monetary standard in the United States, especially since the fall in demand for the metal had been driven partly by nations in Europe and Asia ending the use of silver coins. As it became more obvious that Americans intended to embrace inflation, foreign capital inflows to the United States declined. Exports of gold grew as foreign banks and individuals sought to exchange paper dollars for gold.

So great was the outflow of gold from U.S. reserves that in March 1891 the Treasury suddenly imposed a fee on the export of gold bars from the United States. From this point forward, the export of gold moved to coins rather than gold bars, but the drain continued nonetheless. When the Treasury began to default on convertibility by forcing U.S. banks to take paper rather than gold, the stage was set for a financial crisis. The final act of idiocy came from the Republican-controlled Senate in July 1892, which passed legislation to take all remaining restrictions off the coinage of silver.[6]

The action by the Republican Congress to placate the advocates of free coinage of silver and inflation was a response to internal political pressures and the approaching election, but the results were felt around the world. The Progressive Party polled over a million votes in 1892 based on a platform that embraced the free coinage of silver at the old 16:1 ratio with the price of gold. By then, the price ratio between gold and silver was closer to 40:1, but the Progressives cared not.

President Grover Cleveland led the Democrats to an electoral triumph in the fall of 1892, winning control over both houses of the Congress and the White House for the first time in more than a third of a century. The conservative Cleveland took power just as the U.S. economy was collapsing. Foreign creditors and the country's citizens were fleeing paper assets and demanding payment in gold. Even as the Democrats savored their victory in the five-month interregnum between the election and the inauguration of the new president in March 1893, the global financial markets unraveled.

In February 1893, 10 days before the end of the term of President Benjamin Harrison, the Reading Railroad declared bankruptcy. The Reading was heavily in debt and was in the process of borrowing more to finance the lease of coal-producing lands in northeastern Pennsylvania. Following the discovery of oil in Titusville, Pennsylvania, in 1859, however, many coal-related industries began a slow decline in value.

At the time of the Reading collapse, the Congress had just passed new federal bankruptcy legislation to bring order to the process of insolvencies of businesses that crossed state lines. All of the producers of coal in that part of the United States were controlled by one or more railroad trusts, which were engaged in cutthroat competition that forced them to sell coal at or below the cost of production. And most of these trusts were using debt to subsidize this uneconomic activity. At the time of its collapse, the Reading Railroad controlled the Philadelphia, New Jersey Central, and Lehigh Valley lines. All were financed with debt.[7]

The collapse of the Reading Trust typified the way the use of private debt to finance business expansion and even interest payments had become more and more acceptable. William Janeway, the former vice chairman of the private investment firm Warburg Pincus, in a November 2008 interview, recalled that the first phase in finance is fully secured lending. One makes a loan and gets repaid. The second phase in finance is making loans where only interest expense is covered, echoing the marketing pitch of Jay Cooke. The second phase relies on refinancing to repay principal.[8]

By 1893 the owners of the Reading Railroad were already in the third phase, where even the interest on existing debt had not been "earned" in any economic sense and had to be borrowed to keep the enterprise afloat. This is known classically as cash flow insolvency. The ultimate cause of the bankruptcy of the Reading Trust was the fact that prices for coal had fallen dramatically, below the cost of production in some cases.

When the rail line collapsed, the principals of the Reading were in Europe seeking new money loans in order to pay interest on the company's existing debt and acquire more railroads. In 1900, coal was the chief means of heating homes and powering industry. The owners of the Reading Railroad believed that they could control coal prices if only they could secure control over a sufficient portion of the coal producing properties in the East. The means of gaining control over these physical coal-producing properties was debt and more debt.

The use of debt to fuel speculation, in fact, was an artifice that an increasing number of Americans were employing in 1900. Another notable aspect of the Reading Railroad collapse was how bankruptcy and receivership were transformed from a way to liquidate insolvent companies to a mere stratagem, a political maneuver used to advance the private agenda of the speculative class in a given industry. The

magazine *The Nation* described the evolution of the art of using bankruptcy for speculative gain in the same year that the Reading Railroad
collapsed:

> The old idea of a receivership still lingers in the public mind—
> that an action for that end should be begun before a court only
> in case of total failure to meet obligations, and then only as a
> means of liquidating the affairs or a corporation. Hence, it used
> to be thought that a receivership was to be entered only as a
> last resort and only as the beginning of liquidation or complete
> reorganization. Within the last decade or so we have passed
> beyond this original theory. It was the late Mr. Jay Gould, we
> believe, who first developed the idea of a railway receivership
> until it became merely one of a series of strategic moves for
> the control of a great corporation or for some special finan-
> cial result.[9]

The railroads of the nineteenth century were, in this respect, similar to the "too big to fail" banks and commercial companies of the
latter part of the twentieth century. In the same way that the noted
speculator Jay Gould and his contemporaries employed the guise of
bankruptcy at the end of the nineteenth century to hide their true
strategic agendas, a century later the government-led bailouts of Penn
Central, Chrysler, Continental Illinois, Citicorp, General Motors,
Chrysler, GMAC, and American International Group all were used to
avoid liquidation and to pursue a political agenda. In a sense, the methods of Gould and his nineteenth century contemporaries became the
everyday tools of the American political class a century later.

The Panic of 1893

By the time Grover Cleveland came to power in March 1893, the
Treasury was already limiting the outflow of gold. Banks began to call in
their loans and more businesses failed in what was to become the worst
financial crisis of the modern age. More railroads and scores of other
businesses and banks collapsed during a terrible year that began a decade of privation and economic depression lasting until the turn of the

century and beyond. By May 1893, banks were failing in droves. Notes drawn upon depositories in the South and West could no longer be discounted at the large New York banks, which cut correspondent ties with other banks around the country. Two months later, the silver advocates held a convention in Denver and, as might be expected, blamed the crisis on an international conspiracy to "demonetize" silver by not using it in coins. But the only conspiracy, and one that was not well hidden, was the populist mob of inflation-happy silverites, who saw their salvation, both in economic and religious terms, in restoring the price of silver to the old, 16:1 ratio with gold.

So acute was the government's fiscal situation that J.P. Morgan and other leading bankers put together a bailout for the Treasury, agreeing to subscribe to a $50 million bond issue and to stand ready to do so again if necessary. "We all have large interests dependent upon the maintenance of a sound currency of the United States," Morgan cabled to his London office. "If this negotiation can be made, it will be most creditable to all parties and pay a good profit."[10]

Morgan and the other participants in the Treasury rescue did profit by their investment. But the image of the U.S. government being saved by the House of Morgan was galling to many Americans, who recoiled at the ostentatious power represented by the great New York banks. Robber Barons such as J.P. Morgan were American royalty, men who engendered both admiration and contempt. The latter soon became a central fact in American politics. The economic depression that followed the Crisis of 1893 stretched on for years and ultimately led to the creation of the Federal Reserve System in 1913.

Senator Robert Byrd wrote in *The Senate* that no one could agree on the causes of the great depression that began in 1893. The various political parties blamed one another, while the orthodox Cleveland and his colleagues blamed the purchases of silver and the perceived decline in the Treasury's credit standing. This seems like the obvious explanation, but the political and social factors that first pushed the government to purchase vast amounts of silver and, in the process, inflate the currency, are complex. The rise of William Jennings Bryan of Nebraska as the leader of the pro-silver movement is memorialized in the pages of history books, but the vast social movement behind Bryan may not have been motivated chiefly, or even at all, by economic theories about the nature of money.

Libertarian economist and author Murray Rothbard argued that the conventional view of the economics profession, led by giants such as Milton Friedman and Anna Schwartz, is that the price deflation after the Civil War, especially in agriculture, drove a political conflict between inflationist and pro-gold tendencies in American society. "This conventional analysis has two problems," Rothbard argues. "If Bryan represented 'the people' versus the 'interests,' why did Bryan lose and lose soundly, not once but three times?"

The second problem, raised by Rothbard, is the way the economics profession tends to deemphasize the dynamic political situation in the United States at that time. In this period, the major political parties would go from extremes and great distinctions to increasingly similar centrist platforms of only modestly different colorations, an alignment that remains in force today.

Historian Paul Kleppner observed that the pro-silver forces, despite their political alliance with farm interests, were not "agrarian" parties so much as religious extremists whose purpose was to cleanse the nation of personal and political sin. Biblical references to Bryan illustrate the evangelical tenor of the pro-silver movement. The *silverite* tendency was more a religious crusade than a coherent economic or political faction focused on money. In the twenty-first century, the same true believer perspective is visible with supporters of crypto currencies.

Kleppner wrote: "The Greenback Party was less an amalgamation of economic pressure groups than an ad hoc coalition of 'True Believers,' 'ideologues,' who launched their party as a quasi-religious movement that bore the indelible hallmark of 'a transfiguring faith.'" In addition to embracing a gospel of inflationism and easy money, the silver advocates were invariably in favor of prohibition and public schools and against parochial education, Catholics, Lutherans, and other non-Pentecostal faiths.[11]

The Cross of Silver

None of the proponents of a bimetallic standard for money in America seemed able to grasp, much less to accept, that the falling demand for silver robbed the metal of its role as a store of value or a unit of account. Nations around the world were ending the use of silver for monetary purposes, and demand from industry and for jewelry was likewise depressed. Since a majority of their fellow citizens clearly preferred paper money or gold to silver as a means of exchange, the position of the silver advocates was hopeless in economic terms, even though politically it remained very powerful.

No matter how many objective lessons were visible in the marketplace to refute their adoration for the increasingly common metal, millions of Americans were convinced of the righteousness of the cause of silver. The proponents of silver were indeed "true believers" in the power of silver extracted from the earth to reverse the economic and social pressures that were building throughout the United States. No amount of evidence to the contrary would dissuade them of the righteousness of their position.

William Jennings Bryan, the "Moses" of the *silverite* movement, declared a holy war in the name of silver money and more currency inflation. At the Chicago convention of 1896, Bryan delivered what many consider to be one of the most important political speeches in American history:

> We do not come as aggressors. Our war is not a war of conquest; we are fighting in the defense of our homes, our families, and posterity. We have petitioned, and our petitions have been scorned; we have entreated, and our entreaties have been disregarded; we have begged, and they have mocked when our calamity came. We beg them no longer; we entreat no more; we petition them no more. We defy them! . . . Thou shalt not crucify America on a Cross of Gold![12]

In August 1893, following the collapse of the Erie Railroad in July and the Northern Pacific a month later, President Cleveland called a special session of the Congress and demanded the repeal of the Sherman Silver Purchase Act. To compel quick action, Cleveland used the threat of keeping Congress in session through the dog days of summer in Washington, DC. This charming French-designed city built upon a strip of malarial river sediment and swamp land along the north bank of the Potomac River was generally evacuated in summer months.

President Cleveland had a summer home well past the current location of the National Cathedral today near Newark Street. Of course, Washington has since been raised and filled in by the U.S. Army Corps of Engineers, a wonderful allegory for the history of money and debt in America that concerns this book.

President Cleveland's call for the repeal of the Sherman Silver Purchase Act was a significant move politically. His vice president, Adlai Stevenson, represented the populist tendency in favor of bimetallism and free coinage of silver that was gaining the ascendancy in the Democratic Party. President Cleveland himself was conservative, almost Republican in his views on money and fiscal restraint. He was troubled by what might happen to the financial markets and the economy if his vice president were to assume power.

Despite long speeches by Bryan and other pro-silver members of the House, on August 28, 1893, the lower chamber voted 239-108 to repeal the Sherman Act. This was a tremendous victory for Cleveland, but not the end of the battle over silver. The Senate Finance Committee approved the legislation to end silver purchases to the full Senate for consideration by just a one-vote margin. Then commenced three months of debate in the Senate, during which the pro-silver forces tried to talk the legislation to death via a filibuster. By early October 1893, the White House was growing desperate and, after meeting with key silver supporters, managed to gain their agreement to end the filibuster. On Friday, October 30, 1893, the Senate voted 43-32 to repeal the Sherman Silver Purchase Act.

The Turning Point: 1896

William McKinley, Jr., was the Republican candidate for president in 1896. He was supported by much of the eastern media and political establishment, which in turn supported sound money, the gold standard, and protective tariffs. It was more than a debate over the nature of money, however. McKinley would eventually win because of a reviving economy and a sense on the part of at least some Americans that silver was not the solution to their economic problems. Although fear of the imposition of silver did motivate many Eastern business interests to support McKinley, it was not the only motivator. The Republican sweep of the White House and the House and Senate in 1896 did not equate to a plebiscite on the currency. The process of finally reaching agreement and adopting legislation on currency reform was still more than a decade away.

A key influence over the work done during this period was a paper commissioned to look at the issue of a central bank, entitled "Report of the Monetary Commission of the Indianapolis Convention." The report provided a very detailed discussion of some of the issues that were agitating Americans when it came to money. Whether or not they were for or against the use of silver as currency, most people wanted a more sound and stable money supply to use for the three basic roles that money plays in any economy. The report outlines the three "Functions of Money":

1. A Standard, or Common Denominator of Value
2. A Medium of Exchange
3. A Standard of Deferred Payments

Regarding the first function, the report stated that "a common denominator is as necessary in comparing the value of commodities as is a common language among many persons in any city to enable them to readily compare ideas."[13]

The needs and frustrations of Americans when it came to the nature of money were pretty basic and more related to economic and personal security rather than to an intellectual debate. The public had plenty of reason to be suspicious of banks and other issuers of debt. In fact, the agitation for free silver and the related instability in the U.S. economy during the 1890s did not help to support the solidity of American banks, whether state-chartered or national banks. Even with the restoration of dollar convertibility into gold in 1879, the U.S. economy and financial system were rocked by a series of market panics. Some began to call for a "flexible" currency.

During the period between 1886 and 1933, Congress considered 150 proposals to create deposit insurance plans for the country's banks to address the issue of bank safety and soundness, but none was adopted and little progress was made in dealing with the basic issue of a stable and liquid money supply to support the economy. It took an additional 30 years for Congress to exert federal authority over the issuance of paper currency and end the private free market system of national and state-chartered banks issuing their own private currency.

Following two decades of strong economic growth after the Civil War, when the West was conquered, many Americans in the 1890s began to fear for their prospects. A severe and prolonged economic weakness began to appear in the United States. The reaction of the public was first bewilderment and surprise, followed by anger. Financial panics led to the collapse of railroads and banks, widespread unemployment, and depressed farm prices, and fueled the rise of the populist movement. These events also increased the power of the great "money trusts" vehicles created by the leading banks and industrialists of the day to limit competition and control prices.

The rise of the money trusts confirmed the fears of John Adams and Thomas Jefferson regarding the evil tendencies of private banks, and caused fear and consternation among the public. The political reaction against the Robber Barons and the trusts in the late 1890s and early 1900s helped fuel the rise of the Progressive movement. This included figures from both the Democrat and Republican parties. However, it would take a strange twist of history to bring to the presidency a man who was sufficiently radical and independent to take on the money trusts and the men who controlled them.

When McKinley ran for president in 1896, he had served in the Congress and as governor of Ohio. He ran on a platform of supporting the gold standard and high tariffs to protect American industries and jobs. He had no strong position on silver per se and easily defeated efforts to add a pro-silver plank to the Republican platform. McKinley chose as his running mate Garret Augustus Hobart, a New Jersey legislator and state court judge. Hobart was selected by Marcus A. Hanna, the Cleveland industrialist and political boss who, along with Charles G. Dawes of Illinois, masterminded McKinley's presidential nomination.

The Gilded Age ushered in the age of the Republican machine political bosses such as Hanna of Ohio, Platt of New York, and Quay of Pennsylvania. While generally seen as being in favor of public versus private interests, McKinley's administration was entirely friendly to the large corporations of the day, which flourished and acquired even more financial and political power. However, the rise of the great trusts, and a more general feeling that the promise of American life was not being fulfilled, inflamed the electorate and especially the Progressive movement led by Bryan.

Bryan called the 1896 election "the first battle." McKinley was the last in a long line of Republican presidents—including Grant, Hayes, Garfield, Arthur, and Harrison—who had followed a generally *laissez-faire* approach to government oversight of business, a program that was now heading for a loud but largely irrelevant collision with reform populism.

The victory of McKinley and the Republicans over the Progressives in 1896 was based on a sweep of the Northern states and a modest showing in the Midwest and South. Cleveland had won the South for the Democrats and Bryan did well, as expected. The popular vote garnered by the two candidates was within half a million votes, with McKinley taking a bit over 7 million to 6.5 million for Bryan with the Democrat a distant third. But the election ended the regional balance between the two pre–Civil War parties and vastly changed the nature of national politics for years to come.

The financial and organizational help of business interests such as Hanna, Platt, and other bosses in orchestrating Republican poll activities seemed to have made the difference in this key election. The same powerful political interests behind the Republican Party expected to control the economic destiny of the United States indefinitely. They did not reckon, however, on the strange fate and destiny that would bring a man named Theodore Roosevelt to the White House.

The resounding victory by the Republicans in 1896 brought many new operatives like Roosevelt to Washington. With the crucial support of Henry Cabot Lodge, Roosevelt went to work as undersecretary of the Navy in the first term of McKinley's presidency. He was soon actively engaged in guiding the expansion of the U.S. territory to include the future state of Hawaii.

Theodore Roosevelt was precisely the sort of figure that most Republicans and the machine bosses feared: a man of independent mind and means who was willing to consider new ideas and even risk failure in pursuit of great national goals. Roosevelt presented his case directly in a speech entitled "Citizenship in a Republic," delivered at the Sorbonne, Paris, on April 23, 1910:

> It is not the critic who counts: not the man who points out how the strong man stumbles or where the doer of deeds could have done better. The credit belongs to the man who is actually in the arena, whose face is marred by dust and sweat and blood, who strives valiantly, who errs and comes up short again and again, because there is no effort without error or shortcoming, but who knows the great enthusiasms, the great devotions, who spends himself for a worthy cause; who, at the best, knows, in the end, the triumph of high achievement, and who, at the worst, if he fails, at least he fails while daring greatly, so that his place shall never be with those cold and timid souls who knew neither victory nor defeat.[14]

With the Republicans in control of Congress and the White House, the stage was set for one of the most conservative pieces of monetary legislation in modern U.S. history, the Gold Standard Act of 1900. This law passed by Congress in March of that year established gold as the only standard for redeeming paper money, and prohibited the exchange of silver for gold. For the moment, at least, this reassured the public as to the value of paper money issued by private national banks. The first two paragraphs of the legislation read:

> An Act To define and fix the standard of value, to maintain the parity of all forms of money issued or coined by the United States, to refund the public debt, and for other purposes. Be it enacted . . . That the dollar consisting of twenty-five and eight-tenths grains of gold nine-tenths fine, as established by section thirty-five hundred and eleven of the Revised Statutes of the United States, shall be the standard unit of value, and all forms of money issued or coined by the United States shall be maintained at a parity of value with this standard, and it shall be the duty of the Secretary of the Treasury to maintain such parity.

The Gold Standard Act officially placed the United States on the gold standard and marked the political high tide for sound money in the United States. But the legislation did not preclude the use of silver as money or "bimetallism" as and when international conditions and the "concurrence of leading commercial nations of the world" made a fixed ratio between the price of gold and silver practical.

Referring to the use of silver as money, three members of the Indianapolis Monetary Commission who traveled to Europe early in 1901 found that none of their counterparts in Europe would "even discuss the matter seriously." "The United States thus became a member in good standing of the international financial community," wrote the commission, something that would have been impossible under a bimetallic standard incorporating silver as advocated by Bryan and the silverites.[15]

The pressure exerted by other countries due to trends away from silver appears to have played a role in the U.S. position. It is interesting to note, however, that the formal adoption of the gold standard did not help to prevent the Panic of 1901 nor avoid subsequent swings in public confidence in individual banks or in the currency that they issued. The United States was experiencing success regarding diplomacy and war, including the impending annexation of Cuba and the Philippines. Yet the U.S. financial markets remained fragile and prone to sudden crises, events that were often focused around the harvest time, when demands for liquidity strained banks large and small.

Even though the vast majority of Americans were aware of the nation's shortcomings when it came to the currency, the business community and the bankers were not yet willing to support change. Indeed, with the landslide victory over William Jennings Bryan by the Republicans in 1900, the business community loudly rejected Progressive reform. To the contrary, the money trusts believed that the way was clear for even more bold acts to expand their power and limit competition, particularly in industries such as steel and oil. The members of the Grand Old Party, as Republicans became known during and after the Civil War, did not anticipate Theodore Roosevelt.

Chapter 4

The Rise of the Central Bank

President William Mckinley was the sort of Republican who the business community could rely upon. Just a month before President Mckinley began his second term in office, the U.S. Steel Corporation was formed under the laws of the State of New Jersey. The purpose of the U.S. Steel Corporation was to purchase the stock of numerous steel producers and thereby avoid competition. J.P. Morgan bought out Andrew Carnegie as the controlling interest in U.S. Steel. He put Charles M. Schwab, a Carnegie man, in the presidency, and Judge Elbert H. Gary, a Morgan man, in the chief executive chair of the first billion-dollar trust.

Steel prices were weak in 1900 and many of the producers, which were controlled by Andrew Carnegie or the House of Morgan, were preparing to expand the amount and range of steel production, a move that would have certainly caused steel prices to fall further. Instead, by forming U.S. Steel, Carnegie and Morgan were able to pool their far-flung investments in numerous different steel producers and limit competition, which had an immediate and positive impact on steel prices.[1]

Charles Schwab told Clarence Barron that the merger of the Carnegie and Morgan steel interests came about after J.P. Morgan, at the suggestion of Schwab, called on Andrew Carnegie on the occasion of the latter's birthday. The two men soon reached an accord to combine their steel interests. When Schwab later left U.S. Steel and purchased Bethlehem Steel, Morgan bought him out and held the company as a personal investment, again to avoid competition.[2] Schwab's counterpart, Judge Gary, who served in the Civil War as an Illinois volunteer, would steer the giant U.S. Steel conglomerate through World War I right up through his death in 1927.

U.S. Steel was just one example of the way in which the trust operators manipulated prices and limited competition, and all with the blessings of the Republican Party's candidate in the White House and a majority in the Congress. McKinley's vice president, Garret Hobart, typified the views of the Republican mainstream with respect to the money trusts when he said at the time of his election in 1896 that "corporations and aggregations of capital do not make it impossible for a poor man to climb up. The rich man of today is the poor man of tomorrow."[3]

The death of Vice President Hobart at the end of McKinley's first term illustrates the conservative nature of the government of the United States in 1900. In the first century of the nation's existence, the occupants of the White House were selected from a small group of the country's Founders and their children. In the second century, however, a succession of Republicans from the Northeast dominated the political stage. Hobart was a New Jersey native and an able man. "I am a business man," Hobart was reported to have said. "I engage in politics for recreation."[4]

The election of 1900 was mostly about foreign affairs, particularly the war with Spain and the resulting territorial gains. Bryan again ran against McKinley, who had a kindly personal demeanor and managed to please just about everyone in the country except for the silver evangelists. He chose as his new running mate Theodore Roosevelt, a former governor of New York and war hero in the conflict with Spain.

Roosevelt was too high profile for the taste of Boss Platt, who volunteered the services of the former governor at the Navy Department and allowed him to become vice president under McKinley in order to get Teddy out of New York. The McKinley-Roosevelt ticket focused on the successful war against Spain and an improving economy, and won easily over Bryan, who talked less and less about silver and more about imperialism and the money trusts. Whatever talent he had for speaking, Bryan was like many Progressives, an unsuccessful national politician.

McKinley won a great victory in 1900 polling 51 percent of the vote. Yet fate struck a year later when on September 6, 1901, he was shot and killed at the Pan American Exhibition in Buffalo. Teddy Roosevelt was sworn into office about a week later on September 14, 1901, at the Ansley Wilcox Mansion in Buffalo. Roosevelt said at the time: "The course I followed, of regarding the Executive as subject only to the people, and, under the Constitution, bound to serve the people affirmatively in cases where the Constitution does not explicitly forbid him to render the service, was substantially the course followed by both Andrew Jackson and Abraham Lincoln."[5]

The Progressive: Theodore Roosevelt

Teddy Roosevelt was one of the most radical and brilliant Americans to hold the highest office in the land. The child of a well-off eastern family and educated at Harvard, Roosevelt possessed all of the tools to be an effective technocrat and a great politician. But he added to this a thorough commitment to democracy and reform that made him the giant of the age of reform. It was one thing for a Progressive or a Democrat to attack the money trusts or big business, but to have a libertarian Republican, a Tammany man, and former New York governor become the leader of the Progressive movement was remarkable. Years later, J.P. Morgan remarked to Clarence W. Barron, owner of Dow, Jones & Co: "Who did more than Teddy Roosevelt to smash business?"[6]

Members of the left criticized Roosevelt as a lapdog of the business interests behind McKinley, but Roosevelt actually became more radical as time went on and was certainly more outspoken than many of his Republican and Democratic predecessors. The bankers and political bosses of the age urged the young president to "go slow" and do nothing that might disturb "confidence." Roosevelt ignored these pleas and eventually put himself at the head of the Progressive movement by speaking truth to power.

Like all politicians, he understood that there was real political power in the roar of the crowd, a fact that made Roosevelt even more eager to rail at oppressive business practices. His natural tendency was not to be a Progressive, but his response to the popular clamor for social justice could be quite extreme. The rise of Roosevelt to become the champion of the individual in the age of dominance of large corporations is remarkable. Roosevelt recognized that the money trusts and public companies were antithetical to democracy, one of those rare moments in modern American politics when the random factor of chance dramatically altered history in favor of the individual.

Teddy Roosevelt was an often-contradictory figure. Early in his career he fought against Jay Gould's corrupt inroads into the finances of New York City when the elevated trains were being built in that city. Roosevelt frequently referred to Gould and other moneyed interests of the day in the most colorful terms, playing on the public's growing unease at the role of wealth in American society. Yet he was a personal friend and social peer of J.P. Morgan. Roosevelt never did anything that truly inconvenienced the large banks and corporations of that era—unless he believed them to be malevolent.

Roosevelt played on the popular suspicion of concentrations of economic power, but he was not against big business or even the trusts themselves. He saw the formation of big business as the natural evolution of a growing economy and a necessary step for America to compete in the world. Roosevelt was a strong supporter of tariffs and other trade barriers to protect American industries and jobs from the predatory trade practices of the mercantilist states of Europe. Though not in favor of isolationism, Roosevelt was a nationalist who favored a selective seclusion of America from the evils of the rest of the world.

The major difference between Roosevelt and conservative Republicans such as McKinley was his support for the Progressive approach of balancing big business with an equally muscular government in order to meet the popular anxiety regarding power. Roosevelt was affronted by the belief on the part of the great industrialists of the age that their personal power was greater than that of the federal government.

As a gifted and often inspired politician, Roosevelt also responded to the widely held fear on the part of many Americans that their stake in the collective patrimony, the "American dream" was being stolen. "The ominous sense of a shrinking margin of practical liberties pervaded men," wrote Matthew Josephson in his 1934 classic *The Robber Barons*, "as each successive step in the nationwide consolidation of the country's resources and means of production brought no tangible gains to the population at large."[7]

President Roosevelt did not make money or currency issues a central part of his administration. Yet he did have a significant impact on capital finance for all manner of corporations by starting to address issues of competition and restraint of trade. Roosevelt was not against the idea of large companies, but he was intolerant of companies that restricted trade or used their size to limit personal freedom, "kinder masters" in the socially charged language of the era.

Roosevelt believed not only in legalistic control and break-up of wayward companies, but also in the use of publicity and disclosure to modify the behavior of the speculators and trusts who operated free of limit in the marketplace of the early 1900s. Using the Sherman Antitrust Act and the Hepburn Act, Roosevelt was able to strengthen the enforcement powers of the Interstate Commerce Commission and attack some of the most powerful trusts of the day.

The first antitrust case was brought just five months after he took office, in February 1902. It was against Northern Securities Company, a trust that held the railroad interests of J.P. Morgan in the Northern Pacific and James Hill in the Great Northern railroads. Northern Securities was buying up the stock of other railroads in competition with E.H. Harriman, the great railroad baron and banker who was second only to J.P. Morgan himself in terms of influence during the era of the money trusts.

Roosevelt sought to dissolve the Northern Securities Company and eventually won the case by a 5-4 margin before the Supreme Court. President Roosevelt would bring 45 other suits against other trusts under the Sherman Act.[8] The attack on the Northern Securities Company, however, while politically a very astute move by Theodore Roosevelt, was little more than a nuisance for the House of Morgan.

The irony is that despite the rhetoric, the Roosevelt era saw the continued growth of the trusts and corporate power overall. Roosevelt preferred to persuade company management to effect changes rather than use the blunt club of the Sherman Act to enforce remedies to anticompetitive measures. Sometimes Roosevelt was also overtly friendly to big business, as in the case of the acquisition in 1907 of the Tennessee Iron & Coal Company by U.S. Steel.

The discretion of the White House in deciding whether to sue or not to stop anticompetitive behavior was illustrated by the way Roosevelt pursued selectively his campaign. Clarence Barron records a conversation with Judge Gary, the great chairman of U.S. Steel Corporation, where the latter traveled to Washington, along with the steel magnate Henry Frick, to meet with Teddy Roosevelt. The purpose of the trip was to gain permission for the merger between Tennessee Iron & Coal and U.S. Steel, which had been announced before the 1900 election and the subsequent death of President McKinley. Gary relates that Roosevelt told the delegation led by Judge Gary which represented J.P. Morgan that "while he was President we would not be troubled."[9]

The Tennessee Iron & Coal case was the most prominent transaction by a trust during the Roosevelt era and became so contentious politically that Democrats and Republicans in the Congress demanded an inquiry. President Roosevelt was forced to endure an investigation into the decision to allow the merger to go through.[10]

Most Americans and centrist Progressives loved and supported Roosevelt, yet on the left he was seen as a tool of business interests, albeit one with a taste for imperial expansion. Teddy was, after all, a child of wealth, although not the kind of wealth later possessed by his cousin Franklin Delano Roosevelt. Roosevelt's support for the territorial expansion of the United States through the conquest of Cuba and the annexation of the Philippines evidenced an authoritarian worldview more than a libertarian philosophy. But neither Andrew Jackson nor Abraham Lincoln, Roosevelt's heroes among the American presidents, were opposed to the use of military force to achieve political objectives.

A new age of imperialism was dawning under Teddy Roosevelt, even as an increasingly unsettled American nation drifted to the political left. But given the possible alternatives presented by the growing Progressive leanings of American voters, Roosevelt was a relatively moderate choice. In 1904 when President Roosevelt ran for reelection, some of the most prominent Robber Barons were among the largest contributors to his campaign—banker Morgan, steel and coal magnate

Henry Frick, banker James Stillman of National City Bank, financier George J. Gould, the son of Jay Gould, and H.H. Rogers, director of Standard Oil, to name but a few.

Despite his strong public advocacy of reform, Roosevelt at the end of the day was less of a threat to the industrialists and bankers than was feared. The Reverend W.S. Rainsford, minister of St. George's Church on Stuyvesant Square, the haven where J.P. Morgan sought spiritual solace for four decades, is reported to have said: "The time will come when you will get down on your knees and bless Providence for having given us Theodore Roosevelt as our President."

When Roosevelt spoke at a dinner at the Gridiron Club in Washington where Morgan was in attendance, the president at one point strode toward the banker and, shaking his fist in the face of the financial colossus, shouted theatrically: "If you don't let us do this," referring to reform, "those who will come after us will rise and bring you to ruin." But unlike many other bankers and industrial captains, Morgan was never persuaded by Roosevelt's protestations.[11]

A Flexible Currency

In May 1901, the U.S. stock market suffered a significant decline, but this event was unlike the panics of 1893 and 1873. In the earlier crises, the use of foreign debt to fuel speculative excess made the overall situation far worse. The crisis in 1901, by comparison, was limited to the financial markets in New York and those firms and investors that could absorb the losses without failing. The fact was that the U.S. economy remained hamstrung by a currency system that was prone to swings in the liquidity available based on changes in the public mood, both in the United States and around the world.

Roosevelt was unmoved through the Panic of 1901 and the far larger financial Crisis of 1907. So powerful was the political influence of large business over the Congress that even with Roosevelt's popularity he might not have been able to make headway regarding tariffs or currency reform. By the end of Roosevelt's second term in office, however, a national consensus had formed regarding the need for lower tariffs and other reforms.

Yet the great Republican leaders of the Senate—Orville Platt, John Spooner, William Allison, and Nelson Aldrich—kept the pace of reform at slow to none. Their control over the Senate and thus national policy was an important practical check on Roosevelt's actions, particularly regarding domestic economic and fiscal policy. The uncertain political dynamic of the time, coupled with the power of the Senate chieftains and the great political bosses, may explain why Roosevelt did not focus more attention on the issue of monetary reform.

The question of the "inflexibility" of the banking system was very much in the public mind and the country remained highly vulnerable to changes in sentiment in foreign capitals. Yet the Republican program of fiscal sobriety, high tariffs, and trade protectionism still managed to poll a majority in the Congress and win the White House. This did not mean, however, that President Roosevelt failed to address the question of money and the national currency.

In 1903 in Quincy, Illinois, Teddy Roosevelt said:

It is well-nigh universally admitted, certainly in any business community such as this, that our currency system is wanting in elasticity; that is, the volume does not respond to the varying needs of the country as a whole, nor of the varying needs of the different localities and the different times. Our people scarcely need to be reminded that grain-raising communities require a larger volume of currency at harvest time than in the summer months; and the same principle in greater or less extent applies to every community. Our currency laws need such modification as will ensure definitely the parity of every dollar coined or issued by the government, and such expansion and contraction of the currency as will promptly and automatically respond to the varying needs of commerce. Permanent increase would be dangerous, permanent contraction ruinous, but the needed elasticity must be brought about by provisions which will permit the contraction and expansion as the varying needs of the several communities and business interests at different times and in different localities require.[12]

The comments by President Roosevelt on the monetary system reflected the basic view of Americans of his day, namely the wisdom of avoiding "dangerous" permanent increases or "ruinous" decreases in the supply of money. The public wanted money to be "flexible." Roosevelt called it "elastic." Yet the fact remains that for the public the "flexibility" of the money supply was a visceral political issue. In 1907, for example, interest rates fluctuated from as low as 2 to as high as 30 percent, driven by demand from the major New York banks, which in turn "attracted money from the interior banks into that speculative field."[13]

The purchase of stocks in this period was often financed with credit via margin loans. Fluctuations in interest rates due to factors such as the seasonal harvest or changes in the perceived credit standing of the United States could significantly impact domestic financial markets. The fact that money is "fungible" and moves for value in terms of investment opportunities also meant that credit the Treasury put into the markets with the intention of helping the farm sector, for example, could just as easily end up deployed in the New York financial markets. And that is precisely what occurred.

In his message to the Congress in December 1907, President Roosevelt noted that the currency in circulation had increased more than 50 percent over a period of 10 years, from $21 to $33 per capita. The increased demand for currency visible to all in the fall of each year, and the resulting financial disturbances throughout the economy, showed that the nation still needed basic currency and banking reform. The image of people standing in long lines outside of banks waiting to withdraw their money was part of the American economic experience. Yet it is hard for a politician to sell citizens on the American dream of opportunity and hard work when they cannot depend on the nation's money or the banks that issue it.

The public's concern regarding the adequacy of the money supply in the first decade of the twentieth century is all the more ironic since the money supply was growing at a pretty brisk pace. The increase in money growth can be attributed to the government's reaction to the demand for currency, but this growth came within the context of a government that was loath to use debt or raise taxes for federal spending. Federal revenues and debt were remarkably stable during this period, the former being comprised mostly of the proceeds from tariffs. And still there was no central bank.

Between the end of silver purchases by the Treasury in 1897 and the start of World War I in 1914, the money supply of the United States grew at a reasonably steady rate. This begs the question as to whether the supply of money in the U.S. financial system or the ebb and flow of a growing, free market society was the more important factor behind successive financial crises. The growth in the supply of gold coins and greenbacks was in excess of 100 percent over the 15 years leading up to the first great world war. Yet the United States experienced years of instability in the banking sector leading up to the Crisis of 1907.[14]

The Progressives may have been right; namely that it was where the money was held, not the aggregate amount or supply of currency in circulation, that mattered most to consumers and business. This same reality would be illustrated more than a century later when the Federal Reserve Board almost crashed the U.S. economy in December 2018 because it did not understand the true demand for bank reserves.

Banks in the South and West of the United States did not have the same deep commercial and public sector relationships from which to draw their liquidity, not to mention a close relationship with the U.S. Treasury. The big New York banks were the customs agents for the United States and these banks held the government's cash. When bad times came, banks east of the Mississippi River and, even better, east of the Hudson tended to have superior chances of survival.

The flaw in the U.S. banking and currency system, according to Milton Friedman and Anna Schwartz, was the fact that bank deposits were effectively treated as money. A visualization of this issue is provided by Frank Capra's 1947 film, *It's a Wonderful Life*. When a crowd of panicked customers besieged George Bailey's Building and Loan for cash.

"The contemporary and still standard interpretation of this episode is that an apparently rather mild contraction was converted into a severe contraction by the banking panic and associated restrictions of payments by the banking system," concluded Friedman and Schwartz. "It was this interpretation of the episode that provided the prime impetus for the monetary reform movement that culminated in the Federal Reserve Act."[15]

The Crisis of 1907

The Crisis of 1907 was a century in the making but was also the result of an economy that had far outgrown its monetary system. Unlike previous panics, which began during the autumn farm harvest season, the 1907 event began in March and would last the entire year and beyond. The New York Stock Exchange went into a drastic decline, leading to public panic and depositor runs on banks. These bank runs led to large-scale liquidations of "call loans," short-term loans used to finance stock market purchases. This selling caused further declines in stock prices and widespread insolvency for businesses and individuals.

The natural reaction to crisis by banks and the entire financial system in the early 1900s was to limit the availability of deposits in order to survive. The flow of payments through the U.S. economy slowed, causing personal and commercial insolvencies to soar. By November 1907, the New York stock market averages were almost 40 percent below the levels seen before the crisis began, representing a vast reduction in national wealth and therefore potential for economic growth.

A number of historians and commentators of this period believe that J.P. Morgan and the other members of the money trust precipitated the Crisis of 1907 in order to depress stock and bond prices for certain companies they coveted. Naturally, Morgan disliked the public stock market. He was even less sanguine about individual speculators and the smaller trusts that proliferated and employed bank loans to fund purchases of stocks and bonds. Conveniently enough, the crisis forced the heavily indebted Tennessee Iron & Coal company, a competitor of the great Pennsylvania Steel Trust controlled by the Morgan and Rockefeller groups, to sell itself to Morgan for $30 million, less than 5 percent of its actual worth.[16]

In the fictional work *The Money Changers*, published in 1908 by Upton Sinclair, "a plutocrat very much resembling Morgan provoked a financial panic and turned the people's misery to his own sordid gain," wrote James Grant in *Money of the Mind*.[17] Whether or not J.P. Morgan actually caused the Crisis of 1907 and then arrived as the savior of the nation to counter its terrible effects, many people believed that version of events.

A key event in 1907 was the "run" on the Knickerbocker Trust Company in New York. During the Roosevelt years, trust companies proliferated. National and state banks generally were not allowed to do a trust business. Trusts were based on the fiduciary business, but then added aggressive lending products funded off the street. The trusts of the Gilded Age were not members of the New York Clearing House and did not have the ability to borrow directly from other banks. Trusts were the original "shadow banks" and caused enormous problems in the Great Depression.

Trusts put themselves forward to the public as banks, but these entities more often than not were just lightly capitalized, speculative vehicles for issuing debt and investing in stocks or commodities. The previous discussion of the railroad trusts offers one example of the hundreds of industrial trusts ranging from sugar to commodes formed in order to gain pricing power over a given market. The legacy of Fisk, Gould, and the other Robber Barons was not that of hard work but rather price fixing.

As with the panics of the late-1800s, in the Crisis of 1907 there was no agency in Washington to act when calamity affected the markets. Once again, the colossus, J.P. Morgan, was called upon to save the nation. Morgan and James Stillman of First National City Bank, predecessor of Citigroup today, acted as a *de facto* "central bank" and specifically as a lender of last resort. These banks ensured that the Knickerbocker Trust was able to meet its obligations. Chartered in 1884 by Frederick G. Eldridge, a friend and classmate of financier Morgan, the Knickerbocker Trust was one of the largest trust banks of its day.

The Crisis of 1907 began with a selloff in the stock market and eventually caused a fatal deposit run on many banks. This episode was not unlike the collapse of institutional sources of funding that destroyed Bear, Stearns & Co. and Lehman Brothers a century later.

Terrence Checki, executive vice president of the Federal Reserve Bank of New York, observed about the 2008 financial crisis in a December 2009 speech: "Our system evolved from one funded by intermediaries, to one largely financed by markets. The traditional ties between borrower and creditor were weakened as credit risk became just another commodity to be traded and distributed."[18] And this was precisely the same situation that existed in March 1907, albeit on a far smaller scale.

In addition to the lender role, the failure of Knickerbocker and other trusts featured J.P. Morgan as the *de facto* receiver of failed banks. Morgan liquidated failed trusts and disposed of their assets without the inconvenience of court process. President Roosevelt effectively made Morgan the agent of the U.S. Treasury and provided $25 million in government funds deposited in New York banks to visibly address the panic. Morgan played the same role as played today by the Federal Deposit Insurance Corporation. A team of financiers addressed the crisis, including John Rockefeller, James Stillman of National City Bank, George F. Baker of First National Bank, Edward Harriman the railroad titan, and an assortment of other bankers and lawyers.

As head of the largest bank in the country, Morgan was omnipotent and decided which banks were to fail and which would survive. By putting a great deal of cash on the street, in some cases literally piled up in teller cages to make the point to the public that money was plentiful, Morgan averted a shutdown of the New York Stock Exchange, and thereby engineered a financial bailout of New York City.

Morgan orchestrated an orderly closure of Knickerbocker Trust in October 1907 and then extended loans to Trust Company of America to prevent another large bank collapse, perhaps one of the earliest examples of the moral dilemma of "systemic risk." In a stark example of the reality of collective interest when it comes to matters of finance, Morgan bailed out the larger insolvent trust companies that he loathed and despised in order to keep the entire financial system from crumbling.

Only days after rescuing the trust banks, the head of the New York Stock Exchange told Morgan that the market could not remain open. The failure of the exchange would be a catastrophic blow to public confidence, the banks, and Washington equally. Morgan organized a bailout by the New York Clearing House to support the exchange. Morgan and civic leaders, including members of the clergy, exhorted the public to keep their money in the bank. Yet there were still lines of people standing outside banks on the rainy Monday that followed, waiting to withdraw their cash.

The Crisis of 1907 illustrated that the government was powerless to address the very real problems with the national system of currency and banks, even with the aggressive but limited actions taken by the

U.S. Treasury to supply cash to the banking system. The dislike among Americans for a central government and especially a central bank was too strong. Thus, through inaction, the Congress left the financial sector of the U.S. economy in chaos. The author John Steele Gordon summarized the situation:

> We paid a heavy price for the Jeffersonian aversion to central banking. Without a central bank there was no way to inject liquidity into the banking system to stem a panic. As a result, the panics of the 19th century were far worse here than in Europe and precipitated longer and deeper depressions. In 1907, J.P. Morgan, probably the most powerful private banker who ever lived, acted as the central bank to end the panic that year.[19]

The Crisis of 1907 was one of the sharpest economic contractions in U.S. history and left the finances of many in ruins. It prompted the national Congress to take action that eventually led to the enactment of the Federal Reserve Act in 1913. Yet the path to the creation of the central bank was hardly smooth.

The National Monetary Commission

In a precursor to the Federal Reserve Act, the Congress enacted the Aldrich-Vreeland Act of 1908. The law was a response to the horrible social and economic effects of the Crisis of 1907 and provided for emergency currency issuance by the Treasury during economic crises. At the request of President Roosevelt, the legislation also established the National Monetary Commission to propose a banking reform plan. Chaired by Senator Nelson W. Aldrich (R-RI), the commission examined both the financial and political issues that caused the various crises of the previous decades—but from a decidedly Republican, big city bank perspective.

The Aldrich Commission developed a plan that was largely favorable to the northeastern banks. William Jennings Bryan and the Progressives in all three parties fiercely attacked the proposal. Progressives wanted a central bank under public, not private banker control—echoing a debate that continued until the end of the twentieth century. Aldrich's leadership meant that the Progressives' hopes were dashed.

He was the leading critic of the Progressive movement and a stalwart champion of American conservatism. Aldrich's daughter was married to John D. Rockefeller, Jr. Lincoln Steffens and other muckraking writers of the day referred to Senator Aldrich as "the boss of the United States" and "the power behind the power behind the throne." Aldrich was one of the most visible and unapologetic advocates for big business in modern American history.[20]

The disappointment of the Progressives in the period leading to the creation of the Fed was so fierce that it lingers even today. Republicans were smart enough to pay lip service to the needs of the agrarians, but the agenda was already set by the politicians allied with Morgan and Rockefeller. Laurence Laughlin of the University of Chicago, the author of the Indianapolis Commission report on the U.S. financial system that was produced in 1896, was again pressed into service by the banks, this time as the advocate of "banking reform." Laughlin was a friend of Woodrow Wilson and the obvious champion for the effort—at least from the perspective of the banking industry.

Early in 1913, before Wilson's inauguration, Laughlin began to draft a banking reform bill that was derived from the work of Senator Aldrich and the National Monetary Commission. Laughlin helped to marshal businesspeople and bankers to testify before Congress and persistently disputed the idea of the existence of a money trust, a convenient argument for the House of Morgan and other large banks and industrial groups. There were groups such as the National Citizens League, organized by Laughlin and funded by some of the largest banks, to provide public support for reform legislation.

The blue-ribbon report produced by the National Monetary Commission proposed a National Reserve Association that would issue legal tender notes as required by the financial system. These notes would be backed by a reserve in gold or legal reserve currencies equal to 50 percent of the notes issued. The National Reserve Association essentially would have been a collective owned and controlled by the banks themselves and not subject to direct governmental control. This aspect of private banker control over the new central bank was strongly opposed by Progressives.

While the proposal from the National Monetary Commission offered the promise that the new central bank would provide additional finance to farmers, in fact the Federal Reserve Act eventually drafted by Laughlin did not deliver on any of the Progressive demands, including the availability of farm credit. None of the National Monetary Commission's proposals ever made it to the floor of the Congress.

Paul M. Warburg recalled in his book *The Federal Reserve System: Its Origin and Growth* that in 1910 most Americans were in favor of a central bank, but only if it were "not controlled by 'Wall Street' or any other monopolistic interest."[21] In the 1900s, members of Congress jumped through virtual hoops of fire like trained circus dogs at the command of J.P. Morgan and the captains of other large banks. Then as today, there was no question as to who was boss in Washington regardless of which party controlled the White House or the Congress. And then as now, most Americans were not expert in finance, but they understood well enough that the financial power of the New York banks threatened both the value of money and the political independence of the national government.

In the run up to the 1912 election, the Pujo Committee also focused attention on the power of the large banks, in this case through the underwriting of corporate bonds. The St. Louis Federal Reserve Bank revealed:

In 1912, a special subcommittee was convened by the Chairman of the House Banking and Currency Committee, Arsene P. Pujo (D-LA). Its purpose was to investigate the "money trust," a small group of Wall Street bankers that exerted powerful control over the nation's finances. The committee's majority report concluded that a group of financial leaders had abused the public trust to consolidate control over many industries. The Pujo Committee report created a climate of public opinion that lead to the passage of the Federal Reserve Act of 1913 and the Clayton Antitrust Act of 1914.[22]

The political context of the Pujo investigation is important to understand the final form and adoption of the Federal Reserve Act. Louisiana Democrat Arsene Pujo was actually a supporter of the Republican-sponsored Aldrich plan for financial reform. He attempted to push the plan through the Congress in 1912, but was opposed by

Carter Glass and other Democrats, who wanted to wait for Woodrow Wilson's inauguration in March 1913. Glass also wanted to limit the scope of the legislation to currency reform only, while the Louisiana Democrat had a broader agenda.

The Pujo Committee report detailed the collusive practices among banks and the ownership ties via trusts that connected many banks to one another. Yet despite the public hearings and reformist rhetoric, the Pujo Committee ended its work inconclusively and did not really do more than inconvenience the largest banks. From this perspective, Carter Glass and other members of the Democratic leadership in 1913 were the moderates in the equation, protecting the large New York banks from attacks by the Progressives.[23]

Pujo did not seek reelection in 1912 and thus cleared the way for Glass to become chairman of the House Committee on Banking and Currency. This was a key political inflection point that arguably ensured the Fed's eventual creation—albeit in a different form. Glass, for his part, opposed the work of Senator Aldrich and instead put forward a more decentralized plan for the central bank. Glass did not introduce a bill himself but instead waited for President Wilson to transmit his legislation to the Congress in June 1913.

Given the fierce public debate regarding banking and currency reform, it was remarkable that following the election of Woodrow Wilson in 1913, the Congress actually passed three key pieces of legislation: the Underwood Tariff, the Federal Trade Act, and the Federal Reserve Act. Of all three pieces of legislation, however, the central bank was at the top of the agenda because of the clear need for banking and currency reform from the perspective of a growing number of influential bankers.

Most Americans agreed that change was needed, but still there was far from any agreement on the nature of the change that ought to occur. Banks and business interests generally opposed the legislation proposed by Wilson and Democrats like Carter Glass of Virginia. Bankers envisioned a decentralized system of Federal Reserve Banks to provide liquidity to the banking system and serve as the banks of issue for currency.

Southern agrarians and small business interests in the Democratic Party, however, wanted more radical change. They feared a central bank controlled by the New York banks and the political interests behind them, interests that had controlled the Congress for decades. Ultimately, Chairman Glass, Senator Robert Owen of Oklahoma, and Treasury secretary McAdoo prepared legislation for President Wilson to submit to the Congress. And ultimately the result feared by the Progressives of private bank control over the central bank was precisely what occurred.

During the work of the National Monetary Commission, the banking industry met with key members of the Aldrich group to consider the issue of a central bank. In 1910, Paul Warburg and a small group representing the chiefs of the largest banks and corporations in the United States traveled by rail to Jekyll Island, Georgia, to discuss creating some type of central bank. The Jekyll Island meeting was kept secret because any public hint that Aldrich was consulting the large banks would doom his efforts.

Murray Newton Rothbard described the scene in *The Case Against the Fed*:

> The conferees worked for a solid week at the plush Jekyll Island retreat, and hammered out the draft of the bill for the Federal Reserve System. Only six people attended this super-secret week-long meeting, and these six reflected the power structure within the bankers' alliance within the central banking movement. The conferees were, in addition to Aldrich (Rockefeller kinsman): Henry P. Davidson, Morgan Partner; Paul Warburg, Kuhn Loeb partner; Frank A. Vanderlip, vice-president of Rockefeller's National City Bank of New York; Charles D. Norton, president of Morgan's First National Bank of New York; and Professor A. Piatt Andrew, head of the NMC staff, who had recently been made an Assistant Secretary of the Treasury under Taft, and who was a technician with a foot in both the Rockefeller and Morgan camps.[24]

The conceptual framework for the central bank already was in place long before the Jekyll Island meeting. The architect, Lawrence Laughlin, became the most visible national advocate of the Federal Reserve proposal. Laughlin testified before the Congress and made statements in favor of the proposal. His brainchild not only central-ized and rationalized the nation's currency system, but Laughlin's crea-tion removed the machinations of the bankers from public view. The Federal Reserve Board would come to shield the banking industry from scrutiny by the public and Congress.

The chosen candidate of the large banks, Woodrow Wilson, was elected in 1912 after defeating Robert Taft and Theodore Roosevelt. A dedicated racist, Wilson became the leading light of the now cen-trist Progressive movement and made monetary reform a top priority. The public issue was whether it was even possible to create a central bank that would not fall under the influence and control of the large New York banks. The practical obstacle to moving forward with mon-etary reform was how to clothe the process in sufficiently populist attire to generate support in the Congress.

The Federal Reserve Act

Following his inauguration in March 1913, Wilson's administration worked through the summer of that year to win passage of what would become the Federal Reserve Act. Each time they reached agreement with either the banks or Progressive agrarian interests, the other side would bolt, seeking ever more concessions in a grand example of Wash-ington political theater. The proposal sponsored by Rep. Glass and Senator Owen, the Progressive Democrat from Oklahoma, contained a regional system of 12 banks and was the only legislation that had a reasonable chance of passage through Congress.

Despite the best efforts by the banking lobby to amend the legisla-tion and impose a central bank explicitly controlled by the New York financial community, the superficially more Progressive plan supported by Glass was the clear choice of a majority of the legislature. The New York banks then began a campaign to delay and thereby kill the legislation. This strategy ultimately failed and did so visibly enough to support the appearance of Progressive support for the legislation.

The Progressives rightly viewed the bank-supported central bank as providing political risk but no solution to the lack of credit available for farm communities. The political truth was that the primary impact of the annual surge in demand for funds by western banks to finance the fall harvest was to suppress agricultural prices, something to which bankers and their political allies in Washington raised no objection.

Although the large banks fought the legislation, a growing majority of Americans knew that the recurring financial crises in the United States and the lack of a central bank to supply credit to the financial system generally was a serious disadvantage for the U.S. economy. In the early 1900s, the credit of U.S. banks was considered to be inferior to British banks, which were set up to do business throughout the British empire. London held a tight grip over the financing of American commerce more than a century after the Declaration of Independence. Indeed, while there were many reasons for the Anglo-centric view of the House of Morgan and its strong ties to the London banking market, sheer necessity was one of the most important. J.P. Morgan was seen as a giant in New York, but in the City of London it was still viewed as a colonial upstart right up until World War I. Then the tables of global finance turned in favor of New York.

With the Crisis of 1907 many bankers became convinced of the need for change in the flexibility of the currency, even if their political tendencies had not changed appreciably when it came to the question of sound money and the power of the eastern banks. The debate over the central bank would become an enduring feature of the popular perception of the American dream.

Unemployment, financial panics, and insecurity were now features of the modern American society. As a result, many small-town bankers feared that the system would break without a change and that even more draconian regulation from Washington would ensue. The key shift in the political equation that made the Federal Reserve Act's passage possible was not a populist rebellion in the farm community. The fact that growing numbers of the Main Street banking and business community was willing to revisit the idea of a central bank was the key.

After several months of furious delay engineered by the large New York banks, the Senate passed the Federal Reserve Act on December 19, 1913. The Federal Reserve Act passed the Senate just as the Congress was ending its session. President Wilson signed it into law on Christmas Eve, yet another irony in the history of the American central bank. The following year, the Federal Trade Commission was created and the Sixteenth Amendment to the Constitution opened the way for a permanent federal income tax. The age of reform and regulation—and big government—was in full swing. Senator Robert Byrd (D-WV) summed up the generally accepted version of the event in his history of the Senate:

> The creation of the Federal Reserve System was the crowning achievement of the Sixty-third Congress and, indeed, of the first Wilson administration. Despite the conservative attack in the Senate, its basic structure—the twelve Federal Reserve Banks, privately controlled, regulated and supervised by the Federal Reserve Board—still remains. It proved to be a significant reform of the very heart of the American economy. It destroyed the control of money and credit by a few banks on Wall Street, created a more flexible and sound currency, and permitted a planned supervision of banking reserves to meet the country's needs.[25]

Byrd's quotation is somewhat misleading and reflects a modern-day, sanitized view of the central bank. The Fed's Board of Governors in Washington was not part of the original Federal Reserve Act. The number and geographic location of the Federal Reserve Banks was actually determined by the National Monetary Commission led by Senator Aldrich.

Carter Glass and the other exponents of a decentralized "central bank" deliberately avoided a Washington presence for the Federal Reserve System because of popular opposition. The official version of events said that the decentralized design of the Fed would prevent the New York banks from exercising excessive control, but in fact that is precisely what happened in practice. Lawrence Goodwyn commented on just that point in his landmark 1976 work, *Democratic Promise: The Populist Moment in America*:

> In a gesture that was symbolic of the business-endorsed reforms of the Progressive era, William Jennings Bryan hailed the passage of the Federal Reserve Act in 1913 as a "triumph for the people." His response provided a measure of the intellectual achievements of reformers in the Progressive period. Of longer

cultural significance, it also illustrated how completely the idea of "reform" had become incorporated within the new political boundaries established in Bryan's own lifetime. The reformers of the Progressive era fit snugly within these boundaries—in Bryan's case, without his even knowing it. Meanwhile, the idea of substantial democratic influence over the structure of the nation's financial system, a principle that had been the operative objective of the greenbackers, quietly passed out of American political dialogue. It has remained there ever since.[26]

Virginia Democrat Carter Glass became secretary of the Treasury during President Wilson's second term. Even though a small man in physical stature, Glass was a giant in his day and the authority on financial matters in the Congress. Senator Kenneth McKellar of Tennessee called Glass "one of the finest and noblest characters" with whom he had been associated. "I never knew him to do a small thing; he had a big heart and a great mind."[27]

It can be argued that, at the end of the day, Glass's devotion to core American principles about the need for checks and balances was thwarted by the power of Morgan and the other large banks. The House of Morgan used its massive influence in Congress to shape the outcome of the legislative process. A century later little has changed. The large banks have even more influence, but today inept American legislators have far less grasp of economics and finance.

Glass is credited as the intellectual author of the Federal Reserve Act, but he was hardly the champion of the legislation in that tumultuous year, especially on the floor of the Senate. In fact, all three pieces of Wilson's key legislative reforms were guided through the Congress and to final enactment by Senator John Worth Kern (D-IN), the first member of the Senate to be referred to as the "leader" of the majority and a key ally of Woodrow Wilson. Kern was an unsuccessful Democratic candidate for governor of Indiana in 1900 and was on the ticket as vice president under William Jennings Bryan in 1908. He was defeated in 1917 after only one term in the Senate, but it was Senator Kern, and not Carter Glass, who made the Federal Reserve Act a reality. Glass himself gave credit to Woodrow Wilson for the passage of the Fed legislation.

Benjamin Strong left Bankers Trust Company in 1914 to preside as the first governor of the Federal Reserve Bank of New York. Like all of the Morgan men, Strong was an Anglophile who "wanted to endow the New York Fed with the dignity and prestige of the Bank of England," wrote Ron Chernow in *The House of Morgan.* "Through Strong's influence, the Federal Reserve System would prove far more of a boon than a threat to the Morgan Bank. The New York Fed and the House of Morgan shared a sense of purpose to such an extent that the latter would be known on Wall Street as the Fed bank. So, contrary to expectations, frustrated reformers only watched Morgan power grow after 1913."[28]

President Wilson and other politicians of the day spoke at length about the "cooperative" structure of the central bank and the way the Fed specifically would meet the credit needs of rural farm communities. But the only parties that gained easier access to credit were the banks themselves, who warmed to the idea of a central bank after the Crisis of 1907.

The depression-like conditions and lack of credit affecting the U.S. agricultural sector persisted in the decade after the creation of the Federal Reserve. During the Great Depression and World War II, Washington ladled ample subsidies on large and medium-size farms, but the community of smaller family farms and rural laborers were never addressed by the creation of the central bank nor by any of the myriad of farm credit programs emanating from Washington.

Just as the Progressive movement was marginalized during the debate regarding the central bank, a more corporate political discourse emerged in America after this period. Economics and history textbooks are filled with descriptions of the Federal Reserve Act as a compromise among various political interests, but in fact, the large banks and their political allies in the Congress had their way. In the process, the Federal Reserve System adopted some of the Progressive worldview, particularly the European perspective on private business, economic management, and the role of government. The Aldrich plan for a banker-controlled central bank was more consistent with traditional American values than the corporate world that emerged after World War I. The view of individual freedom and money championed by Thomas Jefferson and Andrew Jackson was not reflected in the final

Federal Reserve Act, even with the populist façade championed by Carter Glass.

The creation of the Federal Reserve, in fact, confirms the cautionary views of Jefferson and Jackson regarding the antidemocratic, authoritarian nature of central banks. Whether located in the United States, London, or the other nations of the world, almost by definition there seems to be something in the character of any central bank that is antithetical to democracy and individual rights, and promotes the expansion of an authoritarian corporate state.

"The Progressive movement that preceded American entry into World War I also drew largely from classic corporatist theories for its industrial relations policies," said Walker Todd, a former Fed official and researcher. "The main unifying principle of classic corporatism was the idea that Marxist or Dickensian visions of class struggle could be avoided if, somehow, corporate owners and managers, agricultural interests, and urban laborers could be brought together cooperatively under the benign auspices of government."[29]

In his classic 1933 book *The Mirrors of Wall Street*, Clinton Gilbert described the scene as the Congress passed the Federal Reserve Act and the subsequent two decades:

It is now almost twenty years since J.P. Morgan and Company, its associates and its satellites attempted to induce Congress to create a central bank of issue instead of the Federal Reserve System. They were determined that control of the national purse should remain in New York. The theory underlying the proposed system that the several sections of the country should control their own finances was preposterous. To them it was anathema. Ten short years later the same group, represented by the same agent who had led their lost cause in Washington, took charge of the Federal Reserve System. For practical purposes the system was transformed into a central bank, and was manipulated to the very ends that its authors had sought to guard against.[30]

Gilbert found that the first Board of Governors of the Fed was comprised of people "distinguished by ability and character." By the time that President Warren Harding succeeded Woodrow Wilson in the White House, though, the New York bankers, led by the House of Morgan, largely captured the Federal Reserve. The slogan "Return to Normalcy" replaced the cries of war and the nation was, once again, more interested in ways to "turn the wheels of commerce and accelerate the movements of trade."[31]

The Federal Reserve Act gave the nation's third central bank a 20-year charter, but without the Washington bureaucracy and staff today known as the Board of Governors. The 12 Federal Reserve Banks were reasonably autonomous entities that set interest rate policy within their geographic territory, albeit with a large degree of communication and cooperation. Over a decade would elapse before the Congress created the expanded Fed Board as an agency of the federal government to supervise the regional reserve banks. By the 1930s, the expanded Fed Board of Governors was firmly in charge. Any pretension at a Progressive, decentralized model for the American central bank ended with the expansion of the Board as a Washington agency.

The expansion of the Board of Governors as an independent agency in Washington not only influenced the evolution of the banking system and the currency, but also played an important role in the trend toward central planning and authoritarian political structures in Washington during and after the 1930s. The creation of the Fed may have seemed a political victory for the forces of sound money, as Goodwyn and other scholars of the Progressive era argue. In fact, the central bank would become an influence supporting inflation, debt, and the rise of even more powerful and largely unaccountable governmental structures in the United States in the 1930s.

Walker Todd noted in "The Federal Reserve Board and the Rise of the Corporate State," the Fed reflected the views of the time, but also remained supportive of statist, antidemocratic governance structures in Washington long after World War I and the Great Depression:

In the history of political economy theory, it generally is believed that a taste for centralization of authority, cooperation and information-sharing to reduce competition, restraint of production to maintain prices and profits, and the coercion of labor by the state into conformance with this design, all die hard once they become embedded in the administrative apparatus of the state. The occasional reappearance and even persistence of some mildly corporatist ideas at the Board since the 1930s might be explained by the hypothesis that such ideas, once having gained sway there in 1931–34, simply have reappeared whenever the economic and political conditions were right.[32]

The tendency of the Federal Reserve Board in Washington to favor authoritarian models of political economy is discussed later in this book. Russell Vought, director of the Office of Management and Budget under President Donald Trump, challenged the existence of the agency in a 2025 interview in the Financial Times: "I can't look at the constitution...and see that that is a place where there deserves to be an exception. I don't even understand who controls the Fed. Where does their authority come from? Are they speaking directly to God?," he asked.[33]

Chapter 5

War, Boom, and Bust

I n the period under Theodore Roosevelt and prior to the administration of President William Howard Taft, the U.S. government's debt hovered around $2 billion, though it began to steadily grow by a couple of hundred million per year to reach almost $3 billion in 1912. With the start of the First World War in Europe and with American assistance, both public and private, however, the public debt began to grow rapidly. This was a significant change compared with the past fiscal behavior of Washington, at least in peacetime. By 1918 the total amount of federal debt outstanding was almost $15 billion, nearly five times the prewar levels.[1]

The change in Washington's spending habits during the period before and during World War I marks the start of a steady increase in federal indebtedness and a tolerance for maintaining these levels of debt, both in terms of direct obligations and indirect contingent obligations, that has been mostly unbroken ever since. Though in some years the amount of debt did decline slightly, overall the growth in the total obligations of the federal government has accelerated. The American approach to debt repayment after World War I stands in sharp contrast to that of the UK, which imposed a draconian regime of taxes and fiscal austerity during and following the conflict to repay the domestic war debt. Unfortunately, the United Kingdom and other European Allies did not repay their war debts to the United States.

With the outbreak of World War I, most of the nations of the world left the gold standard, either explicitly or as a matter of practice. None of the nations involved could afford in economic terms to go to war, so debt and inflation were used to finance the conflict. As with the Civil War, the huge cost of World War I doomed the gold standard and launched investors into a new world of fiat currencies and financial uncertainty. At the start of the conflict, many American investors feared that the war would drain financial reserves out of New York and into London. In fact, the opposite occurred. As raw materials, food, and manufactured goods flowed to Europe, gold and loans came to Wall Street's banks, but this process whereby America became involved in the war on the side of France and Britain was gradual.

At first the Wilson administration did not wish to provide any loans to the British and French governments, a position that infuriated the bankers of the House of Morgan and the other New York businesses. The New York financial community was mostly focused on London. Supporting the British and French against Germany was natural enough and good business besides. The large banks also were very comfortable with the "Dollar Diplomacy" of President William Howard Taft, which was essentially Teddy Roosevelt–style "big stick" diplomacy with a dollar wrapped around it. Like most Republicans who preceded him, President Taft was a conservative, limited or no-government politician who believed that businesspeople could essentially govern themselves.

The noninterventionism of the Wilson White House, and in particular the rhetoric of Secretary of State William Jennings Bryan, made many bankers wish for a return of the good old days of Taft, but the Progressive political surge in 1912 made that impossible. Bryan was no better at being secretary of state than he was as a presidential candidate, but he flattered the nonintervention views of Wilson. President Wilson made staying out of the war in Europe a key part of his reelection campaign in 1916. Having run on the slogan "He Kept Us Out of War," he would change his position immediately following the election.

"What a mess, Oh what an awful mess Wilson is making," President Taft wrote to P.C. Knox in April 1914. "What an opportunist he has shown himself to be, and how entirely he is giving himself up to the political game in his most reckless use of power to involve the country in war in order to take himself out of a political hole!"[2]

Bryan believed correctly that allowing American banks and investors to underwrite loans for the belligerent powers in Europe would undermine the country's policy of neutrality. The Wilson administration also discouraged American banks from participating in a loan for China during the same period. When bankers in France and the United Kingdom asked directly for loans from Morgan and the other major banks in New York, the Wilson administration refused, but the Morgan bankers made no secret of the fact that they were against Germany.

By the middle of 1914, however, other bankers began to press the case for making loans to the governments of France and Britain. Frank Vanderlip, president of the National City Bank, told the French government that he could raise $10 million for them privately. He then went to Washington to challenge Secretary Bryan regarding the matter and specifically contested any authority Washington might claim to have over foreign loans. By October 1914, the Wilson administration completely reversed itself and was telling U.S. banks that it would not oppose investment in bonds issued by the foreign combatants—a position endorsed by the bankers and exporters alike.[3]

The sharp increase in U.S. exports to the governments allied against Germany helped the American economy, which had been in a considerable slump since before the creation of the Federal Reserve System a year before. For many years, the United States had run a trade deficit with the European nations during the first half of the year, and then saw the trade balance reverse when agricultural crops such as corn, tobacco, cotton, and wheat moved from the United States to Europe. The brief prosperity in the United States caused by World War I pushed prices for everything from iron ore to farmland up dramatically, but also caused a major shift in the financial balance of power. In terms of national wealth, the United States went from being an agrarian debtor nation to being a rising industrial power and a net creditor of the European nation–states.

One reason that Wilson may have been persuaded not to restrict the flow of goods and credit to the Allied countries was that America still had a high degree of dependence upon credit from Europe. Just as the cities and states in the western United States were dependent upon credit from the New York banks to meet their seasonal needs for currency, the entire country remained very dependent upon European markets for seasonal loans to finance American agricultural and industrial production. The political ideal of neutrality and nonintervention ran smack into the reality of finance and debt, and the latter prevailed. Charles Callan Tansill noted in his classic book, *America Goes to War*, that in the fall of 1914, the American debt to Europe stood at almost $250 million, "which had to be liquidated either by the export of American goods or by payment in gold."[4] But the debtor position of the United States would quickly be transformed into that of a creditor nation once Britain and France began to demand more and more goods to support the war effort.

News media around the United States were generally supportive of the cause of the Allies, even if most citizens still felt, like Teddy Roosevelt, that the business of America was America; and that it should be pursued without dependence on foreign nations or interference from them. But echoing the Big Stick of Teddy Roosevelt, the growing internationalist tendency in American society had powerful allies. Among them was Clarence Barron, owner of Dow, Jones & Co. He published a book, *The Audacious War*, in support of the fight against Germany. Barron described the cause of wars in Europe with one word: tariffs. Barron expected Germany to impose economic hegemony over the world in the same way that Britain tyrannized the American colonies, through tariffs.[5]

Barron was not at all shy about using the pages of the *Wall Street Journal* to attack Germany and proselytize on behalf of the European Allies, but the truth was that the economic pull of the war was too powerful for the United States to resist. The idyllic, nineteenth-century worldview of an American republic safely isolated from the world by the two great oceans was shown to be impractical in the world of the telegraph, airplanes, and oil-fired warships.

By January 1915, some $500 million worth of munitions and war supplies had already been shipped to the Allies in Europe and the volume would only continue to grow. In fact, by that time, it was apparent to the House of Morgan that the available market for the debt of the European governments in the United States would soon be exhausted and other means of financing war exports had to be found. The Federal Reserve Act limited the ability of the central bank to buy only "warrants issued by the States and municipalities of the United States," but a way was soon found for the Fed to provide financing for the war. The firms shipping war materials to Europe would simply present trade acceptances to the Fed for financing, rather than have the importers in Europe do so.

Not satisfied with this solution of having the U.S. central bank endorse letters of credit for war shipments, J.P. Morgan pressed Washington explicitly to allow the Federal Reserve Banks to accept drafts drawn directly on London banks that had been accepted by a New York bank. By April 1915, the Fed complied with Morgan's request and once again proved that the central bank was always ready to do the bidding of the House of Morgan. The decision by the Fed was an active violation of U.S. neutrality, as many German-language publications pointed out at the time. Even with this concession, however, the volume of war materials and other goods demanded by the Allies overwhelmed the available financing in the United States. On May 7, 1915, when the steamer *Lusitania* was sunk by a German submarine, sentiment in the United States went more sharply against Germany. J.P. Morgan and the Allies took full advantage of the fact. Later evidence would show that the ship may have been carrying munitions in violation of the declared U.S. policy of neutrality.

During this juncture, the press, with the encouragement of Morgan and the other banks, began to carry opinions to the effect that the Allies did not need to pay for purchases of war materials with gold— but instead that the United States should accept payment in paper, that is, debt backed by the future promise of payment in gold. In a May 15, 1915, editorial, the *New York Times* advocated the use of "paper instead of gold for domestic trade" and "the reservation of gold for international use." The *Times* noted that the United Kingdom could no longer maintain the standard of "a pound of gold for every pound of paper" and that hundreds of thousands of dollars' worth of gold "will support almost unlimited millions of purchases from a country that has goods and does not want gold."[6]

Whatever Americans thought about the war on moral grounds, the surge in demand for all types of finished goods and raw materials was a welcome and positive development. The U.S. economy labored to emerge from the harsh economic contraction after 1907 for almost a decade. By the middle of 1915, France alone was purchasing $150 million per month in U.S. goods, frequently using loans from English banks to fund the transactions. In that same time period, H.P. Davidson of J.P. Morgan, writing from London, informed his colleagues in New York that the financing requirement for European imports would reach $400 million by January 1916. This vast flow of goods provided proportionately huge profits for the banks, but even more for the brokers and producers who provided the goods, sometimes under government contracts. The vast majority of the economic benefit realized by the United States during World War I went to a relatively small group of people and companies and was not widely distributed. After the banks, those best situated to take advantage of the war were the industrialists and the transportation interests, followed by the large agricultural firms, and lastly the small farmer.

The House of Morgan was well aware of the funding needs of the Allies. For months after the start of hostilities, the bank effectively supported the value of the British currency at about $5.40 per pound. It was some measure of the commitment to the London market by the House of Morgan that the bank was willing to deploy its own capital for months effectively to subsidize U.S. trade with Britain, especially when it was clear that the Bank of England could not finance its wartime needs.

In the middle of August 1915, Morgan ended its support for the pound, causing the currency to fall almost a full $1 to $4.51 per pound sterling and thereby precipitating a political emergency for the British government. The timing of the crisis, coming just as the flow of commercial orders from French and British buyers was starting to overwhelm the U.S. banks, was a brilliant gambit on the part of Morgan. It forced the U.S. government to become directly involved in underwriting the finances for the European war effort.

In 1917 and 1918, the Treasury issued $17 billion in Liberty bonds to help defray part of the cost of the war, some $30 billion in total expenditures for the conflict. This figure must be compared to the federal budget in 1913, which was less than $1 billion. The massive effort to sell Liberty bonds to the public increased awareness of the world of securities and investing. Not only was the war a huge shot in the arm for the U.S. economy, but the war effort also provided a rallying point for all Americans. A population that only a few years earlier had been voting an increasingly Progressive political line based in part upon bleak economic prospects and rising class tensions was united behind the righteous cause of war.

Thanks to billions of dollars in foreign loans and Liberty bonds, the American economy was surging. The Allies had the munitions and other supplies necessary to support the offensive planned for 1916. As hundreds of thousands of European soldiers went to their deaths, America was rising on a sudden and unprecedented wave of prosperity and wealth. Expectations of global peace and prosperity after World War I were soon dashed, however, a bitter disappointment for a young nation that was only starting to believe in its own possibilities and place in the world.

More realistic Americans in all types of industries took a practical view of the war, namely the opportunity for profit. The prospect of tapping into the vast demand for materials of every description was natural because the role played by America itself, as a whole nation, was widely perceived as that of a war profiteer. Nations around the world criticized the role of the United States as purveyor of materials and sometimes munitions to both sides of the European conflict. Politicians and academic researchers at the time debated whether the quest for excessive gains was not in fact a cause of war, implying that American bankers, munitions merchants, and other businesspeople fomented the war in order to benefit financially.

In the United Kingdom, food prices were subject to government control, and profiteers were subject to imprisonment. In the United States, however, as in most matters, during World War I, the markets prevailed without any real restraint. Prices for many necessities soared. By 1917, the public outcry against inflation and war profiteering became overwhelming. President Wilson signed legislation imposing price controls on food and other products and appointed a Republican named Herbert Hoover as Food Administrator to oversee price controls and punish war profiteers.

The great Wall Street financier Bernard M. Baruch, chairman of the War Industries board during the First World War, demanded government restrictions to eliminate all large profits for industry in wartime. In the event that another war should come, Baruch supported complete federal control over all industries and their workers.

The New York and London banks made good money on the business of war as well. Morgan and other lenders, for example, pocketed nearly $22 million on a $500 million loan for Britain and France led by J.P. Morgan and closed in the last week of December 1915. That amounted to a 4.5 percent commission for placing government bonds for two of the most creditworthy nations on earth, a nice piece of business for any dealer on Wall Street. J.P. Morgan became the purchasing agent for the British government, negotiated London's acquisition of goods in the United States, and also acted as advisor regarding the United Kingdom government's financing.

Profits to the U.S. farm sector from exports of various types of foodstuffs rose nearly 10-fold during World War I, peaking in 1916, a huge turnabout from the previous two decades. Steel exports rose fivefold over the term of the war and the value of farmland likewise soared. Thousands of new millionaires were coined during the period and several companies earned in profits many times their capitalizations. For the vast majority of farmers and industrial workers, however, the opportunity was not shared. America had become banker to the world and was in the midst of an economic boom not unlike that seen at the end of the Civil War—only bigger and fueled by even more plentiful credit from public and private sources.

"World War I marked a great divide in American credit," wrote author and historian James Grant in his book *Money of the Mind*. "Lending and borrowing entered the social mainstream."[7] Grant notes that World War I marked a period when governments, corporations, and individuals gained access to credit on a heretofore unthinkable scale. In 1918 it was clear that some of them could not repay these borrowings.

Wilson, like fellow Democrat Grover Cleveland, was no apologist for debt, nor was he in favor of debt-fueled speculation of the type that increasingly was found on Wall Street. President Wilson fretted over the idea of loans to the Allied nations, and his reservations were well founded. Yet the Allies needed aid and American workers and factories needed work. The fact that the Allies were effectively broke by the time the first year of the war had ended did not prevent America from eventually entering the war, first as a lender and supplier, and later as an active belligerent. But ultimately the U.S. government would underwrite financially the largest part of the war effort.

By the end of the conflict the global balance of financial power had shifted from London to New York. America was rapidly becoming a rich creditor nation, and the influence of America's banks was also growing. No longer were American banks treated with contempt in the City of London. The fact that all of this plenty was the result of a truly horrible slaughter on the fields of France mattered little and, indeed, was turned into a virtue, a crusade against evil in the shape of the menacing German horde often referred to as "the Hun." Authors such as Clarence Barron, who personally covered part of the war as a correspondent for Dow, Jones & Co., painted the conflict in epic proportions and thereby made the tough economic situation and the debt incurred to fund the war seem reasonable.

What is notable about World War I from the perspective of money, debt, and the American dream was the easy, almost painless way in which the country accepted the idea of prosperity via borrowing and also a good deal of monetary expansion. The hard money Jacksonian notions of gold coinage and antipathy to paper issued by banks of any description still lingered in many parts of the country. Yet for a growing portion of Americans and the mass of the large business and banking interests, the idea of an aggressive government presence in the credit and commercial markets was entirely acceptable if the end result was prosperity. The war in Europe had drawn the House of Morgan and the entire New York banking community closer. All of the banks collectively were also drawn closer to the U.S. Treasury and the government in general as first the banks, and later the entire nation, lent money to support the Allied war effort.

An Elastic Dollar

The Fed was created just two years before World War I began and remained a work in progress for years, some might argue decades, thereafter. The emergency authority to issue currency under the

Aldrich-Vreeland Act of 1908 and the more important power to buy or "discount" bankers' acceptances enabled the new central bank to finance the Allied war effort against Germany until the United States officially entered the conflict in 1917.

The efforts by the House of Morgan and Fed Governor Benjamin Strong helped to move the United States toward involvement in the war. During the early years of World War I, both the White House and the Federal Reserve Board were less than enthusiastic about financing the war effort. While the House of Morgan and other banks were vigorous in promoting the debt of the Allied powers, the Fed resisted any endorsement. Even the White House and President Wilson were equivocal at best and embraced the official position of neutrality.

The period from Wilson's reelection in November 1916 to the decision to enter the European conflict a year later was one of the strangest and most significant periods of any presidency. Wilson ran on an explicit platform of staying out of the war. "This country does not intend to become involved in this war," Wilson declared. "We are the only one of the great white nations that is free from war today, and it would be a crime against civilization for us to go in."[8]

There are many reasons advanced for Wilson's change of heart about the war between his election and taking the oath of office for a second time. The prospect of Germany resuming unrestricted submarine operations against shipping in the Atlantic in 1917 was the proximate cause. Wilson himself, after spending much of his first term avoiding the conflict, made the submarine attacks on U.S. shipping by Germany the pretext for entering the war.

The reality was that America's economic resurgence was based upon the flow of goods to Europe. The prewar economic malaise that had stretched as far back as 1907 was gone, and the country was running at or near full capacity in many sectors. Both maintaining the flow of goods and ensuring that the Allied debts were good were priorities for the Wilson government. It is reasonable to ask, though, whether Wilson and the other senior people at the Fed and in the U.S. government believed that the latter was possible and that the Allies would ever pay their war obligations.

The official job of the Fed was to smooth interest rates and thereby prevent the periodic economic crises that plagued the country, yet in the period *after* the creation of the Fed the economy was more volatile than before. Even excluding the Great Depression and the huge swings in income and asset values that occurred after the October 1929 market crash, real levels of economic activity were more unpredictable and displayed greater variation after than before the creation of the Federal Reserve.

The variability in the economy occurred in part because of the Fed's willingness to accommodate the huge increase in exports resulting from World War I. The increase in economic output and employment was all the more remarkable because the seasonal swings in interest rates, which most people associated with the agrarian sector, actually declined following the creation of the Federal Reserve System.[9]

Early on, the primary role of the Fed was to be the purchaser of commercial paper from banks to support the legitimate needs of commerce. This role of financing commerce was greatly expanded during World War I to include foreign trade with belligerent nations. The method employed to finance bank credits was the purchase or "rediscount" of bankers' acceptances and other types of commercial paper. These transactions occurred through the 12 Federal Reserve banks via trades with commercial banks.

Congress empowered the Fed to buy and sell government securities in the open market, thus the term "open market operations," to either add or drain cash from the financial system, again to meet the needs of commerce. "The rediscount operations of the banks were fundamental," Gilbert wrote in *The Mirrors of Wall Street*. "The open market operations were supposed to be incidental."[10]

Almost from inception, the Fed began rapidly to increase the supply of money available to the economy, delivering the "flexibility" in terms of liquidity available to banks that the Progressives had demanded and more. The irony was that the demands for liquidity were no longer coming from the Progressives as much as from the banks, especially larger, foreign-oriented banks intent upon doing business with Europe during the First World War.

The Fed acceded to the demands of the Progressive proponents of silver, effectively substituting the Treasury's purchase of silver prior to the repeal of the Sherman Silver Purchase Act in 1890 with a steady, at times torrid, rate of increase in the supply of paper money. Prior to the creation of the Fed, "high-powered money" consisted of gold, national bank notes, and various other Treasury notes issued over the previous half century. Now deposits at the Federal Reserve, or the actual notes themselves were high-powered money. By 1920, almost three-quarters of the high-powered or "Federal Reserve Money" consisted of Federal Reserve notes and deposits.[11]

Before the creation of the Fed, the movement of gold and the overall trade balance were the chief determinants of the amount of credit available in the U.S. economy. The Fed gave the country and its political class "choices," observed Washington polymath Timothy Dickinson in April 2010. He went on to compare the creation of the Fed with the unanticipated increase in the supply of gold produced in the 1880s and 1890s, necessarily increasing the supply of money and also the means for politicians to buy votes.

The creation of the Fed brought with it a far greater range of alternatives for the national political and business leaders, and thus made possible dramatic changes in how the economy could and would be managed. These were by and large harmful changes that neither Congress nor the public at large thoroughly considered, but which the ancient opponents of a central bank going back to Thomas Jefferson and Andrew Jackson had long predicted.

Milton Friedman and Anna Schwartz compared the period immediately after the creation of the Federal Reserve System in 1913 to the issuance of paper notes under Abraham Lincoln. These two events in American history signified a huge change in the "flexibility" of the money supply but also shifted control over this flexibility from the private markets to the political class. When the Fed was created, no guidance was given by Congress to the central bank as to the money supply or how to handle the ebb and flow of foreign capital. The key powers of the Fed were to discount commercial paper and provide currency, while requiring banks to maintain part of their reserves with the Fed. Initially the Fed was required to keep a gold reserve equal to 40 percent of the money supply and to also keep commercial paper as collateral for the currency.[12]

During the First World War, the world's financial center gradually shifted from London to New York, in large part because of the end of the gold standard. As the conflict in Europe grew, the flow of gold into the New York markets in payment for war materials as well as for safety greatly enhanced the influence of the largest U.S. banks. The massive borrowing program by the United States via Liberty bonds also provided important financial support for the war. As noted earlier, Liberty bonds also introduced millions of Americans to the idea of investing—something other than keeping cash in the bank.

An increased money supply care of the central bank added a dimension to policy that was not anticipated by Congress in 1913. Nor was the idea of the entry into a European war the highest priority in America. Nonetheless, the U.S. banking industry and the central bank financed much of the European war effort and American trade benefitted accordingly. The cost of this effort, however, was inflation, with sharply higher prices during the war and thereafter.

As with the Civil War half a century earlier, World War I was paid for by American workers via higher prices for housing and necessities. In a 1917 editorial, the *New York Times* reminded readers that the increase in prices was not necessarily due to profiteering as much as the sheer weight of expenditure, recalling the words of British Prime Minister Bonar Law: "The remedy is to be found in the control of that expenditure." Unfortunately, the end of the purchases by the Allied nations quickly plunged America into a decade of deflation.

Most of the foreign debt from World War I was never repaid, highlighting the fact that much of the wartime prosperity in the United States had no real economic basis, being the product of borrowing. But perhaps more important was the idea held by political leaders that expecting the Europeans to repay the debt was a reasonable policy in the first place. Americans really believed that the nations to Europe would repay their war debts, even as the United States hoarded global gold supplies and erected ever-higher tariff protection for domestic industries.

Americans clung somewhat to pre–World War I isolation from the world and thought to enjoy the benefits of war without the costs. But the more profound change in the American attitude toward money and debt was the new knowledge that government, operating via the Federal Reserve or by borrowing, could create economic prosperity out of thin air. Over the ensuing decades, this new "flexibility" empowered the American political class and gave it an entirely new role. The power to print money and issue debt and other obligations was a vast new political franchise.

Alexander Hamilton, the great advocate of public debt as a mechanism for national unity, pointed out that government debt was a pretty close one-to-one substitute for money. The realization that government debt could purchase goods and services and even drive the nation to prosperity was one of the results of World War I. This proves yet again that wars are not only about change but usually change of a decidedly negative cast. The revelation about the borrowing power of the fiat state begins with the legal tender laws of Abraham Lincoln and the Civil War, but blossoms into full awareness in the United States during World War I. Many Americans would be violently opposed to such a policy were it clearly articulated and presented for a vote, but the voters were never consulted. Once Americans appreciated that the Europeans either could not or would not repay their war debts, the disillusionment with international cooperation became even more intense.

Wilson spurned requests from Britain and France for debt cancelation and left the problem for his successor. Over the next decade or more, the Allies borrowed yet more money from the United States to drive economic growth on both sides of the ocean. The United States restructured and reduced the Allied loans during the 1920s, but by 1931, the major Allied nations had all defaulted on their war debts. Only Cuba, Liberia, and Finland repaid their World War I loans to the United States.[13]

After the war, the U.S. government paid down the total federal debt, from $27 billion in 1919 to a low of $16 billion in 1931. From there federal debt would climb through the Depression and World War II to reach $250 billion by 1949. Although the federal government generally returned to a conservative, even restrictive stance in terms of spending, the period of the 1920s saw a vast expansion of private debt and speculative financial activity in real estate in venues such as Florida. John Kenneth Galbraith stated the case: "The Florida boom was the first indication of the mood of the twenties and the conviction that God intended the American middle class to be rich."[14]

By the end of 1920, the Republican Congress was facing a revenue shortfall of $3 billion for the next year and cost cutting was the order of the day. The presidential election of 1920 was decided largely on the perceived inability of the Democrats to control spending, an ironic twist given the huge economic benefit that had come from the foreign borrowing and deficit spending by the Congress during World War I. Wilson's popularity and that of the reform program in general was wearing thin long before the end of his second term. The lengthy negotiation for an end to the war and the failure of the process caused the youthful American idealism that fueled support for Wilson to evaporate.

The price controls and taxes imposed during the war also took a toll on Wilson's popularity. By the time the fourth Liberty bond was floated in the United States in 1918, some 21 million Americans participated in the issue. Many had committed to a personal regime of savings and economy to support the war effort. The entire nation had a personal and financial stake in the successful outcome of the war. When it did not materialize as hoped and promised by Wilson, the disappointment felt by Americans was equally great.[15]

A Return to Normalcy

With the conflict in Europe over and the U.S. economy in a slump, control over the federal government swung back into Republican hands under President Warren Harding in 1921. The political shift actually began two years before in 1918, when Congress moved back under Republican control. After Wilson presented the Treaty of Versailles to the Senate for ratification, it failed by seven votes. The promise of global peace and prosperity advanced so confidently by Wilson was seen as a lie by many Americans, a reality already felt in a contracting global economy.

With the alluring promise of global peace and harmony dashed, Americans wanted to return to the relative simplicity of the pre–World War I republic, almost harkening back to the confident days of Teddy Roosevelt and the "Square Deal." But even this familiar and reassuring figure was soon lost. President Roosevelt died in January 1919 in his sleep at his beloved home of Sagamore Hill at the very young age of 60. Had the former president not suffered an untimely death, Roosevelt could have been the Republican presidential candidate in 1920. Americans wanted to return to the confidence and certainty that

President Roosevelt represented. In 1917, President Roosevelt said of World War I: "Peace is not the end. Righteousness is the end . . . If I must choose between righteousness and peace I choose righteousness."[16]

The age of Progressive reform under Wilson and the Democrats was over. In September 1920, just prior to the election, labor leader Samuel Gompers declared that normalcy under Warren Harding meant going backward, and he was right. The Democratic candidate, Ohio Governor James Cox, was a choice for "progress," Gompers reflected, but the American voter would have none of Gompers's advice that year. Harding assailed the Democrats for "extravagance and autocracy" and for being unprepared for war or peace.[17] Cox and his running mate, Franklin Delano Roosevelt of New York, were handily defeated by the Harding-Coolidge ticket and by the largest popular vote margin in modern history, 60.3 percent. The Democrats carried only 11 states and lost Cox's home state of Ohio and Roosevelt's home state of New York.

Harding was the first sitting member of the Senate to be elected president and, as might be expected, he soon proved to be one of the more incompetent if likable chief executives. The infamous "Teapot Dome" oil scandal erupted during Harding's first term and featured some remarkable accomplishments, including the first Cabinet official sent to prison (Veterans Bureau Chief Charles Forbes) and a number of suicides and related events. In July 1924, Representative Cordell Hull (D-TN) attacked the "wholesale corruption" of the Harding-Coolidge administration, but the Republican hold on power was unaffected.

Harding died of a heart attack after just 27 months in office and his vice president, Calvin Coolidge, succeeded to the presidency. Coolidge was "distinguished for character more than for heroic achievement," wrote New York governor Alfred E. Smith. "His great task was to restore the dignity and prestige of the Presidency when it had reached the lowest ebb in our history . . . in a time of extravagance and waste . . ."[18]

Woodrow Wilson reflected nineteenth-century attitudes toward money and debt, yet under Harding and Coolidge cautious attitudes toward finance were discarded in favor of a return to the *laissez-faire* role for the federal government and renewed economic growth, at least internally. Coolidge coined the term "the business of America is business" and proceeded to make that a reality. Despite this focus on business, the Federal Reserve System added to the deflationary tone of the period by restricting credit to deal with the inflation that had existed during much of the war. Inflation quickly disappeared, setting the stage for the brief economic depression of 1921.

With his first message to Congress in December 1923, Coolidge announced his intention to cut taxes on income and also to abolish the nuisance of inheritance taxes. Coolidge made positive statements about collecting the war debts from Europe. But the key part of the "Coolidge Plan" was tax cuts, which drove a final stake through the heart of the Republican Old Guard. The proposal gave Coolidge a direct connection with the business community. Treasury secretary Andrew Mellon led the charge on Capitol Hill and the financial markets surged, but the optimism was premature.

Senator James Couzens (R-MI), the former business partner of Henry Ford and one of the wealthiest men in the country, objected to tax cuts for the rich. The Democrats and Progressives in Congress cut back the Coolidge proposal to a reduction in the top tax rate, from 50 to 40 percent. They added insult to injury by not abolishing the inheritance tax and making tax files open for public inspection. Congress also passed legislation for a bonus for war veterans over a Coolidge veto. The president was able to beat back an effort by farm interests to subsidize food prices.

With the reelection in 1924 of Calvin Coolidge with 54 percent of the vote, the Republican control over Washington was strengthened—this despite the raucous scandals of the preceding years. During his administration the financial markets began truly to roar, fed by the greatest speculative fever since the Great Gold Rush and ample credit from the Federal Reserve. Coolidge was no more inclined to limit the excesses of the banking industry than was his predecessor Warren Harding, although he continued to follow a tough fiscal line and paid down the outstanding federal debt.

The political power of business and the banks grew with the speculative frenzy that gripped the U.S. population after 1924 and became more visible and overt than in many decades. Ron Chernow wrote in *The House of Morgan*: "By 1924, the House of Morgan was so influential in American politics that conspiracy buffs could not tell which presidential candidate was more beholden to the bank . . . The bank's peerless renown in the Roaring Twenties was such that the Democratic presidential candidate was the chief Morgan lawyer, John W. Davis."[19]

The Roaring Twenties

The economic boom experienced by the United States during and after World War I was a striking and welcome reversal of fortune. The nation that had been through seven grinding years of economic depression following the Crisis of 1907. In that earlier slump, production dropped nearly 11 percent in the first year and remained depressed well into the twentieth century. Restrictions on bank payments were lifted in 1908 and the economy slowly began to recover, but by the start of World War I America had still not fully rebounded to the level of economic activity seen prior to 1907.

The renewed prosperity felt by some Americans during WWI created a desire to maintain that level of consumption and opportunity, but equally strong was the feeling by many Americans that they had missed the proverbial party. With millions of people living in poverty in postwar Europe and millions more in America who had not felt the benefit of the war years, the division between rich and poor in America increased during and after World War I. When the economic benefit of the war began to wane in 1917, many of the old issues of social justice and the distribution of wealth that drove the Progressive movement came back into focus.

The end of the war allowed the country to refocus on domestic issues and on that increasingly American pastime—namely consumption—but the road to prosperity was uneven. The economic slump immediately after World War I is one of those details in the historical narrative of the American dream that has been edited out of modern-day treatments of the period. Social tensions that resulted from the slowdown after the war were a function not only of the fall in output and employment all over the Western world, but also of the upheaval across Europe that resulted from the May 1917 Russian Revolution.

The apparent wealth of Americans in comparison to their counterparts in Europe was striking. The product price inflation during the war years, which had seen prices rise by hundreds of percent in some cases, had made Americans seem wealthier than the people of Europe.[20] In reality the wealth felt by many Americans was an illusion resting upon tens of billions of dollars in debt incurred during the war and an inflation rate that had seen consumer prices double in less than a decade.

So sudden and swift was the change in U.S. economic activity that government and civic officials, who had spent the previous several years urging thrift and the purchase of government war bonds, began instead to push for consumers to slow their savings efforts and spend! Cities, counties, and states around the United States followed suit as the boom years of World War I ended, provoking an instinctive, conservative reaction to stop spending money. In April 1917, Howard E. Coffin, a member of the Advisory Commission of the Council of National Defense, publicly called for consumers to spend more money and to "keep the home fires burning" because the thrift on the part of individuals and even local governments was causing domestic output to fall sharply. Austerity once again gripped the nation.

Both in Washington and around the nation, governments responded to the decline in private demand from consumers by cutting spending and attacking deficits, which had the effect of making the overall economic situation even more difficult. The United States refused to make more loans to the Allies by the end of 1919, which caused an abrupt decline in all manner of exports. The momentary feeling of security that many farmers, large and small, had felt during the war years suddenly was replaced with a double-digit decline in demand for their products.

During the European conflict, farm acreage in the United States had grown almost 10 percent. The cutoff by Washington of credit to the Allies and the related efforts by the government to dampen inflation by reducing credit produced a terrible economic contraction. So brutal was the adjustment process for American farm communities that in 1924 the Progressive Party reappeared and fielded a candidate, Robert La Follette, who helped ensure the victory of Republican Calvin Coolidge and his running mate Charles Dawes in that year.

Concerns about the rise of radical political groups and even the threat of revolutionary uprisings in Europe made Americans turn inward and unite against perceived domestic threats. The so-called

"Red Scare" of 1919–1920, caused by the collapse of many industries due to the post–World War I economic slump, was comprised mostly of ineffectual strikes by workers seeking to regain buying power lost during years of stiff inflation and austerity.

New Era Finance

The Roaring Twenties is presented as a time of innovation and rising expectations in America, a time that witnessed an increase in production and productivity that lessened the need for skilled labor to produce goods. The age was symbolized by industrialists such as Henry Ford, who was widely seen as a revolutionary figure who cared for the common man, even though the truth is far less clear cut.[21] The 1920s was a period of extremes. Equal to the changes observed in technology and industry during this period was the evolution of public mores regarding the use of money and debt.

Friedman and Schwartz called the 1920s the "High Tide" for the Federal Reserve System and note that the new central bank immediately embarked upon an exercise in central planning via monetary policy. While the inhabitants of the Federal Reserve System may have believed that they were the "guiding hand" of the economy, the central bank seemed to have little or no effect compared with the massive changes underway in society. Factors such as the electrification of the United States, growing use of consumer credit and the growing acceptance of the use of debt to finance all manner of economic activity, seem to be far more significant factors than the actions taken or not taken by the central bank.

In many respects, it was World War I and the period immediately following the conflict, and not the Great Depression of the 1930s, that was the most significant inflection point for the United States in both economic and political terms. The creation of the central bank and the new feeling of freedom in Washington with respect to the use of public debt was one of the key changes in the World War I era, but the national outlook also changed in important social and political dimensions.

Although there remained a basic fiscal conservatism in society as a whole, the willingness to use debt to fund "necessary" expenditures was a new development. The sale of stocks and bonds, rather than bank loans, to fuel business and speculative operations also grew enormously. The portion of bank balance sheets devoted to investments as opposed to cash and loans also grew, coincident with the sale of government securities to the public. Whereas in the nineteenth century the Treasury sold bonds directly to the banks, by World War I the Treasury was selling most of its debt to individuals. But banks also supported public purchase of all manner of securities with collateral loans on margin, one of the key developments of what was known as the New Era in investing, the phenomenon author James Grant would years later dub the "democratization of credit."

One example of the transformation in thinking on the part of Americans came with a change in how they viewed investments. The 1920s marked a change in focus for analysts and investors from the actual performance of a company or public entity to looking at what might occur with respect to an investment in the future. This alteration in the attitude of the investing public was most pronounced with respect to stocks and was summed up beautifully in *Securities Analysis*, the classic 1934 book by Benjamin Graham and David Dodd. Though *Securities Analysis* is best known as a text on fundamental analysis of companies, there are significant passages in the volume that reflect upon the advent of "New Era Investing" and the social changes occurring in America.

"The new-era concepts had their root, first of all, in the obsolescence of the old-established standards," wrote Graham and Dodd. "During the last generation the tempo of economic change has been speeded up to such a degree that the fact of being *long established* has ceased to be, as once it was, a warranty of *stability*." Graham and Dodd went on to describe how "the new theory or principle may be summed up in the sentence: 'The value of a common stock depends entirely upon what it will earn in the future.'"[22]

The shift in the mindset of Americans from the actual financial performance of a company to what it might do *in the future* had far more significance than merely changing the theory of investing to a culture of speculation. Bernard Baruch defined a speculator as "a man who observes the future and acts before it occurs," a very close analog for the gold rush, risk-taking image of opportunistic entrepreneurship that became the ideal for generations of Americans.

The changes in the nation from the agrarian, work hard, and save your money model of Adams and Jefferson to the opportunism of the industrial baron or gold rush speculator, the shift away from looking at the historical earnings of a company to speculating about its future performance said a great deal about the permanence and stability of the American economy. Today, even among auditors and federal regulators, speculative estimates, surveys, and other "forward-looking" indicators are widely accepted as "data," and thus a reasonable means to monitor the internal workings of companies and markets.[23]

Instead of gradually sharing in the additive growth of a company through dividends, the prevailing investment model became to buy a stock at one price and sell it at a higher price to another market participant—a "greater fool." The rate of change in a given company or industry was so rapid that the traditional buy-and-hold investment strategy could not keep up. This view of money and investing as an essentially speculative activity says a great deal for the way in which contemporary Americans view the world.

Uncertainty or doubt about the solidity of the economy seemed to push Americans into a more tactical, more short-term, and speculative mode of existence. Improvements in communications enabled faster decisions. The rise of the model of speculation as a means to achieve the American dream did not always bring with it positive developments in society as a whole. Minton and John Stuart commented in *The Fat Years and the Lean*:

> The machine brought the Golden Age, making life more complicated but not more significant. The new abundance of material wealth failed to stir the creative energies of the people. The monopolists set the cultural standards of America just as they controlled the political life of the nation. The businessmen were enthroned, the arbiters of taste, the prelates of a civilization that had salesmanship as its art.[24]

The growing role of machines and of mass production in American life is an important part of understanding why the World War I period was such a powerful inflection point for the country. Whereas the English model of industry placed the primary focus on building complex and exquisite tools used by craftsmen to manufacture goods by hand, the American model of industry focused instead on adding speed and productivity to the procedure of transformation from raw material to finished products.

The growing use of standardization and interchangeable parts by industry in the later part of the nineteenth century allowed America to increase production rapidly to meet the needs of World War I—something that never would have been possible in the United Kingdom or in Europe. The "American System" of mass production provided a source of inexpensive consumer goods, from clothes to automobiles to aircraft, the like of which the world had never seen.[25]

The Rise of Consumer Finance

In his 1999 book *Financing the American Dream: A Cultural History of Consumer Credit*, Lendol Calder of Augustana College presents a detailed history of the "culture of consumption" in the United States and how the gradual acceptance of the use of debt to purchase consumer goods represented an evolution in attitudes toward borrowing that developed over a period of centuries. Calder details the slow but steady growth of consumer credit, from its roots in the late nineteenth century, a period he describes as "growth and stigmatization" from 1880 to 1915, to "growth and legitimization," from 1915 through 1930.

Of particular note is Calder's characterization of the tipping point in terms of the broader acceptance of consumer debt as occurring in 1915, the middle of World War I. "It is now generally recognized that just as it would be ridiculous to write a history of a medieval European town without its attention to its cathedral," Calder writes, "so twentieth century America cannot be understood apart from its department stores and shopping malls."[26]

The use of consumer debt to finance immediate purchases based on future income was one of the more important developments of the 1920s. Professor Calder, relying on the work of the noted economist Raymond Goldsmith, notes that the use of consumer debt during the 1920s soared by over 130 percent and that the number of borrowers increased dramatically. A large portion of the increase had to do with one consumer product in particular, the automobile, but installment credit was also used to buy many other types of goods.

"Credit financing made the automobile the quintessential commodity of the American consumer culture," notes Calder. "Credit plans also figured prominently in the selling of radios, refrigerators, vacuum cleaners, fine jewelry, and other expensive consumer durable goods."[27]

Perhaps the most prominent example of consumer finance was the founding of General Motors Acceptance Corporation (GMAC), a remarkable story that came only after GM had been through two financial failures. Founded in 1919 as a wholly owned subsidiary of General Motors Corp., GMAC was established to provide GM dealers with the financing necessary to acquire and maintain vehicle inventories and to provide customers a means to finance vehicle purchases. The company's products and services expanded through the years to include insurance, mortgages, online banking, and commercial finance.[28] GMAC, which was the brainchild of Alfred P. Sloan, the great business executive who led GM's operation from 1920 as a vice president until he stepped down as chairman in 1956, was one of the first "captive" financing vehicles established by a consumer products company.

Although GM was just seven years old in 1920, the company had collapsed under the weight of debt twice and was now placed under the control of the du Pont family. Alfred Sloan was then an executive at the company and was eventually made president by Pierre du Pont, who was chairman of the board of GM from 1915 until 1929. Sloan's genius for operations and sales was enormous, but there were several aspects of his tenure at GM that helped the company take the lead in the auto industry away from Henry Ford.

First, Sloan wanted to have a new product every year, "a product for every purse," whereas Ford manufactured the same car, the Model T, for almost two decades from 1908 to 1927. Second, Sloan realized that the lack of financing for new car purchases after World War I was pushing consumers to buy used cars instead of new models. Even a two-year-old Chevy, Sloan realized, was more attractive than the cranky and increasingly obsolete Ford Model T. And third and finally, Sloan understood that GM's "AAA" credit rating, a function of the support of du Pont and the rational management system that Sloan established within GM, enabled the company essentially to finance manufacturing, distribution, and sales at low cost.

GMAC provided credit to both the dealer and the end customer. When GM manufactured the car, it was "sold" to the dealer, who was required to pay for the vehicle when it arrived. But GM provided financing to the dealers via GMAC, which issued bonds to investors to finance the unsold inventories. Because the cost of the credit for dealers was below the rates charged by banks, the dealers were able to earn more profits for every car sold. And by providing credit for consumers at likewise rock-bottom rates, GM was able to increase new car sales and grow faster than Ford. In essence, by managing its accounts payable to its suppliers and providing financing for dealer inventories and final sales, GM was able to gain up to five months of free float and was therefore able to invest in new manufacturing capacity.

Henry Ford was an extremely conservative man who ran his entire company on a cash basis until after the end of World War II. Suppliers bringing raw materials and parts to the Ford factory were paid in cash. Ford distrusted bankers and hated debt. By 1929 Ford was one of the largest cash depositors in the U.S. banking system. Never thinking of using credit to encourage sales, Ford believed that pushing down the cost of his beloved Model T and making incremental improvements to the perfect car was all the incentive needed to spur sales. And Ford's inability to grasp the significance of financial leverage and consumer credit to expanding demand for his products enabled GM to capture leadership in the auto industry by the mid-1920s, a position of dominance that GM holds to this day—even after a third bankruptcy reorganization in 2009. In fact, through much of the twentieth century, the monoline Ford brand compared its sales not to GM, but to Chevrolet.

America Transformed

Only 1 in 10 people who left the farm to fight in World War I actually went home to rural America once the conflict ended. A huge pool of labor was available in American cities, labor that provided a ready market for the rising consumer products giants of corporate America, which still dominate the market today. Industrial enterprises such as Ford and General Motors arose to challenge the established business giant money trusts like U.S. Steel and Standard Oil. All of these companies and others expanded greatly during the war years and in the process spawned a vast network of suppliers and dealers. Similar national networks of suppliers and sales outlets were created in many other industries so that companies increasingly took on a national scope, unlike the smaller organizations that had been typical in the nineteenth century.

Following World War I, life in urban America was transformed into a continuous quest for prosperity in an economic sense. Every step in life, from early education to professional training was meant to support advancement. Acquisition of certain items of consumer apparatus became the measure of personal affluence and success, part of the journey to "make something of yourself." The vast consolidation and concentration that occurred in many industries during and after World War I encouraged this trend. Larger and larger companies sought to defend markets and brands via media outlets that these same conglomerates controlled through sponsorship if not ownership. Success in life could now be measured by the types of products that individuals owned or consumed, and the use of debt to purchase these products became increasingly acceptable.

The changing social attitudes toward saving and debt that occurred after the Civil War, and especially from the 1920s onward, seemingly made Americans focus on more short-term, forward-looking yardsticks for trying to understand the vast social change occurring around them. These changes were very much evident in the financial world. Graham and Dodd focus on World War I as the demarcation point in terms of broadly accepted American perceptions of investments, yet other scholars such as William Janeway of Cambridge University argue that the change in attitudes about investing began much earlier in the late nineteenth century, a point supported by Calder and others.

When the inflection point occurred in America's view of money and debt is less important than the striking departure this attitude represented for the way Americans acted with respect to borrowing and the basic function of saving. The stay home, work hard, and save model advocated by Thomas Jefferson or John Adams was in complete opposition to the opportunistic, short-term model of the gold rush or the speculator. The traditional rule of prudence defined by Edmund Burke as "the first of all virtues" was a life spent carefully weighing the trade-offs and minding one's own business, Thomas Sowell noted in his book *A Conflict of Visions*.[29]

In the unconstrained world view of writers such as anarchist William Godwin, however, life was seen as ever expanding and man as perfectible beyond the mere rewards of material goods. The optimistic world view of Godwin and his belief in the unlimited potential of human beings is very much reflected today in American attitudes about economic and personal potential. The modern guideposts to the American dream place no finite limit on the advancement of an individual. In that sense, the libertarian political tradition of the United States found economic expression in a decidedly casual and almost libertine view of money and debt all too visible in the third decade of the twenty-first century.[30]

One perspective saw the American dream as a thing to be earned over many years of consistent work, saving, or cash investing. The other view depends mostly upon luck and avarice, the availability of new credit, or a greater fool to ensure gain or immediate gratification as is shown by the world of crypto tokens. The former is the cautious world of cash investing, Graham and Dodd, and deliberate choices made after careful consideration and analysis. The latter an aggressive, imaginative but speculative model of endless vistas and unconstrained vision, the common denominators of any mass movement, religious cult, or financial get-rich-quick financial scheme. The war profiteers of the Civil War like Jay Cooke and Jay Gould, the Robber Barons of the nineteenth century, the even more grotesque war profiteers of World War I, and the stock speculators of the 1920s on Wall Street all used leverage and market power—and luck—to gamble on the future.

The difference between the perspective on money and debt that existed before and after World War I was that by the 1920s, credit had become available to one and all. In the same way that improvements in communication in the latter part of the nineteenth century changed financial panics and bank runs from a local to a national problem, the greater availability of credit enabled more diverse forms of speculation by ever larger numbers and groups of players. The purchase of a consumer appliance and the use of margin credit to buy stocks were seen in some quarters as equally virtuous acts.

Domestic and overseas companies, and even foreign nations and banks, all issued stocks and bonds to American investors during the Roaring Twenties. Newly affluent consumers purchased all sorts of products and began to use consumer credit to satiate their *immediate* demand for goods. Whether in the form of forced savings programs, buying a home appliance on time, or borrowing to finance a speculative investment, American consumers now had access to credit in ways that were not widely known or understood even a generation before.

The financial services industry expanded dramatically during this period, and banks began to offer mortgages, installment credit, and even margin loans to individuals to fund securities purchases. Consumers began to buy bonds and equity securities, and Wall Street expanded capacity to meet and encourage the new demand. Banks began to offer various types of structured assets to consumers and even participated directly in land speculation, conveying at least the image of wealth to America's earliest real estate entrepreneurs. Like the subprime mortgage-backed securities of a century later, these "complex" investments were often a fraud to relieve the credulous investor of their cash. Many of the supposedly "sophisticated" investment strategies of the early twenty-first century were first used in the 1920s.

Among the more popular schemes employed by banks and their securities affiliates in the 1920s was to repackage loans to indebted Latin American nations and sell participation to retail investors in the United States. Much like the complex subprime mortgage paper that would cause a crisis in America a century later, these bonds were completely opaque and the buyers of these securities usually had no idea about the credit standing of the obligors. The securities affiliate of First National City Bank, predecessor of Citibank NA, was one of the more notorious offenders during this period. By the late 1920s, National City Company—as the brokerage firm was known—had more than 2,000 stockbrokers selling risky securities to retail investors. The reckless actions of National City provided a major impetus behind the eventual imposition of a separation between securities dealing and banking via the Glass-Steagall law of the 1930s.

One critical account of the era was a 1937 book by Bernard J. Reis and John Flynn, *False Security: The Betrayal of the American Investor*. The authors chronicle a zoological tour of structured financial instruments that could have come out of Wall Street in the late 2000s, but in fact were being sold in the period after World War I. Under the heading of "investments the public believed to be gilt edged," much of the apparent prosperity during the period resulted from the issuance of debt. As had been the case during World War I, borrowing was employed by many Americans to enable all sorts of activity, from consumption to speculation. The nations of Europe likewise continued to borrow in the United States to fund exports. The authors conveyed the bitterness and anger felt by many Americans after the Great Crash and the Depression of the 1930s:

Simply stated, honesty plays little part in American business. Our morality, on the contrary, in a game of cards or in sports is irreproachable. And so it is that we are gentlemen of honor when engaged in life's pastimes, but devoid of it when engaged in serious pursuits. The public has a subconscious awareness of this state of business immorality, but for some reason remains apathetic to it, and even condones it. True, a simple criminal act is condemned (and when simple it is invariably of small dimensions) but where large profits have accrued or an enormous institution erected on no matter how fraudulent a foundation, we give it respect and applause.[31]

Part of the appeal of the interpretation of the 1920s by Reis and Flynn is the perspective of the aggrieved consumer. Like the work of Graham and Dodd, their description of the public mania regarding "new" investment vehicles in the 1920s could be applied almost word-for-word to the events in the U.S. markets since 2008. The book beautifully illustrates the ancient precursors of modern structured finance with numerous examples of specific transactions and issuers drawn from the time. The authors found that of the $10 billion or so in mortgage-backed securities issued during the 1920s, some $8 billion of original face amount were in default by the early 1930s when Congress launched inquiries into the practices of Wall Street.[32]

The important point to take away from this period is that the very same type of mortgage-backed securities that caused the financial crisis of the 2000s were actually first conceived and sold to the public a century earlier—and by many of the same banks and financial institutions! Billions more worth of bonds issued by foreign nations, states, cities, and other issuers were likewise sold in the United States during this period. Much of this debt was used to purchase American goods for export and most of it was in default by the mid-1930s. The issuers were not only from Europe, but also included many Latin American nations and their internal jurisdictions, exotic entities hitherto unknown to U.S. investors.

In the 1920s, when a bond went into default, the word "shrinkage" was used to describe the reduction in value. With the end of the Roaring Twenties, the U.S. economy not only suffered from the decline in demand due to the inability of foreign governments to issue more debt, but also from the shrinkage of value to American investors who lost money on defaulted debt. The resulting financial deflation and economic dislocation led to the worst economic crisis the American republic had yet experienced.

Prelude to the Depression

In 1927, Congress passed the McFadden Act, which prohibited interstate banking, a limitation that remained in place until the mid-1990s. The McFadden Act also authorized hometown branches for national banks, if allowed by the state, a change that put national banks on a more even footing with state banks. National banks still could not establish branches outside of the city in which they were headquartered, but significantly, the legislation gave national banks authority to buy and sell marketable debt obligations and make loans on real estate. Friedman and Schwartz wrote that when combined with changes to the Federal Reserve Act in 1916, the McFadden Act increased the amount of bank credit available to real estate and other sectors.[33]

The author of the McFadden Act was Rep. Louis McFadden (R-PA), who chaired the House Committee on Banking and Currency during the late 1920s and early 1930s. A banker by profession, McFadden became a staunch critic of the Federal Reserve System following the 1929 market crash: "We have, in this country, one of the most corrupt institutions the world has ever known. I refer to the Federal Reserve Board."

What is interesting about the McFadden Act in terms of our narrative of the evolution of money and debt in the United States is that
the law was initially proposed several years before as a means of allowing national banks to establish branches, yet opposition to the branch
banking measure was so fierce that it was not passed until 1927. The
Banking Act of 1865 had been silent on the issue of branching by
national banks and thus national banks were at a significant disadvantage compared to the far more numerous state-chartered depositories.

The Treasury supported the proposal, but the Federal Reserve and
the state banks opposed it. Indeed, in 1923 the Federal Reserve Board
actually passed a resolution prohibiting member banks from branching
outside a bank's home city and geographic area. After several years of
debate on the issue, Congress finally passed a law that allowed national
banks to establish branches to the same extent allowed by state law for
other banks. The McFadden Act also prohibited national banks from
expanding outside the state where they operated. It is some measure of
the opposition to the law that the Senate invoked cloture for the first
time on a domestic issue during final passage.[34]

The primary logic behind the McFadden Act was to protect banks
from competition, a policy perspective that was in line with the traditional American use of tariffs and a weak currency to protect domestic industries from foreign predation. The boom that was occurring
on Wall Street during the 1920s was fueled by the expansion of the
domestic credit base by the Federal Reserve System and the floatation
of a large number of foreign and domestic bond issues. Not surprisingly, the number of bank failures in the United States rose to alarming
proportions during the 1920s.

Part of the reason for the number of bank failures was the large
number of state-chartered institutions. Even in rural parts of the United
States, there were often more banks in a given state, city, or town than
could survive financially in good times. When times were tough, banks
failed in droves. Over 1,000 banks failed in the United States during
1926 alone, but by that time there were almost 18,000 state-chartered
banks in the country and another 8,000 national banks. These institutions had a powerful political following in their communities. Many
members of Congress during that period were motivated by a desire to
protect banks in their communities. The solution—prohibit banks from

expanding geographically—did not really address the problem. In fact, attempts at protecting banks may have arguably made things worse following the financial market break of 1929.

A final point with respect to this period has to do with the influence of the House of Morgan and its *de facto* agent Benjamin Strong, who served as the first governor of the Federal Reserve and chief executive of the Federal Reserve Bank of New York from 1914 until his death in 1928. In the official history of the New York reserve bank, Strong is described as "a dominant force in U.S. monetary and banking affairs" and indeed he was all of that. But because of his personal links to the management of J.P. Morgan and, through the anglophile tendencies of the Morgan Bank, to the Bank of England, Strong's independence manifested itself in ways that were ultimately at odds with his duties as an officer of the U.S. central bank.

The eminent British economist Lionel Robins, in his classic 1934 book *The Great Depression*,[35] wrote that the credit expansion by the Federal Reserve after 1925 was a deliberate effort by Strong to help the economic situation in Britain. The United Kingdom had gone back onto the gold standard in 1925 and the results on the British economy were so negative that by 1927 the country was facing economic depression and political unrest. The United Kingdom had gone back onto the gold standard at the prewar rate of $4.86 per pound. This move in essence ignored the adjustment that was forced upon English authorities after J.P. Morgan ended its support operations for the British currency in the early years of World War I.

Most historians now accept that the decision by English authorities to return to the gold standard was badly misguided and began a period of deflation in the United Kingdom that soon combined with a recession in the United States starting in the middle of 1927. The Fed's use of easy money in the United States to address the economic weakness in the United Kingdom was the start of a symbiotic relationship between the two nations in monetary terms that is an important part of the history of the post–World War II era. In the United States, too, the economic boom that had accelerated after 1925 was showing signs of ending. Strong and a majority of the Federal Reserve governors supported a policy of easy money starting in 1927 that arguably made the market break two years later more severe when the Fed belatedly tried to deflate the stock market bubble.[36]

Stocks Fall, Tariffs Rise

In the summer of 1927, after eight years of blissful inaction and inattention by Washington to the problems developing in the financial markets and the economy, President Coolidge decided to move the executive offices of the nation to Rapid City, South Dakota, to prepare for the upcoming Republican convention in Kansas City. The economy apparently was booming and the financial markets were soaring, so the president felt no reason not to give his full attention to politics.

Coolidge soon announced in August 1927 that he would not seek the presidency for a second full term, leaving the field to the other candidates such as Herbert Hoover, who was then secretary of Commerce. Of all the possible candidates, Hoover, who unsuccessfully sought the Democratic nomination in 1920, was the only one with the natural talent and who truly sought the job. Coolidge hoped to be asked to take up the Republican standard yet again in 1928, but he underestimated the ambition and political skills of the great engineer.

Hoover was ever loquacious and had no problem speaking to the press. Coolidge, on the other hand, was a man of few words and even fewer real ideas. With the exception of Hoover, he had surrounded himself with men of similar qualities. Chief among them was Treasury Secretary Andrew Mellon, a loyal Republican partisan of Coolidge but a man, like most Republicans of that age, who had trouble assembling consecutive sentences but particularly when in front of the media. By picking Mellon to be his point man at the Republican convention in 1928, Coolidge ensured that he would not run for a third term as president.

The Republican convention of 1928 nominated Hoover on the first ballot. All praised the great technocrat and engineer, the great administrator, the great economist, "the greatest humanitarian since Jesus Christ," as former New York governor and vice presidential candidate Al Smith quipped at the time. Republicans were in no mood to take any controversial positions in 1928 and hoped that Hoover would merely continue the glorious age of prosperity and economic good times. Calls from Progressive elements in the party to focus on the deflation and crisis that existed in the farm sector fell upon deaf ears, as did calls to repeal the Prohibition on sales of alcohol that had been enacted in 1920. The GOP had been returned to power in 1920 on the promise of a "return to normalcy." The goal in 1928 was to continue that successful run, yet the Republicans were unaware that an economic and political catastrophe impended a year later.

Herbert Hoover was the first president born west of the Mississippi River, and he represented a change from his Republican predecessors. He ran on a platform that supported a continuation of the policies of Calvin Coolidge and Prohibition under the mantra of "a chicken in every pot and a car in every garage." He easily defeated the Democratic ticket led by Al Smith, who was a loyal if independent member of the Tammany Hall political machine. Smith was nominated by Franklin Roosevelt, supported the repeal of Prohibition, and had the active support of corporate titans such as John J. Raskob of General Motors. Hoover defeated the Catholic New York governor in a landslide that saw a number of southern states brought into the Republican column for the first time. This result heartened the Republicans even more and convinced them of the correctness of the policies of the previous eight years. Following the election, when the lame duck session of Congress met, President Coolidge told the legislators: "No Congress ever assembled, on surveying the state of the Union, has met with a more pleasing prospect than that which appears at the present time."[37]

Upon taking office in March 1929, Hoover focused on issues such as relief for farmers and reduction of tariffs. He championed federal export assistance for American farmers via the Agricultural Marketing Act and, after considerable debate, the Congress eventually gave Hoover his way. The Act encouraged the formation of farm cooperatives and also provided some early support by the federal government for farm prices. Hoover's action represented a significant victory for agrarian interests, even if a large portion of the aid ended up going to big commercial growers rather than the family farmers.

When Congress next turned to the question of tariff reduction to help the farm sector, as President Hoover requested, the temptation instead to *raise* levies further to protect domestic industries was too great. By raising tariffs, it was believed in the late 1920s, the prices for industrial and consumer goods could be pushed even higher with corresponding increases in profits to big business. In this sense, the American business community had the same mindset as the great speculators of the Gilded Age such as Jay Gould—namely limit supply and competition—and thereby capture higher profits for their goods. The mindset of business leaders and politicians of the day was the opposite of that which prevailed in the United States after World War II, when large corporate interests became the active advocates of free trade and open global markets.

Robert Byrd wrote in his history of the Senate that lobbyists for every industry imaginable besieged Congress to press for greater tariff protection, in some cases hiring special trains to bring the lobbyists to Washington to press their demands. Industrial and agrarian interests actually made common cause to seek higher tariff rates. Even as the stock market was collapsing, the Senate debate on increasing tariffs continued and even intensified as, Byrd wrote, "businesses looked to the tariff as its salvation."

Congress did not pass new tariff legislation—known as Smoot-Hawley after the bill's authors—until more than six months after the October 1929 market crash, in June 1930, but the impact of the increase in the existing tariffs was dramatic. Progressives denounced the legislation, with Senator George Norris (R/I-NE) calling it "one of the most selfish and indefensible tariff measures that has even been considered by the American people."[38]

What is missed by many discussions of Smoot-Hawley during and after that period, however, is the fact that the economic collapse of the 1930s was already a given with or without the new tariff law. The impetus behind the political decision to raise tariffs was a misguided reaction to the collapse of the speculative bubble on Wall Street. It had little to do with the economic depression that occurred in the farm sector following World War I. Support for protectionism was the consistent refrain from the corporate and farm lobbies in Washington in the nineteenth and early twentieth centuries and was provided by members of both political parties. But the real underlying cause of the powerful political push to raise the *existing* tariffs even higher at the end of 1929 may be found in the substantial changes that were occurring in the American economy.

Many historians and economists blame the level of tariffs after World War I and particularly during the Great Depression for making more severe the economic contraction and unemployment following the 1929 market crash. The passage of the Fordney-McCumber Tariff

Act in 1922 symbolized the unique Republican penchant for trade protectionism and inflation that stretched decades back in time to the party's inception in the 1850s.

In his book *Making Sense of Smoot Hawley*, Bernard Beaudreau argues that the imposition of tariff protection for U.S. industry in 1930 was simply a continuation of the policies implemented by the Republican Party after they returned to power in 1920. Beaudreau cites the rising productivity of U.S. factories, the spread of electrification throughout America, and the continued influx of foreign-produced food and manufactured goods as the chief cause of the deflation during this period.[39]

Imports were still perceived to be a threat by the American manufacturers of that day, despite already high tariff levels. Underemployment was the result of the lack of demand and thus falling product prices that resulted in the 1930s. American industry became too efficient too quickly, resulting in a global surplus of goods and an equally dangerous lack of demand. Congress sought to correct this imbalance by limiting imports via the Smoot-Hawley tariff. While there is no doubt that higher tariffs made the Great Depression worse, higher levies on imports may not have been the primary factor.

This alternative view of the role of Smoot-Hawley in turning the market crash of 1929 into the Great Depression of the 1930s is important to our narrative. Following the Great Depression and World War II, the U.S. position regarding tariffs changed dramatically, in part because much of the industrial capacity of Europe and Asia was destroyed by the conflict. Under the rubric of rebuilding the postwar world, America embraced a policy of open markets and free trade. This policy created enormous wealth and prosperity in the first several decades after the end of the Second World War. Later it sacrificed American jobs and industrial capacity to other nations.

Another way of looking at this issue, however, is that once the large business interests realized that they could no longer extract above-normal prices for their products by hiding behind the tariff barriers that were widely supported prior to the Great Depression, they instead chose to pursue growth and new business opportunities by embracing a policy of promoting free trade. This open door enabled the rise of the most extreme modern example of mercantilist predation by a foreign nation, namely China.

The threat of regressive actions in Washington in the form of increased tariffs was barely noticed by the citizenry in 1929, who were too busy celebrating the New Era on Wall Street. Breathless accounts of fortunes made overnight in the markets filled the media of the day, describing the immediate affluence possible by investing in stocks. Media accounts put even the most optimistic sales literature from the banks and their securities affiliates to shame, much like the come-ons used to promote crypto currencies and other frauds today. But even as Hoover took office, there were signs of trouble in a slowing economy.

The Coolidge administration responded to slowing economy with a program of austerity, cutting spending in Washington in response. Hoover continued that deflationary approach, calling for greater economy in Washington even as the nation sank into depression. The federal debt reached a low of $16.1 billion in June 1930 as the government continued to pay off debt and pursued a program of fiscal austerity to match falling tax revenues. This nineteenth-century mentality was the practice in most states, cities, and towns around the country. An already deflationary tendency was only made worse by the belated actions by the Fed to rein in growth in the supply of money.

The interest rate increases by the Fed caused bitter complaints from the speculative class on Wall Street. Bill Durant was by now out of the auto industry and focused instead on his role as one of the great stock operators of the 1920s. Durant traveled secretly to Washington to visit President Hoover early in 1929 and warned that the Fed was making the crisis worse and that catastrophe would follow "unless something is done to limit the Federal Reserve Board to the functions stated in the law that created it." He continued: "Those functions are to stabilize money rates and prevent panic. It did neither. Call money jumped to twenty percent. The country experienced the worst crash in history."[40]

Within the Federal Reserve, a heated debate had been underway regarding the use of central bank credit to fund speculative activities. The surge in stock prices brought the issue to the forefront as differences among the different parts of the Fed system emerged. In February 1929, the Board actually wrote a letter to the Reserve Banks stating that "a member bank is not within its reasonable claims for rediscount facilities at its Federal reserve bank when it borrows either for the purpose of making speculative loans or for the purpose of maintaining speculative loans."[41]

For the next several months, officials of the Federal Reserve Banks and the Board in Washington debated how to deal with the issue of speculation and the increase in credit, which had been expanding at better than twice the rate of growth in terms of business output. George L. Harrison, who was appointed governor of the Federal Reserve Bank of New York to replace Benjamin Strong in November 1928, was an advocate of raising interest rates to cool the expansion of credit. The Fed Board wanted to simply prohibit banks from using the discount window at all to finance speculative loans.

The Fed of New York voted on a number of occasions in the first half of 1929 to raise the discount rate, but each time the Board refused to approve the move, albeit by narrowing margins. The Fed Board continued to hold to the position that "direct action" to keep banks from making or maintaining speculative credits at all was a better course than an increase in the discount rate, in effect preventing the banks from using Fed credit at all instead of simply raising the price. In this period, banks did in fact do business with the Fed on a regular basis and without the stigma that attaches to use of the discount window today. In 1929, the discount rate had real-world commercial and economic significance. Not until August 1929 did the Fed finally approve an application by the Federal Reserve Bank of New York to increase its discount rate to 6 percent.[42]

While the debate raged inside the Fed, the equity markets were slowly starting to fall. The driver behind the rise in the markets had not been primarily the Fed's policies, but instead the marvelous ingenuity of the American people in the form of private debt creation. Hundreds of different types of investment vehicles were available in the marketplace, created by banks, trusts, and other entities. In the 1920s, title and surety companies also were great issuers of bonds and hybrid securities, instruments that look remarkably like the structured finance vehicles of a century later.

Many of these vehicles were listed on the major stock exchanges around the country. The Wall Street firm Goldman Sachs launched a vehicle called Goldman Sachs Trading in 1928 that was listed on the New York Stock Exchange in 1928, even though the firm remained a separate private partnership. The shares rose as high as $121 in 1929 but would close in December 1935 at less than $5.

Deflation and Crash 1929

Although the general level of prosperity in the United States rose during the 1920s, at least as measured by such things as purchases of consumer goods and the use of electricity, the situation in the farm sector was dire. Prices for farm products were going in almost precisely the opposite direction as the rising value of stocks. Between 1920 and 1929, stock prices in the United States had tripled in value, but deflation and bankruptcy were the predominant experience for American farmers.

"The advent of steam railways and the electric telegraph in the nineteenth century provided both objects of speculation and means for more rapidly spreading speculative hype," wrote Edward Chancellor. "The same was true of radio and telephony in the 1920s. Likewise, the arrival of the Internet in the 1990s served as both the medium of speculation and its object."[43]

The speculative updraft caught a number of banks off guard. Banks in many U.S. cities were involved in the underwriting and sale of securities, lending against these securities, and also retained portfolios of these securities for speculative gain. These loans and investments caused numerous bank failures in the 1930s and served as a major impetus for Congress getting the surviving banks out of the securities business through the Glass-Steagall laws.

Some researchers have argued that U.S. stock valuations were not excessive in 1929 based upon an assessment of the fundamental value of the companies included in the major market indices.[44] Friedman and Schwartz argue that the lending policies followed by banks during the 1920s were not necessarily reckless. The expansion in the availability of credit was part of the growing efficiency and productivity of the economy. They go further, however, and state that "the collapse from 1929 to 1933 was neither foreseeable nor inevitable."[45]

This argument may seem quite reasonable from the perspective of an economist, especially revered researchers such as Milton Friedman and Anna Schwartz. When their conclusions are viewed from the point of

view of a credit officer or trader or even a Federal Reserve Bank director, however, a different analysis emerges. Economists from the Chicago
School such as Friedman long believed that the market price of a security
and the intrinsic value of a security in a long-term sense are equivalent.
This view seems to ignore the transient factors such as the availability of
credit, which can greatly affect short-term demand for stocks and bonds.

In the market action in the latter part of the 1920s, the only real
driver was the irrational exuberance of the crowd, the mass of market
participants and particularly their belief that prices would move higher.
As stated succinctly by Friedrich Nietzsche: "Madness is rare in the
individual—but with groups, parties, peoples, and ages it is the rule."

Sylvain Raynes of RR Consulting, who lectured at Baruch
College in Manhattan, put the issue in perspective in September 2007,
just as the subprime financial crisis was unfolding:

> Valuation is not the most important problem in finance; valu-
> ation is not the most interesting problem in finance; valuation
> is the only problem for finance. Once you know value, eve-
> rything happens. Cash moves for value. More price does not
> mean more value. If you do not recognize the difference, the
> fundamental difference between price and value, then you
> are doomed. Now it didn't really matter in corporate finance
> because the two were supposed to remain equal forever. Who
> has been telling us that? These people do not live in New York.
> They live in Chicago. The Chicago School of Economics has
> been telling us for a century that price and value are identical,
> i.e., they are the same number. What this means is that there is
> no such thing as a good deal, there is not such a thing as a bad
> deal, there are only fair deals.[46]

As noted, many "investors" during this period already dispensed
with the old-fashioned idea of using fundamental factors such as profits
or earnings to assess the value of a security. These same investors often
used debt to fund their speculative purchases of securities. When the
securities defaulted and the prices of these bonds collapsed, the debt
accelerated the decline in the markets.

Much of the stock market's valuation in the late 1920s was the result
of the use of credit to purchase stocks and bonds on margin. The cost of

such margin loans was quite high even by modern standards, comparable to using a credit card today to finance stock purchases. Yet the fact that credit was available at all seems to have been the most significant factor in pushing the U.S. financial markets toward the eventual collapse in October 1929.

Valuation in an old-fashioned sense of fundamental analysis does not seem to have been the true driver of the move in stock prices during the Roaring Twenties. Public euphoria created by new products and technologies, an apparently booming economy, and an ample supply of credit seemed to be the true sources of the market surge. This speculative madness was a precursor of the period of the Internet bubble in the 1990s and early 2000s, as well as the subsequent bubbles in residential (2000s) and commercial (2020s) real estate.

Human nature, rather than economic laws or a carefully considered analysis of value, seems to have been the real impetus behind the remarkable ascent of the markets in the 1920s. As the pool of available credit was exhausted and the number of "greater fools" who would buy securities at ever-higher prices gradually diminished, the markets could only go down. This adjustment was then exacerbated by the actions and inaction of the Fed and the White House under Herbert Hoover, neither of which seemed to understand fully the events that were unfolding around them.

Since most economists have never taken risk or traded securities in a hostile market environment, the confusion over the distinction between price and value is understandable. It may be unfair to criticize the economists for failing to understand the true precursors of the Great Depression, namely the ingenuity of the American people and their desire for short-term speculative gain. The catastrophe would change permanently the nature of the relationship between private banks and the U.S. government from implicit support to explicit regulation and oversight.

Galbraith described the problem beautifully in his book *The Great Crash*:

No one can doubt that the American people remain susceptible to the speculative mood—to the conviction that enterprise can be attended by unlimited rewards in which they, individually, were meant to share. A rising market can bring the reality of riches. This, in turn, can draw more and more people to participate. The government preventatives and controls are ready. In the hands of a determined government their efficacy cannot be doubted. There are, however, a hundred reasons why a government will determine not to use them.[47]

Galbraith wrote in *The Great Crash* about how the real economy in the United States was deteriorating for months before the market break, starting with the collapse of commodity prices in the farm sector and then the wonderful boom and bust in land speculation in Florida. Finally, in the autumn of 1929 as seasonal demand for credit peaked due to the harvest cycle in the farm sector, the financial markets turned down sharply and sent the entire nation into what is now known as the Great Depression. In the space of a week, the Dow Jones Industrial Average dropped 30 percent and the previously exuberant business environment was dashed as both consumer and business confidence plummeted.

President Hoover declared after only a week of market upheaval that the worst of the crisis was past. But by July 1932, the Dow closed at 41.22, an 89 percent drop from the pre-crash high and a level that would not be reached again until 1954. After the election of 1932, the public started to horde gold in anticipation of socialist policies from Franklin Delano Roosevelt. Even fellow Democrat and New York governor Al Smith would eventually use the socialist label to attack Roosevelt.

By March 1933 when FDR took office, about half the banks in many states were closed, the nation's economy was imploding under 25 percent unemployment and a decline of 50 percent in GDP. Barter reemerged as bank runs and company closings drained cash from the economy. Many banks that failed did so as a result of margin lending on stocks, one of the enduring lessons of the period leading up to the Great Crash.

Hoover has been somewhat demonized by history, but it is often overlooked by popular accounts of the Great Depression that President Hoover, and not FDR, created the Reconstruction Finance Corporation (RFC) and the Federal Home Loan Banks, two of the most significant and interventionist initiatives ever taken by Washington.

The RFC, operating under Jesse Jones, was empowered to make loans to banks, insurers, and industrial companies almost without limit. The RFC was initially set up with the idea of repaying the government and then some on its investment and would serve as an important part of the government's response to the Depression during the 1930s.

The Great Crash was a political tragedy for Hoover, who was genuinely different from many of his predecessors in the Republican Party. The GOP had been in power, with exceptions such as Grover Cleveland and Woodrow Wilson, for a long time. They looked down upon the Democrats as unfit to govern and especially despised Franklin Delano Roosevelt, Wilson's vice president, as a traitor to his class. But America was still a very young country and had yet to live through anything like the crisis that would unfold during the Depression.

With the bloody exception of the Civil War, Americans lived a fairly safe and stable existence in the country's first 150 years. If World War I represented an opening of American vistas, the Depression was a crushing downward adjustment of collective expectations. Europe collapsed with the financial crisis of 1931, including the failure of several banks and the exit of Germany from the gold standard. The United States also fell into a period of deflation and falling economic activity that would stretch on for many more years.

Like Hoover, the great economist Irving Fisher thought that the financial crisis was past the worst in 1933, but he was mistaken:

The depression out of which we are now (I trust) emerging is an example of a debt-deflation depression of the most serious sort . . . Unless some counteracting cause comes along to prevent the fall in the price level, such a depression as that of 1929–33 (namely when the more the debtors pay the more they owe) tends to continue, going deeper, in a vicious spiral, for many years. There is then no tendency of the boat to stop tipping until it has capsized. Ultimately, of course, but only after almost universal bankruptcy, the indebtedness must cease to grow greater and begin to grow less. Then comes recovery and a tendency for a new boom-depression sequence. This is the so-called "natural" way out of a depression, via needless and cruel bankruptcy, unemployment, and starvation.[48]

Americans had experimented with imperialism, but not in a serious way because they believed that there was more than enough opportunity to be found in the United States. The Great Depression shook that faith. When the financial markets collapsed, it was quickly revealed that Hoover was not the ideal man for the job of dealing with the crisis—nor were the Republicans as a group prepared to lead the nation in a time of mass privation. None of them seemed to grasp the magnitude of the fiscal and credit contraction that was unfolding. The Hoover government spent 1930 and 1931 doing relatively little about the collapsing demand for many goods and services.

By 1932, however, discussions about how to inflate the currency were top of the agenda and the prevention of further deflation and unemployment was a national priority. Hoover appointed Eugene Meyer to head a bipartisan board for the RFC and recruited Charles Dawes as president and chief administrator, and Harvey Couch and Jesse Jones as directors. Ogden Mills, who replaced Andrew Mellon as Secretary of the Treasury, was an *ex officio* member of the RFC board. Finally, the RFC was configured and ready to begin dealing with the lack of financing in many markets, but this was only done belatedly, in the fourth year of Hoover's term. A hesitant Congress actually took away some of the RFC's powers during this period, but the powers of the RFC were restored and more.

During FDR's presidency and under the guidance of Jesse Jones, the RFC was given *carte blanche* by Congress because of the enormous respect and trust that the self-made Texan possessed and the support he had from members of Congress such as Carter Glass as a result. Just as giants like Robert Moses built massive public works in New York during this period, Jesse Jones and contemporaries such as Leo Crowley at the Federal Deposit Insurance Corporation literally restructured the U.S. economy.

Hoover's tidy and beautifully organized memoir is essential reading for students of the period of boom and bust in the first three decades of the twentieth century. Along with Jesse Jones's remembrances of running the RFC for more than a decade, the chronicle of Herbert Hoover is an engineer's report on the progress of the country during and after the financial crisis that began in October 1929.

After his chronicle of the years up to the start of FDR's presidency, the second half of volume two of President Hoover's memoir is a scathing critique of his successor. It features several times the word "fascism" to describe many of the Roosevelt-era prescriptions for fighting the Depression, a blunt reminder that much of what FDR did during these dark years was borrowed directly from the strong men of Europe—Mussolini in Italy, Hitler in Germany, and Stalin in Russia. There were in fact three New Deals in the 1930s, Russia, Germany, and the United States.

Because Hoover handed FDR a country that was on its knees, history has tended to be kinder and more forgiving to Roosevelt and very critical of his predecessor. FDR himself was critical of Hoover, in one campaign speech in 1928 referring to "the Hoover theory of a God-inspired political thinker at the top."[49] The thoughtful engineer Hoover was an easy target for his sharp-witted political opponent FDR, but the former New York governor would soon find himself the owner of the Great Depression.

Chapter 6

New Deal to Cold War

D uring the 1930s, the administration of Franklin Roosevelt caused great change for the perception and reality of money in America. FDR is lionized in many history books while Hoover and the Republicans are demonized. The truth is that neither governing party really understood nor controlled the path of the economy during the Depression. The Democrats actually controlled Congress during Hoover's presidency, so they cannot escape a fair share of responsibility for not foreseeing the catastrophe. But in truth communications in 1930 were inadequate to describe the scope of the disaster.

Franklin Roosevelt and the Democrats deliberately worsened the banking crisis in 1932 by refusing to cooperate with the incumbent Hoover during the long transition period from November to March. The handoff of power between Hoover and FDR in March 1933 was painful, culminating with the oath of office as most of the nation's banks stood closed. The transition in 1933 provided an especially fateful example of why the period of time from the election of a president to inauguration had to be shortened by the Twentieth Amendment to the Constitution, which easily passed that same year.

Hoover declared that FDR intentionally chose not to cooperate openly with his government to contain the banking crisis in 1932 and thereby use the larger emergency in early 1933 as a pretext for imposing a currency devaluation and authoritarian economic controls over American business and labor. But even more, the former president laid the blame for the public's panic in March 1933 at the feet of FDR and particularly the imposition of the New Deal.

"It was the most political and the most unnecessary bank panic in our history," Hoover wrote. Echoing the rhetoric of the Woodrow Wilson and Teddy Roosevelt eras regarding kinder masters, Hoover continued to say that "the breakdown in confidence which sounded the advent of the New Deal is of course a helpful statistical point when they want to show how good they have been to us."[1] The "they" in the previous sentence refers to FDR and his lieutenants, men who the orthodox Hoover described bluntly as "traitors."

The period under FDR was one of the most fateful and significant for the United States over the past century, more because of the statist legacies left behind by FDR than to his accomplishments at the time. FDR ran against the budget deficits of Hoover's years, but ignored the collapse of federal tax revenue caused by the devaluation of the dollar and worsening Depression. Like Wilson, FDR ran against the war, but later involved the United States in assisting the British from the outset of hostilities. FDR subsequently ran even bigger deficits than Hoover and eventually took America back to war. Ultimately it was inflation and war that refloated the US economy.

George Selgin wrote about this period in a 2020 commentary for CATO Institute:

> [T]he recovery that followed FDR's assumption of office was fueled almost exclusively by growth in the Federal Reserve's gold holdings. Those holdings almost tripled during the four years following the nationwide bank holiday, allowing the M2 money stock to concurrently grow to 150 percent of its pre-holiday level. The result was a "Great Expansion" of real GNP that more than offset the "Great Contraction" of the preceding three years.[2]

Ever duplicitous, FDR at first campaigned against tariffs in the months leading up to the 1932 election, promising that trade liberalization would be a key part of his administration. Echoing Democratic leaders such as William Jennings Bryan and Al Smith, FDR made tariff reduction a centerpiece at the start of his campaign against Hoover. By the end of his campaign, however, FDR was singing from the protectionist gospel of the Republican Party. His flexibility in regard to these serious issues of economic and financial policy evidenced an agenda that was first and foremost political, much like authoritarian regimes like China today. The same could be said for FDR's approach to foreign policy and especially relations with Europe.

Whereas Theodore Roosevelt was a libertarian and an advocate for traditional American values of individualism and self-reliance, FDR was an Anglophile and apologist for a European-style unitary federal state and dependence on government. Despite his family's vast wealth, FDR believed in an Americanized version of the corporate statism that arose in central Europe in the 1920s and underpinned the fascist experiments in Italy, Germany, and other nations. Hoover said of the New Deal that it was "an attempt to cross-breed Socialism, Fascism and Free Enterprise" and this was not far from the truth, even if FDR was less than definite as to his actual beliefs. Supporters of FDR claim that times were desperate and thus experimentation was in order, but FDR's attacks on business and seizure of gold were at best politically expedient and evidenced hostility to traditional American society.

Both Teddy Roosevelt and FDR were wealthy men who knew all of the top business leaders and bankers of the day. FDR himself came from very old New York money care of the Roosevelt and Delano branches of the family. The Delanos were the sort of old New Yorkers who traced their origins to the Mayflower, owned an estate in the Hudson Valley, and lived on Colonnade Row in lower Manhattan in the 1830s. They considered the Astors to be *nouveau riche*.

Frederic Adrian Delano, FDR's uncle, was a second-generation railroad baron who spent much of his life focused on the transportation industry. Yet Fred Delano served as the first vice chairman of the Federal Reserve Board. Both presidents knew how to use bankers and business leaders as targets of opportunity when the situation arose. In short, FDR was a wealthy politician but one who was in many ways antithetical to the political views of his cousin Theodore Roosevelt or even his fellow Democrats in Tammany Hall.

Broken Promises

Today the image of FDR in the public mind is larger and more intense than that of Teddy Roosevelt, in part because of the powerful experience of World War II. Teddy Roosevelt was the greater figure in the long run of historical and political events. The proof of the failure of FDR as a transformative figure was the lack of any enduring popular movement from grassroots America in response to the New Deal. Like the years of President Joe Biden a century later, most Americans don't make good socialists. They think themselves than better being mere wards of the state.

In truth, FDR was a machine politician from New York as much as was Teddy Roosevelt, and had little appeal to real Progressives. In that sense, as men of the left, FDR and Wilson both seem to share an establishment respectability garnished with a veneer of Progressive liberalism. Minton and John Stuart wrote in *The Fat Years and the Lean* about the 1932 election that "the campaign was never more than a contest between Hoover and Roosevelt, between the representative of the political machine in power and the nominee of the political machine wanting power."[3]

The members of FDR's "brain trust" were less revolutionary and more bureaucratic at the end of the day, but many on the left saw him as a "transmitting instrument of the new world order," according to the Fabian writer H.G. Wells. A devoted socialist, Wells visited FDR on several occasions and called the president and Mrs. Roosevelt "unlimited" people in a sense of their willingness to discard small-town American values and embrace new, revolutionary ideas.[4] His description of FDR recalls the distinction made by author Thomas Sowell regarding people with "unconstrained vision" in his book *Conflict of Visions*.[5]

Whereas Herbert Hoover was seemingly a man with constrained vision, who saw human nature as comprised of fixed values and characteristics, FDR was a man who came from wealth who deigned to order the affairs of others. FDR was a man of unconstrained vision, a gambler and opportunist, who used the pretense of concern for his fellow man to make seemingly radical changes in society. Like his bitter enemy Robert Moses, FDR thought he knew best how to govern his fellow men. Hoover saw the world as comprised of immutable rules and values that were to be cherished and defended. FDR saw those same rules as factors to be manipulated and, when convenient, violated, to achieve a larger political end.

Contemporary observers such as Eliot Janeway differ with the conservative demonization of FDR and the New Deal. Janeway, who began his writing career at the age of 24, wrote a series of articles for *The Nation* predicting the 1937–1938 recession. In his first book, *The Struggle for Survival*, Janeway argued that Roosevelt had no strong view of theoretical political distinctions or economics:

> Roosevelt was no more a radical than was Queen Elizabeth. Never was a political free-booter more cynical about all theories . . . Temperamentally, the man could not bring himself to believe that good administration ever accomplished or prevented anything. He simply did not believe in Planning—with a capital P—as the answer to the problems of society. And he certainly did not believe in the Planners who looked down their noses at people for being people and at politicians like him for catering to them. No doubt, legend will confuse coincidence with cause, and Roosevelt will be credited with having established Government as the dominant entity in American life. What he actually did was to keep pace with a revolution that no man was big enough to have started or stopped.[6]

Loyal apologists for FDR such as Janeway sought to make his policy caprices seem more reactive than revolutionary, and in large part they are correct, but Eleanor Roosevelt encouraged the president to take ever more radical positions. "Eleanor consistently pushed FDR to the left on key issues and appointments," noted Peter Drier in a 2013 profile. "The left-leaning members of FDR's inner circle (including Labor Secretary Frances Perkins, Agriculture Secretary and later Vice President Henry Wallace, and Harry Hopkins, who formulated and ran many New Deal relief programs) often conspired with Eleanor to make sure he heard the views of progressive activists."[7]

The events moving in the deflation of the 1930s, however, were too large for any one person or country to affect. Franklin Roosevelt was just another American politician from New York, albeit with more than the usual personal flair and affectation due to his inherited wealth. "In Roosevelt's experience, ideology was something to be feared, not embraced," wrote Peter Canellos. "Communism, fascism, Nazism ("National Socialism") and even the unbending capitalist principles of his conservative critics were all looming dangers to the nation's survival."[8]

FDR started his political life as a state senator in New York, a position he had gained over Tammany Hall boss Charles Murphy because of infighting within the organization. As with Teddy Roosevelt, fate helped to give FDR a chance to succeed politically amidst the chaos of Tammany Hall, but FDR ultimately betrayed his predecessor Al Smith. Like his cousin Teddy, FDR was a political accident set in motion by the internal convulsions of New York politics. After serving as assistant secretary of the Navy under Woodrow Wilson and vice presidential candidate with James Cox in the 1920 election against Warren Harding, Roosevelt went home to New York to resume his life as a Hudson Valley landholder, but then fate struck him down with polio.

In 1924, his Tammany Hall mentor Al Smith, convinced the still-recuperating Roosevelt to come to New York City to place Smith's name into nomination at the Democratic Committee to run against President Coolidge. Four years later in Houston, FDR again nominated Smith to a second unsuccessful run for the presidency, this time against Herbert Hoover. At the insistence of Tammany Hall, FDR ran for governor of New York in 1928 and won the most populous state in the union by 25,000 votes. The Catholic Al Smith lost New York in the 1928 presidential election by 100,000 votes.

After turning his back on Al Smith, FDR cleaned Tammany Hall out of Albany and installed his own gang of Progressive thinkers. He launched a series of reforms and state development initiatives that were the testing ground for the New Deal. Despite his popularity, FDR was not a remarkable governor in terms of actual accomplishments outside politics and showed little appreciation for economics. Superficially at least, his main quality seemed to be the ability to please people of all political persuasions. FDR was the stereotype of the modern American politician, never daring to do anything too radical or too controversial.

Roosevelt was "a highly impressionable person without a firm grasp of public affairs and without very strong convictions . . . He is an amiable man with many philanthropic impulses, but is not the dangerous enemy of anything," Walter Lippmann concluded. "[FDR] is a pleasant man who, without any important qualifications for the office, would very much like to be President."[9]

Lippmann was one of the most influential and powerful journalists of his age. He soon completely changed his view of FDR.[10] As one observer remarked, FDR entered the White House in 1933 as the best-liked man in America. Even after a none-too-successful year in office, he was still more popular than when he was elected—but the nation was truly desperate.

In 1930, when Hoover and the Republicans lost control over Congress to the Democrats and the Progressive party, then–New York Governor Roosevelt saw his opportunity. Assisted by long-time supporters such as Louis McHenry Howe and James Farley, FDR began to plan his ascension to the White House. By the time the Democratic Party met to nominate a presidential candidate, FDR had almost sufficient votes to win the prize, but still had to work hard for the nomination.

In the 1932 Democratic platform, the party promised economy in government, a sound currency—and "a competitive tariff for revenue" with other nations. Democrats called for the repeal of Prohibition, self-determination for the Philippines—and the collection of war debts from the European nations. Al Smith hoped to be picked for a third time to lead the Democratic ticket, but his protégé and former subordinate in the Tammany Hall organization stole the prize—with help from House Democratic leader Sam Rayburn of Texas, former Treasury secretary William McAdoo, and publisher William Randolph Hearst. These men provided the key support from California to get FDR the nomination.

In addition, FDR was also helped by Joseph P. Kennedy, who donated and raised hundreds of thousands of dollars for FDR and traveled with him on the campaign trail. Kennedy claimed to have been the decisive force in winning the active support of Hearst for FDR at the 1932 Democratic convention in Chicago. He was also responsible for suborning significant defections from the pro–Al Smith camp, including Honey Fitz and Jim Curley from Boston.

"Roosevelt could not afford to shut the door on anyone with money," Richard Whalen wrote in his 1964 biography of Joe Kennedy,

The Founding Father: The Story of Joseph P. Kennedy. "Alone among
the party's contenders, he indicted erring business leadership for the
country's misfortunes . . . Such radical sounding talk alarmed John J.
Raskob, now chairman of the Democratic National Committee. He
dropped all pretense of impartiality and threw his weight behind the
party's 1928 standard bearer, Al Smith."[11,]

Had the Republicans not been caught completely flat-footed by
the Great Crash of 1929 and the ensuing two years of economic contraction, they might have had an opportunity to win the election of
1932—the Republican political machine remained so powerful. But
with Hoover predicting that "prosperity is around the corner" nearly
every day and without any success to back his claims, the Republicans
got slaughtered and rightly so. FDR and his running mate John Garner
won against Hoover and Charles Curtis with 57 percent of the vote
and carried all but a handful of northeastern states.

The first 100 days of the Roosevelt administration are presented
in most of the FDR hagiographies in dramatic and heroic terms
not unlike newsreel footage from the Soviet Union or Communist
China. The suffering in the country did make the times dramatic. The
response of the federal government was equally serious and substantial, including an initial, almost Republican effort by FDR to cut federal spending. Later in his term, FDR recalled the lessons of Abraham
Lincoln and deficit spending became the order of the day, first for
fighting the Depression and later to finance another war. But early on,
many of FDR's efforts to repair the economy were quite conventional.

FDR's first task was to respond to the economic crisis and in particular the banks. The Emergency Banking Act was introduced on
March 9, 1933, passed the same day, and signed into law. Congressman
Henry B. Steagall reportedly walked into the House chamber with the
text of the legislation newly transmitted from the White House and
waving it in the air said "Here's the bill. Let's pass it."

After a few minutes of debate and no amendments, it was passed
and the Senate soon followed suit. The first section of the law simply
endorsed all the executive orders given by the president or secretary
of the Treasury since March 4. Congress gave FDR the power to confiscate gold, seize banks, and impose currency controls, a remarkable
agenda of socialist expropriation that terrified American citizens. It also

authorized the Treasury to issue $2 billion in new fiat paper dollars that were not convertible and instead were secured by the private assets of the U.S. banking system.

Gold Seizure and Devaluation

The Banking Act authorized the Fed to make loans to any individual based on Treasury bonds as collateral, very tough requirements that would be changed decades later to enable the bank bailout of 2008. The law also authorized the Reconstruction Finance Corporation to invest in the preferred stock and capital notes of banks and to make secured loans to individual banks.[12]

Even a century after the fact, most Americans don't know that the model for the New Deal was fascist Italy. Benito Mussolini organized the *Istituto per la Ricostruzione Industriale* (IRI) in January 1933 to accomplish, with respect to large business trusts in Italy, some of the same functions that the RFC performed for insurance companies and banks. IRI came to own much of Italian industry and continued to operate as a state holding company through World War II and well into the end of the twentieth century.

Even before the Banking Act was passed, the Federal Reserve Board announced that it was preparing lists of people who had withdrawn gold from banks in the previous weeks, a none-too-subtle reminder that hoarding gold now carried criminal penalties. The Fed never questioned the propriety or economic efficacy of the FDR gold seizures. Nearly 15 percent of the currency in circulation in the United States disappeared in the weeks prior to FDR's taking office. An immediate means of bringing that cash back into the banking system had to be found.

Within hours of the Fed's announcement, long lines formed outside banks and Federal Reserve Banks to exchange gold for greenbacks. The Fed then announced that it was widening the hunt for gold hoarders to withdrawals made in the past two years. By the end of the first week of FDR's term, enough gold had been returned to the banking system to support nearly $1 billion in new currency issuance.

That same week, the Bureau of Engraving in Washington began to print money—$2 billion worth of new greenbacks to be precise.

So urgent was the emergency and so short the time that the Bureau printed dollars with old plates that bore the legend "Series of 1929" and used old signatures from the 12 Federal Reserve Banks. By Saturday, March 11, planes filled with newly printed dollars began to leave Washington to deliver badly needed funds to banks around the country. The emergency was far from over, but the rapid distribution of new cash around the country enabled FDR to slow the deflationary aspect of the banking crisis he had willfully exacerbated and buy some time to formulate the next steps.

FDR's abandonment of the gold standard and confiscation of gold coins in 1933 was among the most memorable actions taken in American history. FDR's decision to take the United States off the gold standard and devalue the dollar had a far more profound impact on the country and the world than many of the dozens of other programs that were put in place during the period. Assistance for the unemployed, relief for farmers, and many other programs came later, but his decision to devalue the dollar had global ramifications.

Under Herbert Hoover, the Fed pursued an aggressive, inflationist policy, especially in the last year of his term. For most of 1932, the Fed aggressively added cash and purchased government securities, yet the bank deposit base and the supply of cash continued to contract because people could flee paper for gold. After the election of 1932 and as FDR began his term, the run on paper accelerated. This period in history bears a troubling resemblance to the behavior of the markets in 2009–2010 when the Fed likewise tried to encourage new credit creation and a higher rate of turnover or "velocity" for money as investors fled the securities markets for the safety of cash.

The Emergency Banking Relief Act renewed the powers granted to the president after World War I to exercise authority over all foreign exchange transactions as well as all payments by banking institutions. FDR signed an executive order confiscating all private gold as it became clear that the public was reacting negatively to his presidency by hoarding gold coins and shunning paper dollars. There was essentially "a run-on FDR" between November 1932 and the inauguration in March 1933. He banned banks from making payments in gold, forcing U.S. citizens to accept legal tender dollars for all payments. All of these coercive measures were needed to prevent the Roosevelt government from collapsing financially.

The Democratic "rubber stamp" Congress did not object to and even ratified the decision by FDR to leave the gold standard with the Gold Reserve Act of 1934. Treasury Secretary Henry Morgenthau, Jr., announced on March 11 that "the provision is aimed at those who continue to retain quantities of gold and thereby hinder the Government's plans for a restoration of public confidence."[13] The government was broke and needed to prevent Americans from fleeing dollars for gold. FDR made this weighty decision only weeks after the collapse of the nation's banking system, suggesting that his decision to confiscate all gold was under consideration for some time.

Farm prices and wages had been falling for months. Many Americans and a majority of the Congress anxiously called for the old palliative of currency inflation to stem the terrible depression that affected the entire country. What they got from Roosevelt, however, was not incremental inflation based upon the existing gold regime, but a completely different financial order. Anticipating FDR's actions to deliberately inflate the dollar, in February 1933 the financier Bernard Baruch, who had been an adviser to President Hoover and also to FDR, told the Senate that only by keeping expenditures within income can the people of the United States retain confidence in its credit. Inflation is "the road to ruin," Baruch declared. Without confidence, he continued, money loses value and sinks beneath the level of commodities that can be consumed.

Baruch recalled that inflation had been going on for years during the Depression. The Federal Reserve Banks had been purchasing nearly all of the debt issued by the Treasury to fund federal deficits since the Great Crash of 1929. The Treasury itself, Baruch observed, had been producing inflation by "coining a deficit" to pay for greater government expenditures. Baruch warned: "We have kept that credit above reproach for so long that people think that it can stand any abuse," he told the Senate. "But this is an era of broken precedent. We are witnessing the disintegration of the institutions of an era."[14]

In 1933, most members of Congress were not in the mood for lectures about gold or sound money. Senator Tom Connally (D-TX), who won election to the House in 1917 and to the Senate in 1929, questioned Baruch closely on the issue of inflation. A staunch advocate for the farm community in Texas and of currency inflation, Connally hammered Baruch over the question of whether a little inflation now would not help the American farmer in an immediate sense. Baruch conceded that in the past inflation had provided temporary relief to farmers as in the period during World War I, but he stated that he did not believe that farm prices would necessarily rise with greater inflation, because of the lack of demand.

Senator Robert La Follette likewise endorsed the powers granted to FDR, illustrating the strong support in Congress for inflation at that time. Baruch was unimpressed by the inflationist tendency in the Democrat-controlled Congress and rejected their thinking:

I regard the condition of this country as the most serious in its history. It is worse than war. In war there is a definite enemy. We know what and where he is and how to fight him. We can measure the necessary sacrifices and make them with certainty of effect. But this enemy wears no uniform and takes no position on any front . . . So far as I am concerned, there is no sacrifice I would not be willing to make to fight this terror—no plan, however revolutionary and bold, that I would not try if I could see in it an even chance of success. If I did not know that there was nothing but destruction to be derived from the project of inflation, I would be the first to advocate its trial. But I am as certain as that we are sitting here that the path proposed is the road to ruin.[15]

Regardless of how one feels about the contemporary conservative indictments of FDR, the seizure of gold owned by individuals, companies, and the private banks that were members of the Federal Reserve System was an extreme step that did not help the nation recover from the Depression. As in the case of the financial rescue of 2008, which was financed with trillions of dollars of monetary expansion by the Fed, in the 1930s elected officials were unwilling to raise taxes to pay the nation's bills.

The economic emergency of the Great Depression gave our leaders sufficient political cover to disregard past precedents and established rules, and to print money with a level of recklessness that only a few years earlier would have ensured their political destruction. The FDR move with respect to gold actually hurt public confidence in the

United States and the dollar, which was already badly damaged by the banking crisis. But FDR's motivation also was ultimately political, to prevent the declining value of the dollar measured in gold from sinking him politically. Richard Whalen observed in discussions about this book that FDR's decision to leave the gold standard "was about keeping the people out of the streets," but it is not clear that the decision had any positive impact on the economy.

Though the appearance of growth was created by inflating the currency in the 1930s, prices generally rose with the start of World War II and have risen by an order of magnitude since then. The dollar has lost more than 98 percent of its purchasing power since the Great Depression, but living standards in the United States have also risen dramatically. The use of debt to finance purchases of homes and consumer services, and to finance public expenditures, also increased. Once the link to gold was removed, the government was free to inflate and borrow without effective limitation. This freedom with respect to the uses of debt has also spread to the private sector.

Ogden Mills, President Herbert Hoover's Treasury secretary, said that "it was not the maintenance of the gold standard that caused the banking panic of 1933 and the outflow of gold . . . [I]t was the definite and growing fear that the new administration meant to do what they ultimately did—that is, abandon the gold standard." James Bovard summarized the FDR actions with respect to gold:

Curiously, FDR retained his denigrating tone toward so-called gold-hoarders even after he defaulted on the federal government's gold redemption promise. Even though people who distrusted politicians' promises were vindicated, they were still evil people because they had not obeyed FDR's demand to surrender their gold. In the moral world of the New Deal, justice consisted solely of blind obedience to political commands. FDR had absolutely no sense of embarrassment or shame after he defaulted on the federal government's gold promises—it was simply political business as usual.[16]

The Roosevelt devaluation of the dollar in 1933 was a dismal failure, even though the value of the dollar measured in other major currencies was cut in half. Commodity prices in 1933 were roughly half of the levels in 1926, and there was little relief in sight. Production rose by almost 50 percent between 1919 and 1927, but the advent of electricity and the impact of tariffs caused producer prices and factory employment to plummet. Throughout the 1930s, in fact, the U.S. economy arguably had excess capacity—extra production capability that would conveniently be absorbed by the onset of World War II.

Always astute politically, FDR decorated his administration with a goodly portion of Bryan Democrats, men who were advocates of inflationism and ending the gold standard. In June 1934, FDR even asked Congress to make the dollar convertible into silver at the same time that he sought further legal powers to confiscate private gold. The advocates of the use of silver as money would be disappointed, however. FDR's seizure of gold and the devaluation of the dollar only increased the price ratio between the two metals. After the Roosevelt era devaluation of the dollar, the price of gold was set at $35 per ounce but silver traded around $0.40 per ounce, a ratio of 80 to 1 versus gold.

Devaluation and Tariffs

While there was no appreciable recovery in terms of commodity or producer prices in the 1930s, the drop in the value of the dollar cut the cost of debt repayments to the United States for the nations of Europe and also cut the cost of U.S. exports. But American imports from Europe and other nations fell dramatically. This drop in U.S. consumption of imported goods suggests that it was the Roosevelt era currency devaluation, more than the Smoot-Hawley tariff, that caused the further contraction of the global economy in the 1930s. Gold flowed out of Europe to the United States because our trading partners were still obliged to pay their debts in gold, but the devaluation did not increase prices or employment in the U.S. economy.

Hoover noted that the dollar devaluation by FDR was effectively an increase in the tariff from the perspective of the cost to American buyers: "The Democrats have made a great issue out of the disasters they predicted would flow from the modest increases in the Smoot-Hawley tariff (mostly agricultural products). The fact was that 65 percent of the imported goods under the tariff were free of duty, and that legislation increased tariffs on the 35 percent dutiable goods by somewhere around 10 percent. But the greatest tariff boost in all our history came from Roosevelt's devaluation." Hoover goes on to illustrate that both imports and exports per capita declined in the United States between 1935 and 1938.[17]

In addition to a selection of Bryan Democrats around FDR, there was also a cadre of left-wing operatives that openly took inspiration if not direction from fascist regimes in Rome and Berlin. These New Dealers were true believers and welcomed the permanent debasement of the dollar as part of the road to world socialism.[18] The bankers and communists alike who populated FDR's "brain trust" ultimately agreed on the government's policies regarding gold, even if many of FDR's more conservative advisers were aghast and some even resigned in protest.

The bankers who were then in charge of the House of Morgan provided intellectual support for FDR's move against gold, something that would have shocked J.P. Morgan, who fought to restore the gold standard only decades earlier. But the fact was that the seizure of gold was more than anything else a political move by FDR. He knew that Americans and foreigners were voting with their feet and running away from the Democrats, selling paper dollars and buying gold even as he tried to resuscitate the sagging U.S. economy.

Morgan banker and New Dealer Russell Leffingwell, along with legendary Morgan banker Thomas Lamont, met with the prominent newspaper writer Walter Lippman in early April 1933 to discuss leaving the gold standard. Lippmann then wrote a column advocating an end to the gold standard that appeared in the *Herald Tribune* on April 18, 1933. FDR, who trusted Leffingwell perhaps more than any other member of his inner circle, announced to his advisers that day that the United States was moving off the gold standard. The president made a statement regarding the negative effects of the hoarding of gold on the following day.[19]

Not surprisingly, the FDR strategy regarding gold was good for stocks and caused an immediate rally on Wall Street. The move to leave gold, however, was much the same as other aspects of the New Deal economic program, namely to create scarcity in order to defeat and ultimately reverse deflation. FDR's Republican and Democratic opponents did not understand, however, that when Roosevelt spoke of maintaining *sound money,* he was not promising to restore the pre-Depression gold value of the dollar. Instead, FDR proposed to make money entirely a function of government policy. Part of this change was clearly meant to address the nation's economic crisis, but part was also political, namely to remove the dollar value of gold as a daily barometer of FDR's political standing.

Unfortunately, the lack of understanding by FDR and his economic team as to the true nature of the crisis rendered the change in the dollar largely ineffectual in economic terms. Members of the New Deal team, as already noted, wanted to foster inflation and thereby get domestic prices to start to rise. Most of the policies implemented by FDR, however, had the opposite effect. FDR's efforts to boost farm and industrial prices by manipulating the price of gold and the value of the dollar during the period 1933–1934 were an abject failure.

Rise of the Corporate State

Apart from his departure from the gold standard, FDR's initial approach to economic problems was not revolutionary. His method was precisely the same as that used by generations of Republicans before him, namely to manage prices and markets via scarcity. He took the process further by borrowing from European fascism with corporatist initiatives such as the National Industrial Recovery Act, which created a nationwide network of industry boards to set wages and prices. These initiatives had dubious value in terms of fighting the Depression, but the times were desperate and "new" solutions were being sought.

Walker Todd set the scene in his classic monograph on the New Deal, "The Federal Reserve Board and the Rise of the Corporate State, 1931–1934":

Once one understands the degree to which politicians, jurists, businessmen, and economic policymakers of the early 1930s were attracted to any political economy model that held out the promise of relieving the symptoms of what Friedman and

Schwartz (1963) called "the Great Contraction, 1929–1933," it becomes easier to understand how quickly and how thoroughly corporativist ideas like the National Recovery Administration became permanent fixtures of the Washington political environment.[20]

Instead of trying to increase consumption and therefore firm prices, the New Dealers actually took a page from World War I, or even from the likes of Jay Gould and Andrew Carnegie, and attempted to firm up wages and prices by squeezing and managing supply.

During this period the British economist John Maynard Keynes formulated his theory regarding business cycles and the need for countries to leave the gold standard in order to foster at least nominal growth. In a meeting with Walter Lippmann in June 1933, Keynes described why nations needed to float away from gold and to run fiscal deficits to spur consumption and investment in order to generate economic expansion. So long as consumer demand remained stagnant, Keynes argued, businesses would not increase investment and employment would not grow, regardless of the level of savings. His arguments ran directly counter to the conventional wisdom of spending cuts and tax increases in times of recession, a tendency that persists within business and government to this day.

What is peculiar about the discussions between Keynes and Lippmann is that the former's views on restoring growth in the Western economies seemed to be completely at odds with his changing view on free trade. Writing in the *Yale Review* in 1933, Keynes condemned free trade in no uncertain terms. He made clear that the global interconnections between financial markets had worsened the Depression, a view that runs directly counter to the neoliberal view of free trade after World War II.

"I was brought up, like most Englishmen, to respect free trade not only as an economic doctrine which a rational and instructed person could not doubt, but almost as a part of the moral law," he wrote. "Yet the orientation of my mind is changed; and I share this change of mind with many others . . . I sympathize, therefore, with those who would minimize, rather than with those who would maximize, economic entanglement among nations. Ideas, knowledge, science, hospitality, travel—these are the things which should of their nature be international. But let goods be homespun whenever it is reasonably and conveniently possible, and, above all, let finance be primarily national."[21]

Expanding on his work of a few years earlier in the *Treatise on Money*,[22] Keynes argued that government should use debt to support public works and other types of expenditures during bad times and tax during good times to retire the indebtedness. His very British view of the need to repay the debt immediately upon the end of a war or economic crisis reflected the custom in the United Kingdom.

Keynes was not an apologist for debt or inflation, but he did advocate a strong role for government in times of deflation—precisely the prescription that fit the times. After all, he was a mathematician and speculator first and foremost; a man who understood and played the markets. Grasping the fact that growth, or at least the desire for growth, had outstripped the capacity of the gold-based monetary system was not an arduous process for Keynes.

Three years later, Keynes would elaborate upon his hypothesis regarding the role of government in *The General Theory of Employment, Interest and Money*,[23] a work that radically changed the way that nations and their political leaders looked at money and debt. As with the creation of central banks, the new fiscal mechanics articulated by Keynes created novel alternatives for political leaders such as FDR and at precisely the time when conventional policies were failing. The alternatives of deficit spending and public debt had the notable attribute of not requiring the direct assent of the voters, but would be paid for via future inflation. As Lincoln had done in the Civil War, FDR turned to the printing press and inflation as a tool to restore demand.

The traditional response of government during times of depression was clearly creating political instability in the United States and around the world. A wave of global deflation fueled the rise of fascism in Italy and Germany during this same period. Leaders of the major European nations fully expected revolution, thus the idea of government spending and even borrowing to offset extremes of economic and social conditions was greeted enthusiastically. And because Keynes himself was a believer in central planning, his views fit into the rising tide of corporatist thinking that flowed through many western capitals in the early 1930s. These collectivist notions now competed with traditional American conceptions of money and debt.

Keynes believed that the nations of the world needed to end their slavish devotion to the gold standard and to allow their currencies to decline in value by as much as one-third to revive global growth. Years later, in a presage of Modern Monetary Theory half a century later, he argued that the new currency regime was the opposite of the gold standard and the nations of the world were now free to make of it whatever they wished. This thinking impressed Lippmann, who framed the argument for leaving the gold standard in another column in the *Herald Tribune* of June 29, 1933. It also impressed FDR.

In the age of media plentitude in which we live today, it is difficult to appreciate the influence of Lippmann and his internationally syndicated column in the *Herald Tribune*. Newspapers were the shared experience of Americans and the common source of information. The connection among FDR, Lippmann, and Keynes gave momentum to the intellectual process of responding to the deflation visible in the markets of America and Europe. Days later, on July 3, 1933, FDR sent a message to the World Economic Conference meeting in Europe denouncing currency stabilization as "a specious fallacy." Through his emissaries, FDR made clear to the other nations that the United States was not prepared to agree on either tariff reduction or stabilization of the dollar until economic recovery had begun.

FDR's actions with respect to gold and the dollar hurt the reputation of the United States with foreign countries. The dollar devaluation also led many observers, even close allies of FDR, to wonder if the Roosevelt administration was sound in its thinking. Not all of the leaders of Europe disagreed with FDR's actions with respect to gold, however, including a conservative backbencher in the United Kingdom named Winston Churchill.

Keynes subsequently wrote an article supporting FDR's action. More than a few politicians understood that FDR, by following the thinking of Keynes, was essentially creating an alternative, a "middle way" between the *laissez-faire* capitalism of nineteenth-century America and the Marxist socialism that was destroying Russia and threatened Europe and America. But this was a false distinction since the New Deal really represented a gradual decline into socialist malaise for America.

For most Americans, FDR's actions with respect to gold and the dollar marked a repudiation of the past. In the wonderfully sarcastic book *The New Dealers*, published anonymously in 1934 by Simon &

Schuster, the "Unofficial Observer" described the FDR devaluation and repudiation of gold:

> On the one hand, you have the good old traditional way of doing business, which required the entire population of the country to "walk home" at twenty-year intervals in the name of God and the Gold Standard. On the other hand, you have the new technique of the financial sheik who claims that you can use buttons instead of money. The old school claims that buttons belong in button-holes, the new school asks what is the Gold Standard between friends. The times are on the side of the new school, for the financing of a revolution—even an unconscious one—takes a lot of money, and a lot of buttons.[24]

Under the guise of nationalism, FDR took the United States down the path to economic recovery, first by embracing currency devaluation and inflation as the primary tools of national policy, then plunging America into a second world war in Europe and Asia. The former was done, at least in part, out of a very real fear that the weak economy would lead the United States into violence and social revolution. This is a reference to the invisible, "unconscious revolution" in many other descriptions of the New Deal.

But there was a great deal of deliberate calculation in FDR's domestic decisions during the Depression. The U.S. involvement in World War II was also a deliberate plan on the part of FDR and Winston Churchill, who together worked to draw the United States into the struggle. But a large part of FDR's plan was also political. As he told the Democratic convention in Chicago a year before the currency devaluation:

> I pledge you, I pledge myself, to a new deal for the American people. Let us all here assembled constitute ourselves prophets of a new order of competence and courage. This is more than a political campaign; it is a call to arms. Give me your help, not to win votes alone, but to win in this crusade to restore America to its own people.[25]

In an October 27, 1933, letter to Will Rogers, Bernard Baruch predicted that using the RFC to buy gold by issuing debt would lead to "a loss of confidence in government credit." Foreign governments around the world criticized the break from the gold standard as a negative development, but FDR cleverly cast his decision as "a constructive move" that would "aid somewhat to raise prices all over the world."

FDR's nationalistic repudiation of the gold standard and, by implication, adopting a policy to devalue the dollar, convinced our trading partners that America was pursuing currency inflation and protectionism. FDR told his advisers that he hoped that measures to restructure American agriculture via price supports and restrictions on imports would allow for the eventual liberalization of trade and the restoration of a link to gold. But most of FDR's early policy moves were merely a continuation of the protectionism of Hoover and the Republicans, "for the present emergency" as FDR said, with a future hope held out for cooperation with other nations.[26]

The summary version of histories of this period makes it seem that the Smoot-Hawley tariff was a prime factor behind the worsening economy, but the currency devaluation by Roosevelt and his refusal to lower tariffs that were already in place after decades of enlightened Republican rule may have been more significant. It is closer to the mark to say that tariffs did not help, but the devaluation of the dollar seems to have been the larger negative factor for the economy.

FDR stressed on a number of occasions that abandoning the gold standard was necessary because even with the largest gold reserves in the world, by 1932 the United States only had sufficient quantities of the metal to back a tiny fraction of the currency and debt that was then in circulation. The process of currency inflation begun with the Civil War had reached the point of no return, at least in the Roosevelt worldview. But the real force behind the devaluation seemed to be the powerful deflationary forces at work in the real economy, forces that, in the middle of 1933, terrified FDR's inner circle and all Americans.

When the new American president attended a World Economic Conference in Europe in the summer of 1933, FDR's abandonment of the gold standard and his refusal to cooperate at all with the other nations in terms of stabilizing currencies and tariff reduction did nothing to help the dire international situation. Roosevelt gave general support for removing embargos, import quotas, and other arbitrary restrictions, but he had no intention of agreeing to remove trade protections or making any effort to stabilize the dollar against the major currencies.

The fact that the United Kingdom still had not settled its debts to the United States from World War I added to the delicacy of the situation facing FDR in 1933. With the Europeans led by the French demanding some understanding regarding the dollar and Roosevelt still unsure whether and when the U.S. economy would recover, there was no incentive for compromise by either side. Roosevelt returned to Washington empty handed—and happily so.

The Reconstruction Finance Corporation

By the fall of 1933, armed with the new legislative powers granted by Congress, FDR began to devalue the dollar further by purchasing gold with newly minted fiat paper dollars. Agricultural prices had been falling all year and unemployment was worse than when FDR was inaugurated six months earlier. The Fed refused to participate in purchases of gold, so FDR turned to RFC boss Jesse Jones to buy the gold. The RFC issued debt and purchased gold at a price set personally by FDR, who was assisted by Treasury Secretary Morgenthau and RFC Director Jesse Jones. As with the Treasury's purchase of silver decades before, the result was higher inflation.

Jones was one of President Hoover's original appointees to the RFC, a self-made man who was astute in business as well as in politics. A native of Tennessee who moved to Houston to build a fortune in lumber and real estate, Jones was easily the wealthiest man in the New Deal and the most action oriented. By the middle of 1932, Jones put himself in touch with FDR. During the interval between the November 1932 election and the inauguration in March 1933, Jones kept the president-elect abreast of developments in the economy and particularly in the banking sector.

In February 1933 Jones met the northbound train carrying the president-elect to brief him on the severity of the banking crisis. FDR had been traveling at sea for two weeks on Vincent Astor's yacht, but as one contemporary observer noted, "Hoover had been at sea for four years."[27]

In a conference at the White House on February 9, 1933, President Hoover met with members of his cabinet and Congress, including Senator James Couzens of Michigan. Hoover described how Alfred P. Sloan of GM and Walter Chrysler of Chrysler Corporation committed up to $2 million each to support the Detroit banks. The president asked Couzens to match that commitment for Guardian Trust Company, one of the most important banks in his native city.

Couzens, who was a senior member of the Senate Banking Committee, refused and loudly suggested that the financial burden of supporting the Detroit banks should fall upon Henry Ford. Couzens refused a request from Hoover to speak with Ford about the matter even though the former business partners had reconciled to some degree. Ford ultimately refused to support the Detroit banks and precipitated the Banking Crisis of 1933.

On February 14, 1933, fearing a threat by Ford to withdraw his funds from the Detroit banks, Governor William A. Comstock ordered all banks in the state of Michigan closed for eight days. This began a domino effect that would lead to the collapse of the nation's financial system three weeks later. Michigan was forced to default on its bonds and the state government was crippled, an event of default that rippled through the savings and balance sheets of individuals and companies around the world.

In March 1933, after much of the Hoover-appointed board resigned, Jones elected himself chairman of the RFC. If Roosevelt had someone else in mind for the RFC job, the president never let on who that might be. Jones never gave him an opportunity to make another selection. The RFC quickly became a key part of the New Deal because Jones was willing to do jobs that were difficult, even where the legal authority was less than clear.

Most people in the Roosevelt administration thought that using the RFC to purchase gold was illegal, but Jesse Jones sold bonds to raise the necessary cash and purchased the gold as per the president's orders. Jones particularly enjoyed the gold purchase operations because they were executed by the Federal Reserve Bank of New York. Like much of Wall Street, New York Fed Governor George Harrison opposed FDR's gold policy but was compelled to execute purchases on behalf of the RFC.

The role of the RFC in this early stage and the divergence in views on gold with the Fed illustrates the powerful political role played by Hoover's creation under FDR. The RFC was a parastatal corporation created from examples out of fascist Italy that gave both Hoover and FDR choices in 1933—choices that would not have existed otherwise about how to borrow money and purchase assets to manipulate prices and the economy.

Since the Fed was unwilling to get involved in the decision to devalue the currency, the RFC provided a powerful fiscal agency that could implement government policy. The RFC was an alternative to the Fed. This was especially true when the RFC became empowered to purchase stock in and/or lend money to banks. President Roosevelt and many of his inner circle believed that the government needed to act directly to stem deflation.

When the Treasury and the Fed moved too slowly to deal with failed banks, in a snap Jones volunteered the RFC to take over the problem and within weeks the backlog of failed institutions was being reduced. Jones was precisely the type of direct, no-nonsense leader who fit beautifully into the unorthodox world of the New Deal. Such was the urgency of the times that the appearance of Jones as a forceful and motivated leader of the RFC must have seemed a godsend to FDR and certainly was fortuitous for the United States. And nobody in Washington was dumb enough to argue with Jesse Jones.

Leo Crowley, the financier behind FDR, organized the Federal Deposit Insurance Corporation in 1933 and then later ran the Lend-Lease program through World War II. If your bank could not qualify for FDIC insurance after the 1933 bank holiday, then you went to see Jesse Jones at the RFC. He'd tell you to go home and raise new capital, which he'd match. Otherwise, he'd throw you and the other bank directors in jail.

Jesse Jones and the RFC restructured the US economy, including hundreds of banks and dead companies. Jones eschewed partisan politics at the RFC and relied upon the private sector to do much of the work of restructuring. The RFC performed a receivership function for busted banks and companies through the Great Depression and World War II. It was wound up only in 1957, a year after Jones's death.

The dollar price of gold was gradually increased between October 1933 through January 1934, Hoover comments in his memoirs, with the idea being that "if the number of inches in the yardstick were lessened then there would be more cloth in the bolt."[28] Bankers around the world reacted with horror. Montagu Norman of the Bank of England said: "This is the most terrible thing that has happened. The whole world will be put into bankruptcy." John Maynard Keynes, who was an early supporter of Roosevelt, characterized the gyrations of the dollar under FDR "more like a gold standard on the booze" and characterized as "foolish" the idea "that there is a mathematical relation between the price of gold and the price of other things."[29]

In January 1934, Congress ratified all of FDR's executive actions taken during the previous year and regarding gold by passing the Gold Reserve Act. The next day, FDR set the price of gold at $35 per ounce and was to purchase the metal at that price but sell to foreigners only. Roosevelt abolished gold coins completely but, in a bow to the silverite tendency in the Democratic Party, retained silver coins and set about purchasing silver to add to the national hoard. Not all members of Congress were entirely intimidated by FDR, however, including Senator Carter Glass of Virginia, who attacked FDR's decision in private and in public statements.

When FDR called the senior Democrat Glass to the White House to reveal his plans to "profit" through the revaluation of official gold stocks, the widely respected senator and former Treasury secretary under Woodrow Wilson ridiculed the notion with open contempt. FDR believed that by merely changing the dollar price of gold upward, the government would gain a "profit" of some $2 billion measured in fiat paper dollars, but Glass immediately saw through the fiction.

"That isn't a 'profit' as you call it—it is nothing more than a bookkeeping mark-up," Glass told Roosevelt. "Furthermore, the gold you are proposing to confiscate belongs to the Federal Reserve Banks, and the Treasury of the United States has never invested a penny in it. You are proposing to appropriate something that does not belong to the government, and something that has never belonged to the government."[30]

Several years later, on April 27, 1937, Glass criticized FDR on the floor of the Senate regarding the decision to leave the gold standard. Significantly, he was still the only Democrat willing to publicly challenge FDR:

England went off the gold standard because she was compelled to do so, not by choice. Why are we going off the gold standard? With nearly 40 percent of the entire gold supplies of the world, why are we going off the gold standard? To me, the suggestion that we may devalue the gold dollar 50 percent means national repudiation. To me it means dishonor; in my conception of it, it is immoral.[31]

Despite the elite's disdain for Roosevelt, the voters went for the Democrats big in 1936. FDR won reelection in a lopsided vote that saw Democrats take 76 seats in the Senate with only 16 Republicans and 4 Progressives to keep the minority party company. In the House, the Democrats were 331 to 89 Republicans, giving FDR a comfortable margin in Congress. With this type of mandate, FDR's approach to managing the economy became even more aggressive in his second term—in part because of his lack of success regarding unemployment and growth generally.

America under FDR was seen by Hoover and the Republicans as an imitation of Mussolini's Italy or even Stalin's command economy in the Soviet Union. George Creel, one of Roosevelt's intimates over two decades, would later denounce American "liberalism" as "anti-American" because the people operating under that label gave "allegiance to a foreign power."

This bitter debate over whether members of the New Deal, and the American political and business community, held allegiance to foreign capitals such as Berlin or Moscow went on for decades, through World War II and beyond. But the fact remained that FDR ran up some considerable deficits through his first four years in power. He spent $31 billion on public works and other relief efforts, and had little to show for it. And many liberal observers did not like the authoritarian nature of the New Deal.

Even Walter Lippmann eventually turned sour on the autocratic nature of FDR's New Deal and wrote in *The Good Society*:

A reaction, definite and profound as that which in the late eighteenth century set in against the *Ancien Régime*, which in the nineteenth century set in against the crudities of laissez-faire, has, I believe, already begun. But the popular and influential leaders of contemporary thought are in a quandary . . . They do not like dictatorships, the concentration camps, the censorship, the forced labor, the firing squads or the executioners in their swallow tail coats. But in their modes of thinking, the intellectuals who expound what now passes for "liberalism," "Progressivism," or "radicalism" are almost all collectivists in their conception of the economy, authoritarians in their conception of the state, totalitarians in their conception of society.[32]

Central Planning Arrives in Washington

The various experiments in central planning in the United States in the twentieth century started with World War I, a period when many of the players involved in government during the Depression were in their formative years. Hoover, for example, played a key role in organizing food and other production during the war and coordinating other matters for President Wilson. Later, as president, Hoover organized and encouraged currency support loans to foreign central banks, and organized syndicates of bankers willing to lend funds to troubled banks.[33] Next under Hoover came the creation of the RFC and subsidies to banks and to the states, but not to the degree that would come under FDR and the New Deal. Hoover created the potential of the RFC, but FDR greatly expanded the scope of its operations.

FDR's efforts to implement central planning in the United States were somewhat thwarted by the U.S. Supreme Court during the early Roosevelt years, but later the White House managed to intimidate the Court. While the Supreme Court early on voided 6 of 14 New Deal laws passed by Congress at the behest of FDR, after the 1936 election the president began direct attacks on the Court in the media and threatened to "pack the court" with new appointees. The Court subsequently upheld New Deal laws such as the Railway Labor Act and the Social Security Act, actions that were evidence to Hoover and other conservatives that FDR had successfully forced the Supreme Court to back down in favor of his *revanchist* campaign against private business.

Such was the level of fear and the very real economic crisis in the United States that FDR was able to obtain and exercise huge powers from a frightened Congress. Members of the public were genuinely fearful of revolution from abroad, but were also reluctant to criticize FDR as well. A large number of anonymous critiques of the New Deal were produced during this period by mainstream publishers. The growing ranks of the Socialist and Communist parties in America, wrote Robert Byrd in his history of the Senate, "forced Democratic leaders constantly to reassess their programs. While there was a 'New Deal Boom' in 1933, improving economic conditions, the nation was still locked in a terrible depression and millions of people were still out of work."[34]

Roosevelt had openly discussed his plans for price fixing to solve the problems of the farmer, borrowing a page from earlier efforts to institute federal price controls and supports for farmers during World War I. Hoover had created the Federal Home Loan Banks, the RFC, and convened a special session of Congress to seek modest farm support. He had also begun many different types of public works, but FDR was far more aggressive and willing to go outside the norms of the time because of the seriousness of the economic situation. Hoover, it seems, never truly understood the magnitude of the problems facing the country, but FDR certainly did. By 1934, there were more than 17 million unemployed out of a total U.S. population of 130 million.

Under FDR, Congress held hearings on the suspicion first stated by Herbert Hoover that "bear raids" by Wall Street speculators were behind the country's economic woes. Some speculators did, in fact, admit to selling the markets short when President Hoover made positive statements about the economy. Known as the Pecora investigation after Ferdinand Pecora, the chief counsel of the Banking Committee, the inquiry involved all of the major banking figures of the day. Charles Mitchell, head of the National City Bank, was forced to resign after testimony that he evaded income taxes. Morgan partners likewise were shown by Pecora, a former New York prosecutor, to have paid no income taxes in 1931–1932.[35]

The Pecora inquiry was part of a broad attack on business and Wall Street that was both politically calculated and focused with the precision of a Madison Avenue ad campaign. FDR employed a command economy model that demonized business and used a preponderance of penalties to enforce compliance, all the while glorifying FDR and the federal government and its various agencies. One after another, government programs and agencies emerged from Washington to address some part of the economic crisis. These oppressive attacks on business and expansion of the federal government actually encouraged less private production and employment.

The National Recovery Administration was one of the more notable of FDR's attempts at centralization that was eventually voided by the Supreme Court. It prescribed work rules for most industries and was almost immediately attacked from all sides. Consumers thought it unfair and arbitrary. Conservatives complained about higher prices while liberals warned that the NRA was protecting monopoly. FDR's prescriptions for the economy and industry implied a degree of regimentation and control that Hoover and many other Americans found repulsive.

During the 1930s, numerous schemes were put in place to use the government's credit to raise capital for housing and for commercial activities, all this while FDR inveighed against "economic royalists," his reference to financial and business interests. But at the end of the day, FDR was merely substituting the federal government and various agencies thereof for the "kinder masters" who directed the money trusts of the nineteenth century.

Federal Deposit Insurance

Congress was largely cowed during the first four years under FDR, passing legislation drafted by the White House almost without question. The Securities Act of 1933, for example, was passed without specific hearings by Congress on the legislative provisions. Many other pieces of legislation during that era were enacted in similar fashion as was the TARP bailout legislation in 2008.

The Banking Act of 1933 was a response to the collapse of the U.S. banking system earlier that year. Known as "Glass-Steagall," the Banking Act separated traditional banking from commerce, including securities dealing and underwriting. Sponsored by Senator Glass and Rep. Henry Steagall, this legislation was actually their second effort. The first Banking Act was passed in 1932 and signed by President Hoover to expand the Fed's lending authority. The better known 1933 law also created the Federal Deposit Insurance Corporation, which immediately examined nearly 8,000 state-chartered banks that were not members of the Federal Reserve System and allowed only solvent banks to reopen.

Of interest, neither Senator Glass nor Rep. Henry Steagall envisioned the FDIC becoming a permanent agency, but that is precisely what has happened. Said Senator Glass: "This is not a government guaranty of deposits . . . The Government is only involved in an initial subscription to the capital of a corporation that we think will pay a dividend to the Government on its investment. It is not a Government guaranty." Rep. Steagall: "I do not mean to be understood as favoring the Government guaranty of bank deposits. I do not. I have never favored such a plan."[36]

Despite his other governmental creations, FDR was not a big supporter of federal bank deposit insurance nor was it supported by the banking industry. The deposit insurance fund put in place during the dark days of 1933 was meant to be temporary and was only made permanent in 1935, above vigorous opposition from the banking industry. The idea for the FDIC was proposed by Rep. Steagall and Senator Arthur Vandenberg (R-MI), who were big supporters of federal deposit insurance because they saw it as a way to stem the decline in the number of banks and the destruction of money due to bank failures. The final model for the FDIC as a liquidating corporation was influenced by the Fed, which advanced its own proposal for the agency during this period.

An average of 600 banks per year had failed in the United States during the 1920s, but these banks were mostly in rural areas. Big city bankers discounted such attrition and bragged that tough standards made the industry stronger, but that song would soon change. The "tough love" policy regarding funding support for banks was also adopted by the Fed, which took the position that bank failures, which were mostly among non-Fed member state banks, were beyond the control of the central bank. The Fed's refusal to lend to nonmember banks greatly exacerbated the crisis and, ironically, forced the issue with respect to federal deposit insurance. The Fed was unwilling to lend to state-chartered banks because there was no federal receivership function for failed banks prior to 1933. This meant that if a state-chartered, nonmember bank failed, the Fed would be a general creditor dealing with a state court–appointed receiver. The state court receiver could reject any claim by the Fed with respect to collateral pledged as security for a loan.

By 1933, with larger banks in urban areas failing in droves and most state insurance funds in shambles, Steagall and Vandenberg finally got their way and federal deposit insurance became a reality. The eventual legislation to make the FDIC permanent provided for all member banks to back the bank insurance fund and assessments of insurance premiums on the banking industry to cover the cost. The fact of federal backing for the FDIC has always been secondary to the support of the industry itself. Charles Calomiris of Columbia University contended in his book *United States Bank Deregulation in Historical Perspective* that making federal deposit insurance permanent and allowing state-chartered banks to join was a big win for smaller community banks. "In particular, access to federal insurance did not require small banks to pay the high regulatory costs of joining the Fed, and insurance protected virtually all of their deposits."[37]

The legislation making the FDIC the insurer of retail bank deposits and, more important, the federal receiver for failed banks, was ultimately popular with the electorate, but was resisted by the banking industries for decades afterward. The increase in the type and number of bank failures in the 1930s captured the attention of the public and federal officials, and made it easier to get Congress to agree—especially with the Fed quietly pushing for the legislation.

As the rate of bank failures rose into the thousands per year in the early 1930s, the glaring inadequacy of the policy stance taken by the Fed forced Hoover to attempt to fill the gap using loans from the

RFC. However, when the Democrat-controlled Congress required that the RFC begin to disclose the names of banks borrowing after August 1932, use of the RFC by banks declined. Echoing the debate over requiring the Fed to disclose the names of banks and other entities that used emergency credit facilities in 2008 and 2009, the FDIC found in the early 1930s that "the appearance of a bank's name was interpreted as a sign of weakness."

The pressure on the U.S. banking system would intensify through the fall and winter of 1932, when fear of a currency devaluation by FDR was in the streets and this fact effectively helped to drive the nation into the banking crisis of 1933. Most of the banks that failed during the 1930s were not FDIC insured, but the agency was able to help to deal with hundreds of bank resolutions.

Over the decades since its creation, the FDIC has evolved into a highly successful, industry-funded insurance scheme that also acts as a regulator and data collection agency, and as the statutory receiver of insolvent banks. Today when an FDIC-insured bank is declared insolvent, by process of law the FDIC is automatically appointed receiver of the bank to protect depositors and maximize the recovery on the failed bank's estate.

Centralization of the Fed

With the passage of the Banking Act of 1935, the Fed acquired a Washington headquarters that institutionalized the Board of Governors as the supervisor of the 12 regional banks and destroyed the decentralized model for the central bank. In practical terms, from the mid-1930s onward the central bank became a unitary central bank and lost any pretense of federalist representation via the regional federal reserve banks. The reserve banks became sources of local political patronage but lost control over monetary policy to Washington.

Of greater interest than the physical centralization of the Fed into Washington is the intellectual role the Board of Governors played in advancing and supporting the Progressive evolution of the federal government. Indeed, the Fed Board played an aggressive role in terms of managing the economy years before the election of FDR during the term of Hebert Hoover.

In "The Federal Reserve Board and the Rise of the Corporate State, 1931–1934," Walker Todd notes that Hoover's first encounter with the Fed's Board was in 1925 when he communicated with Governor Daniel Crissinger, a friend of President Warren Harding, about the Fed refraining from backing the United Kingdom's progression back to the gold standard.

Later in 1927, Hoover again tried to dissuade the Fed from running an easy money policy to help the United Kingdom preserve the sterling exchange rate with the dollar. A hopeless Anglophile, Governor Ben Strong at the Fed of New York pushed easy money to help the Bank of England. Hoover offered the following wonderful appraisal of the Fed in his memoirs:

Crissinger was a political appointee from Marion, Ohio, utterly devoid of global economic or banking sense. The other members of the Board, except Adolph Miller, were mediocrities, and Governor [Benjamin] Strong [of the New York Reserve Bank] was a mental annex to Europe. I got nowhere [arguing with them]. President Coolidge insisted that the Board had been set up by Congress as an agency independent of the administration, and that we had no right to interfere.[38]

Hoover had no illusions as to whether the Fed should take its lead from the Treasury and executive branch, especially on matters affecting foreign relations. President Hoover, upon becoming president-elect in November 1928, urged the Fed to jawbone banks against making loans for speculative purposes. Reflecting his experience in World War I, Hoover preferred a method of "credit rationing" to control speculative credit, a policy that was ultimately deflationary.

Hoover's view was adopted by the Fed in Washington, while the Federal Reserve Bank of New York advocated a policy of raising the discount rate and targeting the cost of credit to control speculative loans. The Fed was acquiescing to the policies of Hoover in the period leading up to and after the 1929 market crash, signifying that the incorporation of the central bank into the Washington equation was already well established even before FDR.

But perhaps more important to the Fed's evolution as the premier economic management agency in Washington was when Hoover selected Eugene Meyer as governor of the Fed in September 1930. With the resignation of Roy Young, Hoover made one of the most significant appointments to the Board of the central bank during its entire history. In the brief few years he served as governor, Meyer would lay the groundwork for the Fed's expanded role in the New Deal and in supporting the growth of a European-style, neo-Keynesian world view within the Washington bureaucracy that would be capped with the tenure of Mariner Eccles as chairman.

Meyer headed the War Finance Corporation (WFC) in World War I, which made loans to exporters during 1919 and 1920, but lapsed in 1921. Later, when it was reactivated by Congress over the veto of Woodrow Wilson, the WFC was used to bail out banks from bad loans in the farm sector. The WFC was one of the earliest examples of a government-sponsored entity at the federal level in the United States, and it expanded into agricultural lending under the encouragement of Meyer and then-Commerce Secretary Hoover. The WFC served as the operational model for one of the government's most significant assistance efforts during the Great Depression, namely the Reconstruction Finance Corp.

Meyer was a respected Wall Street financier of generally Democratic persuasions who not only led the Fed Board, but at the request of President Hoover, encouraged the establishment of, and organized the RFC when it was first created in 1932. From the time he joined the Fed and even before, Meyer urged President Hoover to create a new government agency to deal directly with the economic crisis. But that said, Meyer was not nearly as radical in his views on what should be done to help the economy as the New Dealers who would follow him.

Jesse Jones opined in his classic memoir *Fifty Billion Dollars: My Thirteen Years at the RFC* that neither Meyer nor Atlee Pomerene, who succeeded Meyer as RFC chairman in 1932 and remained until FDR's inauguration, "was in favor of boldly making credit available on all fronts in an effort to stop the downward trend in our whole economy. Neither of these men can necessarily be censured, for it was only fair to say that the country was in a situation that it had never before experienced. Few members of Congress probably thought that the government could afford to put its credit behind our whole economy, which we later did under Roosevelt."[39]

Jones knew from firsthand experience about the coming banking crisis. In 1931, Jones led the recapitalization of two Houston banks. He organized the city's bankers and business leaders and asked each to contribute capital to the rescues. After several days of round-the-clock meetings in the headquarters of his own bank, the National Bank of Commerce, Jones announced the purchase of one failing bank by his institution and the purchase of the other, Houston National, by the family of another prominent member of the Houston business community. In this fashion, Jones acquired some very relevant experience in rescuing insolvent banks, familiarity that would stand him in good stead in the difficult years that followed.[40]

Meyer was drafted to chair the RFC only after Bernard Baruch turned President Hoover down for the job. Baruch did not accept any formal role during the Great Depression or World War II, but he was an important adviser to FDR and other New Dealers. Baruch had long warned of the need to prepare for war. "Far from being a power behind the scenes," Baruch wrote of the FDR years with the banker's modesty, "my role during the New Deal was largely that of observer and critic. There was much in the New Deal that I applauded. But there was also much that disturbed me, and moved me to protest."[41]

Meyer "may initially have been approached on this matter by representatives of J. P. Morgan," Todd notes regarding the creation of the government's vehicle for providing emergency credit to the U.S. economy.[42,] Recalling the role of the House of Morgan in supporting the United Kingdom in World War I, it would have been remarkable for the bank not to have a view on the need to revive government support for commodities and industries. As an organization, J.P. Morgan had always taken a keen interest in the larger picture and had operatives monitoring most industries where the bank had credit exposure—especially the railroads.

The RFC made over $1 billion in loans during its first year in operation, many to politically well-connected banks such as J.P. Morgan and Kuhn, Loeb & Co. Governor Meyer supported lending tens of millions in RFC loans to rail companies to be used to repay bank loans and thereby "promote recovery." In fact, the loans were a bailout for the banks with loans to insolvent rail companies, such as the Missouri Pacific, which was allowed to slide into bankruptcy after the Van Sweringen brothers repaid their loans to J.P. Morgan.

"The extent of Meyer's humanitarianism in this affair may be gauged from the fact that his brother-in-law, George Blumenthal, was a member of J.P. Morgan and Company, and that Meyer had also served as a liaison officer between the Morgan firm and the French government," Murray Rothbard wrote in *America's Great Depression*.[43]

As the Depression worsened and the number of bank failures grew, Meyer and the Fed staff encouraged Hoover to declare a bank holiday, an event for which the Fed had prepared since the previous year. Hoover instead wanted simply to guarantee 80 percent of all bank deposits to stem withdrawals and restore confidence, reflecting the cautious world view of a nineteenth-century Republican engineer.

Hoover offered to make the bank closing proclamation in the waning days of his presidency, but FDR turned him down. Hoover apparently wanted FDR to agree to temper his New Deal program in return for Hoover issuing the bank closure proclamation. Later Hoover compared the refusal of FDR to cooperate regarding the bank closings as a supreme act of selfishness. "It was the American equivalent of the burning of the Reichstag to create 'an emergency,'" Hoover wrote in his memoirs.[44] But this would not be the last time that FDR was accused of duplicity when it came to a national crisis.

Meyer was a frequent target for populists such as the crusading Father Charles Coughlin, who referred in his broadcast sermons to the "Four Horsemen of the Apocalypse" of Wall Street as Morgan, former Treasury Secretaries Andrew Mellon and Ogden Mills, and Eugene Meyer. Yet as the man who organized the RFC, Meyer attracted criticism from Progressives outside the northeastern United States, who viewed him as another New York banker. Meyer was far, far more than merely a financier from New York. He was a thoughtful public citizen and a statesman who would end a long and successful career as the owner of the *Washington Post*, succeeded by his daughter and granddaughter. Meyer, who bought the newspaper in 1933, said: "The newspaper's duty is to its readers and to the public at large, and not to the private interests of its owners."

In the 1930s, Huey Long of Louisiana chastised the New Dealers for their tolerance of "the same old clique of bankers who had controlled Hoover." Arthur Schlesinger recounted Long's commentary: "Parker Gilbert from Morgan & Company, Leffingwell, Ballantine,

Eugene Meyer, every one of them are here. What is the use of hemming and hawing? We know who is running the thing."[45]

The Louisiana populist disliked Wall Street bankers and disparaged FDR for being subservient to them. Long made great political use of these facts in his unremitting diatribes. But Meyer, significantly, resigned from the Fed at the start of FDR's presidency, which he saw as unlikely to instill confidence in the country.

In the classic biography of Carter Glass by Rixey Smith and Norman Beasley, *Carter Glass: A Biography*, the encounter between Glass and FDR on the eve of the latter's inauguration shows how doubtful was the legal authority for the president to declare a bank holiday in March 1933. FDR proposed to use the World War I Enemy Trading Act, even though the general counsel of the Treasury had advised that the law was inadequate. But the president-elect had the will to act and, again, he had clearly been considering these issues for many weeks and months before taking office.

FDR told Carter Glass that Meyer and the Fed Board asked President Hoover for a declaration of a bank holiday just prior to the inauguration, but neither Hoover nor FDR thought that such a step was necessary. After taking a telephone call from Hoover, Roosevelt turned to Carter Glass, the most respected Democrat in the country and the dean of Congress when it came to financial questions. FDR explained that he would not give Hoover his support to declare a bank holiday despite the fact that the Fed Board had made such as request several times in as many days.

"I see. What are you planning to do?" asked Glass after hearing FDR's report about his telephone conversation a few moments before with Hoover regarding the banks.

"Planning to close them, of course," replied Roosevelt, referring to his plan to do precisely what Hoover had suggested—but only upon taking office himself.

Glass then went on to protest that Roosevelt did not have the authority to even close national banks, much less order the closure of banks chartered by the states. But Roosevelt replied with the assurance that comes from great wealth that "I will have the authority." Roosevelt proceeded to make a series of proclamations on the following day closing the nation's banks without the benefit of authority from Congress.[46] The giant of the Senate on financial matters, Glass knew the law, but FDR acted nonetheless because the times were so desperate that no one questioned his authority.

Once FDR was president, the Fed under Meyer and Eugene Black helped engineer the seizure of gold and the devaluation of the dollar in an eager and rather shameless fashion, disregarding the fact that the gold belonged to the Fed's member banks. Walker Todd recalls, for example, that when FDR made his first "fireside chat" radio broadcast to the American people after ordering a bank holiday, the text of the comments was published in its entirety in the *Federal Reserve Bulletin*.

"A circumstance," writes Todd, "that in light of everything else that transpired then, causes one to wonder who actually drafted that text for Roosevelt." Rep. Hamilton Fish of New York, after hearing Roosevelt's first "fireside chat" on March 12, "proudly pronounced the new regime 'an American dictatorship based on the consent of the governed without any violation of individual liberty or human rights.'"[47]

Despite the strong current in favor of central planning and control in Washington in this period, the RFC never realized the full potential to become an agency of the state for the simple reason that the chairman of the RFC, Jesse Jones, did not allow it. Such was Jones's stature upon taking over at the RFC that when he was given broad powers by Congress to buy and sell commodities, make loans, and take equity stakes in banks and businesses, the personal confidence of Carter Glass was all the endorsement he required.

Instead of making the RFC into a vehicle for central planning, Arthur Schlesinger observed, the RFC "took on the character of Jones" and was run like a profitable but flexible merchant bank, lending money and buying and selling assets and businesses. Schlesinger suggested that Mills and the other bankers saw the RFC as a backstop for the *rentier* class—"for people anxious to ensure steady returns for stakes they already had"—while Jesse Jones was more inclined to support the rising class of promoters and entrepreneurs. The difference between Jones and the Wall Street bankers who populated much of the New Deal government, Schlesinger concluded, helped to shift from "the hard money, gold standard, coupon-clipping groups in the East to those who, for better or worse, were prepared to risk monetary inflation because they deeply believed in economic growth."[48]

The lending powers eventually granted to the RFC and the Federal Reserve were somewhat overlapping and led to different results, but the Fed was a less aggressive lender than the RFC. This period is especially significant because it introduced Washington to the idea of the government-sponsored enterprises (GSEs) such as the RFC and the Fed as lenders and guarantors of loans, a practice that continued through World War II and into the postwar period.

The existence of the central bank and its balance sheet created possibilities for politicians that did not heretofore exist—and empowered them to deliver certain results and outcomes to voters in the short run without recourse to new taxes. The RFC too was funded from the markets and did not require taxes to make loans. But neither the loans by the Fed nor from the RFC had a great impact on the economy or employment in the 1930s. Both expanded credit and without great result. American consumers were still not buying enough goods to restore balance to the economy.

Eccles and the Corporatist Revolution

When Eugene Meyer resigned from the Fed Board in May of 1933, he was replaced by Eugene Black of Atlanta, who resigned just over a year later in August 1934. Treasury Secretary Henry Morgenthau recommended an official from the Treasury, Mariner Eccles, to replace Black as governor of the Board, as the chairman of the central bank was called before the creation of the Board of Governors in 1935. Eccles was a Mormon from Utah whose family had operated banks in that state for many years. More important, Eccles drank deeply from the cup of Keynesian economics. He was quickly recognized by Morgenthau and others as an effective advocate for deficit spending to address the lack of private consumption and reduction in capital investment during the Depression.

In 1932, FDR and Morgenthau both contended that the surest path to economic recovery was a balanced budget and cuts in government spending, but Eccles believed just the opposite. When FDR asked him to become governor of the Fed Board in November 1934, Eccles stipulated that he would take the job only if he were given a free hand to reform the Fed. Eccles and his collaborator, Lauchlin Currie, a Canadian-born economist and a member of the New Deal "brain trust" at the Treasury, became one of the chief architects of the new U.S. central bank. Currie, one of America's foremost socialist economists, prepared a memo for FDR that outlined basic changes in the operations and governance of the Fed.

As part of the larger group of collectivists that included Harry Dexter White, author of the IMF, Eccles and Currie had two main goals: first, to centralize control of Open Market Operations under the Board and second, to subject all of the governors of the reserve banks to annual appointment by the Board. His ultimate proposal was less radical than the earlier work of Currie, which envisioned a complete nationalization of the Reserve Banks and a unitary, European-style "Federal Monetary Authority." Currie's extensive work on the organization of the Fed informed the debate on the issue.

The stage was set for the Board to become the focus of the economic and legislative drama of the second half of the 1930s, featuring the Banking Act of 1935, the doubling of reserve requirements in 1936–1937, the overhaul of discount-window policies, and the regulatory agreement of 1938.[49] But neither Currie nor Eccles recognized even then the powerful political constituency behind the reserve banks among the banking industry and the local and national politicians.

More than simply acting as the governor of the Federal Reserve Board, Eccles became a leading advocate of change in government fiscal operations, to make federal spending more countercyclical in terms of increased public sector spending when private sector activity failed. Echoing Kamala Harris in the 2024 election campaign, Eccles favored a more equitable distribution of wealth, high taxes on the wealthy, and a national planning board to coordinate public and private activities. John Kenneth Galbraith would later describe the Fed under Eccles as "the center of Keynesian evangelism in Washington."[50]

Allan Meltzer recorded in *A History of the Federal Reserve: 1913–1951* that Eccles opposed the FDR wage and price controls and applauded when the Supreme Court struck them down. Meltzer added in the same portion of his landmark book that Eccles was not an apologist for deficits generally, but only to offset deficits in investment spending. Remarkably, Eccles claimed never to have read Keynes's books nor to have derived any of his own views on deficit spending from Keynes.[51] Todd provides some illumination on this period:

The political economy model followed by most orthodox, mainstream American economists before 1931 was classically liberal, albeit occasionally with peculiarly American permutations. After the United Kingdom suspended convertibility of sterling into gold (the bedrock of orthodox financial principles) in September 1931, American economic policymakers, including President Hoover and Eugene Meyer, governor of the Federal Reserve Board, became increasingly unorthodox in their prescriptions. Although central planning measures of the corporate state variety had manifested themselves vigorously but briefly in policymaking circles during and immediately after World War I, the Harding, Coolidge, and early Hoover years were supposed to be a return to prewar "normalcy," as the slogan associated with Harding's campaign had it.[52]

Meltzer documents how Eccles came to be associated with the famous term "pushing on a string" in 1935 during testimony before the House Committee on Banking and Currency. He knew that monetary expansion did not work in the Depression because people were unwilling to spend or borrow. But Eccles went further than many of his contemporaries and attributed the excess of savings to inequitable income distribution. "Eccles differed from his predecessors in his belief that government had to take responsibility for the economy," wrote Meltzer. "He devoted much of his time to advocating fiscal measures, especially increased spending on investment financed by government borrowing to expand demand."[53]

Part of Eccles's fascination with income and consumption came about as a result of his observations of the Depression, where he saw time and again the process of deflation and liquidation destroying lives. His Mormon upbringing and keen business sense enabled him to discern the value to the economy of thrift. Yet he also saw the available wealth of the nation being drawn into a very few hands, including his own.

Like James Couzens decades before when he was the general manager of Ford Motor Co., Eccles felt a sense of frustration at the fact that his fellow citizens could not consume the products America produced.

The boom and bust of the 1920s was due not to profligacy, Eccles came to believe, but overmuch thrift. "We did not as a nation consume more than we produced," Eccles said. "We were excessively thrifty." Eccles noted. Many Americans already knew very well that economic contractions built upon themselves, deflating the economy until internal and/or external forces reversed the trend and expansion began again.

Eccles saw the "external force" to counter deflation as the federal government and deficit spending, a conclusion he came to himself and spoke about three years before Keynes published *The General Theory of Employment, Interest and Money*. "Eccles was an untutored pioneer," wrote author Bill Greider. "An American banker from Utah, a man who had never studied economics or even attended college, who was able to see what the great British economist himself saw, and Eccles had the uncommon courage to articulate this thinking before it became fashionable."[54]

A recess appointment by FDR, Eccles was not confirmed by the Senate until April 1935. He was opposed by Senator Glass, who disliked Eccles personally and also did not care for his proposals to centralize the Fed Board in Washington.For example, Eccles proposed to limit the Federal Reserve Bank presidents to a purely advisory role and give the appointed governors full voting control over open market operations. The compromise advanced by Glass and other members of Congress kept a role in monetary policy for the Reserve Bank "presidents," as the governors of the individual banks are now known. Glass made it very clear during the debate that he was not in favor of any of Eccles proposals.

At several stages, Glass suggested unsuccessfully that the portion of the bill dealing with the structural changes at the Fed be put aside. The final provisions of the Banking Act of 1935 completed the centralization of the Fed's Board of Governors. It also expanded the type of loans that the Fed could make, particularly in time of emergency. But in a larger sense, the Banking Act of 1935 completed the transition of the Fed from an institution that at least nominally paid homage to the gold standard and an asset currency, to one that was entirely devoted to a fiat currency that was not convertible into anything.

"Currently, the American monetary system is composed of a series of procedures based on statutes and statutes based on procedures, which reflect no integral concept of money but, rather, a series of residual concepts," wrote Jane D'Arista in *The Evolution of U.S. Finance: Federal Reserve Monetary Policy, 1915–1935.* "Since at no point is any concept of money firmly repudiated, the system may be said to accommodate a process of selection among alternatives. It preserves the procedural framework of an asset currency system but in reality is closer to fiat money."[55]

D'Arista writes that like the Federal Reserve Act in 1913, the Banking Act of 1935 is silent on monetary policy and gives no guidance as to what metrics the Fed will use to judge the effectiveness of its policy actions. At the end of the day, the legislative changes made to the Fed in 1935 did not entirely resolve the internal contradictions raised by traditional American exponents such as Carter Glass, who wanted the regional reserve banks to retain autonomy.

The imperfect Fed system is precisely consistent with American ideas of check and balances, with friction between the different players and regions. But it also confirms the long-standing pattern in America of bankers calling the shots in Washington. The fact remains that bankers still control the Boards of Directors of the Federal Reserve Banks and thereby get a seat at the monetary policy table of the Federal Open Market Committee.

While Eccles was successful in bringing the conduct of Fed open market operations into the public domain and under Washington's control, he was not entirely successful in destroying the independence of the 12 regional reserve banks. The bailout of American International Group by then–New York Fed president Timothy Geithner illustrated the fact that the Board was still unable to control the Federal Reserve Bank of New York. But since 2008, the reserve banks have been largely emasculated as the Board has centralized most functions in Washington.

The irony of the Eccles period at the Fed is that much of the time and attention of the central bank was dominated by dealing with secular deflation. The activities of the RFC and, in World War II, the national priorities of global war, provided new debt leverage and investment. Most measures of the money supply tracked by the Fed in those days stayed remarkably stable from 1933–1941, when America threw itself into a two-ocean war and a national mobilization that far exceeded that of World War I.

The Fed of New York cut its discount rate from over 3 percent in 1933 to 1.5 percent in 1934 and did not change this rate until 1936, when Governor Eccles increased reserve requirements from 12.5 to 25 percent. When interest rates rose and a recession began to materialize, the Fed reversed course in 1937, when it dropped the discount rate down to 1 percent. The discount rate in New York remained at 1 percent from 1937–1951 as the central bank adopted what Galbraith described as a passive posture.

Low private demand for capital funds in the United States and the growing flight of private capital from fascism in Europe combined to make Federal Reserve policy largely irrelevant during this period and through World War II. Ironically, for much of the period of the Depression, the solvent commercial banks in the country had record levels of excess reserves. There was simply a lack of demand for loans, so banks bought Treasury bonds. Many of the great minds wondered if the democratic, market economies had lost the ability to foster economic growth—at least short of war or inflation.

The experience under FDR in the 1930s does suggest very strongly that a sustained economic rebound was elusive. Even if one accepts all of the conservative views on the negative financial and political impact of the New Deal on the economy, the fact that the private sector did not heal itself to a larger degree raises troubling questions. A more reasonable view seems to be that much of what FDR and the New Dealers did in the 1930s was ineffective due to the effects of technology and the resulting economic changes around the globe, changes that manifested themselves in powerful deflation and unemployment.

America Goes to War

Between 1929 and 1938, the outstanding debt of the federal government more than doubled from $16 billion to $40 billion, but private balance sheets of banks and companies were just barely growing. After the terrible years of Great Contraction in the early 1930s, the U.S. economy rebounded modestly, followed by the mini-depression of 1937–1938. Wages for those workers fortunate enough to be employed had risen in real terms during the FDR era, but unemployment and inflation remained stubbornly high.

Federal Reserve Board Chairman Ben Bernanke (2006–2014) allowed, in an essay on the period, that "maybe Herbert Hoover and Henry Ford were right" in terms of understanding that paying workers more increased their ability to consume goods and services. The key insight of Henry Ford's business partner James Couzens, who was the author of the wage increase, was the reality that a factory worker at Ford Motor Co. in 1914 could not afford to own a Ford car.

Bernanke found that "Higher real wages may have paid for themselves in the broader sense that their positive effect on aggregate demand compensated for their tendency to raise costs."[56] The trouble in the Depression was that wages and prices had fallen and the overall flow of economic activity contracted as predicted by the great economist Irving Fisher. The result of the high tariffs left as a legacy from the Republicans and FDR's devaluation of the dollar was lower U.S. exports, including farm exports.

With over 10 million men unemployed or on government make-work jobs, the U.S. economy could not be said to be prospering after eight years of FDR. William Manchester wrote in The Glory and the Dream[57] that the unskilled workers building the East River Drive in New York for Progressive giant Robert Moses were being paid less than $1,000 per year. This would have seemed a reasonable wage only a few generations before, but inflation had eroded the purchasing power of the dollar to such a degree that it was a remarkably small sum in the late 1930s.

The failure to address employment before World War II is a notable shortcoming of the New Deal. Malnutrition was rampant and nearly half of all of the men examined for military service in that period were rejected by U.S. authorities. Overall, America was lean and hungry after a decade of deflation and depression, and wanted a break. Nothing done by Congress or FDR had much changed that grim outlook. Harkening back to the period during World War I, the idea of entry into another war was almost an attractive prospect for some Americans in terms of giving the nation purpose and a sense of momentum.

One of the more remarkable statistics from the Depression period is the degree of underemployment faced by many Americans. From the boom years of the late 1920s, hours worked per adult dropped to just 70 percent of the pre-bust levels and did not recover even after the end of the 1937–1938 economic contraction. By 1939, hours worked per adult were still just 80 percent of 1929 levels, again illustrating the degree of deflation and slack in the U.S. economy.

Milton Friedman and Anna Schwartz found that an unusually large portion of economic output through 1937 was focused on nondurable goods intended for government purchase, part of a strategy meant to offset the huge decline in private capital investment. By the end of the decade, the United States was still operating at levels of private industrial capacity and investment that were significantly below 1920s levels. Friedman and Schwartz also determined that FDR's policies to artificially raise wages and regulate business served to push down private capital formation and arguably made the Depression longer and more severe than necessary.

With all of the government stimulus, increased spending, taxes, and debt, the U.S. economy still had not really found its footing—even as Europe once again edged toward war. Deflation in central Europe in the 1930s was as bad or worse than in the United States, causing the revolution in Russia in 1917 and the terrible economic situation in Germany due to World War I reparations. The rise of Mussolini, Hitler, and Stalin in Russia all owed their origins to the economic and political collapse of Western Europe following World War I.

FDR took the United States to war consciously and even deliberately, and there is ample documentation of both. Supporters of FDR point out that the war mobilization saved the U.S. economy and created jobs. The point to take though, is the degree to which the fact of the war and the mobilization to support it masked underlying structural defects in the U.S. economy—shortcomings that would remain concealed for half a century thereafter.[58]

President Roosevelt assumed dictatorial "emergency powers" to set prices and ration all types of goods and materials, and greatly increased spending. During World War I, the profiteering occurred in the streets, with all manner of vendors and companies vying for government contracts. By World War II, under the bureaucratic aegis of the federal government, defense spending and procurement had become an entirely inside-Washington game. The supply and logistical support for the war effort greatly increased the power of the federal government and embedded defense and other types of federal procurement as important elements of the economy of each state.

Even as the United States was beginning to mobilize for the conflict in 1940, Keynes published a pamphlet *How to Pay for the War,* which set forth the three ways a war can be financed: taxation, inflation, and forced savings. Keynes favored the last and believed that along with taxes and debt, savings by individuals should be the way government not only financed the war but also managed supply and demand. Keynes was no apologist for big government, however, and believed that other than regulating aggregate demand, the government should basically leave the private sector to its own devices.[59]

By making allowance for intervention by the state to remedy the imperfections of the free-market system during higher unemployment or war, Keynes opened the door to the enlargement of the corporate state. Ever a weaver of schemes and political scenarios, perhaps Keynes's advice should be taken lightly, to season his speculative imagination. But he was clearly among the most influential economic thinkers of his age, even though he was very conservative in his social views. Robert Skidelski, in his book on "the master" economist, included this comment from 1938 by Keynes discussing his losses in the 1929 Crash:

I find no shame at being found still owning a share when the bottom of the market comes. I do not think it is the business of [a serious] investor to cut and run on a falling market . . . I would go much further than that. I should say that it is from time to time the duty of a serious investor to accept the depreciation of his holdings with equanimity and without reproaching himself. Any other policy is anti-social, destructive of confidence, and incompatible with the working of the economic system. An investor . . . should be aiming primarily at long-period results and should be solely judged by these.[60]

Keynes spent the rest of his life until his death in 1946 working to help the United Kingdom manage its war finances and the British economy. The British government needed all of the help that it could get given the "nationalist" foreign policy of FDR. When Winston Churchill succeeded Chamberlain in May 1940, he sent a very specific note to FDR seeking all manner of war support, including the sale of steel and old warships on credit, part of a voluminous correspondence between the two men during the war.

FDR governed the country as a dictator to a large degree, but not entirely. For example, he did not have the authority to sell warships or to go to war without the consent of Congress. But in his conduct of foreign policy as the head of government and head of state, FDR certainly played the autocrat. "It is obvious that Churchill regarded Roosevelt as an American dictator who had little concern for the opinions of the Congress and the American people," Professor Charles Tansil wrote in *Back Door to War*. "With reference to the matter of war, the Churchill cablegrams reveal that he believed Roosevelt could plunge America into the conflict in Europe any time he desired. The French Cabinet apparently had the same viewpoint."[61]

With the fall of France in June 1940, FDR's willingness to assist Britain with material and warships increased. This was the start of a massive mobilization and transfer of resources to the Allies in Europe. With his election victory in November 1940, Roosevelt could, like Woodrow Wilson before him, put aside his nonintervention rhetoric and more actively help Britain. Churchill pressed FDR to make his assistance free of immediate requirement for payment because the moment was approaching when the British government would no longer be able to pay cash for nonmilitary imports. Britain was already broke.

By January 1941, FDR and his lieutenants began drafting Lend-Lease legislation and the law was passed by Congress and signed by Roosevelt in March. FDR and many Americans believed the propaganda that the Lend-Lease program to provide ships and other armaments to Britain was "peace insurance." The reality was closer to the prediction by Senator Robert Taft that America could conduct an undeclared war "without actually being on the shooting end of the war." By May 1941, however, President Roosevelt not so secretly ordered the U.S. Navy into the battle of the Atlantic, occupying Iceland and beginning destroyer escort operations for U.S. merchant vessels. World War II had begun.

Wartime Finance

Friedman and Schwartz record that between 1939 and 1948, wholesale prices in the United States more than doubled and the money stock nearly tripled, resulting in stiff inflation at the consumer level.[62] But even though these statistics are eye-popping, the degree of inflation experienced during and after World War II was less than either the Civil War or World War I—although significantly the money creation was greater in World War II. Gold poured into the United States during World War II as nations in Europe and around the globe sought a refuge for their monetary assets.

By the time the Japanese attacked Pearl Harbor on December 7, 1941, the United States had already created a rationed economy and many consumer goods were unavailable. Big banks and companies monopolized finance to support the war effort. The Fed, acting under FDR's authority, imposed controls on consumer credit, but such moves had little effect since consumer goods of all descriptions already were very scarce.[63] In stark terms, from the 1929 market crash through the end of the 1940s, Americans lived with constrained incomes and choices, making the collective image of the American dream one of privation and survival.

During the Depression and going into the World War II years, the Fed took a very accommodative policy and explicitly supported prices for Treasury bonds, at the expense of inflation. This policy ended in 1951, amounting to a declaration of independence for the Fed from wartime subservience to the Treasury.

Friedman and Schwartz documented the sensitivity of the New Dealers within the Washington community to the idea that the Fed would no longer subsidize government borrowing. "The Great Contraction and the New Deal," they wrote, "had bequeathed both an increased sensitivity to fluctuations in economic activity and a widespread acceptance of the view that government had direct responsibility for the maintenance of something approximating 'full employment,' a view that found legislative expression in the Employment Act of 1946."[64]

A depressed private sector economy and the large government borrowing during the war pushed the ratio between the federal debt and GDP above 100 percent during and after the war years. As the U.S.

economy began to expand and grow after World War II, the ratio of federal debt to GDP would fall to a low of about 30 percent during the presidency of Jimmy Carter.

In addition to selling bonds to individuals during World War II, the U.S. government also sold them to commercial banks and to the Federal Reserve Banks, resulting in a substantial growth in reserve bank credit during the conflict. But after the war, 60 percent of the assets of U.S. banks were invested in government debt. The Fed actively sponsored and nurtured a nonbank dealer market for Treasury debt, which would eventually support the growth of the U.S. economy for half a century; in many ways the domestic monetary indicators of demand became less and less relevant because the dollar had become the world's currency. By 1945, the dominant assets on the books of most banks were government debt and cash, and consumer finance existed in only the most primitive, local form.

During the years immediately following World War II, the United States pumped the equivalent of $100 billion in today's dollars into the European economies, half of which was provided on a grant basis and the rest as loans that would mostly not be repaid. The growing Cold War confrontation with the Soviet bloc nations was not immediately the focus of the Marshall Plan, but American support for Europe soon became part of a larger American strategy of containment. An even bigger and more significant result of the American aid effort was the movement toward the Treaty of Rome and European unification.[65]

In the United States, the expenditure of billions of dollars per year to help Europe at a time of slack in the economy following the war did not sell easily. Eventually it did gain support, however, when posed as an alternative to a future war. President Truman proposed the expenditure of $17 billion in 1947 as part of the Marshall Plan. After months of lobbying by its namesake, Secretary of State George Marshall, it was adopted in 1948. Marshall later reported that American women were vastly in favor of the plan and "electric" in persuading Congress to go along with the proposal.

Bretton Woods

The Marshall Plan to rebuild Europe, followed by the establishment of the International Monetary Fund and the World Bank, created the conditions for European recovery and eventually political union in Europe. Under the Bretton Woods accord, the financial and economic discussions ongoing through the war years were brought together. The goal: an ambitious effort to impose a multilateral model on the world and particularly on Europe. In keeping with the popularity of central planning among economists, a coordinated policy on trade and financial flows was envisioned. A liquidity facility was provided to stabilize global financial flows and avoid the extreme movement of cash and gold from one nation to the next. Responsibility for maintaining "equilibrium" in the global system fell upon the United States, a reflection of the influence of Keynes and the British side in the negotiations.

With the benefit of the commerce clause of the Constitution and the Civil War, Americans had settled most issues with respect to internal trade and commerce, but Europe at the end of World War II had not. The genius of Marshall and his inner circle was to require joint action by the states of Europe in return for American assistance. The Marshall Plan and Bretton Woods created a structure for global trade and finance measured in and supported by the dollar. This construct supposed the existence of an international currency based upon not gold, but the economy of just one large, geopolitically dominant nation.

The Bretton Woods agreement of 1944 also marked the end of Great Britain as a significant global power in financial and strategic terms. With the economic collapse of the United Kingdom after the war, the United States assumed responsibility for much of the colonial possessions of the British Empire and, once again, bailed out London financially. The mechanism for the bailout was a regime of fixed exchange rates pegged to the dollar. The U.S. currency retained some residual link to gold via its relationship with other central banks. Otherwise FDR had ended the link to gold with the currency devaluation of 1933.

The guns in Europe had barely fallen silent before the United Kingdom was seeking accommodation with respect to its obligations under the Lend-Lease Act of World War II. The British also sought further loans or grants-in-aid and justified these requests as consideration for the suffering of Britain at the hands of the German air force. In September 1945, Keynes himself led a British delegation to the United States seeking precisely those terms. He received a correct but friendly reception from the new administration of President

Harry Truman. Truman was as conventional and cautious in his thinking about the economy and foreign affairs as FDR had been aggressive
and willing to experiment.

Opposite Keynes was the equally new secretary of the Treasury, Fred Vinson, a former member of Congress from Kentucky who
would later become chief justice of the Supreme Court. In the classic
book *Sterling-Dollar Diplomacy in Current Perspective*, Richard Gardner
described the interaction between the two men as the United States
and Britain negotiated the forgiveness of much of the latter's war debt
and another loan. Both Baruch and Hoover spoke strongly against the
new loan to Britain, insisting that American needs first be reckoned.[66]

Vinson had not reached Washington by taking risks. In 1947, with
Truman down badly in the polls and the American electorate restive,
selling Congress on forgiving the Lend-Lease loans to Britain, much
less make new loans to London, was difficult. Public opinion, led by
major media organs like the *New York Times*, condemned Bretton
Woods and trade liberalization—unless the United Kingdom and other
nations of Europe followed suit and dropped their tariffs as well.

Eventually, after lengthy negotiations and sometimes difficult
exchanges between Keynes and Vinson, the two sides agreed on forgiveness of the Lend-Lease obligation and low interest rate loans to
finance Britain's balance of payments deficit. The United States agreed
to this formulation in large part to get the United Kingdom to follow
up with a multilateral trade agreement removing the prewar tariffs. But
the bitter reality for the British was that they were broke. Agreement
with the United States was a necessary condition for the country to
ratify the Bretton Woods agreement at the end of December 1945.

The American side made more than a few concessions to the
British during the final talks to ratify Bretton Woods, balancing the
increasingly isolationist mood of the American people after World War
II with the need to be generous to an ally in victory. The sad fact was
that Britain badly needed American help to avoid real economic hard-
ship. Britain's earnings from foreign trade and investment had fallen
during and after the war. The country's military obligations included
shouldering much of the cost of the occupation of Germany and supporting military installations around the world. But the British empire
was rapidly dissipating.

By 1947, British reserves of gold and foreign exchange had fallen to dangerously low levels and the country was headed for a serious fiscal crisis. The loan agreement between Washington and London signed in 1946 contained a commitment by the British to maintain the convertibility of sterling. Yet it was increasingly doubtful that a devaluation could be avoided—even with the flow of further loans from the United States.

Much of Europe and also the United States were headed into an economic recession by the end of 1947 and the prospect of a lengthy standoff with the Soviet Union loomed. The end of World War II was not as cheerful as the residents of the victor nations might have hoped—but things would soon start to improve. Under the powerful push from the Marshall Plan starting in 1948 and the movement toward lower tariffs and multilateralism in terms of trade policy championed by the United States in the years that followed, the global economy started to expand rapidly and bring renewed prosperity to the United States and the nations of Europe. The combination of the Cold War and Washington's embrace of trade liberalization provided a rising tide that would lift all boats.

Chapter 7

Debt and Inflation

At the end of March 1945, President Roosevelt traveled to Warm Springs, Georgia, to rest before his appearance at the conference in New York to celebrate the founding of the United Nations. Two weeks later, on April 12, 1945, FDR collapsed while sitting for a portrait. A few hours later, the president was declared dead of a brain hemorrhage. Former senator Harry Truman, the vice president whom FDR scarcely knew, became the thirty-third president of the United States. FDR led his country through 15 terrible years of depression and war.[1] He was the only leader that a generation of Americans had ever known. The nation was still at war and still struggling to find its way back to economic stability.

The advent of the Cold War, a term originally coined by Bernard Baruch, had some significant economic effects on the United States and Europe. First and foremost, instead of a total demobilization after the conflict as was the case following World War I, the United States and the Western Allies were compelled to maintain a substantial military presence in Europe to counter the perceived threat from the Soviet Union. In Asia, the United States undertook the occupation of Japan and was required to maintain a large ground, sea, and air presence in the region. In 1945 alone, the United States spent almost $1 Trillion

INFLATED

on defense, a vast sum compared to the size of the U.S. economy, which only generated $223 billion in gross domestic product (GDP) in that last year of the war effort. The chart in Figure 7.1 shows military spending as a percentage of GDP.

Figure 7.1 illustrates the fact that for nearly three decades following World War II, military expenditures as a portion of GDP were extremely high and were arguably the single most important portion of the peacetime economy. Margaret Myers estimates that the direct expenses of the war were estimated by Treasury Secretary Henry Morgenthau at $325 billion in mid-1945, but added that "the cost of the war to all the countries involved is simply incalculable."[2] The same could be said for all wars.

Later estimates of the overall cost of the war would be much higher, especially when compared to the cost of World War I and including the cost of debt forgiveness for the allies. The cost also included the reintegration of 12 million people into the American civilian economy via

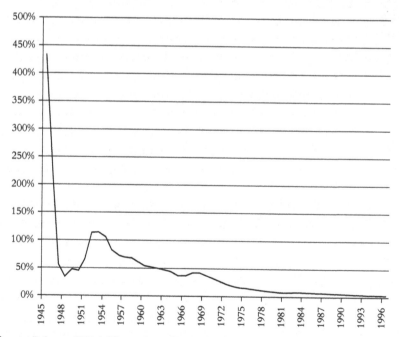

Figure 7.1   U.S. Military Spending as a Percent of GDP (1945–1996).
Source: BEA, DOD/Center for Defense Information.

such measures as the GI Bill of Rights, which was passed by Congress in June 1944. War mobilization had absorbed a large part of the slack in the predominantly male U.S. workforce of the 1930s, and drew millions more women into the workforce as well. This was not the same as gainful employment in the private sector, though. The GI Bill provided cash for returning service personnel, unemployment insurance for up to a year, and loans for housing or to purchase a farm or a business. Most important, the GI Bill provided higher education to veterans, many of whom missed completing their formal education in order to go to war. As with Lincoln at the end of the Civil War, Congress was generous with the returning soldiers. The GI Bill helped to define and fulfill the American dream for generations of citizens in the twentieth century.

Only in the 1970s, as the economy grew, did U.S. military outlays drop well below 40 percent of GDP and from then on dropped to single digits by 1980. From 1948–1991, the United States spent $13 trillion on defense, according to the Center for Defense Information. Annual military spending by the United States would average almost $300 billion per year during this period and is only slightly lower if direct spending for the Korean and Vietnam Wars is excluded, illustrating the fact that the vast majority of the expenditure was focused on the Cold War with the Soviets.

Yet the fact of rising output and inflation, accommodated by the Federal Reserve and driven by the demographic surge of the Baby Boom, made military outlays and the level of federal debt shrink in comparison to the overall economy. From a high of 120 percent of GDP at the end of World War II, the federal debt remained stable in nominal terms and fell as a portion of the economy through the 1960s and 1970s, but began to grow again in the 1980s as economic growth slowed.

The other observation to be made about the period of the Cold War is that it illustrates the inflation experienced by Americans since that time—a loss of purchasing power that tracks almost precisely the expansion of public and private sector debt. Using the constant dollar series from the Bureau of Economic Analysis, if one compares the nominal GDP in the United States in 1945 of $223 billion in inflation-adjusted current dollars, that amount of national economic output would total *$2 trillion* measured in today's money. That represents a 90 percent loss in the purchasing power of the dollar today versus the real, inflation-adjusted value of the dollar at the end of World War II. Figure 7.2 shows nominal GDP, total federal debt, and military expenditures over the Cold War period.

Figure 7.2 illustrates several interesting trends during the Cold War period. First, from the end of World War II until almost 1970, federal debt outstanding was relatively stable. This period spans the presidencies of Harry Truman through John F. Kennedy and includes the relative increases in spending during the Korean and Vietnam wars. During the same period, the U.S. economy was relatively free of financial crises until the early 1970s, when the United States finally left the pegged currency system of Bretton Woods and stopped redeeming dollars for gold upon demand by foreign central banks.

The U.S. government essentially paid its way for two decades after World War II, then unilaterally defaulted on an agreement with other nations. Unlike the United Kingdom after World War I, however, the United States did not increase taxes in order to pay down the war debt. As in earlier conflicts, Congress was not willing to pass on the cost of the war to the taxpayer. Instead, Congress funded the wartime outlays

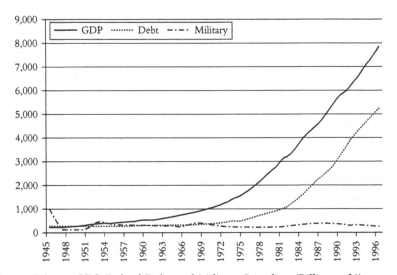

Figure 7.2   GDP, Federal Debt, and Military Spending (Billions of $).
SOURCES: BEA, DOD, U.S. Treasury.

with borrowing and simply rolled the debt over for decades thereafter. The tolerance for debt since World War II has since blossomed into the looming fiscal crisis of the twenty-first century.

Another striking aspect of the chart in Figure 7.2 is the divergence of GDP and debt from military spending after the end of the 1960s, when Washington began to greatly expand nondefense outlays in a variety of different areas of social spending. Military spending was a very significant part of the U.S. economic expansion during the first two decades after World War II, but gradually, as the threat of imminent major conflict receded, domestic priorities and related spending and borrowing grew. Again, the taxpayer was not asked to shoulder the full burden of these outlays and, again, the spending was financed with public debt.

With the Civil War, World War I and World War II, and the Cold War, Americans used debt to finance military expenditures rather than carry the burden through increased taxation. This was not such a great evil after World War II since in absolute terms the level of military spending remained stable even as the overall economy expanded. The problem came several decades later, when nonmilitary discretionary expenditures were likewise funded with federal debt, necessitating an expansion of the currency by the Fed. In that sense, not a great deal has changed since President Lincoln saved the Union and emancipated the slaves with a Grand Army financed with unconvertible paper dollars. The scale of the enterprise and the rate of erosion of the real value of the dollar has simply increased.

In recognition of the decline in purchasing power of the dollar, in 1946 Congress passed the Employment Act, which directed the federal government to "promote maximum employment, production, and purchasing power." Taxes were cut to stimulate the economy after the war concluded, so that the United States did not experience a severe downturn in economic activity, as was the case following World War I. This act marked one of the early instances of Congress mandating full employment as a matter of government policy and giving responsibility for this goal to Washington. Like the promises made by Washington of financial regulation or consumer protection, the promise of full employment helps define the American dream.

Consumer prices rose slowly in the late 1940s and 1950s as wartime shortages were satisfied, but soon abated. Economic busts could be avoided, it was believed, through the use of "compensatory finance" to counter cyclical downturns. With unemployment still stubbornly high even during the war, the political focus on job creation was understandable even from a domestic perspective, but the priority of avoiding a repeat of the downturn after World War I and the needs of the Cold War gave these efforts even more urgency. G.J. Santoni of the staff of the Federal Reserve Bank of St. Louis noted regarding the Employment Act: "The new theory promised the success of centrally directed economic stabilization policy and provided the nucleus around which the proposed legislation was built."[3]

Fortunately, the US economy did promptly recover in the 1950s and 1960s, independent of the actions of Washington. Unemployment dropped from the double digits seen after World War II back to the 4–4.5 percent joblessness that had prevailed in the three decades before the Great Crash of 1929. This return of prosperity and single-digit unemployment prevailed until the early 1970s, when jobs again became a hot political issue.

Revenues Grow

Despite the imposition of the income tax under FDR, tariffs and corporate taxes still generated the majority of U.S. government revenues until 1943. That's when personal income and other taxes surpassed these two traditional sources of revenue for the federal government. The U.S. government never asked the taxpayer to pay the full cost of World War II, the Korean War, or the Vietnam War, but there was little immediate need to do so. The strong post–World War II economic recovery that occurred following the war and especially after 1949 increased federal revenues even with a reduction in the tax base. The Revenue Act of 1945 took millions off the tax rolls by increasing the exemption to $500. In 1948, Congress passed further tax reductions over President Truman's veto.

The United States never made any attempt to reduce or even extinguish the federal debt accumulated during the World War II years. In the subsequent decades of rapid economic expansion in the 1950s and 1960s, federal outlays were still relatively small compared to the size of the U.S. economy. These were also the years when the U.S. external account was in surplus and exports exceeded imports in most years.Yet Congress never pursued any serious effort to reduce debt.

The primary reason for this accumulation and maintenance of federal debt was the Cold War mobilization and the need to maintain a relatively high level of military spending. There was also the traditional argument of economists that a great nation needs to have some debt in order to function in the financial and commercial markets.

With the domestic political emphasis on employment and the continuous crisis atmosphere surrounding the strategic standoff with Moscow in the international sphere, debt reduction was not at the top of the Washington political agenda during the Cold War. The fear of communism provided a very convenient rationale for many policy decisions in Washington and justified continued military spending at high enough levels to buoy the economy. In the end there was no war with the Soviets. Hundreds of billions of dollars were spent on weapons systems that were never used. The end of the largest period of expenditures on the military saw a slowdown in the U.S. economy and a rapid increase in the outflow of gold from the U.S. Treasury.

Recalling the earlier political reluctance of state governments during the nineteenth century to impose property taxes and other levies to finance their operations, the unwillingness of Congress to impose the burden of debt repayment on taxpayers after the war is not that surprising. In the early 1960s, for example, political and opinion leaders wanted to hear about jobs and increased exports, not higher taxes.

As the economy accelerated in the late 1950s and early 1960s, in fact, policymakers worried that the growing government revenues would hurt economic growth. This made life difficult for a young President John Kennedy, who wanted to increase spending and expand the scope of government for the same reasons as FDR—creating a political base and a political legacy. The Democratic Congress was way ahead of Kennedy in this regard, however, cutting taxes and increasing federal spending without any encouragement from the White House.

Even in those days, many observers knew that a large portion of the prosperity of the post–World War II period was built upon federal spending and debt. Two years after President Kennedy defined the future with his "New Frontier" speech in 1960, the *Richmond Times*

Dispatch ridiculed the young leader. "Yale would have done well to have created a special degree for J.F.K.—Doctor of Mythology—not the old, but the New Frontier mythology, based on the illusion that a nation can spend its way to prosperity." But Kennedy put the priorities in plain terms:

> What is important to discuss are the matters of full employment, how to generate buying power which can consume what we produce, how to build up U.S. exports and staunch the outflow of gold, how to provide adequate profits and wages. These, Mr. Kennedy said, are the economic problems that political parties should be talking about . . .[4]

The partisan ire directed at Kennedy for the relatively modest deficits of the 1960s seems almost ridiculous today with tens of trillions of dollars in federal debt. JFK was elected just a decade after the U.S. economy really began to recover from the Great Depression and World War II. Some Americans who endured the worst part of the Depression felt that the government should do more, while affluent Americans looked upon the FDR years as a betrayal of core values and an act of socialist theft. The reality was that both feelings were genuine and sincere, but the politics of the 1960s leaned in favor of more spending and inflation.

Only with the death of FDR and the assumption of the presidency by Harry Truman from Lamar, Missouri, did investors begin to feel comfortable increasing private investment. At the time the political constituency for direct government action still was strong and reinforced by a largely Democratic Congress. Conservatives had begun to win back seats in the Congress in the late 1930s, but the business community was not ready voluntarily to come back to the political bargaining table until it was certain that FDR-style big government was dead and buried.

Robert Higgs, editor of The *Independent Review*, analyzed the postwar boom in his essay, "Regime Uncertainty: Why the Great Depression Lasted So Long and Why Prosperity Resumed After the War." Higgs writes that the information we have about economic output and inflation during World War II is largely useless because of government price controls and rationing under the New Deal and wartime meas-ures such as the Work Projects Administration (WPA), the largest New Deal agency.[5]

Higgs finds that FDR's New Deal delayed the start of the recovery in the U.S. economy to almost 1950 and the Korean War mobilization: "In 1945 the death of Roosevelt and the succession of Harry S Truman and his administration completed the shift from a political regime [that] investors perceived as full of uncertainty to one in which they felt much more confident about the security of their private property rights . . . Only in 1946 and the following years did private investment reach and remain at levels consistent with a prosperous and growing economy," he concludes.[6]

World War II was called truly "the New Dealers War." During the conflict, Washington ran the private economy with a heavy hand. Rationing and shortages were the shared experience of a generation of Americans. Wartime profits were high for businesses and their execu-tives. "Excess profits" were taxed at punitive rates. In California, a new movie star named Ronald Reagan found that the government took 92 percent of his pay. The common popular reaction against decades of privation and unfulfilled dreams was about to explode and propel the American economy forward.

The Fed Regains Independence

Part of the reason for the reluctance of private investors to invest during the Depression was the government's aggressive manipulation of interest rates through the 1940s. "In April 1942, after the entry of the United States into World War II, the Fed publicly committed itself to maintain-ing an interest rate of 3/8 percent on Treasury bills," wrote Bob Hetzel and Ralph Leach of the Federal Reserve Bank of Richmond in a 2001 research paper. "In practice, it also established an upper limit to the term structure of interest rates on government debt. The ceiling for long-term government bonds was two and a half percent. In summer 1947, the Fed raised the peg on the Treasury bill rate. However, the Treasury adamantly insisted that the Fed continue to place a floor under the price of government debt by placing a ceiling on its yield."[7]

When the economy bottomed in 1949 and began a strong rebound, the Federal Open Market Committee (FOMC) under the leadership of Federal Reserve Bank of New York President Allan Sproul began to discuss increasing interest rates. Fearing a surge in prices after years of wartime controls, discussions began in the middle of 1950 about raising rates. By August, Sproul was openly challenging Treasury Secretary John Snyder over the interest rate issue. Eventually the FOMC allowed rates to rise.

By the end of 1950, the Chinese had entered the Korean War and there was an open confrontation between the Fed and the Truman administration. The president imposed wage and price controls on non-agricultural sectors of the economy and demanded that the Fed maintain a cap on interest rates for the duration of the conflict to prevent holders of war bonds from seeing their securities trade below par. But Fed Chairman Thomas McCabe, who had replaced Marriner Eccles in 1948 when Truman declined to reappoint Eccles as Fed chairman, refused and thereby won back the independence of the central bank.[8]

The heroic faceoff between Eccles and McCabe against the populist political bullying from Treasury Secretary Snyder and Harry Truman was one of the great moments of the American central bank as an independent agency. Eccles in particular bore the full brunt of Truman's populist anger, but refused to resign as a Fed governor and served out the balance of his term to support McCabe. More significant, the Fed's effort to regain its independence from the Treasury in 1951 led to a period of financial stability and growth fueled by the growth of consumer finance.

Though not reappointed as chairman, Eccles remained on the board and fought for the Fed's independence during the remainder of his term as governor until he resigned. McCabe was pressured repeatedly by President Truman and Snyder to continue supporting artificially low interest rates, publicly and privately. Yet he, Eccles, Sproul, and the other members of the FOMC stood their ground. But more important, McCabe and other Fed Board members wanted to end the direct purchases of Treasury debt and create a dealer network to finance government needs.

With the famous Accord of 1951 between the central bank and the executive branch, the Fed and Treasury agreed on a set of rules with respect to their respective operations. The Fed agreed to seek to maintain the Treasury's ability to issue debt while limiting the degree of monetization of federal obligations. McCabe was eventually forced out of the Fed in March 1951 by President Truman, who nominated Assistant Secretary of the Treasury William McChesney Martin as chairman.

Martin had led the negotiations with the Fed for the Treasury when Snyder became ill and Truman assumed that he would take a more cooperative stance than Eccles or McCabe. Robert Hetzel recalls that Truman believed Martin would capture the Fed once McCabe and Eccles were out, but Martin turned out to be a supporter of Fed independence and a strong dollar. Chairman Martin put the case for low inflation in his acceptance speech:

Unless inflation is controlled, it could prove to be an even more serious threat to the vitality of our country than the more spectacular aggressions of enemies outside our borders. I pledge myself to support all reasonable measures to preserve the purchasing power of the dollar.[9]

Compared to the capitulation by Chairman Bernanke and the FOMC in the 2008–2009 market collapse, when the central bank subordinated itself to the Treasury in order to bail out private banks and markets, the posture of the Fed in 1950 was heroic and remarkable. Mariner Eccles, Tom McCabe, and Allan Sproul were unsung champions to American consumers in the story of money and debt.

In a telling lesson for today's policymakers, only when the Fed regained control of monetary policy in 1951 and ended direct purchases of Treasury debt were market rates truly reflective of investor sentiment instead of the wartime fiscal priorities of the Treasury and Defense Department. America was on a war economy from the mid-1930s until into the 1960s, a legacy of the full-scale mobilization that made victory in World War II possible. Whole industries worked on cost plus government contracts that helped build and maintain America's massive productive advantage over the Axis nations of Germany, Italy, and Japan. Yet in peacetime, more than pleasing the vanities of economists, an independent central bank that protects the value of money is the ultimate consumer protection agency.

Postwar Growth

In the early 1950s, when unemployment was still in double digits, only ardent conservatives spoke about budget deficits or debt. But as employment and output did eventually grow with the end of wartime controls, the Keynesian crowd in the economics world looked with satisfaction as GDP grew faster than the federal debt. Growth accelerated in the 1950s and 1960s, conveniently reducing the ratio between debt and GDP. This served to confirm the Keynesian view of the growth that could be obtained via deficit spending—even if it were only nominal growth. Even in those uncertain days, there was plenty of comment about federal deficits, but soon the policy focus would swing back to inflation.

The Federal Reserve under Chairman Martin consistently maintained support for price stability. This task was made easier by the election of President Dwight Eisenhower in 1952 and the fact that inflation moderated during his two terms in office. As Hetzel concluded: "Under Chairman Martin, the Fed's overriding goals became price stability and macroeconomic stability."[10]

There were also new calls for greater federal involvement in areas such as housing. In 1950, for example, the Truman administration explicitly focused on housing as a key area of private investment, but with federal guarantees for the debt used to finance home purchases. The widespread use of government loans and guarantees to fight the Depression and World War II opened the door for a more aggressive role for government generally. And in the early 1950s housing slowly started the booming ascent whereby it soon would supplant the defense sector as the focus of government activity. The GI Bill offered low-cost mortgage loans to ex-servicemen. Newly formed families pushed into the exploding suburbs springing up from corn and potato fields around major U.S. cities, fulfilling the American dream of home ownership. More than a return to normalcy, the victors of World War II set about making up for lost time and then some.

The great unspoken secret in modern American life is the refusal to maintain anything like fiscal balance in the national government. The refusal of successive governments in Washington to ask taxpayers to truly pay their way is a key thread in the contemporary version of the American dream. As with the gold rush and the silverites, modern-day Americans want and feel entitled to a certain living standard, but in the twentieth century we showed a growing unwillingness to pay for it. The relatively new, post–World War I tendency to bail out European allies from their war debts and to use subsidies to boost U.S. employment and exports encouraged even more liberal uses of debt for all purposes in the years beginning in the 1950s and after.

Half a century on and into the twenty-first Century the end result of America's fiscal lack of discipline is growing government debt and an underlying level of inflation far higher than official statistics suggest. The steady erosion in the real value of the dollar has eaten away at the purchasing power of American consumers and reduced real long-term growth and employment opportunities. The tendency to fabricate the appearance of growth via debt and inflationary fiscal policies began with the U.S. aid program for Europe after World War II and became institutionalized in the decades that followed.

The power of demographics, innovation, and technology propelled America's growth naturally for several decades. The Cold War and the growing tolerance for public deficits during the Vietnam War all contributed to fiscal disarray. The overarching logic of the Cold War justified any expenditure or policy prescription that fulfilled the main objectives of containing the military advance of Soviet communism and promoting the economic stability of the Western nations. But soon that extraordinary rationalization would be applied to any and all domestic priorities as well as mere desires became priorities.

Henry Hazlitt mused in a 1947 article that making heavy loans or outright gifts to unstable European nations was not the best way to fight world communism. Entitled "Will Dollars Save the World?," it argued that "if the overriding emergency seems to demand it, let our government give food, not money to Europe. Demand no government reforms in exchange for it; but stamp an American flag, literally or figuratively, on every package." Hazlitt made the case that the U.S. policy of flooding the world with dollars, via loans, grants, and other measures, would not generate wealth in the United States or the recipient nations.[11]

Milton Friedman and Anna Schwartz calculated the growth in the U.S. money supply over the period of their classic study of American money from 1867–1960:

The public held 50 times as many dollars of currency at the end of the 93 years spanned by our figures as at the beginning; 243 times as many dollars of commercial bank deposits; and 127 times as many dollars of mutual savings deposits. The total we designate as money multiplied 157-fold in the course of these nine decades, or at the rate of 5.4 per cent. Since the population of the United States nearly quintupled over the same period, the stock of money per capita multiplied some 32-fold, or at the annual rate of 3.7 per cent.[12]

And yet this brisk expansion of the supply of money, described by the two great monetary economists of the twentieth century, stretching over the period from the Civil War to the election of John Kennedy in 1960, was only the start of the great American infatuation with inflation and debt. A large part of that inflation was driven by the expansion of the U.S. government in all aspects, a growth that is best measured by the portion of the annual output of the United States attributable to the public sector.

Before 1933, the share of gross domestic product represented by government at all levels of the United States was about 10 percent. Today the national average of the share of GDP accounted for by government, including the Federal Reserve System and the housing agencies such as Fannie Mae, Freddie Mac, and the Federal Home Loan Banks is more than half and rising.

The expansion of the federal government during the Depression and World War II and afterward is understandable given the fact that the U.S. economy was still extremely soft at the end of the war. Private debt financing essentially collapsed after the 1929 Crash and FDR's 1933 dollar devaluation. In 1929, private debt outstanding in the United States equaled nearly twice the level of GDP, but by the end of World War II the level of private debt capital was just 50 percent of domestic output, a grim illustration of the staggering deflation and deleveraging that occurred during that terrible 15-year period.

While the level of private debt in 1929 was peaking, an outlier that was closely related to the issuance of speculative debt during the 1920s, the post–World War II level of debt was still well below the average for this indicator between the two world wars. Not until the late 1990s, or half a century later, did U.S. economic growth levels begin to slow and financial speculation again grew to significant levels. The amount of private debt to GDP would again reach 200 percent and then go even higher as the twentieth century concluded.[13]

Benjamin Friedman found that there were three major trends in the U.S. financial markets in the postwar period: an increase in private borrowing, the rise of the use of financial intermediaries, and the increased reliance upon government guarantees, regulation, and financial intermediation by government agencies.[14] The sustained rise in private debt financing observed following the end of World War II was made more dramatic by the sharp decline in the previous 20 years. Likewise, the introduction of government support for housing and other types of domestic infrastructure projects, such as roads, bridges, and other improvements, slowly changed the nature of the U.S. economy and made possible the real estate boom of the 1990s and 2000s. We shall discuss both in the next chapter.

By the 1970s, when post–World War II growth slowed and unemployment began to rise, total federal debt and GDP began to climb even more rapidly. The United States ran larger and larger deficits each year due to growing domestic spending. By the early 1980s total federal debt began to grow far more rapidly than either spending or federal revenues, boosted by accrued interest and, most important, the accumulation of surpluses in the Social Security and other federal trust funds. How America reached the early twenty-first century and raced down the road to national insolvency and hyperinflation is closely bound up with the changing reasons behind America's shift to free trade following the two world wars.

Cold War, Free Trade

In the years immediately following World War II, and especially with the start of the Korean War in 1950, many political leaders in the NATO

(North Atlantic Treaty Organization) countries believed that a war with the Soviet Union and its growing group of Allied nations was inevitable. The classic example of the public's perception of the imminent threat of war during these years was the 1964 election between Democrat Lyndon Baines Johnson (LBJ) and the Republican from Arizona Barry Goldwater, who ran with former New York Congressman William E. Miller. Democrats sponsored the infamous "Daisy Girl" television ads, which showed a little girl plucking the petals of a flower followed by an ominous countdown to a nuclear explosion. This ad demonized Goldwater as a nuclear war monger. Although the ad was aired only once, it showed the deadly immaturity of Democratic image-makers exploiting the "balance of terror" that threatened world peace.

The Republican candidate made the mistake of suggesting the use of tactical nuclear weapons in Vietnam. The Johnson campaign pounced on the opportunity. But long before that, Americans came to know and understand that their lives were at risk because of the background threat of nuclear war. The buildup of United States and Soviet military forces and strategic systems capable of delivering nuclear warheads was front-page news in the United States and around the world for decades. Events such as the Korean War in the 1950s and the Cuban missile crisis in 1962 brought the reality of war home to the entire world. In American politics, the means of response to the "Soviet threat" was a key point of debate for decades.

While the wartime scenario may have been fictional, the perception of the nearness of nuclear war was not. The Cold War colored the thinking of generations of Americans and especially in Washington. The domestic political contest between the Democrats and Republicans turned on how the Cold War was or was not being won. JFK gained the upper hand in his campaign against Richard Nixon by alleging that a "missile gap" between the United States and the Soviets had developed under Eisenhower. The widely shared view of the likelihood of global conflict was captured in phases such as "mutually assured destruction" and influenced many areas of American policy, including the international role of the dollar and the growth of U.S. trade with nations outside the Soviet bloc.

American leaders in politics, business, and the defense community believed that increasing the flow of goods between the United States and the other nations of the free world was an effective bulwark against communism. They believed that free trade was more effective than merely lending nations money—but the United States did plenty of lending as well, directly and indirectly through the IMF (International Monetary Fund) and the World Bank. The United States "dollarized" the world to defend it.

The American aid effort after World War II began with a primary focus on the Marshall Plan and helping to rebuild Europe. The effort soon became more global and was focused on expanding trade between the United States and other nations, not only to help the U.S. economy but also to fight against the Soviet Union. The United States dropped most of its protectionist import barriers while allowing Germany, Korea, and Japan to protect their markets. These nations used very similar trade barriers to those the United States had employed prior to 1945. The United States embraced free trade, at least to a degree, but encouraged its former enemies to rebuild their economies behind tariff and nontariff barriers and quotas.

The Bretton Woods Agreement of 1944 and the multilateral trade framework created under the auspices of the United States essentially allowed participating nations to peg their currencies to the dollar and direct resources to domestic economic recovery. By basing the postwar world on the dollar *and* gold, the Allies sought to avoid competitive currency devaluations between nations and thereby sidestep the sharp swings in growth and reserve balances that had characterized the pre–World War II period.

The Bretton Woods scheme and the related proposal to form an international trade body was entirely statist in conception and utopian in its objectives. It envisioned macroeconomic central planning and management on a global scale, but without a political structure to enforce it. Bretton Woods explicitly sought to control the free flow of capital around the world. In the mindset that governed thinking in many world capitals in 1945, it was the free movement of capital around the world that destabilized national economies and set in motion the path to war.

This authoritarian thinking among the post–World War II powers is hardly a surprise given the strong political and intellectual current toward central planning and fascist models of political economy seen in Europe, the United States, and around the world. To one degree or another, the mobilization for war made the United States and Allied nations become like the enemy and more in terms of military might, but there was a political cost along with the financial burden. Members of the U.S. political community of all stripes discarded traditional American values regarding individual liberties and the rule of law to embrace the collective theology of Bretton Woods.

It seems to be in the nature of all people to be fatally attracted to "new ideas," in much the same way that "new era" thinking described by Ben Graham and David Dodd spread through the world of investing at the start of the twentieth century. The horrors of the Great Depression and the two world wars were so great that any expedient was seen as valid. The *laissez-faire* system of Robber Baron capitalism that prevailed in the United States prior to 1913 seemed to offer no alternative to a larger role for government.

Yet after World War II, the governing elites in U.S. business and political spheres seemingly signed on for a very comfortable codependency, first in defense and later in housing and other areas. This cooperative relationship had its roots in the mobilization effort for the great wars and also perhaps the fear that once the war effort was done, the global economy might slip back into the deflationary malaise of the 1930s. Combined with the priority of commerce that underlies the American dream, the union of the two primary political parties with the corporate relations community produced a uniquely American form of statism that endures to this day.

Author George Orwell famously concluded: "The real division is not between conservatives and revolutionaries, but between authoritarians and libertarians."[15] Once business and government became fully aware of the possibilities for profit and political gain created by cooperation in such formulations as price controls and government allocation schemes, an alliance of convenience was created that was far more extensive than the particular influence of a J.P. Morgan or Standard Oil in the pre–World War I era. The template for this "public-private partnership" was the defense sector, which Dwight Eisenhower called the "defense military industrial complex" as he left office in January 1961. He warned:

We must never let the weight of this combination endanger our liberties or democratic processes. We should take nothing for granted. Only an alert and knowledgeable citizenry can compel the proper meshing of the huge industrial and military machinery of defense with our peaceful methods and goals, so that security and liberty may prosper together.[16]

Eisenhower's warning was prescient and not limited to the defense sector. Not only had the defense industry become intertwined with the federal government during World War II, but what Eisenhower called the "military industrial complex" was entirely subsumed inside the government. The wartime mobilization in World War I and in the 1940s for World War II institutionalized the existence of corporatist structures not only in the defense sector, but also for managing and directing the nondefense sectors of the economy. These structures included the Fed and became part of a framework for "deficit government," as Iwan Morgan describes it, which in concert with the Treasury made use of the federal budget to manage the economy.[17]

With powerful motives such as fighting communism and preventing economic depression, the rationale of total mobilization for war was gradually expanded to include all areas of government policy and public endeavor. And with the equally powerful enabling theology of neo-Keynesian economics to justify what we today label "countercyclical" fiscal policy, the way was made for many of the attempts by government to manage employment, currency movements, and even commodity prices during the second half of the twentieth century. Most of these attempts failed miserably, but the fact remains that the policy mindset of government intervention, of management from above, became an acceptable viewpoint—even if it was entirely erroneous.

Thomas Paine observed: "A long habit of not thinking a thing wrong gives it a superficial appearance of being right." During and after World War II, the notion of managing government from the national or macro level, a "God's Eye View" in classical terms, was received as wisdom and gospel. Members of both major political parties in the United States became convinced that deficit spending could employ unused resources, correct market failures, and produce optimal economic results. This narrative, this deliberate act of collective delusion, has governed the direction of the U.S. economy ever since. The author Nassim Taleb talks about the importance of narrative in how human beings come to believe that they understand a complex issue:

> The narrative fallacy addresses our limited ability to look at sequences of facts without weaving an explanation into them, or, equivalently, forcing a logical link, *an arrow of relationship*, upon them. Explanations bind facts together. They make them all the more easily remembered; they help them *make more sense*. Where this propensity can go wrong is where it increases our *impression* of understanding.[18]

Generations of American politicians became aware of the possibility of spending more money on more different things and thereby building a direct, commercial relationship with the voters as well as with foreign countries. The flow of fiat dollar subsidies from Washington became a flow of political influence that touched every American and the citizens of many of the other nations of the world. Since the fiat paper dollar was the center of the post–World War II financial world, America's ultimate victory in the Cold War was assured. But as with the Civil War, the cost of victory has been extremely high measured against consumer purchasing power and inflation.

The Golden Age

The 1950s and 1960s are considered the golden age of modern American culture, albeit one that existed in a highly controlled economy. Today the idea of using price controls or a currency peg to manage an economy may be considered laughable. Price controls only create a target of opportunity for hedge funds and other global speculators—the modern-day heirs of Jay Gould—to attack. But in the restricted financial markets of the 1950s and 1960s, when much of the global economy was still recovering from decades of depression and war, the system of pegging other currencies to the dollar appeared to work initially. A trade expansion initiative under the General Agreement on Tariffs and Trade (GATT) was meant to be the companion to this managed currency arrangement, ultimately culminating in the creation of the International Trade Organization (ITO).

The utopian vision of one world guided by a collective, cooperative political union of nations, managed by a new class of international bureaucrats, was very much in vogue immediately after World War II. But the United States ultimately refused to go along with the ITO. The World Trade Organization, as it came to be known, would not be approved until the end of the Cold War in January 1995, but this did not prevent the United States from pushing for greatly reduced trade restrictions during the 50-year interregnum—albeit for reasons seen through the prism of the East-West conflict with the Soviet Union and China. This change in focus from the internationalist vision of the United States coming out of the 1930s to the Cold War focus of the United States following World War II is a very important turning point in the American dream.

In the 1930s, mainstream thinking within the Democratic Party came to the conclusion that trade barriers and shifts in the flow of capital—that is, gold—were a major cause of both world wars. Even before World War II ended, the Roosevelt administration drafted a document authorizing the ITO and enabling legislation from Congress for broad powers to reduce tariffs at the discretion of the executive branch. The support for trade liberalization was consistent with the traditional Democratic opposition to tariffs, which Progressives saw merely as a means of enhancing the monopoly profits of big business for the benefit of the rich.

Republicans, on the other hand, were the traditional protectionists and built the government's limited finances on tariff revenue. But the most important domestic factor behind the broad and largely bipartisan support for trade liberalization was the fact that while much of the world lay in ruins, U.S. industrial capacity had grown to first in the world. The "hegemonic trade and payments position," to quote Robert Baldwin, of the United States required a policy of openness since American industry was the exporter to the world and American banks the lenders.[19]

From the early 1930s through the Tokyo Round of the GATT from 1974–1979, the United States oversaw a process of trade opening that, in theory at least, reduced tariffs around the globe by almost 80 percent compared to pre–World War II levels. This trade opening largely benefitted the U.S. economy, which generated an abnormally large share of manufactured exports and services for decades. Most of the other nations of the world did not liberalize their trade very much, leading some researchers to argue that the economic recovery following World War II was not primarily a function of U.S. trade opening. In Japan and Germany, for example, the size of imports relative to these rapidly growing economies actually fell during the Cold War period. This suggested to some observers that "freer" trade rather than free trade was the more accurate description of the goal of U.S. policy from 1950–1996.[20]

As the Cold War progressed and the cost of the military confrontation with the Soviets and related assistance to Allied nations grew, the United States showed a growing disinclination to continue the policy of pursuing free trade. Whereas global trade liberalization and the expansion of world trade were regarded as synonymous by U.S. policymakers at the end of the conflict, by the 1950s the focus had been narrowed to rebuilding Europe as a bulwark against Soviet expansion. The need for rearmament to meet the threat from Moscow and fight the expansion of communism in Asia during the Korean War conflicted with the original "internationalist" vision of Bretton Woods.

By the time Dwight Eisenhower was elected president in 1952, the commitment of U.S. leaders and the public at large to the liberal vision of free trade was increasingly in doubt. Congress had already begun to erect barriers to imports from our NATO allies. The infamous "cheese amendment" to the Defense Production Act of 1951 placed import quotas on foreign dairy products from all nations.

In addition to manifestations of these types of pre-1930s protectionism, the United States also saw legislation to limit trade with the Soviet Union and China, as well as their satellite nations. The fact that commodity prices suffered a series of sharp declines during this period did nothing to quiet the desire among American politicians to lash out at unfriendly nations. All trade concessions were withdrawn from Soviet bloc nations, including Czechoslovakia, which was a member of GATT, ironically enough. The shift away from the previous American policy of tariff reduction in the early 1950s did a great deal to undermine America's position at the trade bargaining table.[21]

The shift from a global commitment to free trade to a targeted strategy to beggar the communist nations marked a change in strategy that was not easy for the United States to sell around the world. Not only did the United States attempt to embargo trade with the Soviet bloc, but it also threatened to impose sanctions on nations that did not agree to follow the embargo on the Soviets with respect to strategic materials. Sanctions were most harshly imposed on the Soviets and "front line" communist states such as Fidel Castro's Cuba, while Eastern European nations such as Poland and Czechoslovakia were treated with more flexibility.

The period of the 1970s marked a transition point for the United States as it moved from being a net lender to the world to being a net borrower, an "importer of capital" in the popular language of economics to finance growing fiscal deficits. America's trade balance also moved into the red as Americans started to import more than they exported to the world. Figure 7.3 shows the trend in imports, exports, and the net balance of the overall current account (commercial and financial flows) from 1960–1972.

As the Cold War years progressed, the industrial nations of Europe and Asia were rebuilt and more, new industrial societies began to emerge in Asia and Latin America. Much of this industrial development

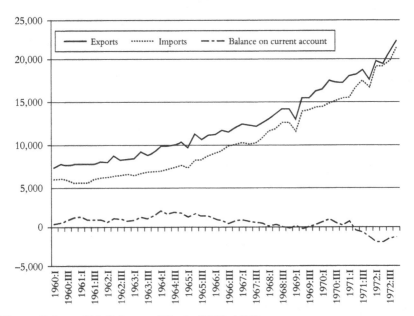

Figure 7.3 U.S. Balance of Trade (1960–1972).
SOURCE: Bureau of Economic.

came about not as the result of U.S. aid, but because these societies made industrial policy a priority. The old policy of beggar thy neighbor was replaced with a modern version of the mercantilist model. By the 1970s, the United States showed new focus on exports and a renewed interest in international lending to finance them. Once many of the nations of the world were rebuilt and their economies had stabilized from the trauma and stress of war, however, the same global pressures and instabilities that were in evidence prior to and after World War I again began to emerge.

Two key events in the reemergence of these financial disturbances after almost three decades of stability were the 1971 decision by the United States to end the dollar peg to gold entirely and the reemergence of sovereign borrowing to fund balance of payments deficits. For the United States, funding external deficits did not require borrowing because the government could simply finance these shortfalls via government debt and monetary expansion. The world did business in U.S. dollars—a unique American monopoly.

Other nations were not so fortunate. As two researchers at the Federal Reserve Bank of New York observed in 1998: "The current account deficit allows the United States to maintain a higher rate of investment spending than would be possible by relying on domestically generated savings alone. However, the corresponding foreign capital inflow is essentially a loan; therefore, it represents claims on future national income."[22]

Global Imbalances Return

Under the pegged currency arrangement created at Bretton Woods in 1944, a global financial institution for countries was created—the International Monetary Fund—which was authorized to make changes in the agreed exchange rates in the event of "fundamental disequilibrium." The idea was for nations to accumulate sufficient foreign currency— that is dollars—to manage their trading relations, and in the event of an imbalance adjust their pegged rate downward rather than resorting to trade barriers. Nations that did not wish to devalue could borrow from the IMF for the purpose of short-term adjustment, with the idea being that the nation would make changes to its economy to eliminate the imbalance and repay the adjustment loan. This all assumed, of course, that nations could maintain a roughly balanced trade relationship with the rest of the world.

In simple terms, the IMF was a bank from which nations could borrow to help balance their short-term imbalances in trade and capital flows. This facility was intended to avoid situations such as those that affected Great Britain before and after World War I, when the country almost ran out of foreign reserves. More modest fluctuations in currency values were meant to be managed by the various members of the IMF or by drawing upon "special drawing rights" (SDR)—a form of ersatz global currency that, like the dollar, was and is backed by nothing. This arrangement did not really address the underlying economic problems in the various nations, but merely obscured the reality with a veneer of government intervention.

John H. Barton, Bart S. Fisher, and Michael P. Malloy put the key issue succinctly:

> The obvious question was how currency values were to be maintained at a fixed relationship, even though governments might engage in inconsistent economic policies. The answer was through a duty of exchange market intervention. When its currency fell more than a defined percentage in comparison with others, a state was obliged to buy its currency and sell the foreign currencies in order to maintain the desired relationship. And a state whose currency rose above the margin was to sell that currency and buy others. The practical limiting factor was the state's store of foreign hard currency, a major component of its currency "reserves." A creditor state could always print more of its own currency to sell to maintain the price relationship. But a debtor state had to buy its currency and sell foreign currency.[23]

Essentially, participating nations had to accumulate foreign currency sufficient to manage their trade position or borrow from the IMF or international investors. This arrangement worked—or appeared to function—for three decades after World War II, but only because it was underpinned and lubricated by the wonderful stuff of inflation and debt. The United States provided loans and grants to the developing nations of the world and expanded the supply of dollars to accommodate both domestic and international need for liquidity.

Much of the assistance provided to Europe under the Marshall Plan, like the loans to Europe in World War I and World War II, were largely forgiven. The Bretton Woods Conference in July 1944 was organized, opined Henry Hazlitt, because of the widespread existence of inflation. But rather than return to the gold standard or some other fixed discipline for maintaining the real value of global currencies, the Bretton Woods Agreement crafted by John Maynard Keynes and his contemporaries institutionalized global inflation under the aegis of the U.S. dollar. "And in spite of the mounting monetary chaos since then, the world's political officeholders have never seriously reexamined the inflationist assumptions that guided the authors of the Bretton Woods agreements," noted Hazlitt.[24]

One of the key measures of the global role of the dollar and inflation in helping to float the world economy after World War II was the growth of the offshore market in dollar deposits—the so-called "Eurodollars." From $1 billion in 1950, the offshore market in U.S. dollars grew to $10 billion at the end of 1965, $100 billion in 1990, over $5 trillion in 2000, and reached more than $10 trillion by the end of 2009 and was measured in tens of trillions by 2024, according to the Atlanta Federal Reserve Bank.

As U.S. trade and external deficits increased after the 1970s, offshore holdings of dollars grew along with the global economy. More than the International Monetary Fund, the Federal Reserve System became the *de facto* liquidity provider to the world, a role now made explicit in the wake of the 2008 subprime crisis. While the IMF could act as a lender of last resort to smaller nations, it does not have the ability to create money out of thin air as does the Fed.

Paul Blustein notes that "[t]he Fed's duty is to lend as much cash as the banks need to cover their depositors' demands—and keep lending until the panic eases, because otherwise the whole system may crash."[25] But when the Fed's domestic priorities as liquidity provider are extended to the entire world, the result is the very global inflation and financial market instability that the classical economists warned against.

The type of crashes that the world has experienced with increasing frequency since the 1970s seem to be the financial legacy of Richard Nixon and the other political leaders of that day. It is easy to criticize the Bretton Woods Agreement from the enviable position of perfect hindsight, but it was very much a product of an uncertain world that existed at the end of World War II. From the years of war and government mobilization, a centralized system of managed currencies made sense to the leaders of that day. When the military and strategic threat of the Cold War is layered atop this existing propensity to embrace statist solutions and mechanisms, the Bretton Woods framework has a certain logic—but only so long as the United States itself maintained fiscal discipline.

Unfortunately, the United States never paid down its debt after World War II. Instead, over the next half century America created a culture of debt and deficits that has only grown with the succeeding decades. Under Bretton Woods, all of the major currencies of the world were defined in dollars, thus when chronic external deficits brought the need to devalue the U.S. dollar, the entire pegged arrangement disintegrated.

The beginning of the end of Bretton Woods started in the late 1960s, as the Federal Reserve Board attempted to balance the inflationary impact of the Vietnam War spending with the powerful domestic political imperative for growth. In 1966, the Fed tightened interest rates to slow domestic price increases, almost leading the United States into a serious recession a year later. Mortgage money was tight, consumer prices were rising, and civil rights protests drove many southern white voters into the arms of the Republican Party. The GOP picked up several governorships including Ronald Reagan in California and Spiro Agnew in Maryland. The Fed subsequently loosened policy and Congress moved to increase domestic spending in 1967. The intense public protests against the Vietnam War and the slack economy eventually caused President Johnson not to seek another term in March 1968.

James R. Jones, who was appointments secretary to President Johnson in 1968, wrote that the most important reason LBJ "decided not to run again was his passionate desire to conclude the Vietnam War honorably."[26] But the political reality was that Johnson was a lame duck following the 1966 election, when the Republicans picked up the seats lost in 1964 and then some. By 1968, Republican partisan politics intersected with the international crisis of the dollar and the return of Richard Nixon.

Nixon's Betrayal

The decision by President Johnson "to walk away from power" was under consideration for more than a year, Jones writes, and dates back to a meeting between LBJ and Texas governor John Connally, who urged him to retire. Connally then became Nixon's Treasury secretary. The eventual determination by President Johnson to leave public life threw the race for the presidency open for both parties.

For the Republicans, moderates led by George Romney and Richard Nixon were set against the left wing of the GOP led by New York Governor Nelson Rockefeller. Ronald Reagan was "an ideal television candidate," wrote Richard Whalen in *Catch the Falling Flag*, "but had never spent a day on duty in Washington."[27] The eventual contest came down to Nixon versus Rockefeller for the Republican nomination, but the dull and serious New York governor was no match for the devious Nixon.

Seeing how LBJ was savaged by the media over the war and the direction of the U.S. economy, Nixon felt vulnerable on the question of jobs. Nixon eventually embraced a left-wing economic program out of political expediency and because he did not see any politically palatable alternatives. What passed for mainstream economic thinking at the time called for more spending and increased deficits, but this policy was stymied by the failure of increased spending to create jobs.

"Watch what we do, not what we say," was the famous advice Nixon's first attorney general, John Mitchell, gave the press at the onset of the Nixon presidency in 1969. That admonition was essential when it came to the confused economic policy of Nixon.

Nixon's policies quickly alienated conservatives. In his first campaign, Nixon declared his intention to start "getting people off the welfare rolls and onto payrolls," but then initiated an income maintenance program that added 15 million Americans to public assistance. This stroke of genius was engineered by Daniel Patrick Moynihan, one of the cadres of Rockefeller Republicans who turned the Nixon years into the "New Deal III" or what Nixon eventually called the New Economic Policy or "NEP."

Time magazine wrote in 1971: "Welfare reform, cutbacks in defense spending, advocacy of deficit spending, and Keynesian economics were difficult enough for Nixon's conservative supporters to tolerate, but for many, rapprochement with Communist China was the final straw." But Nixon's final repudiation of Bretton Woods and devaluation of the dollar had far more significant impact on issues conservatives hold dear, particularly the value of the currency and the stability of the U.S. economy.

Under the Bretton Woods arrangement, gold and dollars were established as the reserve for all of nations outside the Communist sphere. Since in the 1940s there was not sufficient gold to underpin global trade and financial flows except in a fractional way, Keynes and the other Bretton Woods framers essentially made the dollar equal to gold as a backstop for the global economy.

Since the United States had virtually all of the monetary gold in the world at the end of World War II with some $35 billion in gold (valued at $35 per ounce), this arrangement seemed to make sense, and for a while it appeared to work. But as the nations of the world recovered and the United States exported capital and jobs, the gold stocks of the United States dwindled. The United States had just $11 billion in reserves in 1970. Since federal law required that the U.S. Treasury have $25 in gold for every $100 in greenbacks in circulation, Washington was reaching a tipping point.

The Dollar Peg Ends

By 1970, when inflation was starting to rise and the United States was running its first trade deficit in the twentieth century, the global financial markets essentially began a run on the dollar. U.S. official gold stocks fell precipitously. Like FDR 40 years earlier, Nixon was faced with the political fact of the market's lack of confidence in the fiscal integrity of the United States. Increased domestic spending and external deficits caused an outflow of gold from the U.S. Treasury, effectively forcing Nixon to abandon what remained of the gold standard.

Although FDR had confiscated the right of Americans to hold gold as money, under Bretton Woods the United States still maintained the legal commitment to honor gold convertibility of the dollar in its dealings with other nations. Only a month after President Nixon announced his trip to China, he went on national television, announced that the United States was in the worst crisis since the Great Depression, and took the dollar off the gold standard. Nixon effectively devalued the U.S. currency for the second time in 40 years.[28]

By unilaterally ending the gold convertibility of the dollar, Nixon brought an end to the Bretton Woods system of managed currencies and ushered in a period of floating exchange rates. Taking a page out of the Democratic playbook of FDR and Truman, Nixon also imposed a 90-day freeze on wages and prices and a 10 percent surcharge on imports. Following the Kennedy-Johnson administration in the United States, there was a massive effort to manage the marketplace, in part by controlling wages.

In their book *The Commanding Heights*, Daniel Yergin and Joseph Stanislaw described the bizarre fact of Richard M. Nixon, a California Republican and conservative stalwart, taking America once again down the socialist road of FDR to government wage and price controls:

> This initiative was not the handiwork of left-wing liberals but of the administration of Richard Nixon, a moderately conservative Republican who was a critic of government intervention in the economy. As a young man during World War II, prior to joining the navy, Nixon had worked as a junior attorney in the tire-rationing division of the Office of Price Administration, an experience that left him with a lasting distaste for price controls.[29]

Such was the severity of the perceived crisis in 1971 that Richard Nixon, who was elected in 1968 in a very close contest against Senator Hubert Humphrey of Minnesota, veered to the left in terms of economic policy and betrayed all of his past positions and views. Yergin and Stanislaw describe how Nixon declared himself to be a "Keynesian" in 1971, a change that the economist himself might have found troubling. Nixon was uncomfortable with economic issues and allowed his administration to be hijacked by the Rockefeller wing of the GOP—and by his own fears and paranoia. Gary North described Nixon's betrayal of conservative principles after winning the 1968 election:

In 1968, millions of Republicans voted for Richard Nixon. They voted for him overwhelmingly in 1972, the year after he had unilaterally severed the dollar from gold. He had run back-to-back deficits of $25 billion—a huge annual deficit in that era. It is unlikely that the ineffective gas bag Hubert Humphrey would have had the courage to destroy the last traces of the international gold standard. Yet Humphrey almost won in 1968. Republican die-hards had kept this from happening. In the summer of 1972, Richard Whalen's book, *Catch the Falling Flag: A Republican's Challenge to His Party*, documented the story of the takeover of the [Nixon] Administration by Rockefeller operatives. Whalen had been a speechwriter for Nixon during the 1968 campaign. He knew firsthand what had occurred. Republicans paid no attention to his book in November. "Nixon is ours." They re-elected him in November.[30]

Nixon represented a milestone in American economic development, where deficit spending was explicitly embraced to maximize employment even though the economy was not in recession or at war. The leadership for this evolution of the culture of deficit spending came from the left wing of the Republican Party, which at the time was led by New York governor Nelson Rockefeller. Nixon won the White House because of conservative support, but ultimately migrated from pretend Goldwater conservative to Eisenhower moderate to deficit spending socialist a la FDR by the early 1970s.

Hugh Sidey observed of Nixon that "he abandons his philosophy, his promises, his speeches, his friends, his counselors. He marches out of one life into a new world without any apologies or glancing back."[31] But Sidey's description of Nixon could have also applied to FDR and to many other modern American politicians. Nixon's actions were a repudiation of the original vision of Keynes as well as the American framers of Bretton Woods, none of whom were apologists for inflation or borrowing except in times of emergency. Nixon's final repudiation of gold and his explicit embrace of deficit spending to ensure "full employment" was a radical departure from the stated practice of either political party.

Lyndon Johnson established the Great Society programs to fight poverty and improve education, yet the impact on the federal budget was modest compared to the federal spending authorized under President Nixon as part of his Soviet-style New Economic Policy. Federal revenues grew strongly during the Johnson years, but growth stagnated under Nixon in the 1970s. The response from Nixon to economic stagnation was more federal spending combined with price controls to mask inflation. President Hoover resisted massive federal expenditures in the early 1930s for fear of permanently expanding the size of government. Nixon delighted in a growing federal budget as he felt, just as Johnson did, that more spending would insulate him politically. Doing so did protect him from defeat in the 1972 election, when he overpowered George McGovern handily on a platform of economic growth and national security, but at the expense of higher inflation.

Nixon beat Hubert Humphrey in 1968 because of the public's concern over the Vietnam War and mounting budget deficits, but by 1972 Nixon was spending like there was no tomorrow—like a Democrat, in fact. "To improve his chances of re-election, he would pre-empt any position that the Democrats might take in the 1972 campaign," wrote Richard Whalen, "as he had done by adopting their program for the economy."[32]

In July 1971, Fed Chairman Arthur Burns (1970–1978), who was outspoken about inflation, told the Joint Economic Committee of Congress that "the rules of economics are not working in quite the way that they used to . . . I wish that I could report that we are making substantial progress in dampening the inflationary spiral. I cannot do so."

Burns headed the Council of Economic Advisors from 1953 to 1956 under Eisenhower and knew Nixon well, but when he was named chairman of the Fed in 1970 his relationship with the president deteriorated. The fiscal priorities of the White House and the inflation-fighting priorities of the Fed were in direct conflict. Burns was in favor of defending the dollar and, if necessary, selling all of the U.S. gold if need be. "What the hell are reserves for?" Burns thundered. The Fed chairman also believed that the United States should begin borrowing in other currencies to manage the dollar's value, but neither of these suggestions were well received by the Nixon White House.

In that same month of July 1971, the Fed hiked interest rates a quarter of a point and indicated that higher interest rates were likely. From 1952 to almost the end of the 1960s, the Federal funds rate had tracked an unremarkable pattern between below 1 percent in the slack years and as high as 6 percent in years when the economy was near capacity. Prices began to rise. The cost of short-term funds rose in the late 1960s close to double digits as the Fed attempted to act alone to cool inflation. President Johnson refused to propose a tax increase in 1966 or thereafter to pay for the Vietnam War, thus the result was rising inflation, more than doubling by the 1968 election. By 1971, inflation was over 5 percent, but then cooled for several years due to increased interest rates engineered by Arthur Burns and the Federal Open Market Committee.

In punishment for committing the crime of speaking the truth in public, Burns was subject to an ugly campaign of vitriol and personal attacks by members of the Nixon White House staff. The attacks on the Fed in that summer of 1971 only further weakened confidence in the United States and the dollar, but in the Nixon White House the priority was keeping the old man happy. In October 1971, Nixon warned Burns that he was worried that the slowing economy would force him "to go out of town fast," a reference to losing the election in a year's time. Incredibly, Nixon also said that his would be "the last Conservative administration in Washington," referring to the political pressure for even more federal spending. The president also opined that the problem of too much liquidity in the financial system was "just bullshit."[33]

Nixon saw unemployment rise from 3.4 percent late in 1969 to 6 percent in 1971, "but with no abatement in inflation," wrote Bob Hertzel in *The Monetary Policy of the Federal Reserve: A History*, a development that "created intellectual consternation among mainstream economists."[34] More concerned was Nixon, who feared that the Fed was sinking the economy in front of the 1972 election, in a repeat of the process that forced Johnson out of the presidency. Nixon subsequently beat Hubert Humphrey by less than a million votes and thus worried that he could be vulnerable politically in a soft economy.

In early August, at the insistence of Treasury Undersecretary Paul Volcker, Nixon held a secret meeting at the Camp David retreat to discuss the economy. Congress gave Nixon broad powers over wages and prices in 1970 via the Economic Stabilization Act, and Nixon was determined to use them.

Treasury Secretary John Connally, who Nixon recruited for the cabinet in 1970, laid out the plan to the assembled staff, including the wage and price controls, an import surcharge, and closing the gold window. Nixon admitted at the time that he was not sure of the impact of the decision to close the gold window. Fed Chairman Burns was against closing the gold window, but was in agreement with the other aspects of the Nixon NEP. Connally said after the summit meeting that when Nixon announced the unilateral United States departure from Bretton Woods: "We have awakened forces that nobody is at all familiar with."

Chairman Burns, for his part, urged Nixon during the discussions not to close the gold window when he announced the other measures, feeling that these policy changes were more than sufficient to stop the outflow of gold. "If we close the window, other countries could double the price of gold . . . Paul Volcker should go ahead and start negotiating with other countries on a realignment of currencies," Burns argued. He allowed that President Nixon could close the gold window later if these other measures did not restore confidence in the dollar.

Nixon was shrewd enough to know that if he announced his other policy moves that the markets would next anticipate a change in gold convertibility of the dollar. Paul Volcker did not want to close the gold window either, but also worried that speculators would drive up the price of gold. "We have to come up with a proposal to demonstrate gold is not that important," Volcker told the meeting. "Maybe we should sell some," echoing the thinking of Burns.[35]

Sovereign Dollar Debt

By finally ending the gold standard in August 1971, Nixon devalued the dollar for many of the same political reasons that drove FDR's decision in 1933, but Nixon was toppled by the Watergate scandal and cover-up two years later. The difference between the two decisions was that unlike in 1933, the dollar was now the predominant means of exchange in the global economy.

While the United States could devalue its currency and borrow *in dollars* to fund internal spending and external deficits, other nations of the world with balance of payments problems were faced with devaluation—or taking on foreign currency debt. The chief miscalculation of Keynes and the other framers of Bretton Woods was not identifying the risk of national borrowing in dollars to fund internal local currency deficits, a problem that mushroomed in the 1970s and continued to grow, expanding global demand for the dollar.

The decision by President Nixon to devalue the dollar not only set the United States free of fiscal boundaries, but also set a very poor example for other nation–states. The flow of dollars into the global markets created a surfeit of greenbacks so large that they warranted a separate category—Eurodollars. And foreign nations began to borrow dollars in the same way as had occurred between the two great wars. Walker Todd wrote in his 1991 monograph, "A History of International Lending":

The Bretton Woods framers never intended that such commercialized international lending resume—yet such loans were made increasingly after 1973. There are some significant, still largely unexplained gaps in the logic of economists and policy makers who advocate a greater role for commercial banks' loans, ostensibly for development purposes. Somehow, in the mid-1970s, we leaped almost overnight from the supposedly desirable original environment, in which there was no development lending by commercial banks, to primary reliance on such lending.[36]

One of the chief rationales for adjustment lending in the 1970s, at least among the political leaders of the major industrial countries, was the oil embargo in 1973. The weakness of the dollar and the sharp increase in energy costs imposed a heavy tax on the global economy in terms of lowered growth prospects. But equally harmful to many exporting nations was the steady decline in the value of the dollar, which became unstable as early as 1967–1968 when gold outflows from the United States increased. GDP growth in the United States was cut in half, unemployment rose, and the visible level of inflation also surged from low single-digits to twice those levels and more. David Gordon described the chaos and uncertainty caused by the final interment of Bretton Woods:

> When Bretton Woods was formally buried in 1973, the dollar was still apparently overvalued, resulting in a continuing decline of 2.9 percent per year in 1973–1979. No longer officially the world's key currency, the dollar's sharp decline underscored how artificially inflated its value had become at the end of the boom years. The international hegemon had begun to seem more and more like a paper tiger.[37]

Paper tiger or not, the United States still had a vast advantage in the global marketplace compared to other nations. It could print money and issue debt in dollars, and essentially be indifferent to the movement of the currency. Other nations, however, including the largest industrial nations of Europe, were not so lucky. Generally speaking, in the 1970s a debtor nation other than the United States that came to have balance of payments problems had three choices:

1. Loans from and austerity measures imposed and supervised by the IMF. Present and future consumers in these nations would see living standards decline, and political unrest would ensue.
2. Overt default and devaluation, meaning an end to all foreign borrowing and the loss of access to even short-term credit to clear trade transactions. Cold turkey and an all-cash economy. Political unrest would ensue.
3. In the case of less-developed countries, debt forgiveness by the creditor nations whose citizens (mostly the United States) would bear the losses. This was the preferred choice.

During the years of the Cold War, the default choice was always more lending, from the IMF, the World Bank, and/or private lenders. The alternative in the form of a harsh economic adjustment was politically unpalatable for the inhabitants of Washington and for the banks that lent money to the debtor nations. Concerns over the prospect of a left-wing swing in the nations of the Americas, Asia, or the Middle East were sufficient to propel more lending to the subject debtor nation. And even in the case of the largest countries, repayment was never assured or even likely. Over the past 150 years or so over the history of international lending, Todd notes, repayment of foreign loans almost never occurred.

Gerald O'Driscoll of the CATO Institute, who worked at the Federal Reserve Bank of Dallas in this period, wrote in a 1984 paper that "[g]etting from where we are today to a resolution of who is, in fact, going to bear the losses is the key to restoring credibility to international lending."[38] These losses on foreign loans, O'Driscoll noted, had already occurred but were yet to be recognized. But this was precisely the point. These "loans" were never really meant to be repaid. Even Great Britain, once considered the second-best sovereign credit risk after the United States, defaulted on every foreign loan it contracted since the end of the Boer War in 1902.

"Instead, every such loan has been subjected to major currency devaluation, rolled over, suspended, rescheduled, or otherwise restructured, repudiated, reduced, cancelled, or forgiven. The more drastic steps, leading to eventual, partial or complete cancelation of debt have been surprisingly frequent," Todd notes.[39]

The views of researchers such as Walker Todd and Gerry O'Driscoll on foreign lending are confirmed in the more recent work of Carmen Reinhart and Kenneth Rogoff, *This Time Is Different: Eight Centuries of Financial Folly*. The book is another monumental research effort in the fine tradition of Freidman and Schwartz's *Monetary History of the United States* and Allan Meltzer's updates of that work, albeit focused on the largely underappreciated foreign debt component of the economic story of the twentieth century.

Reinhart and Rogoff document the fact that foreign lending between sovereign states or private parties always was problematic, but in the post–World War II era the fiscal and external imbalances of the United States became the key factor. Reinhart and Rogoff set an inflation rate of 40 percent as the threshold for describing an inflationary "crisis," yet their work also suggests that since the 1970s a larger and larger percentage of nations were captured by global financial crises. As the use of what Reinhart and Rogoff describe as financial repression of domestic markets and price controls ended in the 1970s and 1980s, and the U.S. deficit and debt grew, the frequency and number of nations affected by periodic economic crises also increased.[40]

From the closing of the Suez Canal in 1956, the United Kingdom and France had been the primary recipients of IMF adjustment loans. Even in those times, the availability of dollars was so limited that it would have been difficult in a practical sense for foreign nations to incur large amounts of dollar debt. As late as December 1973, the total of all U.S. bank claims on foreigners was just $20 billion—about in the same as the U.S. budget deficit in that year—and one-third of this amount was held against Japan. By the late 1980s, however, total U.S. claims on foreigners had risen to $388 billion, a 20-fold increase in dollar debts in less than 15 years.[41] The total claims on foreigners rose to $4.7 trillion by the end of 2023, an increase of more than 1,000 percent in 35 years, according to the U.S. Treasury.

The return of international lending as a significant factor in the global economy in the 1970s and the explosion of foreign debt as a problem in the 1980s was at its roots no different from the neo-Keynesian economic policies that were being followed in the United States. Policymakers in the industrial countries, aided by armies of economists and bankers, pretended that foreign loans would be repaid. But the reality was that none of these dollar loans, particularly to the established industrial nations, would ever be repaid. The goal of Washington's foreign and economic policy was to keep the level of aggregate output in the non-Communist world rising, at least in nominal terms. Inside the United States, deficit spending, debt, and inflation were the primary means to keep growth on an upward-sloping curve. Foreign loans, trade subsidies, and other means were used to maintain the appearance of output increases internationally.

So long as the supply of dollars already very visible in the growth of Eurodollar deposits continued to expand and the United States was willing to run external deficits, political leaders in the industrial nations could claim that the collective economic pie represented by global trade and commerce was expanding. But once the assumption of constant growth and expansion of international output was questioned, then the United States and other nations were faced with a problem of distributing real income from a static or shrinking global economic pie. In that event, as O'Driscoll and other researchers predicted decades ago, the world economy would be right back in the position of the 1930s, with a contraction of world economic output and reduced living standards in both debtor and creditor nations.[42]

By the end of the 1970s, with the second oil price shock, the use of debt to offset the decline in output and income caused by a quadrupling of energy prices became as much a part of the established practice internationally as deficit spending was accepted as a domestic policy tool within the United States. Despite all of the work and study and discussion by generations of economists before and after World War II, the same problems of growth and debt dogged the United States and the other nations. The role of the dollar as the international reserve currency was in doubt. None of the great thinkers and theorists of the day seemed to have a clear idea in what direction to head next.

The next three decades following Nixon's closing the gold window would see the problems of global debt and inflation intensify even as the growth potential of the United States and Europe seemed to wane, and all with little or no suggestion of a solution to get the global economy onto a less volatile, more stable footing. "I recently commented to some of my economist friends that I'm not aware of any large contribution that economic science has made to central banking in the last 50 years or so," Paul Volcker told Gary H. Stern of the Federal Reserve Bank of Minneapolis.[43]

Volcker would probably chuckle at the thought that central banking hasn't made any contribution to economic science, either. Perhaps the fact that little has changed in the issues and constraints facing the evolution of global economies is what makes the search for solutions so challenging. As Robert Kennedy put it in his famous election speech in 1968, "it [GDP] measures everything in short, except that which makes life worthwhile."

Chapter 8

Leveraging the American Dream

With the final end of gold convertibility of the dollar, banks and dollar-based investors were irrevocably tied to the fiat currency as a means of exchange and store of value. Unlike the process leading up to the Bretton Woods agreement, there were no meetings, no international consultations. The decision to end the gold convertibility of the dollar came down to the unilateral calculus of the president of the United States, who was seeking to manage his domestic political—that is economic—problems. The end of convertibility allowed Nixon to avoid the immediate embarrassment of seeing the Treasury run out of gold. The end of convertibility also cleared the way for increased deficit spending by Congress and monetary expansion by the Federal Reserve to accommodate it.

Fed chairman Arthur Burns later said in a conversation with Richard Whalen that the choice to end gold convertibility was a "terrible decision" that should never have happened, but one that "had to happen." Treasury secretary John Connally at first did not realize what Nixon had done, thinking that merely another dollar devaluation had occurred a la FDR. Burns opposed the move and also Nixon's demands to stimulate the economy, but ultimately the political pressure for growth prevailed. In 1972, Fed Chairman Arthur Burns kept monetary policy sufficiently expansive to help Richard Nixon win reelection by a landslide, taking 60 percent of the popular vote. The *quid pro quo* to Burn's easy money posture was Nixon's imposition of price controls the year before, which made inflation at least appear to be low compared to the official statistics. But the economy was weak, no matter what the figures suggested, and Americans knew it.

"Once past the election, the price controls began to break down. Inflation jumped to 8.7 percent in 1973 and 12.3 percent in 1974," wrote Bruce Bartlett, who was a domestic policy adviser to President Ronald Reagan. "Another recession began in November 1973 and didn't end until March 1975. These poor economic conditions created fertile soil for Nixon's enemies when the Watergate scandal broke. Had the economy been stronger, Nixon might have survived it, just as a strong economy unquestionably helped former President Bill Clinton weather the Monica Lewinski scandal."[1]

The rising inflation and unemployment of the 1970s was known as "stagflation," standing for low growth and inflation, a description for something that many Americans had thought impossible. The modern-day version of the American dream, as interpreted by FDR, LBJ, and Richard Nixon, was to use the government to deliver or at least promise a modicum of prosperity. This objective was not so different from the political goals and pretensions of American politicians of the past. But the consequences in terms of inflation and public debt were far greater now that the dollar was the world's reserve currency. The basic role of the dollar remained the same, though the rules set by the industrial nations after World War II were no longer being followed.

When Gerald Ford took over the presidency from Nixon on August 4, 1974, inflation was in double digits. Americans barely knew of Ford, a veteran congressman from Michigan who had worked his way up the Republican ladder to the position of leader. Ford is the only president who succeeded to the office without being elected. He was made vice president under the terms of the Twenty-Sixth Amendment after the resignation of Spiro Agnew. The Constitution provides for the replacement of the vice president when the office is made vacant by resignation or death. Ford then succeeded President Nixon as the 38th president of the United States.

Ford entered into a political and economic maelstrom, yet at the end of the process he remained one of the most likable presidents in recent memory. "Nixonomics, the highly variable sequence of economic doctrines that left the country simultaneously overstimulated and underemployed gave way now to President Ford's economics of candor and moral uplift," wrote Leonard Silk in September 1974. "The time has clearly come to take a look at what is right with the economy."[2]

Few people of that time held Silk's optimistic view. Ford tried to hold the line on federal spending, but without success. Had he been able to prevent Congress from passing any additional legislation during his short tenure in office, the budget deficits would have climbed because of the actions of past governments. The rising red ink in Washington ultimately resulted in his defeat at the hands of former Georgia Governor Jimmy Carter. Ford wanted to cut taxes to stimulate the economy, but with estimates of a $35 billion deficit for the following year floating around the White House at the end of 1974, Ford did not have a lot of easy options. By March 1975 the same aides inside the White House were projecting a deficit of $100 billion in the next fiscal year.

In congressional testimony during that period, Treasury Secretary William Simon told Congress that the deficit for 1976 would come in around $80 billion, inclusive of a planned tax cut. A young assistant director of the Office of Management and Budget named Paul O'Neill, who would later serve briefly as Treasury secretary under George W. Bush, worried that many of the "temporary" emergency spending initiatives being put in place by Congress in that year would become permanent. He was right. The Ford administration, while asking for modest tax increases, attempted to convince Congress to slow fiscal stimulus efforts. Senator Edmund Muskie (D-ME) dismissed the idea that Congress would ever pass anything like a budget with a $100 billion deficit. Muskie knew that the Ford administration was right that the public was getting angry at these growing budget shortfalls. And he worried that "adding up our spending proposals we may find that we have already used up our options."

In the summer of 1974, the Federal debt was $475 billion, up a little over a $100 billion from the start of the Nixon administration in 1969. The budget deficit actually fell in that momentous year to just $7 billion, but then climbed from that point to $70 billion by the November 1976 election. In that year the government was going to spend about $390 billion and take in $291 billion, including a cut in taxes of about $25 billion. The chart in Figure 8.1 illustrates the federal government's spending in that period.

Ford had the bad luck of serving in the worst economy since the Great Depression. The mid-1970s were difficult years in the United States, with the oil shock and double-digit unemployment breaking the renewed sense of confidence that had prevailed in the post–World War II era. The fact that the fiscal deficits were rising at a time of slack economic demand made the public uneasy. Members of both political parties tacitly accepted the need for deficits, yet the public at large was still largely unaware of the change in the basic assumptions of government that had occurred during the Cold War. The boom years of the 1950s and 1960s gave way to the years of crisis and uncertainty of the 1970s. Competition from Japan and Europe put the United States into an unaccustomed position of being a debtor. This caused many Americans to question whether the country was headed in the right direction. The added factor of runaway inflation, which had only been a problem in wartime, complicated the political equation in a new and unfamiliar way.

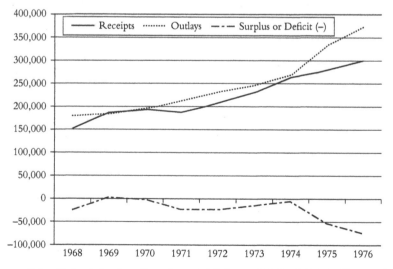

Figure 8.1   Federal Outlays, Receipts, and Balance (1968–1976) (Millions of $).
SOURCE: Office of Management and Budget/The White House.

President Nixon appointed Alan Greenspan as head of the Council of Economic Advisers in the summer of 1974, one of Nixon's last significant official acts prior to his resignation. Greenspan made it clear to the Nixon staff that any resort to further price controls would trigger his departure as well. "He stayed on after Nixon resigned in 1974 and Gerald Ford assumed the presidency," Bob Woodward wrote of Nixon during this period. "Greenspan thought that Ford was the bravest and most correct when he didn't meddle with free markets during the recession of 1974–1975, even at the risk of his own political future."[3]

Ford attempted to address inflation with a program of voluntary restraints on consumption that were meant to reduce demand. Millions of red and white buttons with the word "WIN"—for "Whip Inflation Now"—were produced in 1974 at the instructions of President Ford. The campaign was pretty much a failure, but it made clear that Ford was in political trouble. Americans could not help but sympathize with a man who had made a political career of being affable and honest. "Jerry Ford was the most decent man I ever encountered in public life," Greenspan said in a statement after Ford's death in 2006. "It was a great privilege to work for him. I will miss him."[4]

The New Uncertainty

In his excellent 1995 book on federal budget deficits, *Deficit Government: Taxing and Spending in Modern America*, Iwan Morgan divides the post–World War II periods into four segments:[5]

- The Age of Equilibrium, 1945–1960
- The Age of Activism, 1961–1968
- The Age of Uncertainty, 1969–1980
- The Age of Excess, 1981–1988

The years of Richard Nixon, Gerald Ford, and Jimmy Carter were uncertain times and the first hint that the economic "equilibrium" under the domination of the United States in the global marketplace was ending. None of the policymakers in Washington in either party had any idea what to do—except spend more money. The result was inflation rather than jobs and prosperity. Neither Ford nor Carter held any broad vision about finance or economics. Both men were mere accidents of history—yet again—in the proud and oftentimes peculiar story of the American presidency.

Ford was a loyal friend and had stood with Nixon through the Watergate scandal. He eventually granted Nixon a presidential pardon in September 1974, sealing Ford's fate in the 1976 election. In that sense, the choice of Ford to deal with the aftermath of his resignation made sense for Nixon personally and was not a bad choice for the country.

The tragedy of the Watergate scandal was that Nixon had intended to appoint John Connally as vice president when it became clear that Spiro Agnew was in serious trouble. Agnew resigned as Nixon's vice president in 1973 after authorities learned he had taken bribes and kickbacks—including free groceries—going all the way back to his years as Maryland governor in Annapolis. The Watergate scandal would make the Connally scenario impossible, however, and left the presidency in the hands of a man with no clear agenda when it came to the economy. How different the American political and economic map might look today had Watergate never happened and John Connally succeeded Nixon to the presidency in 1976.

Instead, America got Jerry Ford and Nelson Rockefeller, the latter who had to wait four months until the Democratic Congress deigned to ratify his appointment as vice president. Ford was a moderate Republican who, like Ronald Reagan, had a disarming personal charm and facility with people. He had a remarkable capacity to remember people and names, and used this talent to great advantage in his dealings with Congress. Even during partisan battles, Ford maintained a level of personal decorum with all members of Congress that was and is still remarkable today. A former football star for the University of Michigan, Ford understood the chemistry of teamwork and was always most proud of his athletic achievements.[6]

When he assumed office in the middle of a midterm election in 1974, Ford was dealing with a Democratic and decidedly activist Congress that was emboldened by Watergate and the popular opposition to the Vietnam War. If the years under Richard Nixon had been the imperial presidency, then the brief tenure of Ford was decidedly non-royal and very down to earth. But still Ford was an appointed president.

The addition of New York Governor Rockefeller made the Ford administration one of the most superficially conservative since Dwight Eisenhower, but without Ike's strong sensibilities about avoiding budget deficits and unnecessary defense spending. Writer Richard Reeves commented on Ford's selection of Rockefeller in *New York Magazine* in 1974:

Still, Rockefeller *was* the best choice for Ford, for the Republican party, for the country. It's a cruel world, the one the rest of us have to share with the Rockefellers, and Nelson Rockefeller is a very capable man. Capable of anything, perhaps, but whatever else he is, Rocky is a heavyweight. Despite all the talk about lists and sealed envelopes, I don't think the president seriously considered anyone but Rockefeller.[7]

During the years of the Vietnam War, many Democrats migrated to the antiwar, antidefense spending camp, but John Kennedy had run against the Republicans in 1960 based on the Eisenhower administration being soft on defense and being unprepared to resist a Russian missile onslaught. Eisenhower, for his part, dismissed the idea that war with Moscow was imminent and resisted bipartisan Congressional efforts to increase defense spending.

By 1974, the center of the Democratic Party was moving to the left—so much so that southern conservatives would soon start to change parties. Ford and Rockefeller were only as far to the right of center as the mainstream Democrats were to the left—and the differences between the parties and among Americans were widening. Whereas in 1963 a Democratic Congress was pushing a tax cut to help stimulate the economy, by 1974 the political equation was again changing between the two major parties. The Democrats focused on spending, and the Republicans resisted these initiatives from the position of a seemingly permanent minority.

In 1974, concerns about the rate of increase of expenditures for the Great Society programs and the cost of the Vietnam War forced Congress to pass the Congressional Budget and Impoundment Control Act.

"The Act attempted to strengthen the congressional role in the making of the budget by beefing up and centralizing its budgetary capacity," noted a 1993 report by the *Joint Committee on the Organization of Congress.* "The House and Senate Budget Committees were created to coordinate the congressional consideration of the budget, and the Congressional Budget Office was established as a source of nonpartisan analysis and information relating to the budget and the economy. Indeed, perhaps the most important early role for CBO was to provide an alternate economic forecast to the Congress." Alice Rivlin was the first director, and she established a reputation for being neutral and objective.

It is generally agreed that the 1974 act, while an important step forward in terms of organizing the annual budget process for Congress, was not a success in reining in deficit spending. Nor did it help the government do a better job of anticipating the revenues and expenditures of the Treasury, either immediately or in the longer term. The problem in 1974 was that nobody knew what was happening with the U.S. economy, oil prices, or the trends shaping the rest of the global marketplace. The Arab oil embargo largely fooled most contemporary forecasters when it came to anticipating the decrease in growth and increase in unemployment. The negative impact on employment of the increase in energy prices was felt for years thereafter and forced Americans to begin adjusting the way energy is consumed.

Forecasters from the Conference Board to Herbert Stein believed that unemployment would peak at or below 6 percent, but instead it came in over 7 percent. Nominal growth came in at 6.5 percent in 1974, but with visible inflation at 12 percent. The stunning actual result for the year was a real, inflation-adjusted *decline* in U.S. output of 5 percent.[8] As much as any year since the end of World War II, 1974 began to shake the public's belief in the ability of Washington to engineer positive economic outcomes.

Paul Volcker recalled that when his predecessor Arthur Burns gave his valedictory speech in 1979, the Fed chairman confessed to feeling helpless in the face of the powerful forces that seemed to be moving markets and prices. Volcker also repeated his view that leaving the gold standard in 1971 did not necessarily drive the subsequent inflation in the United States over the next decade. Soaring energy costs did.[9]

The problem faced by Presidents Ford and Carter was that the rate of inflation was higher than the growth in the money supply, forcing the central bank into a quandary. If the Fed expanded the growth of

money to help boost demand, which had been the priority throughout the postwar period, then inflation would also increase. Real money
balances, which is the money stock divided by the inflation rate, had
been falling during 1973 and 1974. This development was shocking to
many observers. Unlike in past periods, when the growth in the money
supply had slowed while prices remained stable, in the 1974–1975
period the opposite situation occurred. Economist saw a stable money
supply, lower velocity of money in terms of the turnover visible in the
economy, but with double-digit inflation. The quadrupling of energy
prices in that period had rendered one-fourth of the U.S. economy
obsolete and uneconomic to operate.

For the Democrats, the answer was more spending and more
debt, while President Ford made inflation his chief point of attack.
The Republican platform in 1976 identified inflation as the number
one obstacle in dealing with unemployment, but the Democrats, led
by such luminaries as Edmund Muskie, ridiculed Ford's 1977 budget
and its $50 billion estimated deficit as inadequate. "The party's 1976
platform decreed full employment as the answer to the nation's problems," wrote Iwan Morgan, "on the grounds that the consequent boost
to consumption would lead in turn to business expansion, higher profits, and greater investment."[10] But with low or no growth and already
accommodative monetary policy, the notion of even more federal
spending to spur the economy was not welcome at the Fed or among
the Republicans in Congress.

By 1976, a real battle was brewing in the Republican Party
between the Ford loyalists, who felt that the incumbent president
deserved a chance to lead the party in an election, and the supporters
of California Governor Ronald Reagan, who wanted to make growth,
big government, and the Democrats the issues in the election. Reagan
was not shy about taking on the Democrats and the Great Society in
1976. Echoing Donald Trump half a century later, he attacked "the
erosion of freedom that has taken place under Democratic rule in this
country, the invasion of private rights, the controls and restrictions on
the vitality of the great free economy that we enjoy."

Nelson Rockefeller was dumped from the ticket and Ford was
looking for something or someone to energize his candidacy. Jimmy
Carter was running away with the Democratic nomination and selected

Walter Mondale as running mate. A former actor and TV commentator, Reagan was written off early on, but came back late in the game with a series of primary wins that turned the Republican nomination process into a real contest. Though Jerry Ford was the favorite in the race, Reagan clearly was the man of the future by the time the GOP delegates met in Kansas City. Ford actually considered Reagan as a running mate in 1976, but eventually picked Senator Bob Dole (R-KS)—fortunately for Reagan.

When Ford and Reagan did meet at the Republican convention, the incumbent president never asked Reagan to consider the vice presidency. Ford only asked if the former governor of California had "any ideas," Reagan told Richard Whalen after his one-on-one private meeting with Ford. What some Republicans called the dream ticket of Ford and Reagan was not to be.

At the end of the 1976 Republican convention, however, when President Ford, Senator Dole, and Nelson Rockefeller stood with their spouses on the platform amid the applause from the delegates, Ford beckoned to Reagan to come down to the platform and join them. The delegates gave Reagan a standing ovation as he delivered a crisp, six-minute statement of values, a call to action that asked what they were willing to do today to protect freedom that would be remembered at the tricentennial celebration of America's independence:

> This is our challenge; and this is why here in this hall tonight, better than we have ever done before, we have got to quit talking to each other and about each other and go out and communicate to the world that we may be fewer in numbers than we have ever been, but we carry the message they are waiting for.[11]

By inviting his adversary to share the platform with him that night in 1976 Jerry Ford fulfilled his stewardship as the unelected president and gave the future of the Republican Party to Ronald Reagan, whatever happened in the election that year.

Even as the Ford-Dole ticket went down to a close defeat in 1976, with 297 electoral votes for Carter to 241 for Ford, the seeds of the Reagan revolution were already starting to grow. By the midterm election in 1978, the insurgent conservatives in the Republican Party were beginning to effectively target liberal Democrats in southern states with the basic Reagan message of tax cuts and smaller government. Only weeks before the election in 1978, a New York congressman named Jack Kemp and Senator William Roth of Delaware won initial approval of a 25 percent across-the-board cut in tax rates, but the measure was dropped from the legislation. It took four more years and the election of Ronald Reagan for the Kemp-Roth tax cut to be adopted by Congress.

Full Employment

The political reaction by the Democratic majority in Congress to the election of Jimmy Carter and Senator Fritz Mondale (D-MN) was to greatly increase federal spending. Among even mainstream Democrats, the answer to the years of uncertainty and unemployment during the 1970s was to embed in the law the right to full employment. Senator Hubert Humphrey (D-MN) and Rep. Augustus "Gus" Hawkins (D-CA) sponsored legislation in the early 1970s to do just that, and in 1978 the Congress passed the Humphrey-Hawkins Full Employment and Balanced Growth Act.

The law established a maximum unemployment rate of 4 percent and did not mandate a government-paid job for anyone who sought one. It was described as the "the last gasp of the New Deal generation's struggle for economic justice," according to Randy Shannon, a Progressive from Pennsylvania. "Its passage occurred at the beginning of the neo-liberal campaign to reverse the New Deal policies."

In chronological terms this description is correct, but it also reflects the economic reality that was already visible in the slowdown of growth over the previous decade. After decades of recovery and expansion, the stagflation of the 1970s took a great deal of the momentum out of the popular confidence in the economy. By 1978, the impact of high oil prices and the novel idea of an external constraint on American economic power created an enormous feeling of anxiety and uncertainty.

The fact that the Democrats, at this late date, were still fiddling around with the leftovers from the New Deal is a pretty tough indictment of the lack of creative thinking among liberals of that era. When one pushes aside the rhetoric of the past half century and more since

World War II, the United States had not contributed anything more original to thinking on economic management than more and more public debt. Even the sacred "four freedoms" articulated by FDR depend upon the continuance of government in order to fulfill these promises. In his state of the union address in 1941, FDR articulated "four freedoms," including:

- Freedom of speech and expression
- Freedom of religion
- Freedom from want
- Freedom from fear

These "four freedoms" were Roosevelt's way of reducing the Bill of Rights down to four simple objectives: mandates, and entitlements rather than rights and responsibilities. These "freedoms" were the promise of the corporate state and, indeed, FDR was offering these freedoms to all of the people of the world. Reflecting FDR's support for Wilson's vision of a unified community of nations, the four freedoms were the New Deal adapted for a global audience.

The first two freedoms are taken from the Bill of Rights and are, in traditional American terms, rights that existed even before the federal government. The last two "freedoms," however, can be interpreted as statements of dependency on government. Freedom from want and freedom from fear are essentially the promises of safety made by the paternalistic welfare state, the very unfortunate situation in which hundreds of millions of people live today in Europe and Asia. The United Nations has adopted these goals as well.

While the American model of political economy saw free people free to live and worship as they choose, the model of the four freedoms is decidedly positivist and European in perspective. Isaiah Berlin, in his classic essay "Two Concepts of Liberty,"[12] defines negative liberty as being able to fulfill our projects without coercion, a direct analog to the American ethic of freedom or the American dream being "life, liberty and the pursuit of happiness."

Positive liberty, on the other hand, is defined by Berlin as the freedom afforded by a deterministic and oppressive regime much like the political configurations visible today in America, Europe, and Asia.

"Since liberalism has spent half a century trying to define itself against totalitarian ideologies," Stanley Hoffman observed in 1998, "these distinctions have been found very useful."[13]

The Soviets defined freedom as the right to support the Party and build Socialism. The four freedoms of FDR conjure up George Orwell's book *1984*, where Big Brother is ever present and the reduction of vocabulary is used to limit dangerous thinking. Of course, most people forget or never knew that Orwell was hardly a conservative. In fact, he fought for the Republicans in Spain and agitated for an English socialist revolution during World War II. After the war, Orwell was a staunch supporter of the Labor Party, but always from a position that was keenly aware of the primacy of individual freedom.

"The sin of nearly all left-wingers from 1933 onwards," Orwell wrote in his essay on Arthur Koestler, "is that they have wanted to be anti-Fascist without being anti-totalitarian." In a similar vein, most members of the political left in the European Union and United States do not appreciate or care that in order to "guarantee" anything resembling the four freedoms, you must embrace a totalitarian and fascist political and economic model.

A majority of Congress rejected the vision of Senator Humphrey and Rep. Hawkins, two men who for decades made a career out of representing the wants and needs of their respective communities in Washington. But despite their optimism about the government's ability to provide a living for any and all citizens, Humphrey-Hawkins was an attempt to legislate an economic reality that could not really be achieved. It took several years for Congress to agree on the final legislation. The legislation started in 1974 as a firm and hard proposal to make the U.S. government the employer of last resort, but was altered and amended to compromise with Republicans and also President Carter.

Jimmy Carter was far more conservative and less "worldly" than the neo-Keynesian socialists who populated the Democratic Party at the end of the 1970s. The South was insulated from many social and intellectual currents prevalent in the more Europe-focused northern states until well into the twentieth century—among them the novel idea of deficit spending. Every state except Vermont has some form of balanced budget amendment, which is one reason why states often must cut services dramatically in the event of a recession. State governors understood the idea of fiscal constraints, but these rules did not apply in Washington after the administration of Richard Nixon in the 1970s.

As South Carolina Senator Ernest Hollings, who also served as governor of that state (1959–1963), recalled: "Every governor, every mayor, has got to pay next year's bill. He's figuring out how to keep his credit rating and pay the bills. But when we get to Washington, well, oh no, you become an economist and you've got a percent of the GNP."[14]

Hollings confirmed what politicians and economic analysts were only starting to suspect in the late 1970s, namely that the efficacy of fiscal stimulus is just about zero. Other means such as capital investment must be sought to encourage growth and employment, especially in real, inflation-adjusted terms. But such subjects were just starting to be discussed in a serious way as Jimmy Carter began his term as president.

When it came to spending, Jimmy Carter was far more cautious than the average for the Democratic Party in 1976. With a background as a child of the Depression and a U.S. naval officer, he viewed federal deficits as a serious problem. But the harsh political realities of unemployment and gasoline rationing made politicians in both parties on Capitol Hill desperate. At first, he attempted to work with the Democrats in Congress, but within only a matter of months President Carter was making public his view that increased deficits would only further stoke the fires of inflation. His close friend and budget director, Bert Lance, was a fiscal conservative and powerful influence on Carter.

Carter in his memoirs chastises himself for "the obvious inconsistency in my policy" of trying to craft further economic stimulus and also fight inflation at the same time. But Carter's worldview was decidedly nineteenth century in character. He would eventually resolve that "my major economic battle would be against inflation, and I would stay on the side of fiscal prudence, restricted budgets, and lower deficits."[15]

Carter was caught between the Democratic Congress and even the liberals within his own administration on the one hand, and the Federal Reserve Board under Arthur Burns on the other. The Fed had early on drawn a line regarding the trade-off between further fiscal stimulus financed with debt and higher inflation—and higher interest rates. In November 1976, Burns said that he wanted to "cooperate" with the

Carter administration, but apparently his statement was interpreted as a warning to Carter that the Fed was prepared for a confrontation. In so many words what Burns was saying was if the new administration sought to promote a faster recovery by applying greater fiscal stimulus, then the Fed would raise interest rates further. From easy money in 1976, the Fed's tighter posture in 1977 generated tensions within the business and political communities. The tepid economic growth achieved in the previous few years began to ebb. Liberals called for increased spending and assailed the Fed for excessive concern over inflation. Yet Carter stuck to his message of fiscal restraint and a focus on wasteful government spending—an almost Republican message from a former governor of Georgia.

With inflation continuing to rise after 1976, however, the debate over fiscal policy quickly began to change. After decades of Soviet-style ideology from the Democrats and their fellow travelers in the academic community in support of deficit spending, doubts were heard. Henry Hazlitt published his classic book *The Failure of the "New Economics": An Analysis of the Keynesian Fallacies* in 1959, but it would take another 20 years for the reality of the link between deficit spending and inflation to become understood at a popular level.

Richard Ebeling described Hazlitt's view of Keynes 35 years after the book's publication:

> The central flaw in Keynes's thinking, Hazlitt insisted, was his unwillingness to acknowledge that the high unemployment in Great Britain in the 1920s and the United States in the 1930s was caused by government intervention, including the empowering of labor unions, that made many prices and wages virtually "rigid." Political and special-interest power prevented markets from competitively re-establishing a balance between supply and demand for various goods. Hence, the market was trapped in wage and price distortions that destroyed employment and production opportunities, resulting in the Great Depression.[16]

America was and is a very young country. Until the 1970s, the United States only experienced sustained inflation during wars. There was and is even today a very limited appreciation for the link between how Washington manages or fails to manage its budget and the dollar, and the result in terms of employment and economic opportunities generally. Ford and Carter both were forced to confront this reality during a period of international upheaval and two oil price shocks. Half a century later in the 2020s, Fed chairman Jerome Powell almost never mentioned fiscal deficits and certainly never threatened to raise interest rates in response to higher federal deficits.

The low point for inflation in the United States during the 1970s would, ironically, be 1976, a fact that did not help the Ford-Dole presidential ticket at the polls. In the years that followed, the rate of price increase trended higher until inflation reached double digits in 1979. Ultimately, inflation continued to race ahead and unemployment was growing, leaving President Carter facing worsening inflation despite interest rates close to 20 percent. The reality of stagflation, when growth is below the level of inflation, brought a chilling new economic reality that destroyed the Carter presidency.

Balanced Budgets and Inflation

In 1970 when Richard Nixon appointed Arthur Burns to succeed William McChesney Martin as head of the Federal Reserve Board, Burns was taking the reins from the Fed chairman most synonymous with sound money and monetary stability. After almost two decades at his post, Martin had enhanced the standing and independence of the central bank, albeit during a time of stable economic growth and relatively low inflation. Only during the Vietnam War did Martin and the Fed Board give in to pressure from President Lyndon Johnson and the White House to keep interest rate policy easy in 1967, a decision that caused inflation to rise to over 6 percent by 1969 as Richard Nixon returned to Washington as president.

The 1950s–1960s in the United States were years of torrid growth but still restrained financial markets, both domestically and internationally. The relationships between the public and private sectors, particularly between public and private debt, also remained very stable for most of Martin's era with no crises to disturb the appearance of Washington's intelligent design. But the artificial stability of the first two decades of the post–World War II period was about to end.

When Burns took over at the Fed in January 1970, there were already significant changes occurring in the U.S. economy and global markets as well. But the fierce velocity and daunting breadth of the changes that occurred during the term of Arthur Burns at the Fed almost seemed the antithesis of the previous two decades under Chairman Martin. Burns had to deal with the end of the post–World War II economic order and the related changes to the U.S. economy. These changes were often not welcome to many Americans and certainly not to the major political parties.

During Chairman Burns's term at the Fed, the amount of debt in the United States, both public and private, began to grow dramatically relative to the size of the real economy. Even though the amount of federal debt had grown during the Cold War, the U.S. economy grew much faster. Initially the burden of servicing the federal debt actually shrank in real terms because of the high rates of economic growth. But in the 1970s the total of all nonfinancial debt, public and private, began to rise relative to the U.S. economy and continue to rise in the decades that followed. Just as World War I was an important inflection point for America in its relationship with the rest of the world, the 1970s marked a point of departure for Americans in terms of how we understood and attempted to manage the changes in the economy.

When the term of Chairman Burns ended in March 1978, President Carter appointed G. William Miller, a successful businessman and investment banker who had served as the chairman and CEO of Textron. Like Carter, Miller was a fiscal conservative but also a bit of a neo-Keynesian in terms of his belief in demand-side stimulus. Miller believed that the United States could grow its way out of a recession while also addressing inflationary pressures. Miller, in fact, was adopting the very "inconsistency" to which President Carter later discussed in his memoirs, namely thinking you can fight inflation and grow public deficits at the same time.

"Unlike his predecessor, Arthur F. Burns, who had tried to limit economic expansion in the belief that inflation was the far greater peril, Mr. Miller insisted that inflation and unemployment could be fought simultaneously," the *New York Times* observed.[17]

Within months it was clear to many that Carter made a mistake in putting Miller at the Fed. There was even a line of thinking at the time that perhaps President Carter had inadvertently picked the wrong Miller by mistake. The global markets were not impressed by Miller and the dollar dropped sharply during that fateful year. Roger Kubarych, who worked for Paul Volcker at the Federal Reserve Bank of New York, recalled the period in late 1978:

> The Carter people were beginning to realize that Miller was not fitting in. He was a CEO, not an academic collegial guy. It's like the TV ad with the firemen. The chief says: You want lower interest rates? Hands go up. Done in 15 minutes. So, the Carter people approached the late Bob Roosa, of Brown Brothers Harriman and Treasury under-secretary under his pal Jack Kennedy. He said "You really should go to Volcker," then president of the Fed of New York. The White House had thought about Volcker before, but decided to go in a different direction. Miller was one of the few business CEOs who really took all of this corporate governance and responsibility seriously. He did a very fine job as secretary of the Treasury. Miller was not a bad guy, he just did not belong at the Federal Reserve Board.[18]

By July 1979, rumors of a cabinet reshuffling were flying around Washington and eventually appeared on the front page of the major newspapers. The dollar slumped in global markets. Gold passed $300 per ounce for the first time, illustrating just how far out of line was the official $35 per ounce gold price set by FDR half a century earlier. When Nixon ended convertibility for other nations only eight years earlier, it was a sobering indicator of the pace of inflation. The irony was that Carter's stand on reducing federal deficits in order to fight inflation may have been entirely erroneous. Because of Carter's efforts to reduce federal spending, and surpluses from the Social Security and other trust fund payments by Baby Boomers, the public deficit in 1979 was a mere $2.4 billion on an economy of almost $3 trillion in gross domestic product.

Whereas the inflation of the 1960s was arguably due to the fiscal policies of Presidents Kennedy and Johnson, the inflation of the 1970s was seemingly a function of external shocks from oil prices. Though few contemporary observers understood the problem at the time, the proper response to the external oil price shocks might have been a combination of fiscal stimulus, tax cuts, and oil conservation measures. Even had Carter actually achieved a balanced budget, it might not have significantly reduced inflation during his term in office.[19]

Carter's orthodox views on inflation and debt made it impossible for him to propose the obvious solution to the weak economy, namely tax cuts. He was focused on balancing the budget, reflecting an almost Jacksonian obsession with purging the evil of debt and deficits from public life. Jefferson said famously that "the principle of spending money to be paid by posterity, under the name of funding, is but swindling futurity on a large scale." Jefferson continued: "It is incumbent on every generation to pay its own debts as it goes. A principle which if acted on would save one-half the wars of the world."[20]

By taking a conservative line on deficits, Carter gave the issue of economic recovery to the Republicans in 1980. Carter had adopted the fiscal conventions of Gerald Ford without questioning the basic assumption that fiscal deficits were linked with inflation and in so doing associated federal deficits with rising prices. Deficits and debt clearly had inflationary consequences, but the United States and many other industrial nations were responding to the external shock of oil prices with monetary tightening and fiscal restraint. Everyone was essentially following the old economic playbook from the nineteenth century. With little or no consideration, Carter effectively did what conservatives had failed to do for decades and discredited the world of Keynesian mechanics.

At the end of July 1979, President Carter nominated Paul Volcker to become chairman of the Federal Reserve Board. Such was the gravity of the situation in the financial markets that in just three weeks Volcker was confirmed by the Senate and sworn in on August 6, 1979. Kubarych recalled that on the day of his appointment by Jimmy Carter, Volcker kept a foreign visitor waiting for him for hours at the Federal Reserve Bank of New York. "Finally, Volcker comes back apologizing profusely and meets with the visitor for a few minutes," he recalled. "Then he came out and said to me: 'Thanks for doing the meeting. We've got some work to do in the morning.'"[21]

Shock Treatment

Volcker, a self-described "Brooklyn Democrat" was born in Cape May, New Jersey, and grew up in Teaneck. He was appointed by President Jimmy Carter at the end of his term in 1979 and inherited by Ronald Reagan, a converted Democrat and former labor leader and California governor. Reagan understood the connection between money and inflation. During a talk to the Prosperity Caucus in Washington in the early 1990s, syndicated columnist Robert Novak revealed that Reagan's favorite economist was Fredric Bastiat, a nineteenth-century French economic philosopher and author of *The Law*. It was the fact of inflation that led to the defeat of both Gerald Ford and Jimmy Carter, and created groundwork for the election of Ronald Reagan. Years later, in 2024, inflation was the leading issue with voters still.

By October 1979, the United States was facing its most serious economic crisis in generations. Inflation was rising and the dollar was falling. Saudi Arabia's finance minister said that his country was considering new cutbacks in oil production because of the eroding value of the dollar. Wall Street welcomed the appointment of Volcker, but the honeymoon would be especially short for the economist from New Jersey.

As Volcker moved from New York to Washington, statisticians at the Labor Department confirmed that over the previous six months the United States experienced the steepest spiral of inflation in nearly 30 years. But more disturbing were the comments seen more and more in the media, and in the political discourse, of a nation living on accumulated wealth. Concerns about foreign trade and offshore competition were growing especially sharp in Washington during this period and increased in the 1980s.

In 1979 with the Iranian hostage crisis as a backdrop, Americans worried about losing their economic edge in the world; that the situation might be too far gone to correct. The income of the average American household doubled during the 1970s, but real purchasing power had risen only one-tenth that amount. For many Americans, the reality of the two-income household was already becoming the norm.

The inflation of the dollar was widely seen as the villain in the global economic bust, which had seen a series of mini crises erupt after the Nixon decision to close the gold window at the Treasury in 1971.

The dollar slid dramatically over the decade prior to the appointment of Paul Volcker as Fed chairman. He had been deeply involved in managing the process, first at Treasury and then at the Fed of New York. Bringing Volcker to Washington to lead the Federal Reserve Board was the perfect move at the right time, but one that occurred only because of the intervention of a number of people, including Tony Solomon. Kubarych relates how Tony Solomon, who served in the Treasury as undersecretary for Monetary Affairs, was tasked by Mike Blumenthal and Charlie Schultz to convince Jimmy Carter to appoint Paul Volcker to the Fed. Solomon succeeded and took over for Volker as president of the Fed of New York, a fitting culmination to a remarkable career of public service.[22]

The Volcker appointment also allowed President Carter to replace Treasury Secretary Michael Blumenthal with Fed Chairman Miller, an arrangement far better fit the latter's talents, including leading the federal bailout for Chrysler. Miller was better suited for politics than the world of the central bank, which in those days was seen as being "above politics." This meant, of course, that the Fed was entirely political, but in a nonconfrontational way. Miller was far too honest and direct for the world of central banking. Volcker, on the other hand, was an economist from New Jersey who worked for Chase Bank. He knew how to behave in public—namely, to be vague, noncommittal, and inoffensive in a political sense.

Volcker needed all of his considerable credibility to convince the world that the United States had not lost its way. Since 1971, foreign nations had accumulated tens of billions of dollars in offshore deposits—Eurodollars—and they were anxious about further erosion in value. As already noted, under Fed chairmen like Burns and even Martin, the Fed had responded to political pressure to lean in favor or ease at critical periods. Volcker had to do the opposite and govern monetary policy by a clearer set of rules in order to help the U.S. Treasury and the dollar regain the respect of the world markets.

In late August 1979 the Federal Open Market Committee raised the federal funds rate from 10 to 10.5 percent, a record. The Fed continued to keep policy tight, driving the U.S. economy into recession in 1980. The Fed paused in its efforts to throttle inflation prior to the 1980 election, but when prices started to again rise—by now inflation was 1 percent per month and mounting—Volcker and the Federal Open Market Committee took U.S. interest rates up until the federal funds rate almost reached 20 percent. Yet in addition to fighting inflation, the actions of the Volcker FOMC marked the effective nationalization of the private market for overnight bank reserves, aka "federal funds."

Noted economist Frederic Mishkin made an important comment about Paul Volcker in the *Financial Times*. The former Fed chairman and president of the Federal Reserve Bank of New York was both a good economist and an astute politician. Truth is, every Fed chief since Governor Charles Hamlin needed to consider political trends and events, but especially since the end of World War II. Mishkin wrote:

> Paul Volcker is considered to be a GOAT (greatest of all time) central banker because he and the US Federal Reserve broke the back of inflation in the early 1980s. However, less talked about is the serious policy mistake that the Volcker Fed made in 1980. The result was a more prolonged period of high inflation that required even tighter monetary policy, which then resulted in the most severe US recession since the second world war up to that time.[23]

The fateful mistake Mishkin describes was the decision by the FOMC to reduce interest rates in May 1980 even though inflation was still rising, a situation not unlike 2001. "This action was taken despite the fact that inflation reached a peak of 14.7 per cent in April," Mishkin recalls nearly half a century later. Fact is, Paul Volcker blinked and Ronald Reagan won the White House in 1980.

By dropping interest rates, the FOMC seemingly helped President Jimmy Carter, a fellow Democrat, but in fact the election of Ronald Reagan was already done by midyear. Inflation-related interest rate hikes over the previous year and the Iran hostage crisis sealed Carter's fate. Volcker knew that Reagan was the likely winner, in large part because of the political advice he received from Richard Whalen, who had been a confidant and speech writer for Reagan going back to 1976 and for candidate Richard Nixon before that. He also remained a loyal friend and political confidant to Volcker and his successor, Alan Greenspan.

Independent or not, Volcker and the Federal Open Market Committee in 1980–1981 put the U.S. economy into a wrenching recession that would see unemployment soar into double digits.

In heartland manufacturing states such as Indiana, Michigan, and Illinois, joblessness reached into the teens. The U.S. economy was mired in recession for three years. This illustrated the level of adjustment that the two oil price increases of the decade, 1973 and 1979, required literally to squeeze the inflation out of the system.

In a 1982 memo from Paul Krugman and Larry Summers, who were both then working in the Reagan White House, to William Poole and Martin Feldstein, the two economists predicted that inflation would again begin to accelerate because the reduction in inflation engineered by the Fed was only temporary. But Summers, Krugman, and many other liberal economists were wrong about inflation. The relentless rate squeeze by the Fed and a lot of positively coincidental and mostly external trends broke the inflation in the United States, but did not really instill fiscal sobriety. Paul Volcker broke the momentum of inflation and also took sufficient demand out of the economy to give the crucial impression of price stability for a short time.

The underlying rate of inflation, represented by internal prices in the United States and the value of the dollar, remained high enough so that, in real terms, the cost of energy and particularly oil dropped for almost two decades afterward until the end of the twentieth century. While the dollar rallied sharply from 1980–1985 because of the towering interest rate regime imposed by Volcker and the resulting rebound in U.S. standing with global investors, the overall trend continued to be one of steady inflation of the dollar and decreased purchasing power for U.S. consumers—except in the case of energy.

Because of the dollar's gradual decline after 1985, in real terms adjusted for inflation, energy prices would not reach the levels of the early 1980s again until well into the 2000s. This decrease in the real cost of energy prices added a deflationary bias to this entire period of U.S. economic history, a rare positive factor at a time of secular consumer and producer price inflation. The period after the mid-2000s, when real energy prices in the United States began to rise rapidly, may be an important reason for the sluggish economic growth and job market seen after the 2008 Financial Crisis. Like the 1990s after the S&L crisis, the 2010s were a period of deflation, sluggish growth, and flat home prices.

The other important change that came about after Volcker took over at the Fed was the growing imbalance in the U.S. financial relationship with the world. Until the 1980s, the United States supplied as much capital to the world as foreigners invested in the United States, a remarkable balance that is the subject of a great deal of scholarly research. Benjamin Friedman asked the key question coming out of this period in a March 1987 paper for the National Bureau of Economic Research, namely "Does the continuing large federal government deficit impair the economy's ability to undertake productive capital formation?"[24]

None of the political or financial observers in that period imagined that the imbalances between public and private debt, and between what the United States owes the world and American investments abroad, would grow so great. "The sharply changed relationship since 1980 between total debt and income in the U.S. economy—and, within the total, between the respective debt of the economy's public and private sectors—presents such a puzzle, and correspondingly provides an opportunity," Friedman concluded.[25]

"In 1981 Ronald Reagan entered the White House and immediately implemented a dramatic new economic policy agenda for the country that was dubbed 'Reaganomics,'" noted the CATO Institute in 1996. "Reaganomics consisted of four key elements to reverse the high-inflation, slow-growth economic record of the 1970s: (1) a restrictive monetary policy designed to stabilize the value of the dollar and end runaway inflation; (2) a 25-percent across-the-board tax cut enacted (The Economic Recovery Tax Act of 1981) designed to spur savings, investment, work, and economic efficiency; (3) a promise to balance the budget through domestic spending restraint; and (4) an agenda to roll back government regulation."[26]

Unfortunately, other than cutting taxes, the Reagan administration did not accomplish any of these other objectives. The monetary policy followed by Paul Volcker was only restrictive until the visible rate of inflation was knocked back down to low single digits. Unlike Burns, Volcker did not threaten higher interest rates if deficits were not curtailed. Through the 1980s, the Fed continued to tolerate underlying inflation that was arguably mid-single digits per year.

Ronald Reagan's promise to deregulate was fulfilled, but in the case of the financial services reforms created the circumstances for future financial crises. Subsequent calamities were made inevitable because presidents before and after Reagan found it impossible to rein in federal spending. No amount of tax cuts will save American consumers from the ravages of inflation if Congress refuses to eliminate fiscal deficits. Even Ronald Reagan, with all of his rhetoric about scaling back the size of government, was reluctant to pay the political price of confronting Congress over spending. The bubble economy was simply passed to the next generation.

The Crisis Managers

Such was the parlous state of the U.S. economy in 1981 that, for the next several years, the Reagan White House wisely and expediently let Paul Volcker take the heat on inflation, while advancing the conservative political agenda on Capitol Hill. The Kemp-Roth tax cuts, deregulation of the oil industry, and a tough attitude toward organized labor were all part of breaking the embedded public psychology of inflation. Paul Samuelson explained that many observers of the post–World War II period missed the importance of inflation in the American narrative, a story that was fundamental to the career of Paul Volcker and many other financial professionals with whom he worked:

We have arrived at the end of a roughly half-century economic cycle dominated by inflation, for good and ill. Its rise and fall constitute one of the great upheavals of our time, though one largely forgotten and misunderstood. From 1960 to 1979, annual U.S. inflation increased from a negligible 1.4 percent to 13.3 percent. By 2001 it had receded to 1.6 percent, almost exactly what it had been in 1960. For this entire period, inflation's climb and collapse exerted a dominant influence over the economy's successes and failures. It also shaped, either directly or indirectly, how Americans felt about themselves and their society; how they voted and the nature of their politics; how businesses operated and treated their workers; and how the American economy was connected with the rest of the world.[27]

One of the symptoms of the increasing inflation visible in the United States in the 1970s and 1980s was volatility in the financial markets and, with this volatility, greater opportunities for market crises and the failure of large banks. Because his institutional experience extended back to the Nixon administration, Volcker understood the monetary and fiscal roots of the crises that erupted during his tenure at the Federal Reserve.

Volcker formed one of his most important relationships during those years with a young economist then at the Fed of New York named E. Gerald Corrigan. Corrigan would become Volcker's heir as crisis manager at the Fed and would succeed Tony Solomon as president of the Federal Reserve Bank of New York. Even after his departure from the New York Fed post in 1993, Corrigan continued to exert great influence over the U.S. financial markets.[28]

Corrigan's unlikely rise to the top of the American financial system started in 1976. As corporate secretary of the Federal Reserve Bank of New York, he was befriended by then-President Volcker. Other senior officers of the New York Reserve Bank still were a bit standoffish toward Volcker because of policy disagreements, most notably, America's abandonment of gold for international settlements at Camp David in August 1971. Corrigan extended himself for the new Fed president and quickly became his trusted adviser and friend. Corrigan was the man doing the difficult jobs behind the scenes as Volcker attracted the public limelight as the supreme crisis manager.

When Volcker was appointed Fed chairman late in the summer of 1979, Corrigan followed him to Washington as the chairman's aide and hands-on situation manager, although he remained on the New York Fed's payroll and was subsequently promoted. He was quickly thrown into the crisis-control fray when Bunker and Herbert Hunt's attempt to manipulate the silver market blew up into a $1.3 billion disaster in 1980, an amusing but also deadly serious repeat of the machinations of Fisk and Gould in silver following the Civil War.

In May of that year, Chairman Volcker was compelled to make a statement about Fed awareness of the Hunt brothers' attempts to corner the silver markets, including an admission that the Fed had asked banks to cease "speculative lending." Volcker also confirmed that the Federal Open Market Committee had taken into account concern about speculation in silver and other commodities as part of its decision to tighten monetary policy further.

Volcker's statement regarding the Hunt brothers was one of the first and most direct admissions by the Fed of an active interest in overseeing the financial markets, even though Volcker went out of his way to disavow any particular interest in these modern-day successors to Jay Gould. The collapse of the Hunt brothers' commodity pool affected other legitimate enterprises and lenders. It was a side effect of the boom in metals that the inflation spawned and was one of the first modern "systemic" crises in the post–World War II era. The far larger crisis involving the collapse of the nonbank market for savings and loans (S&Ls), which were the primary providers of residential home mortgages, loomed ahead.

Corrigan managed the unwinding of silver positions, providing the moral suasion necessary to convince reluctant banks to furnish credit to brokers who made bad loans to the Hunts to finance their silver purchases. In 1982, when Drysdale Government Securities collapsed, Corrigan was again the man on the scene to do the cleanup job, working to avoid the worst effects of one of the ugliest financial debacles in the postwar period. Drysdale was the first in a series of shocks during the 1980s that included the Mexican debt default (1982) and the collapse of Penn Square Bank (1982) and Continental Illinois (1984).

Drysdale threatened not only the workings of the government securities market, but the stability of a major money center bank, Chase Manhattan, which saw its stock plummet when rumors began to fly as to the magnitude of losses. Volcker was a former employee of Chase and had spent a good bit of his early career as a research officer at the bank. Corrigan fashioned a combination of Fed loans of cash and collateral, and other expedients, to make the crisis slowly disappear, even as Volcker again received public credit for meeting the crisis.[29]

While Volcker and Corrigan were managing a series of problems affecting the solvency of large U.S. commercial banks, the S&L crisis was starting to fester in the United States. Congress and the states had liberalized the powers of S&Ls for years, allowing them to take risks and ignore solvency issues until the problem grew to huge proportions. Starting with the State of Texas in the 1960s, state and federal regulators opened the door for thrifts to get into new business activities.

Because S&Ls tended to pay floating rates on deposits, but issued fixed-rate mortgages, fluctuation in interest rates quickly caused many thrifts to be insolvent. The history of the response to the S&L crisis by Congress and the states is a tale of stupidity and corruption. The homebuilders and realtors prevented any substantive response until the thrift industry had already collapsed.

"From 1982 to 1985, thrift industry assets grew 56 percent, more than twice the 24 percent rate observed at banks," notes the official history of the period prepared by the Federal Reserve Board. "This growth was fueled by an influx of deposits as zombie thrifts began paying higher and higher rates to attract funds. These zombies were engaging in a 'go for broke' strategy of investing in riskier and riskier projects, hoping they would pay off in higher returns. If these returns didn't materialize, then it was taxpayers who would ultimately foot the bill, since the zombies were already insolvent and the FSLIC's resources were insufficient to cover losses."[30]

What is fascinating about this period and the lack of public statements by Volcker regarding the S&L crisis during the 1980s is that almost a decade earlier in 1973, the Federal Reserve Board under Arthur Burns had created a plan for the Fed to lend to the Federal Home Loan Banks to support the S&Ls. In 2024, researcher Nathan Tankus, as a result of a series of freedom of information requests, unearthed a secret plan by the Fed to lend to another government agency to support the thrift industry. The August 16, 1973, FOMC minutes, which were still secret at the time, lay out the genesis of the plan:

> In a memorandum of August 6, 1973, the Committee on Federal Reserve Credit recommended approval in principle of a proposed plan to provide emergency credit assistance to the savings and loan industry, with a view toward further discussion and negotiation of the plan with officials of the federal Home Loan Bank Board. Additional documentation included a memorandum of August 15, 1973, from the Division of Research and Statistics, which discussed the current circumstances and future prospects of the savings and loan industry.[31]

Fortunately, the Fed was not called upon to rescue the S&L industry in the 1970s, but that period was also the last time that the U.S. government liquidated insolvent institutions on such a large scale. The next major deflation event following the S&L crisis would be involuntary and occur in 2008, when the U.S. government was compelled to intervene.

In the 1980s, federal officials used liquidation to fix the problem of insolvent S&L after a decade of obfuscation and policy errors. Both state and federal agencies ignored and exacerbated the S&L problem at the behest of the housing industry. The Garn-St Germain Depository Institutions Act of 1982 allowed insolvent banks to stay open and greatly increased the scope of the S&L crisis. The eventual resolution of the S&Ls and the high interest rates of the early 1980s caused enormous economic damage, leading to a lost decade for the economy in the 1990s. But this was the last time the Fed deliberately used high interest rates and deflation to manage the economy.

"What is crystal clear to me is that the regulators did not have to fail all thrifts and create financial and economic chaos, destroying billions in value for shareholders, bondholders, borrowers and owners of real estate," noted Gary Jacobs, former CEO of the Laredo National Bank. "Regulation Q limiting deposit rates only worked as long as commercial banks and S&L's (with a few small credit unions) captured all deposits. The hidden villain back then and perhaps today was allowing Merrill Lynch et al. to form money market mutual funds. Those totally unregulated funds were unfair competition for banks and thrifts and still are even though many holding companies which own them are now regulated."

The FOMC minutes that contain the discussion of the S&L bailout and many other topics remained secret for two more decades, until the author reported their existence in the *Wires Washington* news service in October 1993. I wrote in the *Chrisitian Science Monitor* about the congressional hearing with Fed chairman Alan Greenspan to discuss the minutes. Greenspan was almost forced to reveal the existence of the minutes under oath:

> After last week's congressional hearing, Greenspan was overheard telling one Fed bank official that, had Roth been allowed to ask another question (he was cut off by a punctual Gonzalez gavel), he might have been compelled to reveal the existence of an entire set of secret written transcripts. Dr. [Anna] Schwartz likewise says, "Gonzalez cut Roth off from asking a further question." Whatever Greenspan's reasons for not addressing the issue, the ambiguous result of the Oct. 19 hearing makes it clear that neither Congress nor Gonzalez will soon drop the subject of Fed reform. Roth was shaken by the hearing and warned that the Fed soon must accept the political and practical necessity of releasing more information about the FOMC's deliberations.[32]

Of course, money market mutual funds were encouraged in the 1970s and 1980s as alternative buyers of Treasury debt, this as banks slowly reduced holdings. After the demise of the S&Ls, for example, banks would gradually get into the residential and commercial real estate markets in a much bigger way. Paul Volcker primarily blamed the losses on the expansion of S&Ls into investments outside their traditional role of mortgage lending and serving family financial needs. He also blamed the inability of inexperienced S&L examiners to monitor the new businesses.

"The whole atmosphere during those years was not conducive to strict supervision and strict regulation," Volcker said in congressional testimony in 1990. "It was not in the air, so to speak," Volcker was particularly critical of S&Ls' direct investment in commercial real estate projects as part-owners rather than as lenders. "That is the single area that's bankrupted more savings and loans than any other area," he said. "I thought that was a bad idea to start with."[33]

After the substantial losses accumulated during the S&L debacle, the Fed and other agencies abandon deflation as a policy tool. Because the central bank needed to intervene in larger and larger liquidity crises as the century progressed, benevolence rather than liquidation was clearly the superior policy in terms of economic benefit. When the choice is a 1930s- or 1980s-style liquidation and deflation, or a bailout where asset prices eventually rise, the latter course usually results in higher nominal wealth and less political angst, but also higher inflation.

Latin Debt Crisis

In 1982 Mexico devalued its currency and defaulted on $80 billion in public sector debt, an event that almost caused the world financial system to collapse. The growth in foreign lending by U.S. banks, which was virtually nonexistent only a decade before, made these institutions vulnerable in a new and unexpected way. "Under the leadership of Fed Chairman Paul Volcker," Federal Reserve researcher Walker Todd wrote in 1999, "a temporizing strategy was devised under which the bank lent new funds to the debtors, who then repaid the same amounts to lenders to cover interest payments falling due. Principal owed was never reduced (in fact, it usually increased)."[34]

The cost of fixing the 1982 financial crisis was tiny, a couple billion dollars, petty cash compared to the looming default on tens of billions of dollars' worth of hard currency obligations of private Mexican companies and banks. When Mexico defaulted in August 1982, the Reagan administration immediately extended $2 billion in order to refloat the country's battered economy and insure a smooth political transition for the new government of Miguel de la Madrid. Another $2 billion came from the Commodity Credit Corp. and U.S. commitments to buy Mexican oil for the Strategic Petroleum Reserve.[35]

Through the mid-1980s, foreign banks refused to make new money loans to Mexico and even pressed demands for repayment, although the IMF and other multilateral agencies continued to lend. A steady flow of new money loans from multilateral agencies, as well as direct investment flows, kept Mexico's single-party state afloat for the balance of the decade. By 1987, net flows of capital from Mexico back to its creditors in the industrial world were actually positive as it slowly repaid its hard currency debts. Unlike the United States, Mexico could not merely print money to fund its external obligations.

In 1987, Brazil declared a moratorium on foreign loans and Washington feared that Mexico would follow. The larger banks, led by Citibank and J.P. Morgan, reluctantly began to reserve against the eventual write-off of loans to Mexico and other debtor nations. Fed chairman Volcker, a fierce opponent of debt forgiveness and making the banks write down bad loans, left his post later that year. In the July 1988 elections, Carlos Salinas de Gortari was defeated by Cuauhtemoc Cardenas Solorzano. Through electoral fraud and another $1 billion "bridge loan" from Washington to the de la Madrid government in August of that year, Salinas prevented Cardenas, the son of nationalist hero General Lazaro Cardenas, from taking office and fulfilling his vow to repudiate Mexico's then $105 billion foreign debt.

The impact of the debt crisis on American consumers was, very simply, more inflation. The Fed had to maintain an easy monetary stance through much of the period in order to help the largest banks regain profitability. It is interesting to note that none of the large U.S. banks issued new equity between 1982 and 1989, when Treasury Secretary Nicholas Brady put aside the policy of temporizing on Latin debt embraced by Chairman Volcker and Treasury Secretary James Baker.

In February 1989, food riots in Venezuela caused nervous bankers and their servants in Washington to capitulate on the issue of repayment and extend new loans to Latin debtor nations. The abortive debt reduction plan named for then-Secretary Brady was completed roughly a year later. It afforded Mexico little real debt relief, but did provide the first substantial new money in almost seven years. The Brady Plan was followed with a proposal for a "free trade" agreement between the two nations by former CIA director and then-President George Bush.

More than 15 years before, when he worked in the oil business in Texas and Mexico, Bush built a close personal relationship with Salinas and his father, Raul Salinas Lozano, the power behind the state oil monopoly, Pemex. George Bush may have been a CIA asset through all of his years in the oil business, his congressional campaigns, ambassadorships, and eventually as director of central intelligence. His attention to Mexico and close political contacts in that country, and Bush's eventual pursuit of a free trade agreement with Mexico, make a great deal of geopolitical sense in terms of helping to stabilize that country.[36]

The Latin debt crisis illustrates how Paul Volcker and many of his contemporaries laid the intellectual and practical foundations for policies such as "too big to fail" for the largest banks. The tendency to bail out large financial institutions and eventually whole countries in the 2008–2010 period dates from the late 1970s and the tenure of Paul Volcker at the Fed and James Baker at Treasury.

Whether one speaks of the World War I and World War II loans to Europe or the bad foreign debts of the largest banks, Washington's tendency in the twentieth century was to paper over the problem with more debt and inflation. Yet in terms of real economic growth, bailing out the debtor nations made a lot more sense than embracing a debt deflation a la the 1930s. When we asked Chairman Volcker why he and FDIC chairman William Issac (1981–1985) allowed the big banks to inflate their leverage after the Latin debt crisis, Volcker said over lunch in 2017: "They were broke. What else was I going to do?"

Lunch at 30 Rock (2017).

In the 1980s, many analysts in that era, including the author, despaired of Mexico, Brazil, and other "developing" nations such as Russia ending their dependence on foreign borrowing and loans from the IMF. In fact, all of the debtor nations have repaid their debts or at least ended their reliance on new borrowing. Mexico, Brazil, China, and many of the emerging industrial nations today have no need to issue foreign debt or use the facilities of the IMF. Indeed, it is the older, more developed and less dynamic economies, such as the European Union and the United States, where debt and inflation are now chronic problems.

By 1982 Volcker, who was by then supervising the unfolding Penn Square situation, pushed for Corrigan to take the open presidency of the Federal Reserve Bank of Minneapolis. Corrigan was president of the Minneapolis Fed for four-and-a-half years before moving to the New York Fed. Volcker later admitted wanting to keep the badly insolvent Penn Square open for fear of wider market effects, but the Federal Deposit Insurance Corporation closed down the now infamous Oklahoma bank, paying out only insured deposits. Comptroller of the Currency C.T. Conover told Congress in December 1982 that Penn Square Bank's failure was inevitable, but the fact remains that Volcker, Corrigan, and other Fed officials would have rescued the badly insolvent lender instead of imposing huge losses on half a dozen other banks.

In his 2010 book *Senseless Panic: How Washington Failed America*, former FDIC chairman William Isaac confirms that Mike Bradfield, then general counsel of the Fed who later held the same position at the FDIC, demanded that the FDIC bail out Penn Square Bank, no doubt with the knowledge of Volcker and other Fed governors. Isaac responded that he would but only if the central bank shared the cost, but the Fed under Volcker balked.[37]

As Volcker promoted Corrigan's career within the Fed, he took extraordinary measures to prevent the nomination or appointment of respected conservative economists and free market advocates like W. Lee Hoskins and Jerry L. Jordan to head other Reserve Banks. Both Hoskins and later Jordan were appointed to the Cleveland Reserve Bank's presidency after Volcker's departure as chairman in 1987.

Hoskins was the antithesis of Volcker, an unrepentant exponent of conservative, sound money theory. Hoskins advocated making zero

inflation a national goal. Volcker and the more liberal economists who
had controlled the Fed for decades were against excessive inflation, but
were more than happy to tolerate inflation of 2 percent if it got the
country close to full employment and kept the big banks afloat.

Hoskins left the Cleveland Fed in 1992 to become president of the
Huntington Bank. He and other free market exponents believed that
ill-managed banks should be allowed to fail, but by the last decade of
the twentieth century bailouts became the norm. He also believed that
federal deposit insurance hurts rather than protects the financial system
by allowing banks to take excessive risks that are, in effect, subsidized
by the American taxpayer. This free market perspective represented
mainstream American economic thought before the New Deal, but is
at odds with the established view of avoiding "systemic risk." Public
subsidies for large banks and other, more generalized types of government intervention in the "private" marketplace are easier to sell politically. While it is clear that bailing out insolvent banks allows society
to avoid 1930s-style deflation, it also makes consumers pay the tab in
terms of inflation and a loss of purchasing power.

Reagan Reappoints Volcker

In his book *Maestro*,[38] Bob Woodward describes how the Reagan inner
circle believed that they needed to keep Volcker at the Fed in 1983
because of the turmoil in the financial markets caused over the previous
year. But the actual reappointment of Volcker was a more problematic
process than is generally appreciated. Volcker had a one-year head start
on Reagan in terms of managing the economy. Nobody in the Reagan
group was paying attention to the politics of the Fed and what the consequences of a V-shaped recession and likely 10 percent unemployment
would be for a new president.

Some members of the Reagan kitchen cabinet periodically met
with Volcker to better understand the timing of the inevitable recession and what the impact of the high anti-inflation interest rates
would be on the economy. The general assumption in Washington in
early 1980 was that Carter would be reelected and that Reagan was,
in Volcker's words, "just an actor." But Volcker was soon made aware of

the fact that Reagan was going to win the election and that the Fed chairman needed to start managing the expectations of the new political leadership.[39]

Volcker was crucially important to Reagan because he had been on the job fighting the key economic battle of the time. With the encouragement of several people around Reagan, Volcker decided to call Reagan long before the election decision and Reagan at once returned the call. The connection enabled Reagan to better appreciate how dire the economic situation really was and to direct his cabinet to act accordingly. Former adviser Richard Whalen recalls the inside politics of the appointment and reappointment of Paul Volcker:

The Volcker appointment was a source of great unhappiness to all kinds of people, including Donald T. Regan, who had been my first client as a consultant many years earlier when he was CEO at Merrill Lynch. Walter Guzzardi and I had both been assisting managing editors at *Fortune*. He became the inside guy at Merrill and I was the outside guy at Merrill. We guided Don Regan, who was an arrogant SOB, ex-Marine colonel, through the minefield of creating the SIPC and burying some of the bodies from various Wall Street firm failures that occurred during the 1970s. He called me one day in the 1980s and said "Dick, I've been asked to become Secretary of the Treasury." And I said, "I know, you're on the list." So he said, "What should I do?" And I said, "If you want it, take it, but for Christ's sake stay away from Nancy Reagan and do not mess around with the Fed. Those are my terms if you want my help." So soon after Volcker had done this brilliant job of saving the economy and making it possible for Reagan to have a successful first term, [Don] Regan tried to impose Beryl Sprinkel as the new [Fed] chairman in 1983. I had to go around Don Regan to Senator Paul Laxalt (R-NV) to carry my recommendation to the President. It was just Laxalt, Reagan and the wives at Camp David. I urged Reagan to call Paul Volcker that Sunday night and ask him to accept reappointment as Chairman of the Fed. I gave Paul Laxalt the telephone number and the call occurred and Volcker stayed on at the Fed until 1987.

Laxalt called me that Monday and thanked me for taking the initiative on this. And I thought is this the way these things always happen in Washington?[40]

Roger Kubarych noted that the group of Reagan conservatives who were in control of the administration by 1987 intended to get the Democrat Volcker next time. "And then we had 17 years of the good and the bad Alan Greenspan, Kubarych observed."

Volcker moved to protect his bureaucratic flank in 1984 when he nominated Gerald Corrigan as a replacement for President Anthony Solomon at the New York Fed, an event that required almost as much lobbying as was later needed to block the appointment of Lee Hoskins to head the St. Louis Fed in 1986. The cigar-chomping Fed chairman, who was known for his affable nature, got on a plane to hold a rare Sunday meeting of the St. Louis Fed's board. He reportedly pounded the table and warned of being outnumbered by Reagan-era free market zealots if the board picked Hoskins. Volcker, it seems, may have still expected to be renominated by Reagan. The St. Louis Fed's board caved in to Volcker's demands and Hoskins was passed over, although he would be appointed president of the Cleveland Fed in late 1987, after Volcker's departure.

Corrigan's impending selection as Fed of New York president late in 1984 caused several conservative line officers and research officials to flee the New York Reserve Bank. Roger Kubarych, who was one of the deputy heads of research in New York and a widely respected economist on Wall Street, actually resigned the day Corrigan's appointment was formally announced, fulfilling an earlier vow not to serve under "Volcker's apprentice" that symbolized earlier internal Fed disputes. Yet Corrigan's personal comportment forced him to leave the Fed a decade later.

Following the 1985 Plaza Accord when the United States and other industrial nations attempted to depreciate the dollar, Corrigan often appeared in the domestic and foreign exchange trading rooms of the Fed of New York at all hours of the day or night during periods of market intervention.

In the mid-1980s, the Fed of New York was open 24–7 because of the cash- and check-clearing operations. The young traders and analysts in the foreign exchange and domestic trading function often worked round the clock. During the market intervention to push down the value of the dollar in 1985 known as the Plaza Accord, Corrigan was on deck in the foreign exchange trading room at the crack of dawn to check market rates—after breakfast, of course, with the bank supervision team at Jim Brady's across Maiden Lane.

The Neverending Crisis

From the first day he took over as head of the New York Fed in 1985, Jerry Corrigan's chief priority was "managing" the Latin debt crisis and in particular its devastating effects on the New York money center banks. Even in the late 1980s, most scholars and government officials admitted that loans to countries like Brazil, Argentina, and Mexico would have to be written off, as J.P. Morgan did in 1989.

Reflecting Volcker's view, Corrigan continued to push for new money lending to indebted countries in an effort to bolster the fiction that loans made earlier could still be carried at 100 cents on the dollar. Even by the early 1990s, when some analysts declared the debt crisis to be over, the secondary market bid prices for Latin debt ranged from 65 cents for Mexico to 45 cents for Argentina and 25 cents for Brazil.

"Anything approaching a 'forced' write-down of even a part of the debt—no matter how well dressed up—seems to me to run the risks of inevitably and fatally crushing the prospects for fresh money financing that is so central to growth prospects of the troubled [less developed countries (LDCs)] and to the ultimate restoration of their credit standing," Corrigan wrote in the New York Fed *Quarterly Review* in 1988. "A debt strategy that cannot hold out the hope of renewed debtor access to market sources of external finance is no strategy at all."

And of course, in the case of Mexico, debt relief was followed by massive new lending and short-term investment, albeit to finance a growing external trade imbalance that was strikingly similar to the import surge that preceded the 1982 debt default. Likewise bankrupt Russia, which was supposedly cut off from new Western credit, received almost $18 billion in new Western loans in 1992–1993—loans guaranteed by the taxpayers of the G7 countries and facilitated by Corrigan.

But in addition to pressing for new loans to LDC countries, Corrigan worked hard at home to manage the debt crisis, bending accounting rules, delaying and even intervening in the closing of bank examinations. He resisted regulatory initiatives such as market value accounting for banks' investment securities portfolios, and initially promoting the growth of the interbank loans, swaps, and other designer "derivative" assets traded in the growing, unregulated over-the-counter (OTC) market.

Corrigan played a leading role in affording regulatory forbearance to a number of large banks with fatal levels of exposure to heavily indebted countries in Latin America. But no member of the New York Clearing House received more special treatment than Citibank. Former Citicorp Chairman Walter Wriston said that sovereign nations don't go bankrupt, in response to questions about his bank's extensive financial risk exposure because of lending in Latin America.

Wriston's supreme confidence in the eventual outcome of the Latin debt crisis was credible because he and other financiers knew that senior Fed officials like Volcker and Corrigan did their best to blunt the impact of bad loans on the balance sheets and income statements of major banking institutions. In 1989, for example, as Wriston's successor, John Reed, was in Buenos Aires negotiating a debt-for-equity swap to reduce his bank's credit exposure in Argentina, Corrigan pressured bank examiners in New York to keep open the bank's examination for 14 months.

Corrigan's decision probably was made in order to avoid charges against earnings by forcing the bank to post higher reserves against its illiquid Third World loan portfolio, an action that would later be taken anyway as Argentina slid further down the slope of inflation and political chaos. Corrigan and other officials pushed the Baker plan after 1985, essentially a new money-lending program, to help buy time for commercial banks—as Volcker, the Chase alumnus, did before him.

Paul Volcker was never a hawk on bank regulation and especially with respect to the largest banks. His concern with the well-being of the financial system essentially made the argument for bailing out particular banks. The good of the many, to borrow the old phrase, was more important than market discipline for the one failed institution, even if that meant embracing public subsidies and moral hazard writ large.

In a very real sense, Paul Volcker and not Gerry Corrigan was the father of "too big to fail" with respect to the largest U.S. banks.

Apart from fighting inflation, Volcker's legacy to the Fed was to support and enhance the tendency of the central bank to bail out large banks. But the actions of both Volcker and Corrigan were driven by the growing reliance of America on inflation and debt. When the Salomon Brothers market-rigging scandal erupted in the spring and summer of 1991, Corrigan was again the key man on the scene to manage fallout from the debacle. Following 1986, when regulatory responsibility for the government bond market had been explicitly given to the SEC, the Fed, at Corrigan's instruction, largely curtailed its surveillance of the market for Treasury debt, particularly the informal "when-issued" market in Treasury paper before each auction.

When the Salomon scandal broke open, it was apparent that the hands-on "management" of markets publicly championed by Volcker and Corrigan failed to prevent one of the great financial scandals of the century.

"Neither in Washington nor in New York did the Fed seem aware that the dangers of failure to supervise this market had grown exponentially in 1991," Martin Mayer wrote on the Salomon debacle in his 1993 book *Nightmare on Wall Street.* "Like the Federal Home Loan Bank Board in its pursuit of making the S&Ls look solvent in 1981–1982, the Fed had adopted tunnel-vision policies to save the nation's banks. And just as excessive kindness to S&Ls in the early 1980s had drawn to the trough people who should not have been in the thrift business, Fed monetary policies in the early 1990s created a carnival in the government bond business."[41]

The Salomon crisis was not the only problem facing the central bank. During December 1990, the Federal Reserve Bank of New York, working in concert with several private institutions, fashioned a rescue package for Chase Manhattan Bank when markets refused to lend money to the troubled giant. The failure of Penn Square Bank and the FDIC's subsequent repudiation of loan participations sold to Chase and other banks, eventually caused six other banks to fail or be sold.

Chase officials vociferously denied that any bailout occurred, yet the pattern of discount window loans during the period and off-the-record statements by officials at the Fed and several private banks suggest very strongly that Corrigan's personal intervention prevented the failure of Chase and a major banking crisis at the end of 1990, the peak of the S&L crisis. A decade later in 2000, a crippled Chase Manhattan merged with JPMorgan & Co, to form today's JPMorgan Chase.

Rational observers agree that the collapse of a major banking institution is not a desirable outcome, but the larger, more fundamental issue is whether any private bank, large or small, should not be subject to the discipline of the marketplace. The same issues of moral hazard and "too big to fail" that were the subject of fierce debate and reform legislation in Congress during 2009 and 2010 have their roots in crises two decades earlier. In the case of Salomon Brothers, Citibank, Chase, and numerous other smaller institutions that received government help in the 1990s, the question remains: Should these banks have been allowed to fail? Corrigan, like Volcker before him, answered with a resounding "no." and thereby failed the public trust, yet probably made the correct call in economic terms.

Volatility Returns

In June 1987, Volcker's term was ending, much as it began, with the dollar weak and the world uncertain about the direction of the U.S. economy. Chairman Volcker was able to get inflation under control, but he was not able to steady the dollar or work out a better means for the management of global markets. "He was brought in to help stabilize the dollar," Lee Hoskins told the *Los Angeles Times* in 1987. "Now after record highs and a steep decline, he was leaving the dollar in the same condition in which he found it—weak. But he saw that the major issue was inflation, and he turned it around."[42]

During the Volcker era, budget deficits had been a fact of life, but the outstanding debt of the U.S. Treasury, inclusive of the obligations of the trust funds, was growing very rapidly, as shown in Figure 8.2.

The other factor that contributed to the growth in the total debt of the U.S. Treasury was the relatively high level of interest rates during much of this period, some years well into double digits. Since the United States never actually ran a surplus during the 1980s period to retire any debt and averaged deficits over $100 billion, the growth in

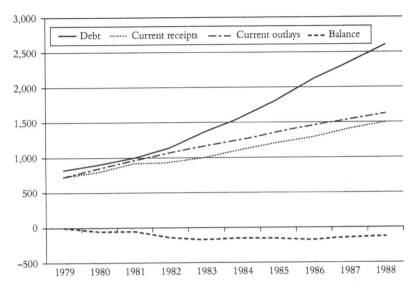

Figure 8.2 Federal Debt, Outlays, Receipts, and Balance (1979–1988) (Millions of $).
Source: Office of Management and Budget/The White House.

the overall corpus of public and internal debt was greatly accelerated by these years of high interest rates.

The inflationary years of the 1980s and the growing public debt also produced greater and greater official sensitivity to the public perception of inflation. "Government statistics are about the last place one should look to find inflation, as they are designed to not show much," investment manager David Einhorn argued in a May 26, 2010, *New York Times* commentary. "Over the last 35 years the government has changed the way it calculates inflation several times. According to the Web site Shadow Government Statistics, using the pre-1980 method, the Consumer Price Index would be over 9 percent, compared with about 2 percent in the official statistics today."[43]

One of the chief methods used by government officials to mask the true rate of inflation is to use estimates of the "core rate" of inflation, excluding volatile items such as food and energy. The net effect of the inflation of the late 1970s and really all of the 1980s was to increase official sensitivity to public disclosure of the rate of inflation, but this did not diminish either the accumulation of public debt in the United

States nor the true rate of price increases. As already noted, underlying inflation kept real energy prices in the United States below 1973 levels for almost three decades. Real economic growth averaged 3.2 percent during the Reagan years versus 2.8 percent during the Ford-Carter years and 2.1 percent during the Bush-Clinton years, but this assumes that the inflation figures used to adjust the government's nominal economic growth statistics are accurate.

A major development during the 1990s under Fed chairman Alan Greenspan (1987–2006) was the renaissance of nonbank finance and the rise of private sector debt to levels not seen since the Great Depression. The nonbank dealer community that had grown from the 1950s traded Treasury debt, which was a relatively easy progression from banking. Yet as a practical matter, secured finance using private debt outside of banks did not exist until the 1980s and then only in limited amounts. Few banks made residential mortgage loans, and access to credit for most individuals was very limited. Although the use of consumer debt had grown from the 1950s onward, borrowing by consumers and private businesses was very restrained through the early 1970s, when the first private sales of consumer loans occurred.

From 1947–1974, for example, total loans to consumers by all U.S. banks tracked by the Federal Reserve Board grew from $4 billion to just under $100 billion. Given the low level of private debt at the end of the war and the sharp increase in GDP over three decades, the growth rate is not that remarkable. Only with the development of a secondary market for mortgage loans in the 1970s, when Ginnie Mae sold the first mortgage securities to investors, did we see the rise of nonbank finance. Credit slowly became more widely available for consumers. Technology and the marketplace combined to create not only enormous opportunity but also some enormous risk when it came to the ebb and flow of interest rates and employment.

From the mid-1970s onward, the amount of outstanding consumer debt doubled to over $200 billion in a decade and doubled again between 1984 and 1994. More telling than the expansion of consumer debt was the overall increase in the use of credit in the U.S. economy. The growth of nonbank finance in the 1990s was largely responsible for the economic growth during the presidency of Bill Clinton (1993–2001). From the appointment of Alan Greenspan to the Fed by Ronald

Reagan in 1987 through to the 2008 Financial Crisis, the total credit outstanding in the United States as a percentage of gross domestic product rose from a little over 100 percent to over 230 percent—more than the pre-Depression peak in 1929.[44]

The key drivers of this debt increase were the boom in the housing market and the related explosion in mortgage and consumer debt, much of it supported by nonbank finance companies. But significantly, the debt was growing much faster than the economy, suggesting that future inflation would be higher.

"When I boil what I've learned all down to one factor that drives the markets and an economy, it is debt," Jerry Flum, CEO of Credit Risk Monitor observed in 2010. "Every dollar of debt moves a future purchase into the present. As credit grows, we spend more of it now. So, if you look at debt versus gross domestic product, we are already at record levels. We can also look at incremental debt versus incremental gross domestic product. In the 1950s, it took $1.50 in debt to produce an incremental $1 of GDP. Today it takes more than $6 in debt to produce $1 of GDP, so we are approaching the end of the game."[45]

Boom to Subprime Crisis

Senator Elizabeth Warren (D-MA) and her daughter Amelia Warren Tyagi, in their 2004 book *The Two-Income Trap*,[46] describe part of the changes in the behavior of Americans that began in the late 1980s and accelerated into the 1990s. The use of two-family incomes to make better homes with better, safer schools and amenities possible for more Americans also reflected the relentless impact of rising prices. The national obsession with home ownership began after World War II with the GI Bill, but by the late 1970s began to evolve into a replacement for the defense industry as an engine of growth—and debt. Just as consumers were taught to want the better job or car or washing machine—and to buy these things using credit—the better home in the better neighborhood with the better school district became the new definition of the American dream.

The progression to a "housing industrial complex" in wartime parlance matured in the 1980s, when the first major real estate bubble was revealed and burst by the Fed's tight interest rate policies. The combination of direct government support for affordable housing, active advocacy, and credit availability by government-sponsored enterprises such as Fannie Mae and Freddie Mac and intense lobbying and marketing efforts by the real estate, home building, banking, and mortgage lending industries, created the subprime bust of 2007–2010. That bust had its roots in the savings and loan crisis of the late 1980s and the first modern real estate recession.

During a 2008 interview at the height of the Financial Crisis, Robert Feinberg, a veteran Washington staffer and observer of Capitol Hill, put the growth of the real estate lobby in historical context:

> When I first started working on the Hill in the early 1970s, there was a conservative Democrat on the Education and Labor Committee named Edith Green who coined the term "Education and Labor Industrial Complex" to describe what she was up against regarding education policy. Starting about that same time there developed what I call the Homebuilder-Realtor-Mortgage Banker Industrial Complex. They created a mythology that said you could not have enough housing and it was up to the government to make sure that happened. The home builders had a quota of 2 million units that had to be constructed every year. They really didn't care what happened to those homes once they were built . . . You must remember that 95 percent of what you hear in Washington is pure propaganda and is not even believed by the people propagating it, so don't feel bad about hurt feelings. People in Washington say that nobody saw this crisis coming, but there were clear signs of trouble for anyone looking.[47]

The respected housing finance expert Josh Rosner told the story of the real estate bust in a September 2007 interview:

> The reasons for the boom in housing in the past decade come from the structural changes in the housing industry over a decade before. Most of these changes were a result of the 1980s recession. We came out of the economic slump and a lot of the industry players had lost their shirts in the S&L crisis.

We saw Fannie Mae insolvent on a mark-to-market basis in 1986 and that was largely because of the portfolio of fore-closed real estate. We saw housing in 1993 and 1994 with home ownership rates stagnant, in fact exactly where they were at the beginning of the 1980s. Home ownership rates have consistently ranged in this country between 62 and 64 percent during the post-WWII period, and yet affordability had actually locked people out.[48]

Rosner argues that the "problem" of home affordability in the 1990s saw the creation of the largest public-private partnership to date, started as the National Partners in Home Ownership in 1994. Supported by the realtors, the home builders, Fannie, Freddie, the mortgage bankers, and HUD (Department of Housing and Urban Development), the push to make housing more affordable was a massive effort, with more than 1,500 public and private participants. The goal of the push for "affordable housing" was to reach all-time high home ownership levels by 2000. And the stated strategy proposal to reach that goal, says Rosner, was: "to increase creative financing methods for mortgage origination."[49]

The precursors of the problems in the housing industry in the 2000s are pretty obvious, namely government subsidies for home ownership. What is not so apparent is the underlying impact of inflation on home ownership. Rising prices and falling purchasing power forced many American households to use the power of two wage earners to make the purchase of a home a reality. And many Americans from the mid-1990s through 2007 saw the value of their homes rise dramatically, in some cases more than 100 percent over that period, leading to many people thinking of homes as speculative investments instead of a place to live.

Yet the most striking fact coming out of the housing crisis was that despite the 25–35 percent drop in value for many homes in major metropolitan areas in the 2010s, the cost of replacing many existing homes was *above the current market value*—grim testament to the reality of the underlying rate of inflation. By 2024, even two incomes still left many American families just surviving, with no savings and no financial security, tough indictments of the American dream.

The Greenspan Legacy

Contemporary observers writing accounts of the collapse of the sub-prime debt bubble in 2008 may blame Alan Greenspan and the members of the Federal Open Market Committee for the crisis. The more accurate observation seems to be that the Greenspan-dominated Fed presided over a two-decade long increase in financial leverage in the U.S. economy as interest rates slowly fell. This occurred under successive Republican presidents, followed by a conservative Democrat and an even more conservative Republican. The gradual change from at least paying lip service to deficit reduction to a formal and effective embrace of inflation and debt as tools of economic policy was a radical shift that culminated in the great financial bust of 2007–2009. Simon White of *Bloomberg* summarized the decline of financial standards in the United States under Greenspan's FOMC:

> Greed reached its apotheosis in the 2008 crisis. Due to the alchemy of finance and complaisant ratings companies, "risk-free" assets could be magicked up from highly risky ones in originate-to-distribute lending models. This meant that when central banks needed to inject liquidity into the system to prevent its collapse, they had to accept as collateral de facto position-making assets of deeply dubious quality, with the Fed's Maiden Lane portfolios acting as one of the main conduits.[50]

The fact that the massive growth in public and private sector debt occurred during the tenure of Alan Greenspan is a little ironic, but only a little. While economist Greenspan is styled as a conservative, like many Republicans today he is really a fan of big government. The former disciple of author Ayn Rand did little to prevent the growth of government or the federal debt during his tenure, but it was the declining quality of private debt that raises even larger questions about the role of monetary policy.

Greenspan occasionally criticized fiscal deficits during his years at the Fed, and had some notable exchanges with members of the Senate regarding the fiscal impact of Social Security, but he hardly confronted either Congress or the White House over fiscal policy as Chairman Burns had done decades before. When Democrats during the Clinton administration congratulated themselves in the 1990s for almost eliminating the federal deficit, Greenspan only modestly protested the accounting gimmickry of counting incoming Social Security payments toward the visible public fiscal shortfall.

In the Randian world view of Alan Greenspan, which is most easily understood as a European-style "positive liberty" perspective versus the negative liberty, "libertarian" world view of the pre–World War I American republic, the markets existed for private agents to exploit. The world of Rand is not a utopia of the sort romantically described by American conservatives, but a state of institutionalized selfishness where government allocates freedom to individuals. The European Union today exemplifies this "tyranny of the consensus," but the Democratic Party post-2000 and particularly post-2024 and the failed candidacy of Kamala Harris fits into the same category of state socialism.

Greenspan's focus on monetary policy and his belief in "self-regulating" markets was partly a reflection of his views forged by long association with Rand. But it was also a passive recognition of the political tide in America and particularly of the fact that the federal regulators had largely curtailed much of the worst tendencies of the banking industry, pushing the real fun and games of finance into the street.

Big government was rhetorically demonized by Ronald Reagan, yet government continued to grow nonetheless. Greenspan made Americans believe that they could have a normal, stable economy despite the growing public debt in Washington, a clear sign of future inflation that Greenspan ignored. Just as past Fed chairmen gave presidents their way with respect to monetary policy, Greenspan did so and more. He gave Americans what they wanted to see, namely the appearance of nominal economic prosperity, without forcing Congress and successive presidents to address fiscal problems.

Presidents Reagan, Bush, Clinton, or Bush had no need to encourage Greenspan to provide easy money, as President Richard Nixon did with Arthur Burns and Ronald Reagan and James Baker had done so bluntly with Paul Volcker. Greenspan and the other members of the FOMC during this period were leading the easy-money parade. This fact simply proves the point made by the Fed's framers about the ill effects of putting the central bank in Washington or having a unitary central bank at all. The Greenspan Fed encouraged and facilitated greater fiscal excesses, diminished value for money, and more overall debt and higher inflation.

Critics of Chairman Greenspan like to blame him for the sub-prime bubble, but not nearly enough attention is paid to the fact that American presidents from Bill Clinton forward allowed the Federal Reserve Board to be dominated by Greenspan and to become narrowly focused on monetary policy and largely indifferent to banks and financial markets. Chairman Greenspan may not have been a particularly good economic prognosticator or bank regulator, but he was an exceptional politician. In 1992, when President-elect Clinton invited Alan Greenspan to Little Rock, Greenspan jumped at the chance and quickly reintegrated himself back into the White House policy loop he knew so well.[51]

By accommodating the political concerns of the White House and also of the banking industry, Greenspan gained effective control over the Federal Reserve Board and the selection of governors through his entire term. As a result, the Board and its staff tended to be focused almost entirely on monetary policy. This predisposition to give Greenspan virtual control over the appointment of Fed governors continued through the administration of George W. Bush, turning the central bank into a compliant monoculture. Successive Republican and Democratic governments and their supporters in the business community became very comfortable with the monetary policy of Chairman Greenspan. To paraphrase Mark Twain, we had the best government money could buy.

After the October 1987 market breakdown, when the Greenspan Fed showed itself willing to provide the credit and access to collateral required to get through the crack in confidence, there was no reason to replace him. The real cost of two decades of Alan Greenspan at the Fed is measured in the successive decades after his tenure, when America's public debt exploded and the Fed became deliberately silent with respect to fiscal issues. The failure of Chairman Greenspan and other FOMC members to address fiscal problems during almost two decades in office left the United States on a trajectory for economic stagnation, rising inflation, and the attendant political and social costs. But in fairness to Chairman Greenspan, any Fed chairman would have done the same, meeting the needs of the White House and the banking industry, just as Chairman Ben Bernanke did after he replaced Alan Greenspan. History does repeat itself.

As we discuss in the next chapter, the institutionalized crisis affecting financial markets and the government's fiscal situation is inexorably moving the United States toward a more centralized and less democratic form of government. The key point of George Orwell's classic book *Animal Farm* is that socialist governments in Germany under Adolf Hitler, Italy under Mussolini, or Russia under Joseph Stalin inevitably became dictatorships.

Without a change in the fiscal and monetary regimes of the United States, government will increasingly be the central player in the economy, surrounded by a heavily regulated "private" marketplace. Individual liberties and opportunities will become a function of politics and administrative mechanisms. Decisions about major business transactions involving large banks and companies will be politicized far beyond what was thought possible even a few decades ago. This fundamental economic change, which has its roots in the response to the Great Depression and the two world wars, is occurring within the world's greatest democracy without an informed public debate. Other than the childish spectacle of crypto currencies in the twenty-first Century, Americans seem to have no serious opinions about the nature of money.

Chapter 9

Financial Crisis and Malaise

The 2008 Financial Crisis was an inflection point in modern American history, a turn in the road when the country's political and business leadership were publicly discredited in a way not seen since the 1930s. After the victory over fascism in World War II and then decades of Cold War ending in the fall of the Berlin Wall in 1989, America's leaders were convinced of their acumen and righteous judgment. Galbraith famously opined about the Great Crash of 1929: "Genius comes after the fall."

The decades that followed the fall of the Berlin Wall in 1989 confirmed the ability of America's leaders to legislate economic and even geopolitical outcomes, often at the expense of other nations and all funded with debt. None in Washington saw the collapse of 2008 as a repudiation of mainstream economic thinking in the United States from the 1970s onward, a uniquely American mixture of socialism and corporate statism.

The decades of borrow and spend since 2008 have only led to greater economic uncertainty and changeability, yet America's leaders barely acknowledge their collective failure. Conservatives in both political parties warned of the coming crisis of confidence that accompanies dissolute fiscal policies. There were plenty of people in and out of government warning of approaching crisis years before 2008, yet America's leaders largely ignored the signs of impending collapse and focused on short-term profits. In the second half of the twentieth century, hubris became a very visible liability for government and private business alike.

Economist Robert Brusca put the 2008 Financial Crisis and subsequent lack of introspection into context in a 2024 interview:

For Alan Greenspan, the obfuscation was out in the open. His middle initial was "O" and he was a believer in all of the Ayn Rand stuff. When the markets fell apart and he discovered there was all of this cheating and cutting corners in finance, he was shocked. Greenspan truly believed that efficient markets would discipline behavior and that people would not commit fraud and do stupid things that undercut reputation. Since 2008, the Fed and other agencies have reassessed the way markets work and changed the rules accordingly, so today it is all about being in the middle of the pack. You can always fail, but if you look like the pack in terms of risk, you are safe because the pack cannot fail.[1]

For the central bank and other regulatory agencies, 2008 marked a considerable failure in terms of both monetary policy and the supervision of banks. The private market for "federal funds" ceased to exist, most of the nonbank primary dealers failed along with roughly half of the large banks in the country by assets.[2] Citibank, Wachovia, Washington Mutual, Bear Stearns, and Lehman Brothers were just the largest bank failures in that fateful year and each was also a significant primary dealer of government securities. Add to that illustrious list the insurer American International Group and the mortgage giants Fannie Mae and Freddie Mac.

The last two names on the list are "government-sponsored entities" (GSEs) that were partially "spun off" by President Lyndon Johnson to hide the costs of the Vietnam War. The GSEs were controlled by the government yet masqueraded as private firms, rewarding private "shareholders" for taking no risk as they purchased subprime mortgages. If you want an illustration of the delusional quality of America economic thinking over the past 50 years, the ambiguous legal status of the GSEs, Fannie Mae and Freddie Mac, are two of the best examples. As President Donald Trump took power in 2025, he promised to again release the GSE's into ersatz private ownership.

The decade that followed 2008 was very similar to the period of slack economic growth in the 1990s following the S&L crisis. But there were many differences. In the 1990s, most Americans still reflected the Depression-era mentality that debt was bad. In contrast to the more liberal social perspectives of the 2000s, people avoided defaulting on their debts because of the social stigma involved.

In the 2010s, however, default became commonplace and the political class responded with more subsidies. Progressive politicians turned housing into an entitlement for poor families that had been overwhelmed by creeping inflation. As millions of Americans lost their homes in the 2010s, the politics of credit and default changed. It took until 2016 for home prices to recover from the massive numbers of home foreclosures and flows of new financing into residential construction to begin to grow.

That fateful year 2008 also marked the abandonment of any pretense of concern for the private capital markets and a new willingness by the Federal Reserve to use massive purchases of government securities and other assets to meet perceived economic needs. The political architect of the strategy of using massive open market operations as "monetary policy tools" was Federal Reserve Board chairman Ben Bernanke, although he was simply copying the policies developed by others and used by the Bank of Japan years earlier.[3]

Many banks and commercial companies in the United States were functionally insolvent or at least illiquid in the months after September 2008, but the central bank provided ample liquidity to refloat the market. This was the correct and necessary response to the immediate needs of the economy, namely providing ample short-term liquidity. But the Fed's immediate liquidity provider role then grew and metastasized into a permanent economic crutch akin to the Reconstruction Finance Corporation of the 1930s. And even though the benefits of quantitative easing after 2008 in terms of boosting employment are greatly in doubt, the Fed continued to include massive purchases of government securities among its policy options into the 2020s.

As the Fed was aggressively growing bank reserves and its balance sheet, Congress also created a toxic mixture of federal spending and new regulations via the 2010 Dodd-Frank legislation that slowed economic growth in the United States for years afterwards. Congress could hardly say no to more spending, especially since the budget process was largely abandoned by both political parties.

The Senate of the United States became incapable of marking up budget legislation and instead rubber stamped bills from the House of Representatives. Congress simply increased spending each year and passed authorizing legislation in what is euphemistically known as a "continuing resolution." And because of low or zero short-term interest rates and the Treasury's preference for short-term debt, the Fed encouraged mounting budget deficits that continued to grow faster every year as interest compounded.

The crisis of 2008 and the rescue engineered by the Fed seemed to weaken any resolve in Congress or the White House to restrain spending, but it also marked a spiritual defeat as any remaining confidence in private markets gave way to bailouts for all. But the financial safety net provided by government also kills the free market. Thomas Hoenig, former president of the Kansas City Fed and head of the FDIC, said of that period in written comments to the author: "One of the worst things I think that's happened, and I've watched is that 'market discipline' has atrophied. There is none."[4]

Chairman Ben Bernanke understood that both the sudden drop in economic output and investor demand that occurred after 2008 had to be offset, otherwise we end up in a classic debt deflation described by Irving Fisher in his famous 1933 essay, "The Debt-Deflation Theory of Great Depressions." Fisher wrote:

When an investor thinks he can make over 100 per cent per annum by borrowing at 6 per cent, he will be tempted to borrow, and to invest or speculate with borrowed money. This was a prime cause leading to the over-indebtedness of 1929. Inventions and technological improvements created wonderful investment opportunities, and so caused big debts. Other causes were the left-over war debts, domestic and foreign, public and private, the reconstruction loans to foreigners, and the low interest policy adopted to help England get back on the gold standard in 1925.[5]

Returning to the gold standard in 1925 was a monumental error by the Bank of England, one that accelerated the post–World War I deflation that ultimately led to the Great Crash in 1929. Bernanke and Harold James noted that by the end of 1925, a long list of nations returned to a gold currency peg at their prewar exchange rates, creating an unstable global economic system that eventually collapsed. They wrote in a 1991 paper for the National Bureau of Economic Research:

> The length and depth of the deflation during the late 1920s and early 1930s strongly suggest a monetary origin, and the close correspondence (across both space and time) between deflation and nations' adherence to the gold standard shows the power of that system to transmit contractionary monetary shocks. There is also a high correlation in the data between deflation (falling prices) and depression (falling output), as the previous authors have noted and as we will demonstrate again below.[6]

The truth reflected in the work of Bernanke and others is that you cannot ignore inflation by attempting to defend a fixed currency, especially once that inflation has already occurred as in the case of World War I. But the key insight for managing a fiat currency system is to maintain balance between capital and investments, and the confidence this balance requires, or else the financial system collapses under its own weight. And this has nothing to do with gold and everything to do with asset price deflation.

"We must," veteran attorney Fred Feldkamp likes to remind colleagues, "Never forget the Fisher/Bernanke combined lesson. It starts with the national income accounting identity that 'savings' must and always will equate with 'investment'. That is an 'identity' because that is how we have constructed the world's national income accounts. It says that the value of all debt and equity must (and always will) equate with the total of all capital investment," he explained in *Financial Stability: Fraud, Confidence and the Wealth of Nations.*[7]

Debt is always an amount set by contract but it is necessarily a "value" that fluctuates with the market by its present value, determined by the "base rate plus spread," to establish the ultimate daily market value of debt. That's why Treasury rates and bond spreads are vital data points for making economic policy, benchmarks that the Fed too often ignores. Spreads set the day-to-day value change of total debt, Feldkamp has long observed. Equity markets are bid up and down by investors, based on expectations regarding earnings and other factors, including the perceived actual future cash flow burden of daily market values for debt. When either equity or debt value "crashes" as in 2008 and later in 2020 during the outbreak of COVID, the current value of "savings" necessarily shrinks and that stark reality undermines the value of the world's total "investment."

What Fisher showed (and Chairman Bernanke understood from his work on the Great Depression) is that capital assets necessarily crash in value unless debt grows to replace any sudden market value drop. Equity values recover when market confidence is restored. An inflexible gold-based standard cannot respond sufficiently to counter such a deflation, but the fact of gold convertibility of the dollar did not cause the great crash and the deflation of the 1930s. Rather it was the expansion and contraction of the paper assets perched atop the foundation of gold-based money that caused the catastrophe.

The bond market data maintained by the Fed shows that bond spreads normalized by 2011, ending the need for further purchases of securities. Yet a combination of partisan politics and hubris caused the FOMC to do too much for far too long after 2008, creating the circumstances for an eventual upsurge in inflation a decade later. Yet there are some who say that critics are too hard on the Fed.

Had the FOMC been focused on financial market indicators and particularly bond spreads in the mid-2000s, then U.S. officials would have seen the trouble brewing in mortgage finance years before 2008. In fact, the huge hit to value that many believe begins in 2008 actually started late in 2005 with the end of the great bubble in the housing market. Less shrewd lenders such as Citibank, Washington Mutual, Wachovia Bank, Countrywide, Bear Stearns, and Lehman Brothers began to fail in

2006, two years before the more general 2008 collapse. These firms were literally choking to death on fringe market subprime assets they could no longer sell to Fannie Mae, Freddie Mac, and private investors.

Overnight, valuations on trillions of dollars in residential mortgage loans and securities were cut in half. Banks stepped back from markets, leaving mortgage companies of various stripes aground without financing. Many of the dealers and funds on Wall Street were insolvent by the end of 2008. At the local barber shop in town, the television was changed back to news or talk instead of CNBC. The decade-long party fueled by home mortgage loans and securities fraud was at an end.

Quantitative Easing

The radical response of Chairman Ben Bernanke and the other members of the Federal Reserve Board after the 2008 financial bust represented an incremental shift by the central bank toward more aggressive and long-term economic intervention and, as a result, more inflation and public debt. But it also marked a political failure by Congress and President Barack Obama to act and provide guidance to the central bank. Unlike Congress and FDR in the 1930s, after 2008, Congress left the Federal Reserve Board on its own to make national policy behind closed doors. The unelected Board became a government unto itself, with no transparency or accountability for its actions.

The start of "quantitative easing" in November 2008 under Chairman Bernanke was an Orwellian reference to massive open market purchases of Treasury debt. Yet what we know as "quantitative easing" marked the beginning of the end of the Fed's credibility as in independent central bank and a major shift toward executive branch control. This fall from grace is measured by the refusal of Fed governors to talk about the federal deficit. Here's how the Federal Reserve press release announced quantitative easing:

> [T]he purchase of the direct obligations of housing-related government-sponsored enterprises (GSEs)—Fannie Mae, Freddie Mac, and the Federal Home Loan Banks—and mortgage-backed securities (MBS) backed by Fannie Mae, Freddie Mac, and

Ginnie Mae . . . Purchases of up to $100 billion in GSE direct obligations under the program will be conducted with the Federal Reserve's primary dealers through a series of competitive auctions and will begin next week. Purchases of up to $500 billion in MBS will be conducted by asset managers selected via a competitive process with a goal of beginning these purchases before year-end. Purchases of both direct obligations and MBS are expected to take place over several quarters.[8]

Quantitative easing is the most radical and, in some ways, irresponsible *fiscal* action ever taken by a federal agency. With quantitative easing, the Fed ended any pretense of separation from Treasury and simply mutated into another fiscal arm financed with debt. The Fed purchased securities with funds raised from private banks. In financial terms, open market bond purchases by the Fed after 2008 look a lot like the gold purchases of the Reconstruction Finance Corporation (RFC) by FDR during the 1930s. The difference is that Congress authorized the latter but ignored the former, leaving the Fed alone to experiment on the U.S. economy. The Fed's actions resulted in massive losses to the central bank and, indirectly, to the Treasury, yet Congress remained largely mute when it came to the Fed's bond purchases. The dilettantes in Congress preferred to simply be spared the task of deciding what to do when faced with global market contagion.

The Fed's capital is authorized by law; but quantitative easing is not. In making massive purchases of securities using funds borrowed from banks, and then incurring equally huge losses as a result, the Fed is essentially operating an illegal hedge fund with the Treasury's money and running it very badly. By purchasing trillions of dollars more in securities after 2011 when bond markets normalized, the Fed cost the taxpayer hundreds of billions in future losses. All this was done in the name of a vague claim to be stimulating the economy. Instead, the Fed stimulated inflation in home prices and financial assets such as stocks and bonds.

The remarkable thing about quantitative easing is that so few economists and policymakers understand what was actually done. The Fed essentially bought bonds from private banks, but used cash taken from these Treasury securities to fund the losses caused when interest rates rose. Like the S&Ls of the 1980s, the Fed's policy of paying market interest rates on reserves but investing in low-coupon Treasury and mortgage securities caused a huge interest rate mismatch. By the end of September 2024, the Fed's accumulated losses totaled over $200 billion and will continue to grow for years to come, depriving the Treasury of income from the Fed's portfolio.

By definition, a central bank is the alter ego of a national treasury and therefore never earns a "profit." The Federal Reserve System is always an expense to the U.S. Treasury on a net basis. Robert Eisenbeis, former research head at the Atlanta Federal Reserve Bank, discussed this point in a 2017 interview:

> The Fed almost by definition cannot make a profit. It baffles me how people inside the system can fail to see the accounting reality here. The Fed issues short term liabilities to buy Treasuries taking duration out of the market. The Treasury makes interest payments to the Fed who takes out its operating costs, including interest payments on reserves and returns the remainder to the Treasury. If this intra governmental transfer were settled on a net basis like interest rate swaps, there would always be a net payment from the Treasury to the Fed. It is too obvious, yet I am not privy to the sidebar conversations on this issue.[9]

Instead of seeking authority from Congress for massive open market purchases of securities, Chairman Bernanke and other members of the FOMC simply made the problem of post-2008 deflation in the financial markets go away. Chair Janet Yellen (2014–2018) continued quantitative easing and added to the absurdity of Fed actions by attempting to manipulate long-term Treasury yields in imitation of the Bank of Japan. By the time that Chairman Jerome Powell took the helm of the FOMC early in 2018, the Fed's staff merely added a "0" to its tab at the U.S. Treasury and kept right on purchasing securities through the COVID pandemic. Chairman Bernanke laid out the rationale for providing liquidity support to the economy via quantitative easing in a 2009 speech at the Bank of England:

The abrupt end of the credit boom has had widespread financial and economic ramifications. Financial institutions have seen their capital depleted by losses and writedowns and their balance sheets clogged by complex credit products and other illiquid assets of uncertain value. Rising credit risks and intense risk aversion have pushed credit spreads to unprecedented levels, and markets for securitized assets, except for mortgage securities with government guarantees, have shut down. Heightened systemic risks, falling asset values, and tightening credit have in turn taken a heavy toll on business and consumer confidence and precipitated a sharp slowing in global economic activity. The damage, in terms of lost output, lost jobs, and lost wealth, is already substantial.[10]

Bernanke's assessment of the need for quantitative easing reflects the corporatist view of economics that predominates within the Federal Reserve and other central banks. After all, a monetary agency that represents the collective credit of an entire society is hardly likely to employ conservative economists or spend a lot of time worried about individual investors and private markets. The Fed is a progressive agency where policy is justified by needs of the many rather than the needs of the few. But whether or not the Fed actually has the means to alter markets and engineer specific economic outcomes is another matter, especially when the Treasury has very large deficits.

After Congress authorized the Federal Reserve Banks to pay interest on bank reserves in 2008, the FOMC now had a tool to manage short-term interest rates—or at least that was the assumption. Nobody in Congress ever dreamed that the Fed would use this new power so aggressively. Prior to 2008, all of the interest earned by the Fed on its portfolio was returned to the Treasury, net of the operating expenses of the central bank. After 2008, the Fed could essentially compete with JPMorgan and the other large banks for liquidity, and also compete with the Treasury directly. By paying interest on reserves, the Fed thought that it could put a "floor" under interest rates. But like many Fed policies, this public promise turned out to be a mirage.

"For some decades now the Fed like other central banks has insisted that its task is to regulate short-term interest rates," noted

George Selgin in a 2019 interview about that period. "So, when interest rates do something that the Fed has not planned for them to do, that's a problem. If the Fed isn't able to control interest rates, then what is it doing and what is it able to do?"[11]

The official view of monetary policy from the Fed and other central banks does not make room for what is the elephant in the room, namely the U.S. Treasury and the federal deficit. When the Treasury is creating so much new "near money" in the form of short-term government debt, the idea that the Fed can combat inflation by merely changing the target for Fed funds is laughable. Economist John Cochrane described the official view of Fed policy, real and imagined, in a blog comment:

> There is a Standard Doctrine, explained regularly by the Fed, other central banks, and commentators, and economics classes that don't sweat the equations too hard: The Fed raises interest rates. Higher interest rates slowly lower spending, output, and hence employment over the course of several months or years. Lower output and employment slowly bring down inflation, over the course of additional months or years. So, raising interest rates lowers inflation, with a "long and variable" lag.

Cochrane notes that monetarist theory requires that money and Treasury bonds be distinct assets. But is this true? Menand and Younger described the scene in a 2023 paper for Columbia Law School. The authors make a compelling case that the fiat currency first created by President Abraham Lincoln to finance the Civil War and Treasury debt are essentially interchangeable. That is, we're all 100 percent practicing Modern Monetary Theory right now when the Treasury is in deficit. How can the Fed profess to control the "money supply" when the Treasury is issuing trillions of dollars a year in new "near-money" debt?

"I get all the discussion about 'near money' etc., but isn't it all way simpler than that?" economist Brian Wesbury of First Trust Advisors told the author in a September 2024 email. "The Fed has separated the money supply and bank reserves from interest rates. It now manages monetary policy like it is playing 'whack a mole' and it is the one that is creating all the moles."

One of the more troubling discoveries made by the Fed after 2008 was that merely dropping the target for short-term interest rates did not mean that markets would respond as desired. "Quantitative easing" as envisioned by Ben Bernanke was a brute force means of forcing market rates down, not just short-term interest rates but the entire yield curve. Any concern for private markets or investors was sacrificed on the altar of expediency, just as the Fed helped FDR seize gold from private citizens almost a century earlier. The end justified the means, even if Congress and the public had no real idea what the Fed was doing in our name.

As Figure 9.1 illustrates, the return on earning assets for all U.S. banks fell from almost 1 percent in 2008 to as low as 55bp in 2021, this before the Fed again began to increase interest rates. Through a vast social engineering project known as quantitative easing, the Fed transferred billions of dollars from the shareholders of banks to private borrowers and the federal government itself. This process of robbing private companies to support the Treasury is known as "financial repression."

Whereas in the 1930s Congress authorized asset purchases and other activities as fiscal operations, in the post-2008 period the Federal

Return on Earning Assets (%) | All Banks

Figure 9.1 Return on Earning Assets.
SOURCE: FDIC.

Reserve mutated into a *de facto* fiscal agency, spending trillions of dollars in Treasury funds and incurring huge financial losses ostensibly in pursuit of the dual mandate of Humphrey-Hawkins. It is pretty clear that the Fed's focus is now more on "full employment" in terms of market stability than "price stability," even as the Fed now defines it. The change in behavior by the Fed is precisely illustrated by the fact that open market operations went from short-term, temporary operations to impact the supply of bank reserves to long-term outright purchases of securities that had more vague economic rationales and objectives, and larger potential risks to the taxpayer.[12]

George Selgin warned against engaging in fiscal quantitative easing because it would "undermine the Fed's independence and credibility, erode democratic oversight and transparency of fiscal policy, and could open the floodgates to backdoor spending. It might also relieve, at least temporarily, the pressure to deal with unsustainable entitlement programs—all while still resulting in higher inflation. The dangers of fiscal quantitative easing are great, the harms would be widespread, and the political temptation to use it will grow," he argued.[13]

We can divide the Fed's grand experiment with quantitative easing into two periods: the time from 2008–2014, when the Fed used massive open market purchases of Treasury and mortgage securities to "ease the stance of monetary policy," and 2015 through the end of the COVID pandemic in 2022, when the Fed greatly increased outright purchases of securities meant to be held to maturity and reinvested principal repayments to maintain the size of the system open market account (SOMA) portfolio. These open market purchases of Treasury debt represented a direct subsidy to the U.S. Treasury itself, net of losses and operating expenses incurred by the Fed. The purchases of mortgage debt were a subsidy to the issuers of MBS and, indirectly, to homeowners and investors.

Seen in the light of experience, the Fed's payment of interest on reserves failed to achieve the desired results and, to the contrary, set up the U.S. economy for a series of financial market crises since 2008. Allowing the Fed to pay interest on reserves gave the unelected members of the FOMC the power to tax and spend without a congressional appropriation. Whatever economic benefit may be conferred by the Fed's cash-raising operations by paying interest on bank reserves is more than offset by the monstrous political conflict raised by this unfettered fiscal activity.

Again, allowing the Fed to pay interest on reserves places the central bank in competition with private banks and the Treasury itself. As the Fed's purchases of securities grew the SOMA into the trillions of dollars, so too did the deposits that were controlled by the central bank, raising some of the issues we discussed 150 years before with respect to the Bank of the United States. Following are some of the major milestones in the Fed's explicit embrace of quantitative easing in a summary prepared by the New York Federal Reserve:[14]

Quantitative Easing 1: From November 2008 to March 2010, the first round of large-scale asset purchases included purchases of $175 billion in agency debt, $1.25 trillion in agency MBS, and $300 billion in longer-term Treasury securities. Including agency and MBS in the Fed's purchases was mean to "help" housing, but over time it caused home prices to rise rapidly but little in the way of new home construction. By dropping the cost of mortgage credit, the Fed enabled Americans to buy bigger homes but there was no appreciable change in net new home construction.

   Following completion of the program, the Federal Reserve rolled over maturing Treasury securities (consistent with historical practice) and, starting in August 2010, maintained the then-current total level of securities by also reinvesting principal payments from agency debt and agency MBS (initially, in longer-term Treasury securities). By reinvesting prepayments back into mortgage securities, the FOMC exacerbated the parabolic rise of home prices during the period of quantitative easing.

Quantitative Easing 2: From November 2010 to June 2011, the second round of large-scale asset purchases included $600 billion in longer-term Treasury securities. Principal payments received from holdings of all domestic securities continue to be reinvested in Treasury securities.

Operation Twist: From September 2011 through 2012, the Maturity Extension Program, commonly known as "Operation Twist," included purchases of $667 billion in Treasury securities with remaining maturities of 6 years to 30 years, offset by sales of $634 billion in Treasury securities with remaining maturities of 3 years or less and

$33 billion of Treasury security redemptions. It also included reinvesting principal payments from agency debt and agency MBS in agency MBS. Again, including MBS in reinvestments of prepayments by the Fed put upward pressure on home prices, but did not alleviate supply constraints. Indeed, by the middle of the 2020s, new homes actually became cheaper than existing homes.

At the commencement of the Maturity Extension Program, the Federal Reserve also shifted its reinvestment policy to reinvestment principal payments from holdings of agency debt and agency MBS in agency MBS rather than Treasury securities. This strategy was incredible from a financial perspective, and caused further losses to the Fed later on, losses that should have never occurred. Reinvesting into MBS forced down mortgage rates and forced up home prices, again without creating any new housing supply.

Quantitative Easing 3: From September 2012 through 2013, the third round of large-scale asset purchases included a colossal error. The Fed made monthly purchases of $40 billion in agency MBS, dropping to monthly purchases of $35 billion in January 2014 and decreasing by $5 billion after each FOMC meeting until October 2014. Starting in January 2013, it also included monthly purchases of $45 billion in longer-term Treasury securities, dropping to monthly purchases of $40 billion in January 2014 and decreasing by $5 billion after each FOMC meeting until October 2014.

In total, the Federal Reserve purchased $790 billion in Treasury securities and $823 billion in agency MBS in the third quantitative easing purchase program. None of the purchases in Quantitative Easing 3 were necessary from an economic perspective and badly exacerbated price distortions in the financial and residential housing markets. By the end of 2017, in fact, it was clear that the Fed's massive purchases of securities had created a duration trap for the U.S. banking system and money market funds. The Fed would need to expand its balance sheet and operations even further to deal with these new challenges, real-world market issues that affect real people created by poorly planned monetary policy.

In the name of consistency, the Federal Reserve resumed reinvestment of Treasury redemptions at the start of the third large-scale asset purchase program, and maintained its existing Treasury and agency debt and agency MBS reinvestment practices throughout and even following the conclusion of the program. Had the Fed simply allowed its portfolio to run off naturally instead of mechanically reinvesting the principal repayments for years too long, the damage to private markets would have been greatly reduced.

Reflecting the statist thinking inside the Federal Reserve Board, the portfolio was maintained for years as a sort of "macroeconomic stimulus," even though the Fed has never described or documented the supposed benefit of these actions in terms of the central bank's legal mandate. Reflecting the oversized view of Fed power, Yellen said in a 2018 interview that the goal of buying assets via quantitative easing was to put downward pressure on long-term interest rates, although she offered no support for this claim. As the Fed unwound the assets there would be some upward pressure on those rates. "But it would be gradual, too," she said confidently. Moreover, Yellen asserted, the unwinding would take the balance sheet to about $2 trillion to $3 trillion, not back to pre-crisis levels.[15] Events would prove both of these judgments by Chair Yellen to be wrong.

Some observers believe that of recent Fed chairs, Yellen may have been the least culpable in the decision to greatly expand the Fed's balance sheet. Lee Adler, a veteran Treasury market trader and publisher of *Liquidity Trader* noted in a 2023 conversation with the author:

> Everybody blames Yellen, but Powell was the one who went big. Yellen shrank the Fed's balance sheet. She started the "normalization" policy. Powell was the one who panicked and reversed course when they had a problem in the money markets because of it. And Chairman Ben Bernanke knew he was setting a trap for anyone who would dare to try to reverse his money printing. He's a financial war criminal. The villains are Greenspan, Bernanke, and Powell. Yellen is the only one who tried to do the right thing. Yet the rabid right loves to lump her in with the real bad guys. They even make her the primary villain. It's wrong.

We must always remember that the Fed is a progressive, New Deal institution. The 1978 Humphrey-Hawkins legislation was an explicitly socialist law imposed by a Democratic majority in Congress that must inevitably lead to inflation. When Fed Chairman Bernanke tried to differentiate between credit easing and quantitative easing in a 2009 speech in London, the world witnessed the last gasps of the dual mandate to balance employment with inflation. Since 2009, quantitative easing has delivered monumental inflation, this justified in the name of short-term expedience that make a mockery of the "price stability" portion of Humphrey-Hawkins. The FOMC since Alan Greenspan, including the terms of Chairman Bernanke, Chair Janet Yellen, and Chairman Jerome Powell, document the consensus view at the Fed over the past decade or more that "inflation is too low."

The Powell Pivot and COVID

After a decade of easy money, the Yellen FOMC began to raise the target for federal funds starting in October 2017. At the same time, the Fed began to slowly reduce its securities holdings. This had the effect of reducing bank reserves and bank deposits dollar-for-dollar. Fed purchases of securities swelled the size of the U.S. banking system by adding new reserves, but running off the Fed's bond portfolio likewise reduced bank reserves and deposits. Because the Treasury is running a deficit, every time a bond held by the Fed matures, the Treasury is forced to immediately issue a new bond. When an investor buys that new bond in the open market, a bank deposit disappears. When the Fed buys a Treasury bond from a dealer, conversely, a new bank deposit is created.

The stated objective of Fed policy in 2017 was to normalize the size of its balance sheet by decreasing reinvestments of principal payments from the Federal Reserve's securities holdings. These adjustments to the portfolio were years too late, looking at the stock market and credit spreads we discussed earlier, but the Yellen FOMC chose to err on the high side of both the size and duration of open market purchases. Since the Fed continued to reinvest the prepayments on Treasury and mortgage securities, this deepened the distortions of the agency and secondary mortgage markets long after the economic necessity for intervention was past. The Fed's actions over most of the decade after the 2008 Financial Crisis suggests that the U.S. economy was and remains in far more fragile condition than any public official will admit. Indeed, market volatility in 2012 and 2016 made some policymakers call for more action from the Fed.

In 2015, the Fed announced the adoption of a "floor system" for managing interest rates, but never notified Congress or published any public explanation for the change. In just a couple of years, however, the accumulated policy missteps by the Federal Reserve Board plunged the financial world into a near collapse at the end of 2018. The crisis in December 2018 was predicted by a number of observers, but none more specific than George Selgin of Cato Institute, who from the outset took issue with the Fed's post-crisis approach to implementing monetary policy. In March 2018 congressional testimony, Selgin noted that "while Fed officials hoped that the new floor system would assist them in regulating the flow of private credit in the face of extremely low and falling interest rates, a close look at the workings of the system, and at its record, shows that those hopes have been disappointed."

After years of massive open market purchases of securities, the idea that the Fed could return to "normal" by simply raising interest rates and ending the purchase of securities was, in retrospect, very ambitious and even reckless. It is important to state, however, that since the Fed models market liquidity versus vague economic factors such as gross domestic product, it is unlikely to have a true understanding of the actual market dynamics among specific counterparties. Bill Nelson, chief economist at the Bank Policy Institute, noted in an October 2024 commentary that the model for liquidity used by the Board was designed decades ago (1968 in fact) by Bill Poole, president of the Federal Reserve Bank of St. Louis, to measure liquidity *intraday*. It was never intended to measure required liquidity over time.

Claudio Borio, head of the Monetary and Economic Department of the Bank for International Settlements, rebuked the Fed on its use of abundant reserves in 2023. Yet the Treasury's growing fiscal imbalances has apparently made the Fed unwilling to relent on "big" reserves. Borio:

> Since the Great Financial Crisis, a growing number of central banks have adopted abundant reserves systems ("floors") to set the interest rate. However, there are good grounds to return to scarce reserve systems ("corridors"). First, the costs of floor systems take considerable time to appear, are likely to grow and tend to be less visible. They can be attributed to independent features of the environment which, in fact, are to a significant

extent a consequence of the systems themselves. Second, for much the same reasons, there is a risk of grossly overestimating the implementation difficulties of corridor systems, in particular the instability of the demand for reserves. Third, there is no need to wait for the central bank balance sheet to shrink before moving in that direction: for a given size, the central bank can adjust the composition of its liabilities. Ultimately, the design of the implementation system should follow from a strategic view of the central bank's balance sheet. A useful guiding principle is that its size should be as small as possible, and its composition as riskless as possible, in a way that is compatible with the central bank fulfilling its mandate effectively.[16]

By reducing reserves at the same time as the FOMC was raising the target for federal funds during 2017 and 2018, the Fed quickly dried up the excess liquidity in the system and created a serious financial crisis. Regulatory requirements for maintaining short-term liquid assets also constrained lending by the larger banks led by JPMorgan, the largest secured lender in the United States. This author watched the short-term mortgage markets during this period at a large broker-dealer in New York.

Although the interest rate increases from 2017 onward were moderate and largely what the markets expected, Chair Yellen and other members of the FOMC clearly wanted to get interest rates up off the zero bound and begin to normalize policy after years of quantitative easing. Yet none of the members of the FOMC seemed to as yet understand the cumulative impact of the Fed's actions on the private markets. Tightening the cost of money while reducing bank reserves held by the Fed was a recipe for disaster.

By 2016, the Yellen FOMC was under growing political pressure to normalize policy. Senator Patrick Tomey (R-PA) said that the Federal Reserve should continue moving monetary policy back to normal, despite the swings in the financial markets. "I'm going to try to be a voice for encouraging a normalization," Toomey told CNBC's *Squawk Box* on February 11, 2016. Yet neither Toomey nor other members of Congress seemed to realize just how radical were the policies of the FOMC in that period and how ending those policies could result in big trouble.

It is important to state that the Fed thinks about liquidity in private markets as a function of reserves in the system held by banks. As late as June 2016, Chair Yellen continued to defend the decision to shift to a floor system that required massive portfolio balances, balances maintained by reinvesting principal repayments on the Fed's portfolio. These enormous increases in the Fed's assets and deposits were not so much to help the economy or create jobs, but to support liquidity in the burgeoning Treasury bond market. Quantitative easing was a huge boon to equity investors and also was an explicit subsidy to the Treasury. Yet it also reflected the fact that the nonbank dealer community that supported the government debt market for half a century was largely annihilated in 2008.

"Maintaining our sizable holdings of longer-term securities should help maintain accommodative financial conditions and should reduce the risk that we might have to lower the federal funds rate to the effective lower bound in the event of a future large adverse shock," Yellen told Congress in June 2016, yet subsequent events seem to disprove Yellen's views.

Jerome Powell was sworn in as Fed chairman in February 2018, taking over for Janet Yellen, who later became Treasury secretary under President Joe Biden. Powell first joined the Fed in 2012 to fill a vacant seat and thus has great experience on the board of the central bank. Powell took over as chair of the U.S. central bank after a decade of extraordinary action by the Fed that had left the banking industry decapitalized and the housing market only starting to recover.

Because of the actions taken by Yellen, Powell, and their colleagues on the Federal Reserve Board, economic intervention became an even more important policy tool for the central bank in the 2010s. Under Powell, the staff of the Board of Governors expanded the central bank's role in manipulating the U.S. economy to a degree not seen for a federal agency since the 1930s and, again, without guidance or ascent from Congress.

Through 2017 and into 2018, the FOMC continued to increase the target for federal funds in quarter-point increments, adding to stress in the short-term money markets that was exacerbated by the unwillingness of JPMorgan and other large banks to lend, even on a fully secured basis.

The various capital and liquidity rules put in place since 2008 retarded private market function. Yet despite the large numbers in the Fed's weekly reports showing trillions in available bank reserves, in fact by the middle of 2018, the accessible liquidity from large banks for smaller dealers, REITs, and funds was rapidly disappearing.

The Fed's macro data was missing a classical economic problem, namely that aggregate economic data does not tell you very much about the particular behavior of specific market participants. Even as the equity markets began to give ground after Labor Day 2018, the FOMC continued to mechanically raise interest rates, focusing on the still-positive picture in macroeconomic data instead of the rapidly deteriorating liquidity in the overnight money markets. The year 2018 would be remembered not just as the worst year for stocks in more than a decade, but a year of great volatility, both outcomes that the Fed's leaders such as Yellen and Powell said large reserve balances were supposed to prevent.

In early October 2018, Powell began a market selloff after an interview with Judy Woodruff of Public Broadcasting Service (PBS). Powell said the Fed no longer needed the policies that were in place that pulled the economy out of the financial crisis malaise. "The really extremely accommodative low interest rates that we needed when the economy was quite weak, we don't need those anymore. They're not appropriate anymore," Powell said. "Interest rates are still accommodative, but we're gradually moving to a place where they will be neutral. We may go past neutral, but we're a long way from neutral at this point, probably."[17]

Powell's frank comments set off a selloff in risky credit market assets that started with high-yield debt and worked its ways up the credit food chain to Treasury bonds and agencies by December 2018. Remarkably, Powell still did not seem to appreciate the extent to which the Fed's open large market operations were supporting the market and, conversely, how little risk the major primary dealer banks could or would shoulder. The Fed continued to raise interest rates, however, even with clear indications coming from the markets that there was a growing liquidity problem.

Fed officials did not appreciate enough that the total reserves in the system were concentrated among a few large banks. These large banks were under growing pressure from federal regulators to maximize internal liquidity—that is, not to lend to other firms. The Fed failed to reckon with the fact that, even though these banks on paper had sufficient liquidity to meet regulatory rules and liquidity requirements, in fact they did not feel comfortable lending out what seems to be a surfeit of reserves—not even in response to high rates and for short periods. The lessons of the 2008 Financial Crisis regarding the "run on repo" documented by a number of researchers was forgotten.[18]

In December 2018, as liquidity in the financial system rapidly disappeared, this author watched as several small dealers and publicly traded mortgage REITs came close to failing. The S&P 500 lost almost 15 percent of its value. This led to the famous "pivot" by Jerome Powell, flanked by Janet Yellen on one side and Ben Bernanke on the other. The Fed chairman "bent the knee" to the markets, setting off a vast equity market rally and related slaughter among credit traders with the audacity to be short volatility. As one trader said at the time, "If you're short volatility, you make money . . . but eventually die. But if you're long volatility, you die before you make money."

Early in January 2019, Powell completed the Fed's capitulation to the markets and also signaled that the Board of Governors staff in Washington badly misjudged the situation and misread its own model and data on reserves and liquidity. Few in Washington outside of the professional staff of the Fed and Treasury took note of Powell's debacle, a failure so public and profound that his two previous successors were compelled to close ranks around the Fed chairman in a public media event. Again, the Fed staff was too busy looking at their models and focused too little on the nonlinear word of financial markets that they routinely take for granted.

One critic summed up the decade when it comes to economic management by central bankers. "It is increasingly common to hear prominent U.S. and European central bankers claim, with respect to the crisis of 2008–2010, essentially the following verdict: "'We did well, '" wrote Simon Johnson in 2011. "But this arrogant claim merely undermines central bankers' credibility, which, ultimately, is the only basis of their authority."[19]

The Fed Goes Big

With the Powell pivot at the very end of December 2018, the FOMC suddenly abandoned any further rate hikes and, in a matter of weeks, began to reduce interest rates and expand liquidity in the banking system. Yields on bonds and mortgages began to fall as the Fed used forward sales of mortgage-backed securities to manipulate markets further. And perhaps more important, the Powell FOMC quietly announced an entirely new configuration for monetary policy in the United States. Economist Komal Sri-Kumar summarized the sudden turnabout by the FOMC:

> Jerome Powell started 2018, his first year in office as Chairman of the Federal Reserve, on a high note. Inflation in the consumer price index had accelerated from 2.2% in February when he became the Chairman, to 2.9% by mid-year despite repeated increases in the Federal Funds rate. By November, inflation was back to 1.9%. Proud of his success, Powell told investors at his press conference on December 19 to be prepared for further monetary tightening during the following year. In response, equities cratered during the final days of 2018, and the Chairman's message abruptly changed on January 4, 2019. The Fed would be patient with monetary tightening, he assured his listeners, and the central bank actually *reduced* the policy rate several times during the year.[20]

Not only did Powell capitulate in January 2019 with rate cuts, but he and the other Committee members then authorized the *de facto* nationalization of the U.S. money markets. By greatly expanding the Fed's open market operations and the size of the Fed's balance sheet, and making other legal and regulatory changes, the Fed essentially subsumed the private markets in a portfolio that was one-third of GDP in 2023. And the FOMC never sought authority from Congress for these changes.

The process whereby the Fed took control of the money markets began in the 1970s, when the FOMC under Chairman Arthur Burns began to target the yield on federal funds traded between banks as a policy indicator. But after 2019, the Fed's control of the markets was complete—at least until investors decided to revolt. The new policy regime requires the Fed to grow its balance sheet enormously, by purchasing securities using Treasury funds and paying interest on bank reserves to maintain it. Powell sought no authority from Congress for this expenditure and merely put the change into effect.

"The record indicates that the FOMC did not appreciate the consequences of its decision at the time," wrote Bill Nelson of Bank Policy Institute, "and the question now is whether the decision will be revisited given how manifest and serious those consequences are." Nelson continued:

> Specifically, the Fed announced that it would conduct monetary policy by over-supplying liquidity to the financial system, driving short-term interest rates down to the rate that the Fed pays to sop the liquidity back up. Previously, the Fed had kept reserve balances (bank deposits at the Fed) just scarce enough that the overnight interest rate was determined by transactions between financial institutions; those transactions consisted of banks with extra liquidity lending to those that needed it. Now the rate is determined by transactions between banks and the Fed. Moreover, the Fed has committed to providing so much extra liquidity that it would not need to adjust the quantity of reserve balances it is supplying in response to transitory shocks to liquidity supply and demand.[21]

In 2019, the FOMC essentially changed course and proceeded to turn the U.S. money markets into a government market, a synthetic representation right out of the 1999 Wachowski film *The Matrix* with the Fed at the center of the universe. The Fed and the New York Clearing House are now the counterparties for all trades in U.S. Treasury securities. More, the 2019 policy change assumed that the Fed would need to get even bigger in the future to avoid market disruptions like December 2018. Yet as subsequent events would show, a larger Fed balance sheet seemed to coincide with greater market volatility, higher inflation, and greater financial losses to the taxpayer. This discredits the chief arguments for going big in the first place going all the way back to the public statements of Chairs Bernanke and Yellen.

Through 2019, the FOMC cut the target rate for federal funds several times and pushed market rates down dramatically using cash and forward sales of mortgage-backed securities. This had an immediate and dramatic impact on residential mortgage interest rates. The duration of the $2.5 trillion in Ginnie Mae MBS, for example, fell from roughly 5.5 years in the beginning of 2019 to barely above 3 years by December, a huge decrease that created equally large market risk for U.S. banks and REITs several years later.

This massive manipulation of the markets caused serious problems for the banking system and massive losses for the Federal Reserve System as well. In simple terms, the mortgage-backed securities created during the peak period of Fed open market purchases in 2020–2021 saw their effective durations explode in 2023 and beyond. The Fed deliberately repeated the mistake of Long Term Capital Management and innumerable other Wall Street houses when it comes to variable duration securities. As late as 2024, the average yield on mortgage-backed securities owned by the Fed and many large commercial banks still averaged less than 3 percent, a disaster in terms of profitability and ultimately solvency. And many large banks led by Bank of America, PNC, and Truist Financial were caught in the same duration trap.

With the start of COVID at the end of Q1 2020, the FOMC pushed interest rates down to the zero bound and caused huge distortions in the bond markets, eliminating the term structure of interest rates overnight. Risk became free, care of the FOMC. For example, the FOMC forced down the cost of residential home mortgages from around 5 percent prior to COVID to just 1 percent by the end of 2020. This represented an extraordinary manipulation of the private mortgage markets that would cause the failure of several large banks in the beginning of 2023 led by Silicon Valley Bank. Whereas past crises involving variable maturity securities like Long Term Capital Management and Kidder Peabody were caused by private hubris, the bank failures of 2023 were caused by commercial bankers who were dumb enough to listen to Fed officials describe the "transitory" nature of inflation. Silicon Valley had 40 percent of its balance sheet in mortgage securities in 2022, ensuring the bank's eventual failure.

When the FOMC eventually allowed interest rates to normalize after 2022, the interest rate risk created by the FOMC's "go big" policy from 2019–2022 was measured in the trillions of dollars. The duration of the Fed's massive mortgage portfolio, roughly a quarter of the total residential loan market in the United States, quadrupled between 2022 and 2024 as interest rates rose and loan prepayments plummeted. The Fed paid over 5 percent on bank reserves and reverse repo transactions, but earned half that much on its mortgage securities, resulting in substantial cash losses to the Treasury that will continue for years to come.[22]

More, because the Fed provided so much excess liquidity to the markets, they were forced to issue ersatz Treasury bills to sop up the flood, like the wizard played by Mickey Mouse in the classic Walt Disney film *Fantasia*. The Fed took deposits from money market funds, foreign banks, and even the GSEs and Federal Home Loan Banks by issuing reverse repurchase agreements or "RRPs." Figure 9.2 from FRED shows RRPs and the Fed's holdings on Treasury bonds and mortgage securities during this period.

Think of the trillions in reverse repurchase agreements issued by the Fed between 2020 and 2024 as a measure of how far the Powell FOMC went beyond what was necessary in terms of providing market liquidity. Gauged against any reasonable standard, the Powell era policy of "going big" with bank reserves from 2019 onward was a

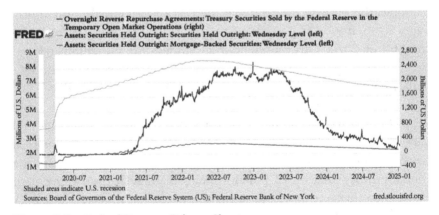

Figure 9.2   Federal Reserve Balance Sheet.
SOURCE: FRED.

decidedly mixed blessing—and one where the downside hazards were largely foreseen by policymakers before the fact yet disregarded by the FOMC.

The sharp decrease in interest rates in 2019 set in motion a vast wave of mortgage refinance volumes that quickly eclipsed volumes for home purchases, an extraordinary event that has vast economic and political ramifications. Half of all mortgages in the United States were refinanced in an 18-month period between March 2020 and September 2021. And this means that half of all homeowners were "locked in" to below market rates, limiting the supply of homes and further boosting home prices. Mark Palim and Rachel Zimmerman of Fannie Mae described the damage done to the housing market by Fed policy:

> An unintended consequence of the policy response to the COVID-19 pandemic was a dramatic decline in mortgage rates that allowed millions of homeowners to refinance their mortgage at rates well below current levels. Additionally, as housing needs changed and mortgage rates moved lower, home sales jumped, growing approximately 14% from 2019 to 2021 compared to a much slower 1% increase from 2018 to 2019. In 2022, mortgage rates doubled. Consumers adjusted to those rising rates, in part, by purchasing fewer homes, and so homes sales declined nearly 18% year over year. This year, while *new* home sales have rebounded, the paucity of *existing* home sales has persisted, declining from a peak annualized sales pace of 6.6 million units in January 2021 to 4.0 million annualized in August 2023. In fact, as of August, the number of existing homes for sale hovered around 1.1 million, 40 percent below the level seen in August 2019, pre-pandemic. As of this writing, in 2023, the 30-year fixed-rate mortgage is at 7.79 percent, more than one full percentage point above where they were at the end of 2022.[23]

An earning warning was sounded by Dan Alpert of Westwood Capital, who noted in a *New York Times* op-ed in November 2023: "The Federal Reserve's relentless attack on inflation is jeopardizing our housing market. The resulting damage is not only having an impact on a critical engine of economic growth but is also, ironically, undermining the war against inflation as well."[24]

By early 2023, however, the damage was done. The value of mortgage securities plummeted, causing Silicon Valley Bank to fail and imposing trillions of dollars in unrealized losses on the banking industry. Mortgage rates doubled and lending volumes fell dramatically, causing a severe recession in the housing sector. Millions of tomorrow's home sales were pulled into the present by the Fed's policy of exceptionally low interest rates. After a huge hiring binge in 2020–2021, nearly one of three people in the mortgage finance industry lost their employment in 2023 and 2024.

The enormous wave of home refinancing and also new home purchase volumes in 2020 onward created an equally huge sea of cash in bank escrow accounts that enabled mortgage lenders to finance two years of loan forbearance for millions of Americans during COVID. The mortgage industry dealt with the mechanics of making legally mandated loan forbearance available for millions of people without any direct compensation or even a thank you from the Biden White House. And the taxpayer bore the ultimate cost of this massive explosion of debt forgiveness driven by the progressive aspirations of the Biden administration. Of course, nobody in Washington thought to thank the private landlords who lost billions due to government mandated loan forbearance and rent moratoria.

Perhaps most important, the huge decline in interest rates engineered by Jerome Powell and the FOMC from 2019–2022 drove up prices for single-family homes by double digits annually, destroying a key component of the American dream in home ownership. The regulatory rules put in place by the Biden administration during the COVID pandemic became permanent, allowing consumers to default on mortgages or leases without any consequence. Giving consumers a free option to default on their mortgage or other debt is economic suicide for a society.

Congress should roll back most of the forbearance and other subsidy programs that were put in place by the Biden administration during COVID, but probably won't. "Without default, mortgage lending becomes an entitlement," argued Tobias Peter at American Enterprise Institute in a 2024 discussion. A number of commercial bankers echoed this view and warn that progressive policies regarding mortgage delinquency only appeared to work because of strong home prices. But getting rid of any entitlement is virtually impossible in twenty-first century America, even when President Donald Trump and the Republicans control the White House and both sides of Capitol Hill.

The Biden administration and Congress pandered shamelessly to consumers during COVID, putting in place moratoriums on mortgage and rent payments that imposed huge cash losses on landlords and private investors, losses that nobody in Washington bothered to notice or address. The debt moratoria legislated in Washington and in state capitals around the country began a deflationary wave in commercial real estate that continues to grow as this book is being completed. And it is pretty clear that the FOMC and the staff of the Federal Reserve banks were aware of these risks.

Almost a decade before, in an essay published by Malz, Schaumburg et al. in a blog post for the Federal Reserve Bank of New York in March 2014, these researchers warned about the risks facing private markets as the Fed grew the size of its portfolio. This argument tracks the work of mortgage banker Alan Boyce, who long warned about the hidden duration risk in the bond market since the start of quantitative easing in 2009. The authors summarized the situation facing banks and private investors at the end of 2022:

> When interest rates increase, the price of an MBS tends to fall at an increasing rate and much faster than a comparable Treasury security due to duration extension, a feature known as the negative convexity of MBS. Managing the interest rate risk exposure of MBS relative to Treasury securities requires dynamic hedging to maintain a desired exposure of the position to movements in yields, as the duration of the MBS changes with changes in the yield curve. This practice is known as duration hedging. The amount and required frequency of hedging depends on the degree of convexity of the MBS, the volatility of rates, and investors' objectives and risk tolerances.[25]

By 2022, the FOMC began to slowly normalize the target for federal funds, but the Committee continued to compound past errors by aggressively reinvesting all redemptions from the Fed's massive portfolio, including $2.7 trillion in mortgage paper. The Fed's asymmetrical approach to normalization in 2022 was illogical and reflected fear of repeating past errors. The Fed did not sell any securities outright and even hesitated to reduce the level of principal reinvestment in its portfolio for fear of causing another repeat of December 2018. The sole tool for normalization was simply to raise the target for federal funds and the rate that the Fed paid on reserves and reverse repurchase agreements, but leave more than $10 trillion in mortgage risk sequestered inside the System Open Market Account.

By the middle of 2022, the Federal Reserve portfolio contained over $8 trillion in securities, including almost $3 trillion in mortgage bonds, and another $2.7 trillion in reverse repurchase agreements. The duration on the mortgage bonds was extending rapidly, making the mortgage position larger than the Treasury portfolio in duration-adjusted terms. More, the Fed arbitrarily set *an above-market interest rate* on reverse RRPs to bail out a lot of private money market funds and banks from the ill-effects of quantitative easing in 2020 onward. Why did the Fed do this? Because what is left of the non-bank primary dealer market for Treasury debt, including money market funds, is in danger of extinction. Once money market funds are forced to shut down, the banks and the Fed will be the main buyers of Treasury debt.

The Fed has issued reverse RPs for more than a decade to maintain a minimum level of interest rates, yet market rates have traded lower than the artificial floor, illustrating the ultimate futility of the Fed's efforts to subsidize money market funds and banks. Meanwhile, the Fed's portfolio of low-coupon mortgage securities will likely remain for many years to come, generating large operating losses for the Treasury.

During the period of the Fed's purchase and reinvestment in mortgage securities, the price of U.S. homes galloped ahead, one of the enduring shortcomings of the Powell strategy of maintaining massive reserves and, indeed, maintaining these reserve levels via reinvestment of proceeds from bond redemptions. The Fed's actions seem to be in direct opposition to the dual mandate because the Committee's actions in the bond market caused home prices to rise dramatically. Only by hiding behind the heavily doctored definition of inflation used by the FOMC in its deliberations, which incredibly excludes home prices, could any economist claim that the Fed had any control over inflation.

Author Felix Salmon noted in May 2024 to the chagrin of many traditional economists: "The meaning of the word 'inflation' has changed. It used to mean rising prices; now it means high prices."[26]

Deficits and Central Bank Independence

As this revised edition of *Inflated* was nearing completion in December 2024, the total national debt was over $36 billion and climbing. During the final years of the Biden administration, the Treasury was creating a trillion in new debt every three to four months. The same hubris that allows Americans to turn the central bank into an engine of inflation also operates on the assumption that the Treasury will always be able to sell debt, what economists childishly refer to as a "continuous market." In Washington the political class worries about budget deficits in a polite fashion, but in fact the United States is already teetering toward default. In a 2024 comment, Robert Patterson and Kevin Kearns set the scene:

> Federal expenditures of trillions of dollars that the country doesn't have—the national debt has soared to an astonishing $34 trillion from $5 trillion in 2000—may create the impression of good times. But it's an illusion. We are clearly living far beyond our means—and stealing growth from future generations while saddling them with repayment obligations. The unprecedented, and unsustainable, trajectory of the twin deficits threatens our superpower status, the dollar as the reserve currency, our living standards, and the viability of most federal programs, particularly the two most relied on by Americans: Social Security and Medicare.[27]

The tough talk from the authors is what approximates concern about the budget in Washington, but the reality in the bond markets is far more serious. Economists make many assumptions about the future, but one of the most outlandish is the idea that the Treasury will always be able to sell more debt to cover interest and principal payments. In fact, the market for Treasury securities—the "deepest and most liquid in the world"—has faltered repeatedly since late 2008. In March 2020, for example, the Fed was forced to buy several trillion in U.S. Treasury debt to essentially prevent a default. Major media in the United States ignored this event with some exceptions,[28] but researchers Lev Menand and Joshua Younger described the near default:

> In March of 2020, as the COVID-19 pandemic spread, Treasury markets became so impaired that simple transactions were difficult (if not impossible) to execute. Prices dropped rapidly even as investors moved toward, not away from, low-risk assets. A financial crisis loomed. To prevent what some warned could be a catastrophe rivaling the 2008 collapse, the U.S. monetary authority, the Federal Reserve, intervened with a massive program of "market functioning purchases." It bought more than $2 trillion of Treasuries and offered to finance trillions more as part of an unprecedented and open-ended commitment to stabilize the market. Although the effort was successful, it raised questions about the line between money and debt issue as mechanisms of public finance, and whether there in fact was one at all.[29]

A number of observers have worried that a large foreign central bank in China or the Middle East could suddenly sell Treasury bonds and thereby destabilize the market for U.S. government debt and the dollar. Such a scenario is not a concern because dollars and risk-free assets such as Treasury debt are infinitely fungible and remain in strong demand. A greater concern for the long-term future of the dollar is the risk from idiocy within Washington, a magical city on a hill where any act of stupidity is possible.

There is a steady erosion in confidence in the U.S. economy because of the action or inaction of the U.S. Congress and successive administrations in Washington. The collection of dilettantes and rent-seekers that fill Washington today would make characters of the Gilded Age described by Mark Twain seem righteous by comparison. The operative term in Washington is omission. Twain said most famously: "Never put off till tomorrow what you can do the day after tomorrow."

In 2024, when Donald Trump or Kamala Harris talked about tax cuts and subsidies for home purchases or auto loans instead of a plan to balance the federal budget, this is not credible behavior. But since the governments in many other nations are in even worse fiscal disarray than the United States, Washington is able to continue the great pretense of fiscal probity while relying upon inflation. Suffice to say that in 2024 both Trump and Harris had long lists of new programs and giveaways, but no way to pay for them save more debt.

A big part of reining in public expenditures is spending less, both domestically and around the world. If you ask most Americans how we should address the federal deficits and debt, the answer is to spend less. Yet when you ask these same Americans to accept less in the way of benefits from government or to pay more in taxes, the response is universally negative. Focus on the cost of inflation on wages and savings as a result of federal deficits gets you scant more attention from the public. But tell them that there are rich individuals and companies with tens of trillions in cash stashed abroad to evade taxes and suddenly the light goes on.

Of course, collecting unpaid taxes is the duty of any responsible regime, but the key issue to remember is that the market for Treasury debt was created by the government. The Treasury began to issue debt more than a century ago to finance World War I and the New Deal, and greatly increased this financing role in World War I. The market for government debt was built upon a foundation of nonbank broker-dealers, many of whom were crushed in 2008. This left the market increasingly supported by hedge funds and other "shadow banks" of unknown origin and substance. The "near-money" represented by Treasury bonds was almost unsalable in March 2020, a dangerous portend for thing to come.[30]

In their important essay, Menand and Younger identify several phases in the development of the Fed as an independent central bank. In the first phase, the Federal Reserve System and the Treasury were separate. With World War I, the Great Depression, and World War II, the Fed incentivized banks to purchase Treasury debt and even bought Treasury debt itself. After 1951, the Fed won its independence from the Treasury, and later focused on developing a nonbank dealer market to support government debt issuance. Since banks and securities firms were legally separate, the nonbank sector grew and supported strong economic growth through the end of the twentieth century.

With 2008, however, the nonbank dealer community was decimated and many primary dealers were acquired by or converted into commercial banks. The golden age of nonbank finance that accounted for much of the economic growth from the 1980s through 2008 ended abruptly. A great deal of capacity for underwriting Treasury debt disappeared in a matter of days. In their heyday, firms like Countrywide, Washington Mutual, Bear Stearns, and Lehman Brothers sold a lot of Treasury bonds and provided capital to the market for government bonds. That dealer capital is now gone.

The final period that brings us through to 2024 and the election of Donald Trump to a second term as president sees the Fed once again as the major buyer of last resort for U.S. Treasury debt, with money market funds, hedge funds, and commercial banks playing a secondary role. If we see the Fed winning its operational freedom from the Treasury in 1951 as the peak of central bank independence, then surely today the U.S. central bank is once again captive and totally subsumed by the fiscal needs of the Treasury. How long will it be before the Fed keeps the target for federal funds artificially low to accommodate the Treasury as it did during the Depression and World War II.

The rise and fall of the nonbank dealer community is a key part of the story when it comes to the Treasury's ability to sell debt. During the golden age of nonbank finance in the United States during the 1980s and 1990s, the primary dealer community formed a deep ecosystem of market makers and funds that supported Treasury issuance. Money market funds invested in government securities and used repurchase agreements to provide liquidity that was as good as cash. But since 2008 and particularly 2020, the private dealer market for Treasury securities has collapsed several times, leaving the central bank as the sole counterparty for government debt.

The Fed was created in 1913 to provide liquidity for private commerce and the currency, but in the years that followed the central bank has come to be more and more associated with the needs of the state rather than private markets. Paul Wachtel and Mario Blejer of CATO Institute wrote in 2020:

> While the overwhelming majority of academic and central bank practitioners continue to support central bank independence, it is clear that, while independence continues to be protected, its golden age ended with the crisis a decade ago, and

it did not end gently. The first wave of charges against central banks was straightforward: the worst financial crisis since the 1930s took place after central bankers worldwide were handed, or thought they were handed, most of the economic-management levers and were given much discretion in the design and certainly the implementation of their economic policies. Given these perceptions, there is no way they can now avoid blame, and preserve intact their prestige and standing. Indeed, the reputation of "independent central bankers" was severely damaged by the crisis, removing partially the implicit taboo involved in asking the unmentionable: perhaps central banks should not be, nor should aim at being, so independent after all?[31]

Or as the Hayek quotation that appears at the front of this book declares, central banks are never independent of the state that creates them. When the state is dissolute in matters of finance, its credibility internally and externally fails. Given that the Fed functions first and foremost on maintaining public confidence, perhaps credibility for the central bank is more important than independence.

"In 2012 when Ben Bernanke promoted and shifted over to 'inflation targeting' the idea was to use Fed credibility to get markets to set expectations on the 2% target," notes economist Robert Brusca in September 2024 at the Lotos Club in New York. "The idea was to have Fed policy and markets pull together for a common goal sort of like the two Mouseketeers: 'one for all, and all for 2%!' One problem . . . there was never any specification about HOW the Fed would do that . . . Another problem . . . there was never any attention paid to what would happen if the Fed lost credibility. And if the Fed did lose credibility there is no clue anywhere as to how the Fed gets it back. The whole shebang depends on credibility and on the Fed having 'the craft' to achieve a 2% inflation target."[32]

As the federal debt grows and the related economic problems multiply, it is interesting to note that the Federal Reserve System has been actively cooperating with the Treasury to avoid a U.S. default for more than half a century. In a memo unearthed by researcher Nathan Tankus, former Treasury Undersecretary Paul Volcker called Federal

Reserve Board Chairman Arthur Burns in 1973 to discuss the federal budget. "A confidential memo documenting this event was declassified on August 21st 2020," Tankus relates. The memo describes the phone call this way:

> Mr. Volcker had telephoned Chairman Burns shortly after 9:30 a.m. on December 3 to ask whether the Federal Reserve, under existing law and regulations, could and would make a formal commitment at this time to refrain from tendering for redemption its holdings of Treasury bills maturing on December 6, in the event that the statutory debt ceiling remained below the amount of outstanding debt on that date. If the Federal Reserve did not tender those holdings for redemption, the Treasury would be able to meet other obligations for a somewhat longer period.[33]

Tankus notes that because the Fed would receive no interest on the debt after the maturity date: "That means the Federal Reserve was both foregoing profits, in addition to effectively providing credit to the Treasury." So much for the independence of the Federal Reserve Board from the U.S. Treasury.[34]

Of course, just as Chairman Burns faced pressure from President Richard Nixon, Chairman Volcker also faced pressure from the White House. Volcker recounts in his 2018 biography that President Ronald Reagan's chief of staff, James Baker, ordered him not to raise interest rates until after the 1984 election. Baker's successor, Treasury Secretary Donald Regan, later tried to replace Volcker with economist Beryl Sprinkel in 1983. Regan was thwarted by the timely intervention of Senator Paul Laxalt, as we discussed earlier. But that outcome could have easily been changed had greater political and fiscal pressure been focused on President Reagan.

Former Fed Governor Alan Blinder famously said in 1994: "The last duty of a central banker is to tell the public the truth." But this, of course, assumes that our political leaders and central bankers know the truth in the first place and have the courage to speak truth to power. The false narrative coming from U.S. political leaders and policymakers after 2008 and again after 2020 was that the U.S. financial system is strong and sound. The 2008 Financial Crisis did serious, long-term damage to the U.S. economy and the ability of the U.S. Treasury to finance its obligations. The subsequent expansion of the public sector is slowly crowding out the world of private finance, both nonbanks and commercial banks alike.

In 2024, the Dow and S&P have repeatedly hit record highs. But even as the value of the stock market grows in dollars, the number of firms traded on the market is shrinking and has been since the mid-1990s. This is a troubling development, both in terms of the fiscal outlook for the United States and also what it says about future economic growth.

First and foremost, the slow demise of nonbank finance, including the U.S. bond market, private equity, and publicly listed stocks, is a big threat to the U.S. economy. In the previous chapter, we referred to the annihilation of the primary dealers in 2008 and how this damaged the ability of the U.S. Treasury to finance its debt. But the greater concern is that the damage done to the world of private finance away from obligations of the United States is considerable and hurts future growth prospects. It is nonbank finance, and not state-supported commercial banks, that supports economic growth and creates jobs.

Government consumes and redistributes economic value, but creates nothing. At best it maintains a civil society that encourages the free enterprise systems, but at worst Washington is a gorgon, robbing the savings of individuals and businesses via inflation to feed the endless needs of welfare state and defense sectors. Despite endless pronouncements and regulations concerning fiscal issues, the reality is that the United States has lost the will to govern itself and collect sufficient taxes to pay for public needs.

Offshore Dollars and Taxes

Alexander Hamilton was a great advocate of national debt as a way to strengthen the finances of the republic, but he also knew that printing money was much easier than paying taxes. "The stamping of paper," Hamilton explained, "is an operation so much easier than the laying of taxes, that a government, in the practice of paper emissions, would rarely fail in any such emergency, to indulge itself too far in the employment of that resource, to avoid as much as possible, one less auspicious to present popularity."[35]

Over the decades, the political will to collect taxes in the United States has failed, often because conservative politicians think (wrongly) that depriving the Treasury of revenue will somehow slow federal spending. If Democrats tend to be too enamored of demand-side policies and debt, Republicans tend to have a nineteenth-century view of money and markets that is entirely antiquated. What the Civil War proved and the New Deal and subsequent decades confirmed, a legal tender fiat currency and Treasury emissions are interchangeable. But when American individuals or corporations avoid taxes, they are essentially forcing the Treasury to borrow.

"It's not right that everyday Americans pay taxes while struggling to make ends meet, but some of the wealthiest in this country have been able to evade payment," noted Treasury Secretary Janet Yellen in August 2023. "This is money our government needs to protect our national security, provide social security and healthcare, and invest in our nation's infrastructure, among many other priorities."[36] Estimates of how much money is hidden offshore vary, but the numbers total into the tens of trillions of dollars, at least as much as the national debt.

A large portion of the amount of offshore dollar assets represents tax avoidance by U.S. individuals and corporations accumulated since World War II. While the national debt measured in tens of trillions of dollars may seem a substantial sum, the total of offshore assets created by American individuals and companies to avoid taxes is arguably higher. In particular, the notion frequently advanced in Washington that lower corporate tax rates will lead to repatriation of untaxed corporate profits stashed offshore, thereby funding increased investment and productivity, and ultimately creating more jobs in the United States is, upon reflection, complete nonsense.

First and foremost, corporate investment decisions are based upon the cost of capital and the prospective equity returns that new investment can generate, not the availability of actual cash in a given country. In a world where corporate bond yields are still low by historical standards and equity market valuations are at all-time highs, the effective cost of capital for many multinational companies is arguably negative. The problem is not funding new investments with cash but finding new endeavors in which to deploy cheap and plentiful capital.

The economists who largely control the major central banks in the industrialized nations may try to manipulate markets and cancel excessive debt through inflation, but they cannot manufacture attractive investments—at least not yet. The Fed's issuance of ersatz T-bills in the form of reverse repurchase agreements with above market rates are a troubling precedent.

The low-interest rate regime put in place by the Federal Reserve, European Central Bank, and Bank of Japan arguably retards new productive investments by driving cash into real estate, commodities, and speculative whimsies such as crypto currencies and electric vehicles (EVs). The same logic that permits incompetent politicians in the United States or China to mandate economic activity in areas such as EVs, and waste tens of billions of dollars in the process, drives capital flight from both nations. When Vice President Kamala Harris proposed taxing unrealized capital gains during the 2024 election campaign, you could almost hear the American business community fret in unison. Yet even committed socialists such as Harris, for some odd reason, will never talk about collecting trillions in corporate taxes that are already owed.

The release of the Panama Papers in 2016 highlighted hundreds of firms as users of secret offshore vehicles and documented that these vehicles are used to finance corruption, avoid taxes, and expropriate value from shareholders via fraud. Yet even this significant look into the opaque world of offshore money is dwarfed by the totality of the tax avoidance. Most of the money secreted away to foreign jurisdictions is hiding in plain sight, in the financial statements of global corporations like Apple Computer and Facebook. The notion that any of this money would return to its home jurisdiction fails to reflect the true nature of offshore tax schemes and how problematic it is to reverse these complex tax transactions.

In 2016, Karen C. Burke and Grayson M.P. McCouch of the University of Florida published an article entitled "Sham Partnerships and Equivocal Transactions" for the American Bar Association's journal

Tax Lawyer. The understated article provides an in-depth look at how U.S. corporations have stashed literally trillions of dollars in offshore venues since the 1990s to avoid domestic taxes. The authors stated:

> Corporate tax shelters proliferated during the 1990s, exploiting the flexible partnership tax rules of Subchapter K to defer or eliminate tax on hundreds of billions of dollars of corporate income. The corporate tax shelters were typically structured as a financing transaction in which a U.S. corporation leased its own assets back from a partnership, generating a stream of deductible business expenses while shifting taxable income to a tax-indifferent party such as a foreign bank. Since the transaction allowed the U.S. corporation to raise capital in a tax-advantaged manner in connection with its regular business operations, it was assumed that the transaction had economic substance. Nevertheless, in scrutinizing these shelters, courts have invoked a sham partnership doctrine, derived from the longstanding Culbertson intent test, which disregards a partnership that lacks a bona fide purpose (or, alternatively, a purported partner whose interest does not constitute a bona fide equity participation).[37]

The Internal Revenue Service is on to these fraudulent scams for which, of note, there is no statute of limitations. In January 2017, the U.S. Supreme Court declined to hear an appeal involving an adverse tax decision by the IRS against an affiliate of Dow Chemical known as Chemtech (*Chemtech Royalty Associates, L.P., By Dow Europe, S.A., as Tax Matters Partner, et al., Petitioners v. United States*).

The two transactions reviewed by the Supreme Court are referred to as Chemtech I, dealing with tax years 1993–1997, and Chemtech II, dealing with tax years 1998–2003. Chemtech I was promoted and marketed to large corporate taxpayers by Goldman Sachs under the trade name SLIPs, standing for "Special Limited Investment Partnerships," and was implemented by Dow with the assistance of tax lawyers at the law firm of King & Spalding. Chemtech II was designed and implemented by the tax lawyers at King & Spalding. Both arrangements are enormously complicated in their construction and operation, but ultimately came down to deliberate tax evasion.

At issue in this case is whether the IRS incorrectly adjusted certain partnership items of Chemtech for the 1993–2003 tax years. In addition, the United States sought and won penalties for 1997–2003 tax years. In dispute, among other things, was whether the investment in the SLIP was debt or equity. Expert Jole Finard provided analysis and testimony related to the capital markets risk and reward attributes of the banks' investment in the SLIP. District Court Judge Jackson ruled in favor of the United States and imposed a 20 percent penalty on Dow. The U.S. Supreme Court affirmed Judge Jackson.

The hundreds of corporations that have used offshore transactions to hide revenue knew that Dow's appeal was their last hope to avoid sanctions by the IRS. General Electric is an example of a U.S. corporation that has been forced by the IRS to reverse a bogus offshore "asset sale" transaction used to hide tax liability. There are tens of trillions in offshore tax shelters that could be recovered by the U.S. Treasury given the funding and political will.

The irony of any discussion of tax avoidance by U.S. residents, of course, is that there are very few places to put illegal funds and even fewer ways to move or deploy these assets. The network of U.S. trade sanctions, antiterrorism and anti-money laundering (AML) mechanisms put in place over the past several decades has essentially created a binary choice for individuals and organizations. Individuals and companies are increasingly restricted in their options to conceal wealth, but corporations continue to use complex financial transactions to avoid taxes.

The United States was among the first nations to adopt anti-money laundering legislation when it established the Bank Secrecy Act (BSA) in 1970. An early effort to detect and prevent money laundering, the BSA has since been amended and strengthened by additional anti-money laundering laws. The Financial Crimes Enforcement Network (FinCEN) is now the designated administrator of the BSA—with a mission to "safeguard the financial system from the abuses of financial crime, including terrorist financing, money laundering and other illicit activity."

In 1989, several countries and organizations formed the global Financial Action Task Force (FATF). Its mission is to devise and promote international standards to prevent money laundering. Shortly after the 9/11 attacks on the World Trade Center and other targets, FATF expanded its mandate to include AML and combating terrorist financing.

In 2024, the United States further proposed expanding regulations and compliance to all financial advisors operating in the United States.

In the world of global dollar hegemony, Washington is able to impose huge legal and operational rules on the financial transaction of anyone who touches the dollar world. Either you are on the grid and compliant with tax and trade laws in the United States and EU, or you are entirely off the grid and avoid touching dollars or U.S. financial institutions entirely. This is particularly true with crypto currencies, private financial tokens that are seen by U.S. law enforcement and financial regulators as vehicles for facilitating money laundering, terrorism, and other illegal acts subject to U.S. sanctions.

In October 2020, the Department of Justice published a lengthy "cryptocurrency enforcement framework detailing its approach to the nascent space and discussing potential crimes," *Coindesk* reports. "The document also suggested the U.S. government would enforce its laws regardless of where exchanges—referred to as virtual asset service providers, or VASPs—are based. In other words, these exchanges should comply with U.S. laws—even for their non-U.S. customers."[38]

"Because of the global and cross-border nature of transactions involving virtual assets, the lack of consistent anti-money laundering/countering the financing of terrorism (AML/CFT) regulation and supervision over VASPs across jurisdictions—and the complete absence of such regulation and supervision in certain parts of the world—is detrimental to the safety and stability of the international financial system," the DOJ framework states.

Just as the infamous American gangster Al Capone was taken down for violations of income tax laws, the world of crypto assets is under an oblique assault by regulators around the world. The particular routes of attack are consumer protection, anti-money laundering (AML) and know-your customer (KYC), to start. Add bank fraud, tax evasion, and facilitating terrorism to the mix and you have a pretty good roadmap for the future of crypto assets that are not 100 percent onshore for the purpose of U.S. law.

Compliance with U.S. law and regulation is the new litmus test for crypto assets. The fact that Treasury secretary Janet Yellen raised the issue with the Financial Stability Oversight Council (FSOC) should be sufficient warning to the wise. Yet apparently intelligent people like

Tesla founder Elon Musk and Twitter and Square founder Jack Dorsey continue to encourage retail investors to traffic in crypto assets that may ultimately be problematic in terms of U.S. law and regulation.

The basic problem with crypto assets is not merely the possibility of financial fraud, a very real risk, but anti-money laundering and know-your-customer rules. The same U.S. financial regulatory regime that has nearly destroyed offshore venues such as the Bahamas is now focused on crypto. The concern is that the market for crypto includes criminals, terrorists, and other parties who are not onshore in terms of U.S. law and regulation. Any individuals facilitating transactions with such parties are tainted by these illegal activities. An innocent American investor or institution could buy crypto assets from a terrorist organization and thereby become implicated in facilitating terrorism.

The special role of the dollar in American finance allows the U.S. government to impose harsh compliance and reporting requirements on foreign nationals and institutions that it does not follow in reciprocity with other states. U.S. AML/CFT rules now cover most of business and finance in the United States, including foreign nationals who happen to have relationships with U.S. individuals or companies. The new 2024 rules apply to non-U.S. entities, even if they do not maintain any offices or personnel in the United States.

Tax evasion, of course, is one of the oldest forms of human endeavor. Two thousand years ago, the priests of the great temple in Jerusalem ran a hidden scheme for gain at the expense of religious pilgrims. When they made a market in temple money, they had a bid and an offer price. But going back to the time of Moses, the Old Testament forbade the use of two measures. The priests were meant to buy or sell temple money at the mid-market price.

Since the temple priests collected taxes on behalf of Rome, when their deception was publicly uncovered by Jesus of Nazareth, the penalty was severe. Christ died for his boldness in 33 CE. Forty years after, in 70 CE, the Roman legions descended upon Jerusalem, destroyed the great temple, taking it apart stone by stone, to find the hidden gold concealed by the temple priests. As Jesus said in the gospel: "Give unto Ceasar what is Ceasar's."

Chapter 10

New American Dreams

I n the course of our journey through three centuries of American monetary and political history, there are a number of recurring themes that become increasingly prominent as the decades pass. Reflecting the classic view of the founders, John Adams expressed hope for a world that was not merely defined by commercial standards but comprised of a society of individuals who were free to pursue their own definitions of liberty and success. This classical liberal design of the Founders has given way to a more commercial egalitarianism copied from the states of Europe that puts government before the rights of the individual.

The American society of the 2020s is built upon failed collectivist principals of equality of outcome rather than the more rigorous world of individual liberty and opportunity. China, the Soviet Union, North Korea, Venezuela, Argentina, and Zimbabwe all testify to the failure of collective economic schemes and the authoritarian governments that spawn them, yet Americans seem bound to repeat this pattern of failure.

Only recent émigrés to the United States who have lived under communist systems like China or Russia seem to appreciate the value of a democratic and free society. "I grew up in a socialist country, and I have seen what that does to people," billionaire Hungarian immigrant Thomas Peterffy said in a 2012 television ad. "There is no hope, no freedom, no pride in achievement. The nation became poorer and poorer. And that's what I see happening here," said the founder of Interactive Brokers.

The financial and economic trends since the turn of the twenty-first century merely confirm the pattern set in the preceding years, with public sector debt and other government obligations growing much faster than the real economy in the United States and also around the globe. As America struggles with its enormous federal budget deficit, societies from the EU to China likewise contend with massive spending imbalances and economic misallocation directed by inept politicians.

The reliance on debt and the unwillingness of Americans to live within their means are some of the primary threads in the modern narrative of the American dream, but those threads stretch back to colonial times. The silverites of the nineteenth century and the crypto traders of the twenty-first century are both looking for a windfall. The greatest ever generation that won World War II and the Cold War celebrated for decades, leaving behind a monumental tab. With consumers already pressed to the wall by the declining real incomes, no politician dares suggest higher taxes on the broad population.

Progressive politicians complain about greedy corporations, but the truth is that inflation caused by public debt and government monetary expansion is the true enemy of all, rich and poor. The 2 percent inflation target enshrined by the Fed since 2008, compounded annually, means that Americans will lose half of the real value of their wages and savings over just two decades. In twenty-first-century America, "price stability" equals at least 2 percent inflation because the global dollar must continue to expand or risk collapse. As Irving Fisher predicted in 1933, America is caught in a vast debt-deflation trap and there is no obvious way out save more inflation.

As office-bearers promise more and more in economic entitlements, the real promise of the American dream dies. The American dream requires not only opportunity, but hard work and risk. Government sponsorship of outcomes focused on certain ethnic and social groups renders the dream irrelevant. Meeting needs without achievement and effort is an empty result that ultimately diminishes the individual. The natural corruption that occurs as government grows into a controlling administrative state further detracts from individual freedom and achievement. The promise of life, liberty, and the pursuit of happiness is dead in the world of big government.

Noted author, philosopher, and longshoreman Eric Hoffer once observed: "Up to now, America has not been a good milieu for the rise of a mass movement. What starts out here as a mass movement ends up as a racket, a cult, or a corporation. Unlike those anywhere else, the masses in America have never despaired of the present and are not willing to sacrifice it for a new life and a new world."[1]

Successive American presidents since the 1980s relied upon steadily falling interest rates to manufacture the appearance of economic expansion, at least in nominal terms. Fed chairmen from Alan Greenspan onward touted the periods of nominal growth while ignoring the broader measures of inflation. These broader inflation indices show that American consumers and businesses were constantly losing ground to rising prices for everything from food to shelter to education. In that sense, the entitlements offered by American politicians in the twenty-first century are a cruel canard, a deception whereby the office-bearer promises some help or benefit, but fails to deliver in real terms.

American politicians, like their counterparts around the world, have essentially run out of ideas when it comes to promoting economic growth without stoking inflation. As debt levels balloon, debt service costs curtail economic growth. Politicians from Joe Biden to Xi Jinping to Donald Trump are unskilled when it comes to making any economic or financial decisions. Politicians usually inhibit growth more than promote it, but the easy policies like merely dropping interest rates, which sufficed in the 1990s and 2000s, are ineffective today.

Unfortunately, the "new" ideas coming from American leaders are no better than some of the outlandish schemes that emerged a century ago, when America's liberal tendency coalesced following the disappointment of World War I and Wilsonian liberalism. Yet at least Wilsonian liberals "remained committed to the free market in the face of war and depression," notes David Steigerwald of Ohio State University, "and continued to oppose interest groups in spite of the emergence of mass politics."

Most Americans are unaware of the deep roots of socialism in the United States going back to the Progressive era a century ago. In the 2020s, calling a politician "progressive" is polite code for socialist.

The fact of World War II and the fight against fascism made a socialist agenda unfashionable in America for decades after the war. After all, there were three New Deals in America, Germany, and Russia, and these systems were in deadly competition. In the economic deflation and political disillusionment of the 1920s, the founders of today's American liberalism—Herbert Croly, Randolf Bourne, H.G. Wells, Sinclair Lewis, and H.L. Mencken—created a vision for an American state governed by liberal intellectuals. These leading lights of collectivism were European in their tastes and allegiances, and like FDR often more loyal to Great Britain than to America. They despised America's ethic of small-town democracy and free enterprise, and served to gradually undermine the free market orientation of the Democratic Party.

Croly, who was cofounder of the *New Republic* magazine, was the Progressive Party candidate for president in 1912. His program called for "a great increase of federal power to regulate interstate industry and a sweeping program of social reform designed to put human rights above property rights."[2] Croly stated the case for using government to impose socialism from above that is heard today from Democrats like Barack Obama, Joseph Biden, and Kamala Harris:

> Democracy must stand or fall on a platform of possible human perfectibility. If human nature cannot be improved by institutions, democracy is at best a more than usually safe form of political organization . . . But if it is to work better as well as merely longer, it must have some leavening effect on human nature; and the sincere democrat is obliged to assume the power of the leaven.[3]

"Today's brand of liberalism, led by Barack Obama, has displaced the old Main Street private-sector middle class with a new middle class composed of public-sector workers allied with crony capitalists and the country's arbiters of elite style and taste," wrote Fred Siegle in his classic 2013 book *Revolt Against the Masses*.[4]

Obama is an American who aspires to be European and despises the white American middle class. His political philosophy is based upon the regime of "rights" created by FDR and America's liberal leaders during the New Deal, Siegle notes: "The assertion of economic rights began the process of displacing a constitutional order that since the Founding had been organized with individuals with natural rights."

And during the Obama administration (2009–2017), America's debt relative to GDP accelerated dramatically to over 100 percent.

As the Democratic Party endorsed an explicitly socialist brand of mass politics and rejected the traditional American system of free enterprise, it has become more authoritarian and intolerant. Many Democrats, for example, believe that the liberal tendency in Americans should have political monopoly and that Republicans and traditional conservatives should not be allowed to run for public office or even speak freely. Radical New York socialist Alexandria Ocasio-Cortez in 2024 openly called for censorship of public speech. Robert Kennedy, Jr., in a statement ending his 2024 presidential campaign, blasted the Democratic Party—his former party and that of his father and uncle—saying that it has become "the party of war, censorship, corruption, big pharma, big tech, big tech, big ag and big money."

In the 2020s, the push for economic "rights" by Democrats reached a point of absurdity. During the televised September 2024 presidential debate, Vice President Kamala Harris proposed a list of giveaways that would make a third-world dictator red with envy. She offered to subsidize new small businesses and give a free $25,000 down payment to poor families to buy a home. Whether or not these poor families can actually afford to buy *and* own a home is another matter.

More than 10 percent of all government-guaranteed FHA mortgages were in default in mid-2024, but apparently Vice President Harris wanted to see that number even higher—regardless of what it costs taxpayers or consumers. The well-worn Progressive strategy of stoking demand for homes or whatever else only results in higher prices for food and shelter for consumers.

"These proposals rest on the faulty premise that housing affordability can be improved through subsidies for construction and home purchases," noted Ed Pinto and Tobias Peter of American Enterprise Institute. "But history offers a cautionary tale: From the 1930s to 2008, Congress passed and presidents signed into law at least 43 housing, urban renewal, and community development programs. Despite their lofty promises, these initiatives consistently failed in making housing more affordable. Candidate Harris's plan will be no different."[5]

President Joe Biden made giving away taxpayer dollars a hallmark of his administration, whether in terms of promoting demand for housing, admitting millions of illegal émigrés, subsidizing domestic production of electric vehicles, lithium batteries, and microchips, or forgiving billions of dollars in government-guaranteed student loans. The Biden administration even considered creating a sovereign wealth fund to invest badly in other industries. Meanwhile, Republican candidate Donald Trump promised to cap interest rates for credit cards and auto loans at 10%, a completely impractical proposal. After his election win in November 2024, Trump proposed to buy Greenland from Denmark to enhance national security.

It is absurd for any American leader to even propose subsidies for basic necessities much less a sovereign wealth fund. The free enterprise system that built America's prosperity did not require state sponsorship. Proponents of an American sovereign wealth fund are essentially the same people who see economic prosperity in government programs, gambling casinos, or crypto currencies. Trading in crypto tokens, for example, creates no new wealth, but does generate new taxable income owed to the Internal Revenue Service. But like many of the economic ideas that have come out of the political community in recent years, a sovereign wealth fund or a "strategic reserve" of crypto makes no sense economically or financially—especially in an economy that is already growing below potential.

"Launching a sovereign wealth fund is probably our least-bad, bad idea," noted Allison Schrager in a 2024 commentary. "Trump floated the idea, but apparently the Biden administration had already been working on it. The concept is to use revenue (likely taxes or money from energy sales—though money is fungible, so it doesn't really matter) to invest in things the government thinks we need. They're confident these investments will pay off big and compensate for the debt we'll incur. This is otherwise known as a leveraged bet—what could go wrong?"[6]

The notion of making new state investments in American industries even as liberal policies stoke inflation and increase the scope of government seems like a great contradiction. To reduce inflation, better to reduce the scope of government and scrap the sovereign wealth fund. Yet in the fall of 2024, both the Democrat Kamala Harris and the Republican Donald Trump were mostly figuring out how to give away more money or cut taxes. Former President Trump, for example, proposed an end to taxes on gratuities and threatened to cap interest rates for consumers, all paid for with higher tariffs. The federal budget deficit was never discussed in their one single debate. The entire political process in 2024 devolved into a bidding war to see who could give America consumer more free stuff.

Successive regimes in Washington have embraced ever more absurd levels of entitlements and public spending and debt, yet the demands from consumers and business for subsidies and relief from higher prices grow ever louder. Just as there is no limit to the market demands for liquidity in the Fed's latest operating model, the demand for new public spending is likewise without effective limit. Yet higher public spending, funded with debt, only means ever higher inflation for businesses and consumers.

Even as America descends into a collectivist dead end, in Argentina libertarian President Javier Gerardo Milei is dismantling decades of mismanagement and debt under that nation's previous socialist governments. How long will it take for Americans to realize that borrowing and printing more and more fiat paper currency is the road to hell in economic terms? Some analysts argue that the United States should adopt Modern Monetary Theory, which is another way of dignifying money printing and hyperinflation. Yet it seems that America has already adopted this irrational view. Author and political analyst Joe Costello put the world of government spending and inflation into context in an unpublished 2024 interview with the author:

> As I used to argue with the Modern Monetary Theory people that we already have such a system that you want to replace. Who really knows what the MMT advocates want, bank-debt money with just straight out printing into the economy? Well, that's been done before too, and it's no cure-all. I never understood MMT as monetary reform, except in just changing some of the centralized chairs of power. That held no interest. The other thing, most especially what's been done since 2008, you can replace wherever they use "stability" with "going up." Everything they've done since 2008 has been to ensure that markets keep going up and they have. Where is Bernie Madoff when you really need him? With this present financial system, it is very hard to argue it provides much in the terms of economic viability, that it offers much of anything except lucre for those participating. Most especially, it's impossible to say it in any way values economic activity in any sort of constructive way, at the very least in providing a helpful measure of value for the hard economy.

The policies of Xi Jinping in communist China and the Democratic Party in America are mostly indistinguishable. Economic mandates for everything from housing to global warming to fully electric vehicles come from the governments of the two global superstates, yet these mandates are severely lacking when it comes to economic and technical design. The ongoing crisis in China's housing sector, for example, will consume hundreds of billions in capital for homes nobody wants and cities where nobody lives. The vast misallocation of economic resources directed by governments over the past decade into various initiatives total into the hundreds of billions of dollars, yet the world has made little progress in slowing global warming or achieving many of the other goals set by various progressive governments.

More than anything else, government directed investments merely confirm the impotence of all nations to address complex problems for society.[7] Yet the same liberal politicians who complain about wealthy individuals or corporate greed richly reward government employees even as private workers suffer a continuous decline in the real value of their income. Wages for government employees, for example, are roughly twice the level of compensation for private sector workers. And today the public sector unions in America are allowed to make political contributions to their political sponsors, a grotesque example of institutionalized political corruption. "It is impossible to bargain collectively with the government," noted George Meany, the former president of the AFL–CIO in 1955. Public sector unions insist on laws that serve their interests—at the expense of the common good.[8]

Over the past decade, the political process of expanding the available pool of credit, driving up asset prices and nominal economic activity, and then deflating the resulting bubble, created the temporary impression of economic growth in the United States. The average American was once again enticed and seduced by the image of the gold rush, of making easy money today by borrowing from tomorrow.

James Grant wrote in *Money of the Mind*: "As the marginal debtor received the marginal loan, the extra car (or house, boat or corporation) was sold. All this worked to enlarge the national income."[9] But did this increase in notional income result in a real increase in personal or national revenue, either for America or the world? America inflated, but did we create more value or cut the same pie into smaller pieces?

The Growth Illusion

"Lending to yourself only works if the newly created and borrowed money will be accepted by the rest of the world in exchange for real stuff," William Dunkelberg, chief economist for the National Federation of Independent Business since 1971, told the author in 2010. "We get huge trade deficits instead of inflation as long as this willingness persists."[10]

Dunkelberg summarized the key assumption made by American leaders decades ago, namely that the world will continue to buy fiat paper dollars and Treasury securities indefinitely. The corollary enumerated by Dunkelberg and Robert Triffin before him is that the only cost to this arrangement is big trade deficits, but in fact this assumption turns out to be incomplete. "Providing reserves and exchanges for the whole world is too much for one country and one currency to bear," noted Henry H. Fowler, U.S. Secretary of the Treasury (1956–1968).[11]

The cost to Americans for the special role of the dollar is not just the abstraction known as "trade deficits," but also high domestic inflation. This seems to be especially the case when the government runs big fiscal deficits, which transfer public resources to debt holders. As we noted earlier, large public debts balanced atop a fiat currency worked in nominal terms for a half century after World War II, but with declining economic returns from new debt, it seems to be a recipe for economic stagnation and default.

Since the Fed's legal mandate described in the 1978 Humphrey-Hawkins legislation is purely domestic in focus, the cost of being the global reserve currency is never mentioned in the Fed's minutes or even discussed by members of Congress. Consider the fact that American policymakers regularly and forcefully engaged on global financial issues half a century ago, yet today such issues are barely given secondary attention by presidents and members of Congress. Yet perhaps the reason for this neglect is that America's contribution to the world as sponsor of the reserve currency grows ever more costly measured against inflation.

Over the past half century, Americans generally lost ground to inflation but made it up on asset price appreciation or financial speculation. The half of Americans with investments in financial assets or real estate often were able to build wealth faster than the underlying rate of price increase. And inflation of real and financial assets actually accelerated the investment returns for wealthy Americans, especially in housing but also in stocks and many other asset classes. The other half of the American population, however, have seen their purchasing power and savings decimated.

The ebb and flow of the federal deficit, as well as the manic rhythm of Fed monetary policy, further boosted profits for astute investors while consumers saw their purchasing power diminished. The disparity between those who benefit from inflation and those who lost ground slowly created a political divide in America over the past 50 years, this even as millions of desperate émigrés from failed societies around the world sought to come to the promised land. The American addiction to inflation and debt is one obvious theme that emerges from our inquiry, an addiction that had contributed to financial market crises and overall volatility even after the creation of the Fed.

One need only consider the erosion in the purchasing power of the dollar since the Great Depression to appreciate just how much of the economic activity in the United States reported during this period was an illusion. Every $1 spent in fiscal and monetary assistance in the 1930s is worth almost $25 in today's inflated money. And we should remember that officially defined measures of inflation understate the true erosion in the real value of the currency since FDR's devaluation of the dollar in 1933.

For several decades, analysts and authors have been predicting that the chronic dependency of the United States on inflation and public debt to stimulate the economy in the short run must eventually end in crisis and default. It may be time to consider another possibility, namely that the United States will continue to use currency inflation to reduce the relative burden of the total load of public and private debt. Far from being a new idea, this is precisely how the United States dealt with the relatively huge public debt load that existed immediately after the Civil War and World War II.

From over 100 percent of GDP in 1945, within a decade the size of the federal debt was cut to just 50 percent of GDP due to strong economic expansion and a brisk rate of inflation. Current estimates of future levels of public debt to GDP for the United States reach over

250 percent before 2050, with the chief drivers being Social Security, Medicaid, and Medicare. As Fed chairman Alan Greenspan told the Congress during an appearance on Capitol Hill, there is no question that Social Security recipients will get their checks. The question is: What will the dollars purchase?

The more important political point to ponder, though, is whether the American people are likely to embrace a regime of fiscal stringency if and when the other nations of the world demand it, if only by selling dollars. Americans are an instinctively self-reliant, isolationist people who might very well turn their backs on the world if given a free choice. The same progression that took President Theodore Roosevelt from blissful isolation of the American continent that he loved so well to the foreign expansionism of the big stick could be reversed given the right combination of circumstances and personalities. Yet the destiny of America lies in global engagement, in competition and leadership, in making real the words of Ronald Reagan that America is "the last best hope of man on earth." But Reagan was no fiscal conservative and neither is Donald Trump.

Economists and political figures have warned the American people about the dangers of inflation, but most Americans don't have sufficient wealth to worry about the value of the dollar next week, much less next year. Even were the United States to return to the gold standard tomorrow, the wizards of Wall Street would find a way to create new vehicles for leverage and speculation just as Gould, Fisk, and Cooke did more than two centuries ago. The world of crypto currencies and other speculative activities illustrate the genius of Americans to create new games. Fraud is only possible in a free society. The tendency of human beings to use debt and other forms of leverage to earn nominal profits today discourages and defeats the sincerest efforts to protect the soundness of money over the longer term.

L.J. Davis wrote in his classic 1981 book *Bad Money*:

With the public currency rendered finite and expensive by the gold standard, private currency can be expected to flourish as the bankers and the businessmen seek to keep the marketplace as liquid as possible, bringing Gresham's Law into operation. Cheap money is more attractive than expensive money.[12]

If inflation and debt are the obvious problems facing the United States, and if the American political class is unwilling to make changes in fiscal and monetary policy to address these problems, then what does the future hold for Americans and the nations that trade with and invest in the United States? For a start, at home the likelihood is for a continuing diminution of real living standards, asset values, and economic opportunities due to inflation. Recalling our earlier point about debt such as greenbacks and Treasury bonds both being forms of "near money" and therefore functionally equivalent, the trillions of dollars in U.S. public sector debt, guarantees, and contingent liabilities represent future inflation—and also economic stagnation.

Author and financier James Rickards, relying on the work of Carmen Reinhart and others, argues that since 2008, the United States has been in a debt trap where increasing levels of public debt have resulted in less and less nominal growth in GDP. Once the U.S. public debt went above 90 percent of GDP during the Obama administration, every dollar borrowed and spent by the U.S. Treasury resulted in less than a dollar of incremental GDP.

"We have been in a depression since 2007," argues Rickards in a 2024 interview before the release of his latest book, *Money GPT*.

> I use the definition of depression used by Keynes in the General Theory, which is a period of below trend growth with neither a tendency to collapse or grow stronger. In other words, a depression is depressed growth. So, if your potential growth is three and a half percent, but your actual growth is two, then you're in a depression. By the way, from 2009 to 2019, the compounded rate of growth was just over two percent.[13]

Despite the clear negative of rising debt levels, today there seems little appetite on the part of Americans to address fiscal imbalances. There is little public clamor to address inflation in the way in which presidents such as Gerald Ford or Jimmy Carter, or Fed chairman Paul Volcker, attempted to do in the 1970s and 1980s. The bitter collective memory of inflation a century ago faded and was only briefly renewed by Chairman Volcker's much acclaimed inflation fight. Post-COVID, a steady, low double-digit increase in the cost of living, regardless of what the heavily manipulated official inflation statistics indicate, seems baked into the model of the U.S. economy.

Rickards notes that Americans "no longer know what money is" and have replaced "money with moneyness." He then describes both why the dollar is the global currency and why Americans may lose this privilege:

> Money is one of the foundations of civilization. Money is not the point of civilization and it's far from the most important feature. Still, it's part of the bedrock and performs crucial roles. Money is an advance on barter. Money is an alternative to violence. Money facilitates commerce and investment, and acts as a store of wealth. Money is among the institutions, along with law, religion, and the family, that enable civilizations to be civil and avoid a Hobbesian war of all against all. Just as money supports civilization, so money relies on civilization for its value. Money's value springs from trust, and trust itself depends on some institution—a central bank, a rule of law, a gold hoard, an AI algorithm—to sustain it. When institutions break down, and trust is lost, the value of money is lost as well, only to await the rise of new institutions and new forms of money so the cycle begins again.[14]

But the major point of vulnerability for the United States may not be inflation per se but diminished economic growth and a gradually weaker dollar, both of which will lessen the influence of America in the world. "It is always easier to borrow as long as someone will lend to you," observes Alex Pollock, a veteran banker and government official. "When the lenders stop lending, that's what forces the change."[15]

Inflation and Stagnation

"We live in an amazing world," former Fed chairman Paul Volcker noted. "Everybody has big budget deficits and big easy money, but somehow the world as a whole cannot fully employ itself. It is a serious question. We are no longer just talking about a single country having a big depression but the entire world. If the world as a whole cannot employ everyone who is ready and able to work, it raises some big questions."[16]

One of the issues facing the United States and the global economy when it comes to generating jobs and economic opportunities is the still-lingering effects of World War II. The Bretton Woods agreement was an arrangement defined by a victor in war that was agreed to by a world that lay in ruins. The children of the victors, the "greatest generation," are the chief actors in our narrative, the demographic bulge in the United States popularly known as the Baby Boom. For decades, the United States has been the engine of global growth in order to meet the wants and needs of the Boomers, exchanging fiat paper dollars for real goods and services.

When President Richard Nixon finished the process of default begun by FDR and ended the last link between the dollar and gold in 1971, the value of the dollar became a function of the political credibility of the United States. But as the growth potential of the U.S. economy wanes and the Baby Boomers reach retirement age, all the while refusing to rein in their insatiable desire for consumption, the ability of the American economy to fulfill the dreams of workers at home and around the world is in doubt. How we deal with the existence of a global fiat currency will define the destiny of America and the world in the next century and beyond.

One of the major themes to take away from this book is that Americans need to develop new models and frameworks for distinguishing between real economic growth and the illusion of growth created by inflation and credit-driven speculation. After the collapse of Bear, Stearns & Co. and Lehman Brothers in 2008, the Fed for years kept interest rates at or near zero, ostensibly to help the banking sector recover from record credit losses. Since then, Fed interest rate policies have transferred trillions of dollars from savers to investors through low interest rates. Little of this social engineering has reached American households, however. We can praise Fed officials for saving "the system" so that the ATM machines and credit cards still function, but at what cost?

The more interesting question raised by Fed policies since 2001 is whether the U.S. economy can generate positive real growth as and when interest rates in the United States return to something like normal levels. In 2001, when the U.S. economy experienced a "mini" recession, Fed chairman Alan Greenspan and the FOMC responded by dropping interest rates to very low levels. Critics of Chairman Greenspan subsequently lambasted the Fed for keeping rates too low for too long and thereby causing the bubble in real estate later in the decade. But what many observers fail to appreciate is that the Fed, operating in the moment, was mostly concerned with deflation inside large financial institutions, not with encouraging employment.

"During the period after 2001, people in the Fed were worried about repeating the deflationary experience of Japan," concludes David Kotok, CEO of Cumberland Advisers. "They chose policies that were designed to blunt the risk of deflation, but they failed to appreciate the other risk, namely encouraging a bubble in the domestic real estate market. It is easy to criticize the Fed in hindsight, but the central bank operates in real time. In this case the perceived solution to one problem created another."[17]

It appears that the Fed's motivation in the early 2000s was not to create a bubble in the housing market, but to keep the level of nominal economic growth and employment above some acceptable minimum level. Large consumer lenders such as Citigroup, a bellwether of an economy where the average borrower is subprime, experienced significant increases in credit losses during the 2001–2003 period, losses far above the bank's peers and also higher than markets expected.

Spooked by the unexpected losses at Citi, the Federal Open Market Committee took the federal funds rate from 5 percent at the end of 2000 down to just above zero by the end of 2003, yet concerns remained. These concerns caused officials at the central bank to consider new policy alternatives for operating in an environment of very low nominal interest rates. A senior Fed official said in June 2010, "Go back to the 1990s and count the number of quarters where we have not had fiscal stimulus or expansionary Fed interest rate policy or both."

Had Chairman Greenspan and the Federal Open Market Committee raised interest rates in the 2000s, the bubble in the housing market might not have been nearly as large, but the U.S. economy might well have weakened rapidly. In 2024, how would the U.S. economy look without a $2 trillion deficit in federal finances? Whereas in the years immediately after World War II the United States had modest inflation but still higher levels of growth, today the situation is reversed, with persistent inflation and weak real levels of economic growth.

"A nation that spends on itself is not spending on physical plant and equipment," observes Vincent Reinhart, former director of the Federal Reserve Board's Division of Monetary Affairs. "I don't think it's an accident that high savings rates and low deficits were associated with fast growth. We forgot that lesson in the 1960s. Financial innovation also made it easier for the government and households to spend more."[18]

The basic question the Fed, the Congress, and the American people need to consider is whether the current load of public and private debt, combined with an overvalued dollar, makes stable, noninflationary growth and job creation impossible. How will the economy and job market perform if the Fed and Treasury are ever forced to defend the dollar with higher interest rates? Most the more than $35 trillion in federal debt is short-term, creating an extremely problematic situation for the United States in the event of sustained dollar weakness.

This precarious position for the Treasury dates back to Undersecretary Peter Fisher in October 2001. He announced that the Treasury would suspend issuing 30-year Treasury bonds. Fisher's decision, made at a time when receipts to the Social Security system were masking the overall federal deficit and the Fed was driving rates down, shortened the duration of the outstanding public debt of the United States.

Up until 2001, as much as one-third of total Treasury debt issuance had been in 30-year bonds. In a 2001 statement, Fisher said: "We do not need the 30-year bond to meet the government's current financing needs, nor those that we expect to face in coming years. Looking beyond the next few years, as I already observed, we believe that the likely outcome is that the federal government's fiscal position will improve after the temporary setback that we are now experiencing."[19]

By 2008, however, Fisher, who by then had gone to work for BlackRock, opined that the Treasury should start to issue 100-year debt. During the COVID pandemic, when the FOMC had pushed long-term interest rates down to near zero, the Biden administration chose to finance the exploding federal deficits with trillions of dollars in T-bills instead of long-term bonds, a political expedient engineered by Treasury Secretary Janet Yellen to hide the true cost of the federal deficit.

In an environment where the United States is forced to respond to demands from foreign investors either to pay higher rates to compensate for risk or issue foreign-currency denominated debt, the United States could face a situation similar to the one confronted by Chairman Volcker and the Fed in the 1970s. Only this time, instead of being focused on restraining domestic inflation, the U.S. central bank and Treasury may instead find themselves fighting to placate angry foreign creditors by maintaining the value of the dollar and access to the international capital markets.

During the 1980s and early 1990s, for example, Mexico was forced to pay double-digit interest rates on T-bills in order to finance its deficits. When Mexico and other heavily indebted nations ran into problems in decades past, currency devaluations and IMF-administered fiscal austerity measures were imposed as a condition of gaining access to new credit.

Some of the debtor nations followed these prescriptions, others did not, but one of the remarkable facts of the twenty-first century is that the United States and the EU have now taken the place of these emerging nations as potential subjects for structural adjustment due to excessive debt. As mentioned previously, Mexico, Brazil, China, and other major debtor nations of decades ago are now self-sustaining, without the need of assistance from the IMF

The question for the United States and other nations is which of these older, more developed economic blocs will be the first to get their fiscal and monetary house in order. But perhaps the single biggest factor preventing fiscal reform is that monetary policy is no longer able to supply easy growth, but instead creates volatility and crises in the financial markets. Targeting the federal funds rate as an instrument of monetary policy in the United States may have finally reached an endpoint.

The entire topography of Western finance going back a century to the Depression and World War II is threatened by growing debt in the United States. In the 1930s, government was at the apex of credit, but today the U.S. Treasury is gradually seeing its standing decline in the global credit markets compared to private corporations. What happens to banks and pension funds when Treasury debt really becomes junk? And despite this dire prospect, not a single member of the media covering the Fed in the 2020s seemed able to ask Fed chairman Jerome Powell any questions about the central bank's balance sheet.

"Monetary policy is, after all, a blunt instrument," noted former New York Federal Reserve Bank official Terrence Checki. "It supports investment and consumption in the real side of the economy by stimulating financial activity, by lowering borrowing costs and boosting financial wealth. But, as we have learned the hard way, easy monetary and credit conditions are also the stuff out of which credit excesses and bubbles can form. So the question many central banks face is whether the benefits of further easing are worth the potential costs: in essence, will we get enough risk-taking on the real side of the economy, before we get too much on the financial side?"[20]

In the post-2008 period, the financial side and particularly financial institutions and professional investors have received the lion's share of the benefits of the monetary policy actions of the Federal Reserve and other global central banks as well. The Treasury, of course, was a major beneficiary of quantitative easing, but consumers also received vast subsidies and wealth transfers via debt moratoria and forgiveness, all engineered by the Federal Reserve Board without any legislation.

The vast amount of debt incurred by governments around the world has forced policymakers to err on the side of ample liquidity in fact, regardless of what the official statements say about encouraging jobs and fighting inflation. In the fall of 2024 on the eve of a presidential election, the Fed decided to end the battle against inflation a little early, a remarkable development given that the central bank had barely reduced the level of bank reserves and home prices had not fallen. Yet the fact was that the Fed was unwilling to reduce market liquidity for fear of causing another systemic event in the bond market a la December 2018 or March 2020.

Even though the Fed goosed home prices with a sharp decrease in interest rates from 2019 to 2022, for example, bank reserves were essentially unchanged from pre-COVID. Indeed, the Fed tightening cycle in 2022–2024 did not reduce the level of reserves in the system much less stop the appreciation of existing homes and land.

"It's been a funny such cycle to say the least," wrote Simon White of *Bloomberg* in August 2024. "Chastened by the repo-market flare-up in 2019 that put an end to its last attempt to shrink its balance sheet, the Fed's current tightening cycle has proceeded along different lines. In fact, from the market's perspective there has arguably been no tightening as reserves—a primary determinant of market liquidity—are unchanged since QT began in June 2022."[21]

The Fed's reluctance to use outright deflation a la Paul Volcker in the 1980s to force prices down illustrates the extent to which the illusion of independent "monetary policy" has been overtaken by the Treasury's vast debt. Lest we forget, the collapse of the Treasury market in 2008 and later in March 2020 were seminal events that forever changed the way that the United States manages national finance. Yet few market observers or economists are aware of the messy details so powerfully documented by Menand and Younger. The official view of monetary policy from the Fed and other central banks does not make room for what is the elephant in the room, namely the U.S. Treasury. When the Treasury is creating so much new "near money" in the form of short-term government debt, inflation is a given.

It is useful to recall that the Fed used to depend upon a chief transmission mechanism—housing—to control economic activity and deflation. The policy mistakes made by the Powell FOMC in 2018 and 2020 broke that connection and contributed to boosting home prices 40 percent in the past four years, a massive increase of consumer inflation.

The unspoken issue for the Fed, however, was whether elevating the cost of buying a home by raising the cost of finance was having any impact on home prices. Again, the need to ride to the rescue of the Treasury in 2020 had a cost, boosting the cost of housing dramatically. In such a scenario, the fact of higher funding costs might actually be inflationary and impact the final cost to consumers as lenders tried to limit losses on loans.

A bigger question is raised by the fact that the Fed pretends to have control over the short-term credit markets, but in fact does not. Few economists and investors appreciate how little control the FOMC retains over interest rates or markets given the size of the public debt. In December 2018 and March 2020, the Fed essentially had to cross the line and bail out the Treasury in a way not seen since the eve of World War II in 1941. John Cochrane:

> But the bigger problem is that this [Standard Doctrine] theory just doesn't apply to today's world. The Fed does not control money supply. The Fed sets interest rates. There are no reserve requirements, so "inside money" like checking accounts can expand arbitrarily for a given supply of bank reserves and cash. Banks can create money at will. The Fed still controls the (immense) monetary base (reserves+ cash). The ECB goes further and allows banks to borrow whatever they want against collateral at the fixed rate. The Fed lets banks arbitrarily exchange cash for interest-paying reserves. Most "money" now pays interest, so raising interest rates doesn't make money more expensive to hold.[22]

Even as the Fed declared success on inflation in September 2024, the central bank's assets and liabilities were more likely to rise with the federal debt than to fall as a result of any decision by the FOMC. The shared origins of the fiat paper dollar and federal debt, going back in time to the Civil War, make future inflation seem inevitable.

In 1959, Milton Friedman told a joint session of Congress that monetary policies "operate with a long lag and with a lag that varies widely from time to time." Over the past half century, the Standard Doctrine followed by the Fed was "leaning against the wind." If the economy is getting too hot in terms of inflation, the Fed should proactively raise interest rates to try to slow it down. But Friedman believed that the effects of monetary policy were too uncertain for this to be an effective strategy.

"We know too little about either these lags or about what the economic situation will be months or years hence when the chickens we release come home to roost, to be able to be effective in offsetting the myriads of factors making for minor fluctuations in economic activity," he told Congress.

Or as John Cochrane wrote in August 2024: "Higher money growth means higher inflation, immediately. Higher interest rates mean higher inflation, immediately. That's exactly how a "frictionless" model should work. Except the sign is wrong relative to the Standard Doctrine we're trying to chase down. Higher interest rates raise inflation? Are you out of your mind? You won't get invited back to Jackson Hole if you say that out loud."[23]

A Flexible Currency

Even as the fiscal and political situation in America deteriorated since 2008, offshore demand for dollars for use in trade and finance kept the U.S. currency relatively strong. From 2009–2011, the dollar actually gave back ground even as the Federal Reserve ramped up purchases of Treasury debt and mortgage securities to reflate a collapsed U.S. financial sector. As prices for U.S. stocks and real estate reached absurd levels, foreign purchases began to decline. In particular, changes in U.S. tax rules for foreign investors in real estate as well as political changes in nations such as China caused the dollar to slump after 2009.

After bottoming in 2012, a flood of new foreign capital began pouring into severely discounted U.S. real estate and also financial assets, which finally began to lift the dollar. More than simply recycling foreign official holdings, private investment into the United States also rose as China and other Asian economies sought returns on their dollars. Despite the economic malaise in the United States during much of the 2010s, the dollar commenced a sustained rise in value that peaked just after the election of Donald Trump in 2016. Trump's volatile personality and preference for nationalist hyperbole shocked many foreign governments.

The strength of the dollar following the existential experience of 2008 begs a key question: Could the same persistent inflation that torments U.S. citizens serve as an incentive to foreign nationals to use the dollar? Is the preference for a large currency expressed by some of the Founders led by Alexander Hamilton so powerful that it offsets parochial concerns about domestic fiscal discipline? The dollar is clearly preferred as a means of exchange in global commerce and finance, and a unit of account, because it is constantly expanding.

Menand and Younger remind us that Hamilton perceived that government debt had a "capacity for prompt convertibility" to currency, potentially rendering transfers "equivalent to a payment in coin." In other words, claims on the sovereign exist in a superposition of states between money and debt. This conveyed a special status on direct obligations of the federal government compared to all other financial assets, especially "at a time when money was in short supply."[24]

The post-crisis peak in the dollar in December 2016 came after years when strong capital inflows helped to reflate the U.S. equity and real estate markets, the latter both for commercial and residential properties. Yet the dollar rose even further into the 2020s, peaking at higher levels in the period of extreme economic stress during the COVID pandemic. Even as the markets madly scrambled for cash in the first quarter of 2020, the global dollar remained strong.

As the revised edition of this book was completed, more than two-thirds of all reserves held by central banks are in dollars, 60 percent of the total debt globally and more than half of all trade were in dollars in 2023.[25] Since the 1920s, when the United States took over the role of reserve provider from the United Kingdom, the dollar has been the dominant currency for trade and finance. By the end of 2020, for example, Borio, McAuley, and McQuire, in a paper for the

International Monetary Fund, projected that the total of undisclosed dollar financial transactions was in excess of $50 trillion.[26]

High and rising prices may have come to be expected in twenty-first century America, yet growing fiscal deficits and financial market turmoil did not appreciably dampen foreign demand for dollars and dollar assets. Quite the contrary, the world has shown an increased preference for dollarizing some or all of national transactions in goods and finance. Reinhart, Rogoff, and Savastano, observed that the degree of dollarization for borrowing and trade has increased dramatically around the globe.[27]

Despite growing signs of fiscal disarray and even authoritarian views in American governments of both parties, the United States is still among the safest venues for private investors in the world. Much of the world, including China, Russia, and many other nations, do not protect private property rights and are happy to expropriate assets when needed. As Milton Friedman famously observed: "A society that puts equality . . . ahead of freedom will end up with neither equality nor freedom . . . a society that puts freedom first will, as a happy by product, end up with both greater freedom and greater equality."

Perhaps the short answer is that access to the dollar and, equally important, "risk-free" dollar assets in the United States is the gold standard for global investments and trade, at least today. This vast demand for dollars and Treasury collateral is never discussed as part of the monetary policy process in the United States. Offshore demand for dollars and dollar credit may be the most significant factors facing U.S. policymakers in the future, especially given the rapid increase in the U.S. public debt. Such macroeconomic concerns, however, still do not seem to dissuade individuals and entities around the world from using dollars as their primary reserve asset.

If you were a family in Argentina a decade ago, for example looking to flee misguided socialist economic policies, you'd move the legal domicile of your family assets across the border to Uruguay. Then you'd place the cash with a family office in Montevideo and custody the assets at Pershing in New York in dollars. And in Uruguay and many other nations around the world, dollarization of large financial transactions such as investments and real estate, and even indexing of wages to the dollar, is now a fact of life.

Tricentennial Dollar?

Will the dollar still be the world's reserve currency in 2076, in time for America's tricentennial? The fact of the fiat paper dollar being the world's default means of exchange, unit of account, and even store of value goes back to World War I and is a precious franchise. Can America retain the global currency monopoly? Or is this a decision made by other nations and often through war?

"The US dollar, still the #1 reserve currency held by central banks, keeps losing share in bits and pieces ever so slowly," notes Wolf Richter, who reports that the dollar is losing share "against a mix of other reserve currencies as central banks diversify their holdings of dollar-denominated assets to assets denominated in other currencies. And they're also adding to their holdings of gold."[28]

Could Americans one day be forced to earn and spend the money of other nations as we did in colonial times? Until the Civil War, we recall, paper notes from English or Dutch banks were more trusted than debt from most U.S. banks. But the deflationary implications of a collapse of the dollar system are alarming for the United States and other nations.

As this edition of *Inflated* was finalized, the dollar fell to 58 percent of global reserve assets through June 2024 versus 66 percent in 2015, according to the International Monetary Fund, the lowest level since 1995. Roughly two-thirds of global trade excluding the EU was denominated in dollars. And neither the EU nor China have grown their share of reserve assets in recent years, suggesting that the dollar consensus may be slowly dissipating in a global example of entropy.

"Nearly 50 years ago, Yale University economist Robert Triffin identified the inevitable future deterioration of the dollar in his book, *Gold and the Dollar Crisis: The Future of Convertibility* (1960)," wrote Walker Todd in a December 2008 article. "Essentially, Triffin argued, under the Bretton Woods system in which the U.S. dollar was the world's principal reserve currency (instead of gold, for example), the United States had to incur large trade deficits in order to provide the rest of the world with the liquidity required for the functioning of the global trading system."[29]

Yet Triffin was fundamentally wrong when he worried that excessive U.S. deficits and a "dollar glut" would erode confidence in the value of the U.S. dollar. Without confidence in the dollar, he worried, it would no longer be accepted as the world's reserve currency. The fixed exchange rate system could break down, leading to instability, he worried, yet the opposite has been proven to be the case.

The nineteenth-century rule attributed to Bagehot said in times of crisis lend freely at a high rate against good collateral. This rule has been replaced by a world comprised of fiat currencies and public debt, which require low interest rates to function. In the pre–World War I world, money—that is, gold—had to be coaxed out of the hands of investors and into the market by offering high rates of return on paper debt. Yet since the currency devaluation and gold seizures of 1933, fiat currencies and below-market interest rates have been the rule. In a global scheme in which government occupies the prime position, the operative term remains "financial repression," whereby governments control markets and artificially suppress rates of return on debt.

The fact that the dollar continues to trade strongly versus other currencies reflects the reality that as the main means of exchange globally, the dollar cannot be easily replaced. One reason for this continued support for the dollar is that the trade in petroleum and other commodities is so large that it requires an equally large currency to accommodate it. Also, neither the Europeans nor the Japanese, the only two possible alternatives, are willing to risk the external deficits or inflation that the United States suffers as the host for the global currency. The demand for risk-free assets denominated in dollars has exploded since 2008 and the United States found a ready market for its debt among global central banks.

If you recall the phenomenon of the greenback's price in gold collapsing in the 1860s then slowly rising back to parity with gold after the Civil War, the demand for a means of exchange is a powerful force and one that seemingly is indifferent to inflation, at least in the short run. This is the essence of "Triffin's Dilemma" in its latest iteration, namely that the United States must run large trade deficits *and* also expand its currency to accommodate the world's liquidity needs. These trade deficits and the related expansion of the currency and risk-free assets, especially when financed with debt, also seems to mean a brisk rate of inflation for U.S. consumers and business.

Triffin wanted to create a new, global currency so that the United States could escape the burden of the reserve currency, but a lot of geopolitical and military considerations accompany the host of a reserve currency. Economist Robert Brusca, who worked as chief of the International Financial Markets Division at the Federal Reserve Bank of New York, believes there is no replacement for the dollar now or on the horizon.

> Reserve currencies in addition to the usual attributes of needing to be liquid and a store of value . . . must be in a country with a legal system others feel is fair and be creditworthy. That is why the pound sterling is still used and why EU, with France as its likely center and its strange Napoleonic code, does not challenge. Aso because the EU is not willing to run persistent (current account and fiscal) deficits to create reserve assets the rest of the world can acquire.

The never-ending U.S. deficits are both the threat to and the life-blood of this system, Brusca argues. How much debt can the United States run up without losing repayment credibility? On the other hand, countries want to acquire more reserve assets and that can only be done if the reserve currency country runs persisting (dual) deficits. He continues:

> The US deficits also are a problem from the standpoint of letting the US repair and improve its competitiveness since that might/ would require the dollar to weaken and that could interfere with the currency's reserve status role. In the early 1970s, when OPEC hiked oil price sharply and then there was an Arab oil embargo, the US ran high inflation in the wake of the just failed Bretton Woods system. The dollar fell and US inflation rose and so the dollar fell more . . . As it fell OPEC raised dollar prices of oil more, it was a reinforcing cycle. At one point the US got the ultimatum from OPEC to either control inflation or OPEC would abandon dollar pricing. So, these conditions can ebb and flow.

As we noted at the start of this book, the fiat paper dollar created by Abraham Lincoln has leverage built in, so adding a lot of public debt atop a structure that is already built upon debt is problematic. Gold is the only form of money that is not debt, yet few Americans think of gold as a benchmark for government. The process of domestic inflation at home and dollar devaluation abroad was barely perceptible to Americans, at least until the COVID pandemic, when double-digit price increases became commonplace. Just as most American consumers are too focused on jobs and family to concentrate on the erosion of the dollar's value in real terms, the major exporting nations likewise live in the present and are focused on maximizing national income today. The last thing that any individual or company or country is looking to do is change the money used to enable day-to-day life.

Endgame

For years analysts have predicted that other nations would one day shun the dollar in favor of some alternative money, but this eventuality has been slow to arrive. In human history, changes in the dominant means of exchange have come after empires have fallen. The dollar's longevity as the largest single global exchange medium supports the classical position of Alexander Hamilton centuries ago that a big currency is better.

The flexible dollar helped to create and sustain the role of the U.S. currency as economic hegemon, but at a high cost in terms of domestic inflation. And the dollar has remained relatively strong even as deficits have grown, hurting the competitive position of U.S. industry. The pairing of fiat paper dollars and risk-free Treasury debt, not gold, is today the foundation of not just global commerce and finance, but the U.S. political economy.

This whole arrangement depends fundamentally on the willingness of people to accept worthless paper in return for tangible goods and work. Gordon Wood described the scene in an essay in the *New York Review of Books*:

> We place a lot of confidence in paper money. We trust in pieces of paper that seem to have no intrinsic value whatsoever. We pass paper bills from hand to hand with little or no questioning of their worth. During some periods of American history people were able to turn in these pieces of paper to some institution or another for specie, that is, for gold or silver, which most people believe do have some intrinsic value; but not anymore. Today the paper bills rest exclusively on faith, on the confidence we have that the notes are genuine and that everyone will accept them.[30]

Although America and the world could probably continue to live with the current global currency system for many years to come, the question for U.S. policymakers is whether this serves the national interest. Experience teaches that so long as American politicians believe that they can borrow to paper over fiscal deficits, they will do so. But the arithmetic of deficits, including compounded interest, may eventually force the United States to default, either explicitly or by converting "near money" Treasury bills directly into fiat cash. The original greenback notes issued in 1863 paid interest, let us recall. National banks were permitted and, indeed, encouraged to double leverage the paper "asset" held as capital in the vault. Dire need and legal tender laws compelled Americans to accept the arrangement.

Dealing with the role of the dollar in the global economy ultimately may be linked to fiscal and political reform in the United States. Conventional wisdom says that there is no way out of the current situation of having the dollar as the global reserve currency. A comment published in 2009 by the Council on Foreign Relations quoted Luo Ping, a director-general at the China Banking Regulatory Commission, on the issue of the reserve currency status of the dollar:

> Except for U.S. Treasuries, what can you hold? Gold? You don't hold Japanese government bonds or United Kingdom bonds. U.S. Treasuries are the safe haven. For everyone, including China, it is the only option . . . We know the dollar is going to depreciate, so we hate you guys, but there is nothing much we can do.[31]

We could deal with the issue of American debt by going back to the original framework for the Bretton Woods agreement and fashion a new global currency mechanism. This would no longer afford the dollar a monopoly and no longer give American politicians a free ride when it comes to fiscal discipline. Bretton Woods was as much about propping up Great Britain and the other bankrupt nations of Europe after World War II as it was an effort to create a truly balanced international monetary system. The path for a new system might be focused on helping the United States restructure its public debt and other fiscal obligations to avoid default, essentially a twenty-first century Marshall Plan in reverse. But is such a plan that reflects old notions of money and debt relevant or even possible in the twenty-first century?

In a historical sense, creating a means for the United States to transition away from bearing the full burden of serving as the reserve currency for the world economy would truly mark the end of the Cold War period and, more broadly, the recovery of the world from the two world wars. Just as it has taken nearly a century for the social and demographic effects of World War I and World War II to work their way through the U.S. political economy, the economic effects of these terrible upheavals are still being felt in the huge fiscal imbalances and inflation visible in the United States today.

A change in the global role of the dollar, however, has significant geopolitical implications that suggests it will not happen voluntarily or short of war or another crisis. If China and the EU, for example, were committed to replacing the dollar as the global means of exchange, how would this be accomplished? Would a nuclear exchange in Ukraine make dollar assets more or less sought after? Contrary to the first edition of *Inflated*, the idea that nations would voluntarily stop using the dollar as a global means of exchange seems outlandish today.

Why would any nation not use the dollar until the United States is finally forced to either hyperinflate or default on its debt? The only cost of holding dollars is the natural diminution of value for what the currency will buy inside the United States, but outside the marketplace for dollar assets is entirely different. As a means of exchange for settlement of global trade transactions, the slow wastage of the American dollar is not an issue. But the value of the dollar fundamentally affects the value of all U.S. assets held by foreign investors.

Perhaps a future American president and Congress, pressed by the sheer interest expense on the public debt, will use the example of Lincoln and mandate that 10 percent of all public debt be purchased by the Fed and converted into new issue greenbacks each year. This is essentially a debt default via currency inflation similar to the dollar devaluation of FDR in 1933, a policy prescription that ultimately failed. It was not the fact of gold that limited the Fed's ability to increase credit in the 1930s, Friedman, Bernanke and others have shown conclusively, but instead the fact of private debt deflation as described by Irving Fisher that pulled the entire system down.

When the U.S. government under Franklin Roosevelt repudiated the promise to covert dollar notes into gold and seized gold in private hands in 1933, that fact generated fear and drove capital out of the system. What would be the world's response to another unilateral American default? Would the EU, China, and other economic blocs reject the dollar? Or would they likewise convert public debt into fiat currency in a global jubilee in order to maintain competitive parity?

Nouriel Rubini said in his book *Crisis Economics* that Adam Smith and other economists spent their time focused on why markets work, not why they falter. Perhaps we are witnessing the slow demise of the dollar system, just as the currency system based on the English pound declined before World War I. The expense of the First World War finally served as the tipping point for the UK and forced them to hand the baton on the global reserve currency to America.

Studying the evolution of the dollar system provides few clues for how the future will unfold. The International Monetary Fund identified several periods since its inception at the end of World War II in terms of global economic development and cooperation.

Conflict and Cooperation (1871–1944)

Destruction and Reconstruction (1945–1958)

The System in Crisis (1959–1971)

Reinventing the System (1972–1981)

Debt and Transition (1981–1989)

Globalization and Integration (1989–1999)

The period from 1959–1971 is dubbed "the system in crisis," ending with President Nixon's decisions to finally close the gold window to other central banks. Franklin Roosevelt had defaulted on the promise to convert paper into gold 40 years earlier in 1933. How would we characterize the period from 2000 onward? Financial crisis and public debt? Whereas half a century ago America's leaders were intensely focused on the dollar's place in the global financial system, today we simply assume the dollar's place in the global economy is permanent.

How America gradually transitions from holding a monopoly on the world's money to being merely one large player in an equal exchange among nations will be a test of national character. In meeting this challenge, Americans will do what they do best: adjust, adapt, and excel in a way that no other people on earth can. Economist Judy Shelton suggested a new strategy in comments for this book:

> The fundamental challenge for the United States is to demonstrate that we intend to be standing tall fifty years from now—proving that we can, as a nation, counter the existential threat of fiscal unsustainability. The key to convincing the world (and ourselves) that we can get back on a path to sound finances and sound money is to restore some measure of gold convertibility to the U.S. dollar. It was an idea embraced by President Reagan—who aspired "to make the dollar the most trusted currency in the world." We can do it by issuing 50-year gold-convertible Treasury bonds.

Shelton then commented on the dollar 50 years hence:

> Will the age of fiat dollar hegemony be ended, or will we still be the world's default means of exchange? It is vital that the U.S. dollar not only retains but enhances its role as the reserve currency of the world. "Fiat" comes from the Latin for "let it be done," implying that dollar hegemony is attained through political, economic, and military dominance. These are advantages, as Nobel laureate in economics Robert Mundell has explained. But monetary integrity is a virtue that transcends geopolitical considerations by gaining the confidence of users around the world as a dependable standard of value.

Do we want to make the necessary adjustment to preserve and strengthen the role of the dollar at a time and at a pace of our choosing? Or do we prefer to wait for events to force change upon us in a time of crisis or worse? Do Americans have the honesty to talk about limiting our national wants and needs to our national income? Do we have the courage to lead another global discussion with other nations about the dollar and America's infatuation with inflation and debt? Or do we simply wait for global events to end the special role of the dollar?

Will the dollar still be the world's global currency 50 years hence when America reaches the tricentennial in 2076? Banker and author Alex Pollock offers a perspective:

> The dominant role of the US and the dollar in the world still reflects the special conditions of the aftermath of World War II, which must fade as the next half century unrolls. If we go back 50 years, it is

1974 and the Bretton Woods system had just collapsed. Back another 50 and you are in the difficulties of the post-World War I monetary events, after the war had destroyed the gold standard, and the Fed is in process of displacing the Bank of England as top central bank. Could in the next 50 there be a renewal of a gold-tied international currency, reflecting many other countries' wishing to escape the ability of the US to use the dollar for political purposes? Might Europe produce an Alexander Hamilton who will create consolidated EU taxation and debt as more successful competitors to US securities? Will the Nixonian monetary world of "our currency but your problem" lose market share, say from 60 to 40 percent or less of international reserves? What will the gold-dollar price be? $7,000 an ounce? Fifty years was long enough for two world wars, four international monetary regimes, a depression and the atom bomb. In the fullness of time?

Perhaps the more interesting question is whether the United States can ever voluntarily shed the "special role" of the dollar. Patterns in global reserves suggest that nations are diversifying away from dollars, the euro, and the Chinese yuan. David Kotok observed years ago during a fishing trip to Grand Lake Stream Maine, the special role of a currency as a global means of exchange like the Roman *Aureus* or the British pound sterling is something that finds you, usually as the result of war. Great nations with enormous military might and powerful economies typically are the providers of the most frequently used means of exchange. But being the issuer of a global currency carries benefits and also terrible costs for the nation so fortunate to be chosen by history.

As with the Greeks, the Romans, and the British Empire, does America's economic and military hegemony forged in a global war 75 years ago have a finite life? Or can the United States tame its fiscal indiscipline and thereby preserve the advantages of a global reserve currency into the twenty-second century? To recall the judgment of mathematician and author Freeman Dyson, as a society we are really good at replication but have not yet learned to maintain metabolism.[32] In a free society as volatile and unruly as America, hoping for stability in fiscal or monetary affairs may be a vain hope.

Author Jim Rickards gave the obvious summation of the future prospects of the fiat paper dollar in a September 2024 interview: "The Treasury should buy gold." He argued: "The Treasury buying gold would restore confidence in the dollar and perhaps make people believe again that the currency has real value. The price of gold in dollars would clearly go up, but buying gold would be a statement to the world that we are not just going to go down the print-the-dollar rabbit hole. This does not mean that we are going back to a gold standard, but it does say that we are going to honor our obligations. But to make it to 2076, we need to think really hard about whether we have lost the thread about what money really is for America."[33]

Americans will debate the meaning of money and debt into the 21st Century and beyond. And they will pursue the ever evolving image of the American dream. But as the great Treasury Secretary Albert Gallatin (1801-1815), whose figure stands in front of the Treasury building in Washington, said two centuries ago: "All our dreams can come true if we have the courage to pursue them."

Notes

Preface

1. Adams, James Truslow, *The Epic of America* (New York: Little Brown, 1931), 404.
2. Selgin, George, The Rise and Fall of the Gold Standard in the United States (June 20, 2013). Cato Institute Policy Analysis No. 729, Available at SSRN: https://ssrn.com/abstract=2282720

Chapter 1

1. Sylla, Richard, "Financial Foundations: Public Credit, the National Bank, and Securities Markets," National Bureau of Economic Research (NBER), (February 8, 2010): 4–7.
2. Homer, Sidney and Sylla, Richard Eugene, *A History of Interest Rates* (Piscataway, NJ: Rutgers University Press, 1996), 274.
3. McCullough, David, *John Adams* (New York: Simon & Schuster 2001), 171.
4. James, Harold, *Severn Crashes: The Economic Crises That shaped Globalization* (New Haven, CT: Yale University Press, 2024).
5. Chernow, Ron, *Alexander Hamilton* (London: Penguin Books, 2004), 346.
6. Costello, Joe, "Election Day Fodder," *Substack*, November 5, 2024.

7. History of the Bank of New York, Bank of New York Mellon Corporation.

8. Dunn, Susan, "When America Was Transformed," *New York Review of Books*, March 25, 2010, 30. Dunn reviewed Gordon Wood's *Empire of Liberty: A History of the Early Republic 1789–1815* (New York: Oxford University Press, 2009).

9. Catteral, Ralph Charles Henry, *The Second Bank of the United States* (Chicago: University of Chicago Press, 1903), 9.

10. Byrd, Robert C. *The Senate, 1789–1989* (Washington, DC: U.S. Government Printing Office, 1988), 66.

11. Byrd, 67.

12. Dunn, 29.

13. Myers, Margaret G., *A Financial History of the United States* (New York: Columbia University Press, 1970), 143.

14. Kamensky, Jane, *The Exchange Artist: A Tale of High-Flying Speculation and America's First Banking Collapse* (London: Viking Penguin, 2008).

15. Grinath III Arthur; Wallis, John; and Sylla, Richard, "Debt, Default and Revenue Structure: The American State Debt Crisis in the Early 1840s," Historical Paper 97, NBER (March 1997), 3.

16. Foulke, Roy A., *The Sinews of American Commerce* (New York: Dunn & Bradstreet, 1941), 151.

17. Grinath, 4.

18. Schweikart, Larry, *Banking in the American South from the Age of Jackson to Reconstruction* (Baton Rouge, LA: Louisiana State University Press, 1987), 167.

19. Grinath, 26–27.

20. Dunbar, Willis F. and May, George, *Michigan: A History of the Wolverine State* (Grand Rapids: Wm Erdmans 1995), 230.

21. Byrd, 105.

22. "President Jackson's Veto Message Regarding the Bank of the United States" (July 10, 1832), Yale Law School.

23. Taylor, George Rogers, *Jackson Versus Biddle: The Struggle over the Second Bank of the United States* (Boston: CD Heath, 1949), viii.

24. Taylor, viii.

25. James, Marquis, *The Life of Andrew Jackson* (Camden, NJ: Haddon Craftsmen, 1938), 583.

26. James, 601.

27. James, 664.

28. Specie refers to metal coins, bullion coins, hard money, commodity metals, and other hard stores of value that are also used as a means of exchange.

29. James, 729.

30. "1995 Annual Report: A Brief History of Our Nation's Paper Money," *Annual Report*, Federal Reserve Bank of San Francisco, 1995.

31. History of the U.S. Treasury, U.S. Department of the Treasury, Washington, DC.

32. Webster, Daniel, *The Works of Daniel Webster, Vol. III* (Boston: Little Brown, 1881), 394.

33. Margo, Robert A., "Wages in California During the Gold Rush," NBER Historical Working Paper No. 101★ (June 1997).

34. Brands, H.W., *The Age of Gold: The California Gold Rush and the New American Dream* (New York: Anchor Books, 2003), 488.

Chapter 2

1. Bloom, Harold, "The Central Man," *The New York Review of Books*, July 19, 1984.

2. Phillips, Kevin, *The Cousins' War* (New York: Basic Books, 2009), 459.

3. Canova, Timothy, "Lincoln's Populist Sovereignty: Public Finance Of, By, and For the People," Paper No. 09-38, *Chapman Law Review*, Vol. 12, 2009, 561–562 (http://ssrn.com/abstract=1489439).

4. Rothbard, Murray Newton, *A History of Money and Banking in the United States* (Auburn, AL: Ludwig von Mises Institute, 2002), 122–123.

5. Phillips, 389.

6. DuBois, W.E.B., *The Suppression of the African Slave Trade in the United States of America 1638–1870* (New York: Social Science Press, 1954), 123.

7. DuBois, 424–425.

8. Byrd, Robert C. *The Senate, 1789–1989* (Washington, DC: U.S. Government Printing Office, 1988), 247.

9. Bloom, Harold, "The Central Man," *The New York Review of Books* (July 19, 1984).

10. Kinley, David, "The Independent Treasury of the United States and its Relations to Banks in the Country," National Monetary Commission, U.S. Government Printing Office (1910), 97.

11. Rothbard, 123.

12. Rothbard, 124.

13. Hixson, William F., *Triumph of the Bankers: Money and Banking in the Eighteenth and Nineteenth Centuries* (Westport, CT: Praeger Publishers, 1993), 143.

14. Josephson, Matthew, *The Robber Barons* (New York: Harcourt Brace & Co., 1934), 36.

15. Rothbard, 133.

16. Guyatt, Edward, "Blues, Grays & Greenbacks," *The New York Review of Books*, May 25, 2023.

17. Wilkeson, Samuel, *How Our National Debt May Be a National Blessing* (Philadelphia: M'Laughlin Brothers Printers, 1865).

18. *History of the Treasury*, Secretaries of the Treasury: William P. Fessenden, U.S. Department of the Treasury web site (www.ustreas.gov).

19. Hixson, 136.

20. Myers, Margaret G., *A Financial History of the United States* (New York: Columbia University Press, 1970), 175.

21. History of the Treasury, Secretaries of the Treasury: Salmon Chase.

22. Rothbard, 152–153.

23. Swanberg, W.A., *Jim Fisk: The Career of an Improbable Rascal* (New York: Longmans, 1960), 123.

24. Hoyt, Edwin P., *The Goulds: A Social History* (New York: Weybright & Talley, 1969), 49.

25. Swanberg, 123.

26. Swanberg, 145.

27. It has been suggested in several published works that Gould and Fisk, in fact, were in league even as Gould seemed to be profiting at his confederate's expense, and that the two men divided the profits on the gold market operation afterward.

28. Rothbard, 138–139.

29. *The Campaign Text Book*, National Democratic Committee (1880), 169–171.

30. Josephson, 167.

31. Rothbard, 161.

32. Rothbard, 163.

33. Holdsworth, John Thom, *Money and Banking* (New York: D. Appleton and Co., 1922), 30.

34. Hofstadter, Richard, "The Paranoid Style in American Politics," *Harper's Magazine*, November 1964.

35. McFeely, William, *Grant: A Biography* (New York: W.W. Norton & Co., 2002), 397.

36. Adams, James Truslow, *The Epic of America* (New York: Little Brown, 1931), 316.

37. Byrd, 348.

38. Myers, 212.

39. Faulkner, Harold, *Politics, Reform and Expansion: 1890–1900* (New York: Harper & Row, 1959), x.

Chapter 3

1. Twain, Mark and Warner, Charles Dudley, *The Gilded Age: A Tale of To-Day* (Hartford: American Publishing Company, 1874), v.

2. Mintz, Steven, (2007). Digital History (www.digitalhistory.uh.edu/), viewed March 6, 2010.

3. Josephson, Matthew, *The Robber Barons* (New York: Harcourt Brace & Co., 1934), 319.

4. Friedman, Milton and Schwartz, Anna, *A Monetary History of the United States, 1867–1960*, NBER (1965), 138.

5. Rothbard, Murray Newton, *A History of Money and Banking in the United States* (Auburn, AL: Ludwig von Mises Institute, 2002), 167. See also Friedman and Schwartz, 106.

6. Rothbard, 168.

7. See "The Reading Receivership," *The Nation*, Vol. 56, No. 1445, The Evening Post Publishing Co., New York (1893), 174.

8. See "New Hope for Financial Economics: Interview with Bill Janeway," *The Institutional Risk Analyst*, (November 17, 2008).

9. "The Reading Receivership," 175.

10. Brands, H.W., *Masters of Enterprise* (New York: Simon & Schuster, 1999).

11. Kleppner, Paul, *The Third Electoral System 1853–1892: Parties, Voters, and Political Cultures* (Charlotte, NC: University of North Carolina Press, 1979), 291–296. Murray Rothbard prepared an excellent summary of Kleppner's work and the evolution of the American political system after 1896 in his *History of Money and Banking in the United States*, 169–179.

12. Nevins, Allan and Comanger, Henry Steele, *A Short History of the United States (Fifth Edition)* (New York: Knopf, 1966), 378.

13. Indiana Monetary Commission, 77.

14. Theodore Roosevelt Association (https://www.theodoreroosevelt.org/).

15. Myers, Margaret G., *A Financial History of the United States* (New York: Columbia University Press, 1970), 221.

Chapter 4

1. Jones, Eliot, *The Trust Problem in the United States* (New York: The MacMillan Co, 1921), 198–201.

2. Pound, Arthur and Moore, Samuel Taylor, *They Told Barron: The Notes of Clarence W. Barron* (New York: Harper Brothers, 1930), 85–86.

3. Magie, David, *Life of Garret Augustus Hobart: Twenty-Fourth Vice-President of the United States* (New York: G.P. Putnam's Sons, 1910), 53.

4. Magie, 41.

5. See "Timeline," Theodore Roosevelt Center (https://www.theodoreroosevelt center.org/Learn-About-TR/TR-Quotes).

6. Pound and Moore, 21.

7. Josephson, Matthew, *The Robber Barons* (New York: Harcourt Brace & Co., 1934), 446.

8. Myers, Margaret G., *A Financial History of the United States* (New York: Columbia University Press, 1970), 256.

9. Pound and Moore, 80.

10. Harrison, Robert, *Congress, Progressive Reform, and the New American State* (New York: Cambridge University Press, 2004), 250.

11. Josephson, 450–451.

12. Speech at Quincy, Illinois, April 29, 1903. See Roosevelt, Theodore and Garrison, Elisha Ely, *The Roosevelt Doctrine: Being the Personal Utterances of the President on . . .* (New York: Robert Greier Cooke, 1904), 153.

13. Roosevelt, Theodore and Carnegie, Andrew, *The Roosevelt Policy: Speeches, Letters and State Papers, Relating to Corporate Wealth and Closely Allied Topics* (New York: The Current Literature Publishing Company, 1908), 667.

14. Friedman, Milton and Schwartz, Anna, *A Monetary History of the United States, 1867–1960*, NBER (1965), 181.

15. Friedman and Schwartz, 163.

16. See *Watson's Jeffersonian Magazine*, Volume 5, Thomas Edward Watson, Editor (July 1910), 1050. See also McCaleb, W.F., *Theodore Roosevelt*, (New York: A&C Boni, 1931), 242.

17. Grant, James, *Money of the Mind: Borrowing and Lending in America from the Civil War to Michael Milken* (New York: Farrar, Straus and Giroux, 1992), 119.

18. "Beyond the Crisis: Reflections on the Challenges," Remarks by Terrence J. Checki, Executive Vice President Federal Reserve Bank of New York, at the Foreign Policy Association Corporate Dinner, New York, NY, Tuesday, December 2, 2009.

19. Gordon, John Steele, "A Short Banking History of the United States," *Wall Street Journal* (October 10, 2008).

20. Steffens reference to Aldrich as "the boss of the United States" is found in his book, Steffens, Joseph Lincoln, *The Struggle for Self Government*, (New York: S.S. McClure Co., 1904), 120.

21. Warburg, Paul M., *The Federal Reserve System Its Origin and Growth: Reflections and Recollections Vol. II* (New York: The MacMillan Company, 1930), 117.

22. "Money Trust Investigation: Investigation of Financial and Monetary Conditions in the United States Under House Resolutions Nos. 429 and 504: 1912–1913," FRASER, Federal Reserve Bank of St Louis.

23. "Oppose Reopening of Money Inquiry; Wilson and Underwood Also Against Embodying Pujo Remedies in Currency Bill," *New York Times*, (May 31, 1913), 13.

24. Rothbard, Murray, *The Case Against the Fed* (Auburn, AL: Ludwig von Mises Institute, 1994), 116.

25. Byrd, Robert C. *The Senate, 1789–1989* (Washington, DC: U.S. Government Printing Office, 1988), 412.

26. Goodwyn, Lawrence, *Democratic Promise: The Populist Moment in America* (New York: Oxford University Press, 1976), 269.

27. "Carter Glass, 88, Dies in Capital," *New York Times*, (May 29, 1946), 1.

28. Chernow, Ron, *The House of Morgan: An American Banking Dynasty and the Rise of Modern Finance* (New York: Grove Press, 2001), 182.

29. Todd, Walker F., "The Federal Reserve Board and the Rise of the Corporate State, 1931–1934," *Economic Education Bulletin*, Vol. XXXV, No. 9 American Institute for Economic Research, Great Barrington, Massachusetts (September 1995).

30. Gilbert, Clinton, *The Mirrors of Wall Street*, New York, Putnam & Sons (1933), 9–10.

31. Gilbert, 15.

32. Todd, 42.

33. Politi, James, Russell Vought: the man on a 'divine mission' to traumatise US bureaucrats," *Financial Times*, February 10, 2025.

Chapter 5

1. "Historical Debt Outstanding," U.S. Treasury web site (www.treasurydirect .gov). The totals for debt outstanding provided by the U.S. Treasury include all physical dollars or "legal tender notes," and any silver and gold certificates that are still in existence. All of the paper issued by the Treasury, either currency or in the form of notes and bonds, are essentially debt, even if the former is not convertible into gold upon demand. This is why conservative,

hard-"money" exponents are so violently against fiat money because it is essentially debt, which promises value but which is never redeemed.

2. Tansill, Charles Callan, *America Goes to War* (Boston: Little Brown and Co., 1938), 69, n7.

3. Tansill, 73–75.

4. Tansill, 79.

5. Barron, Clarence W., *The Audacious War* (New York: Houghton Mifflin Co, 1915), ix.

6. "This War's Finance," *New York Times* (May 12, 1915), 12.

7. Grant, James, *Money of the Mind: Borrowing and Lending in America from the Civil War to Michael Milken* (New York: Farrar, Straus and Giroux, 1992), 145.

8. Seymour, Charles, "American Neutrality: The Experience of 1914–1917," *Foreign Affairs* (1933).

9. Miron, Jeffrey A., "The Founding of the Fed and the Destabilization of the Post-1914 Economy," NBER Working Paper No. 2701, *National Bureau of Economic Research* (February 1990), 3. Miron provides an excellent overview of the research on the economic impact of the creation of the Fed on the direction of the U.S. economy since 1914.

10. Gilbert, Clinton, *The Mirrors of Wall Street* (New York: Putnam & Sons, 1933), 24.

11. Friedman, Milton and Schwartz, Anna, *A Monetary History of the United States, 1867–1960*, NBER (1965), 190.

12. Friedman and Schwartz, 194.

13. Hoff, Joan, *A Faustian Foreign Policy from Woodrow Wilson to George W. Bush* (New York: Cambridge University Press, 2008), 72–73. Regarding the eventual loan default by France and Britain, Hoff notes that the loans to the Allies were not really "business transactions" because the countries were insolvent at the time of World War I and very clearly could not repay their debts.

14. Galbraith, John Kenneth, *The Great Crash 1929*, (New York: Harpers Business, 2009).

15. Minton, Bruce and Stewart, John, *The Fat Years and the Lean* (New York: International Publishers, 1940), 3.

16. "Timeline," Theodore Roosevelt Center (https://www.theodoreroosevelt center.org/Learn-About-TR/TR-Quotes).

17. "Gompers Assails Harding Position," *New York Times* (September 27, 1920), 5.

18. Calvin Coolidge, White House Historical Association (https://www.white househistory.org).

19. Chernow, Ron, *The House of Morgan: An American Banking Dynasty and the Rise of Modern Finance* (New York: Grove Press, 2001), 254.

20. "Tell Why America is Now Unpopular," *New York Times* (May 12, 1920), 2.

21. For example, Henry Ford is credited not only with using mass production methods to make his products less expensive, but with instituting the $5 per day wage in 1914, when many Americans could barely survive. More recent research suggests that, in fact, James Couzens, the general manager of Ford and later the senator from Michigan was the man who actually pressed Ford to increase wages for workers. See Harry Bernard, *Independent Man: The Life of James Couzens* (Detroit: Wayne State University Press, 2002).

22. Graham, Benjamin and Dodd, David, *Securities Analysis* (New York: McGraw Hill, 1934), 307.

23. On April 13, 2010, the Federal Deposit Insurance Corporation issued a proposal that would change the calculation of deposit insurance assessments for "large" or "highly complex" institutions. Pursuant to the proposal, the FDIC would replace fundamentals-based ratings and certain financial measures currently used with a "scorecard" consisting of well-defined financial measures that are more forward looking.

24. Minton and Stewart, 184.

25. Malone, Michael Shawn, *The Future Arrived Yesterday: The Rise of the Protean Corporation and What it Means to You* (New York: Crown Publishing, 2009), 54–55.

26. Calder, Lendol, *Financing the American Dream: A Cultural History of Consumer Credit* (Princeton, NJ: Princeton University Press, 1999), 6.

27. Calder, 18–20.

28. GMAC company history, GMAC web site (https://www.ally.com/about/company-structure/history/index.html).

29. Sowell, Thomas, *A Conflict of Visions: Ideological Origins of Political Struggles* (New York: Basic Books, 2002), 15–16.

30. Marshall, Peter H., *William Godwin* (Yale University Press: 1984).

31. Reis, Bernard J. and Flynn, John, *False Security: The Betrayal of the American Investor* (New York: The Stratford Press, 1937), 1. A facsimile of the original book was republished by Kessinger Publishing.

32. Reis and Flynn, 134.

33. Friedman and Schwartz, 244.

34. See Meltzer, Alan, *The Federal Reserve System: An Encyclopedia*, R.W. Hafer, Editor, (Westport, CT: Greenwood Press, 2005) 243.

35. Robins, Lionel, *The Great Depression*, (London: Macmillan, 1934), 50–62.

36. Cogley, Tim, *Federal Reserve Bank of San Francisco Economic Letter 1999-10 |* March 26, 1999.

37. "Mr. Coolidge's Farewell Warning," *The Literary Digest* (December 15, 1928), 5.

38. Byrd, Robert C. *The Senate, 1789–1989* (Washington, DC: U.S. Government Printing Office, 1988), 447.

39. Beaudreau, Bernard, *Making Sense of Smoot-Hawley, Technology and Tariffs* (Lincoln, NE: iUniverse, 2005).

40. Sparling, Earl, *Mystery Men of Wall Street: The Power Behind the Market* (New York: Greenberg, 1930), 17.

41. Friedman and Schwartz, 257.

42. Friedman and Schwartz, 259–264.

43. Chancellor, Edward, "Waiting to Deflate," *New York Review of Books*, August 19, 2021.

44. McGrattna, Ellen R., and Prescott, Edward C., "The Stock Market Crash of 1929: Irving Fisher Was Right!," NBER Working Paper No. 8622 (December 2001).

45. Friedman and Schwartz, 247.

46. "The Subprime Crisis & Ratings: PRMIA Meeting Notes," *The Institutional Risk Analyst* (September 24, 2007).

47. Galbraith, vii.

48. Fisher, Irving, "The Debt-Deflation Theory of Great Depressions," *Econometrica*, October 1933.

49. "Roosevelt Attacks Theories of Hoover," *New York Times* (November 2, 1928), 11.

Chapter 6

1. Hoover, Herbert, *The Great Depression* (New York: Macmillan, 1952), 359.

2. Selgin, George, "The New Deal and Recovery, Part 7: FDR and Gold," Cato Institute, August 2020.

3. Minton, Bruce and Stewart, John, *The Fat Years and the Lean* (New York: International Publishers, 1940), 284.

4. Hoover, 355–356, n4.

5. Sowell, Thomas, *A Conflict of Visions: Ideological Origins of Political Struggles* (New York: Basic Books, 2002).

6. Janeway, Eliot, *The Struggle for Survival* (New York: Weybright & Talley, 1951), 10–11.

7. Drier, Peter, "Eleanor: The Radical Roosevelt," *Yes* Magazine, January 25, 2013.

8. Canellos, Peter, "What FDR Understood About Socialism That Today's Democrats Don't," *Politico*, August 16, 2019.

9. Raico, Ralph, "*FDR: The Man, the Leader, the Legacy*," Independent Institute, April 2001.

10. Steel, Ronald, *Walter Lippmann and the American Century* (New York: Little Brown, 1980), 292–293.

11. Whalen, Richard, *The Founding Father: The Story of Joseph P. Kennedy* (New York: New American Library, 1964), 118–129.

12. Federal Deposit Insurance Corporation, "The First Fifty Years: A History of the FDIC 1933–1983" 37.

13. Cassell, Gustav, *The Downfall of the Gold Standard* (New York: Augustus Kelley, 1966 [1936]), 118–19.

14. "Sound Money and Balanced Budget Only Way to Revival, Says Baruch; Inflation the 'Road to Ruin,'" *New York Times* (February 14, 1933), 1.

15. "Sound Money and Balanced Budget Only Way to Revival, Say Baruch," 1.

16. Bovard, James, "Money: The Great Gold Robbery," *The Freeman* (June 1999).

17. Hoover, 407.

18. Hoover, 353.

19. Steel, 304.

20. Todd, Walker, "The Federal Reserve Board and the Rise of the Corporate State, 1931–1934," *Economic Education Bulletin*, Vol. 35, No. 9, September 1995, 2.

21. Keynes, John Maynard, "National Self-Sufficiency," *The Yale Review*, Vol. 22, No. 4, June 1933, 755–769.

22. Keynes, John Maynard, *Treatise on Money: The Pure Theory of Money, Volume 1,* (London: Cambridge University Press, 1976).

23. Keynes, John Maynard, *The General Theory of Employment, Interest, and Money* (New York: Harcourt, Brace, 1936).

24. The Unofficial Observer, *The New Dealers* (New York: Simon and Schuster, 1934), 104.

25. Library of Congress, "President Franklin Delano Roosevelt and the New Deal," https://www.loc.gov/classroom-materials/united-states-history-primary-source-timeline/great-depression-and-world-war-ii-1929-1945/franklin-delano-roosevelt-and-the-new-deal.

26. Cohen, Adam, *Nothing to Fear: FDR's Inner Circle and the Hundred Days that Created Modern America* (New York: The Penguin Press, 2009), 237.

27. The Unofficial Observer, 131.

28. Hoover, 398–399.

29. Warburg, James P., *The Money Muddle* (New York: Alfred A. Knopf, 1934), 159.

30. Smith, Rixey and Beasley, Norman, *Carter Glass* (New York: Ayer Publishing, 1970), 358–359.

31. Smith and Beasley, 353.

32. Lippmann, Walter, *The Good Society* (Boston: Little Brown & Co, 1937), 48–49.

33. Todd, 11.

34. Byrd, Robert C. *The Senate, 1789–1989* (Washington, DC: U.S. Government Printing Office, 1988), 471–472.

35. Chernow, Ron, "Where is Our Ferdinand Pecora?" *New York Times* (January 5, 2009).

36. Both quotations come from a paper by Pollock, Alex, "Reprivatizing Credit: Remarks at a Federalist Society Conference on 'The Financial Services Bailout'," Washington, DC, March 19, 2009.

37. Calomiris, Charles W., *United States Bank Deregulation in Historical Perspective* (London: Cambridge University Press, 2000), 200.

38. Hoover, 9.

39. Jones, Jesse and Angly, Edward, *Fifty Billion Dollars: My Thirteen Years at the RFC* (New York: Macmillan, 1951), 84.

40. Jones, 85–86.

41. Baruch, 250.

42. Todd, 15.

43. Rothbard, Murray, *America's Great Depression* (Auburn, AL: Mises Institute, 1963), 298.

44. Hoover, 214.

45. Schlesinger, Arthur, *The Politics of Upheaval, 1935–1936: The Age of Roosevelt* (New York: Houghton Mifflin Harcourt, 2003), 55–56.

46. Smith and Beasley, 341–343.

47. Todd, 23.

48. Schlesinger, Arthur, *The Coming of the New Deal, 1933–1935* (New York: Houghton Mifflin, 2003), 433.

49. Todd, 42.

50. Greider, William, *Secrets of the Temple* (New York: Simon and Schuster 1989), 310.

51. Meltzer, Allan H., *A History of the Federal Reserve: 1913–1951*, 465.

52. Todd, "The Federal Reserve Board and the Rise of the Corporate State, 1931–1934."

53. Meltzer, 478.

54. Greider, 308–309.

55. D'Arista, Jane, *The Evolution of U.S. Finance: Federal Reserve Monetary Policy, 1915–1935* (Armonk, NY: ME Sharpe, 1994), 192.

56. Bernanke, Benjamin, *Essays on the Great Depression* (Princeton, NJ: Princeton University Press, 2000), 253.

57. Manchester, William, *The Glory and the Dream: A Narrative History of America, 1932–1972* (New York: Bantam, 1984), 289–295.

58. Regarding FDR's advance knowledge of the Japanese strike on Pearl Harbor in 1941, see C.L. Sulzberger, "Foreign Affairs: The Dim-Witted Machines," *New York Times* (December 8, 1966).

59. Keynes, John Maynard, *How to Pay for the War: A Radical Plan for the Chancellor of the Exchequer* (New York: Macmillan, 1940).

60. Skidelsky, Robert, *Keynes: The Return of the Master* (New York: Public Affairs, 2009), 74.

61. Tansill, Charles Callan, *Back Door to War: Roosevelt Foreign Policy 1933–1941* (Westport, CT: Greenwood Press, 1975), 588.

62. Friedman, Milton and Schwartz, Anna, *A Monetary History of the United States, 1867–1960*, NBER (1965), 546.

63. Friedman and Schwartz, 553–555.

64. Friedman and Schwartz, 596.

65. Gardner, Richard, *Sterling-Dollar Diplomacy in Current Perspective* (New York: Columbia University Press, 1980), xxx.

66. Gardner, 195–245.

Chapter 7

1. Manchester, William, *The Glory and the Dream: A Narrative History of America, 1932–1972* (New York: Bantam, 1984), 349.

2. Myers, Margaret G., *A Financial History of the United States* (New York: Columbia University Press, 1970), 361.

3. Santoni, G.J., "The Employment Act of 1946: Some History Notes," Federal Reserve Bank of St. Louis, (November 1986).

4. "Opinion of the Week," *New York Times* (June 17, 1962).

5. Higgs, Robert, "Regime Uncertainty: Why the Great Depression Lasted So Long and Why Prosperity Resumed after the War," *The Independent Review*, Vol. I, No. 4 (Spring 1997), 561–590.

6. Higgs, 564.

7. Hetzel, Robert L. and Leach, Ralph F., "The Treasury-Fed Accord: A New Narrative Account," *Economic Quarterly* (Winter 2001), 33–34.

8. Hetzel and Leach, 35–37.

9. Hetzel and Leach, 50–54.

10. Hetzel and Leach.

11. Hazlitt, Henry, *Will Dollars Save the World?* (New York: D. Appleton Century Co., 1947).

12. Friedman, Milton and Schwartz, Anna, *A Monetary History of the United States, 1867–1960*, NBER (1965), 5.

13. Reinhart, Carmen, "This Time Is Different Chartbook: Country Histories on Debt, Default, and Financial Crises," NBER Working Paper 18815, March 2010, Figure 66c, 119.

14. Friedman, Benjamin, "Postwar Changes in the American Financial Markets," NBER Working Paper No. 458, March 1981, issued March 1981.

15. Leys, Simon, Letters, *The New York Review of Books*, September 29, 2011.

16. President Dwight D. Eisenhower Fairwell Address, January 17, 1961.

17. Morgan, Iwan, *Deficit Government: Taxing and Spending in Modern America* (Chicago: Ivan R. Dee, 1995), ix.

18. Taleb, Nassim, *The Black Swan: The Impact of the Highly Improbable* (New York: Random House, 2008).

19. Baldwin, Robert E., *The Changing Nature of U.S. Trade Policy Since WWII* (University of Chicago Press, 1984), 5–7.

20. Lake, David, *The International Political Economy of Trade*, Vol. I, (Cheltenham: Edward Elgar Publishing, 1993), 8–10.

21. The United States in World Affairs: The World Economy in 1951, Council on Foreign Relations, 225–229.

22. Higgins, Matthew, and Klitgaard, Thomas, "Viewing the Current Account Deficit as a Capital Inflow," Current Issues, Federal Reserve Bank of New York (December 1998), 4.

23. Barton, John H., Fisher, Bart S., and Malloy, Michael P., "Regulating International Investment," *International Trade and Economic Negotiation*, 6 (2006).

24. Hazlitt, Henry, *From Bretton Woods to World Inflation: A Study of Causes and Consequences* (Auburn, AL: Mises Institute, 2009), 7.

25. Bluestein, Paul, *The Chastening: Inside the Crisis that Rocked the Global Financial System, and Humbled the IMF* (New York: Basic Books, 2003), 16.

26. Jones, James R., "Why LBJ Bowed Out," *Los Angeles Times* (March 30, 2008).

27. Whalen, Richard J., *Catch the Falling Flag: A Republican's Challenge to His Party* (New York: Houghton Mifflin, 1972), 6.

28. Manchester, 1251–1252.

29. Yergin, Daniel and Stanislaw, Joseph, *The Commanding Heights* (New York: Simon & Schuster, 1997), 60–64.

30. North, Gary, "The Lesser of Two Evils Rarely Is," www.LewRockwell.com (June 8, 2007).

31. Sidey, Hugh, "The Economy: Nixon's Grand Design for Recovery," *Time* (August 30, 1971).

32. Whalen, 266.

33. Abrams, Burton A, "How Richard Nixon Pressured Arthur Burns: Evidence from the Nixon Tapes," *Journal of Economic Perspectives*, 20: 4 (Fall 2006): 177–88.

34. Hertzel, Robert L., *The Monetary Policy of the Federal Reserve: A History* (New York: Cambridge University Press, 2008).

35. Safire, William, *Before the Fall* (New York: Doubleday, 1975), 513–515.

36. Todd, Walker, "A History of International Lending," *Research in Financial Services Private and Public Policy*, Vol. 3. (Greenwich, CT: JAI Press, 1991), 203.

37. Gordon, David M., "Chickens Come Home to Roost: From Prosperity to Stagnation in the Postwar Economy," In *Understanding American Economic Decline*, Michael A. Bernstein and David E. Adler (Eds.) (London: Cambridge University Press, 1994), 54.

38. O'Driscoll, Gerald, "Restoring Credibility to International Lending," *CATO Journal*, Vol. 4, No. 1 (Spring/Summer 1984), 131.

39. Todd, 205.

40. Reinhart, Carmen, and Rogoff, Kenneth, *This Time Is Different: Eight Centuries of Financial Folly* (Princeton, NJ: Princeton University Press, 2009), 205.

41. Federal Reserve Bulletin, 1990, A64.

42. O'Driscoll.

43. "Interview with Paul A. Volcker In Conversation with Gary H. Stern," Federal Reserve Bank of Minneapolis, July 15, 2009.

Chapter 8

1. Bartlett, Bruce, "(More) Politics at the Fed? Greenspan Should Tighten A.S.A.P.—For His and the Country's Good," *NRO Financial*, April 28, 2004.

2. Silk, Leonard, "There's a Brighter Side; . . ." *New York Times,* September 18, 1974, 55.

3. Woodward, Bob, *The Maestro: Greenspan's Fed and the American Boom* (New York: Simon & Schuster, 2000), 35.

4. Grutsinger, Martin, "Ford WIN Buttons Remembered," The Associated Press, December 28, 2006.

5. Morgan, Iwan, *Taxing and Spending in Modern America* (London: Iwan Dee, 1995).

6. Mieczkowski, Yanek, "The Secrets of Gerald Ford's Success . . . 30 Years After He Became President It's Time to Consider What Made Him Tick," *History News Network*, George Mason University, August 2, 2004.

7. Reeves, Richard, "The City Politic: The Nationwide Search for Nelson Rockefeller," *New York Magazine*, September 2, 1974, 8.

8. Roesch, Susan R., "The FOMC During 1974: Monetary Policy During Economic Uncertainty," Federal Reserve Bank of St. Louis, April 1975, 2.

9. Interview with Paul Volcker, March 18, 2010.

10. Morgan, 127.

11. Anderson, Martin, *Revolution: The Reagan Legacy* (Stamford: Hoover Press, 1990), 69.

12. Berlin, Isaiah, *"Two Concepts of Liberty," an inaugural lecture delivered before the University of Oxford on 31 October 1958* (London: Clarendon Press, 1958).

13. Hoffman, Stanley, *Redeeming American Political Thought* (University of Chicago Press, 1998), 111.

14. Whalen, Christopher, "Do a Good Job: Interview with Senator Ernest Hollings," The Institutional Risk Analyst, May 3, 2010.

15. Carter, Jimmy, *Keeping Faith: Memoirs of a President* (Little Rock: University of Arkansas Press, 1995), 82.

16. Ebeling, Richard M., "Henry Hazlitt and the Failure of Keynesian Economics," *The Freeman,* November 2004, 17.

17. McFadden, Robert, "G. William Miller, 81, Former Top Economic Official, Dies," *New York Times,* March 20, 2006.

18. Whalen, Christopher, "Fed Chairmen and Presidents: Roundtable with Roger Kubarych and Richard Whalen," The Institutional Risk Analyst, October 30, 2008.

19. Morgan, 134.

20. Letter to Antoine Louis Claude Destutt de Tracy, 1820.

21. Whalen, "Fed Chairmen and Presidents."

22. Whalen, "Fed Chairmen and Presidents."

23. Mishkin, Frederic, "The Fed Must Avoid Volcker's Mistake on Inflation," *Financial Times*, September 14, 2022.

24. Friedman, Benjamin, "New Directions in the Relationship Between Public and Private Debt," *National Bureau of Economic Research*, Working Paper No. 2186 (March 1987).

25. Friedman, "New Directions in the Relationship Between Public and Private Debt."

26. Niskanen, William A. and Moore, Stephen, "*Supply-Side Tax Cuts and the Truth About the Reagan Economic Record*" (Washington: CATO Institute, October 22, 1996.

27. Samuelson, Paul, "Lessons from the Great Inflation: Paul Volcker and Ronald Reagan's Forgotten Miracle Created a Quarter Century of Prosperity—and a Dangerous Bubble of Complacency," *Reason Magazine*, January 2009.

28. See Whalen, Christopher, "Gone Fishing: E Gerald Corrigan and the Era of Managed Markets," *Herbert Gold Society*, 1993.

29. Volcker and Corrigan were close friends and liked to steal away for some fishing around the United States. Volcker told this author of a trip to Pocomoonshine Lake in Princeton, Maine, which is about 10 miles south of Grand Lake Stream.

30. Robinson, Kenneth J., *The Savings & Loan Crisis*, Federal Reserve Board, November 23, 2013.

31. Tankus, Nathan, "Revealed: The Federal Reserve's Secret 1973 Plan to Bailout the Saving & Loan Industry That Very Nearly Happened," *Substack*, September 24, 2024.

32. Whalen, Christopher, "Fed's Secretive Decisions Need 'Sunshine'," *The Christian Science Monitor*, October 28, 1993.

33. Skidmore, Paul, "Volcker: Blame S&Ls, not Fed, for Crisis," *Tampa Bay Times*, October 4, 1990.

34. Todd, Walker, "Latin America, Asia & Russia: Have the Lessons Been Learned?", *Research in Financial Services* (Stamford, CT: JAI Press, 1999), 116–117.

35. Then California governor Ronald Reagan had met with Mexican president Jose Lopez Portillo before the election and was personally aware of the importance of the U.S.–Mexico relationship.

36. Whalen, Christopher, "Going South," *The Nation*, January 23, 1995.

37. Isaac, William, *Senseless Panic: How Washington Failed America* (Hoboken, NJ: John Wiley and Sons, 2010), 30–31.

38. Woodward.

39. Whalen, "Fed Chairmen and Presidents."

40. Whalen, "Fed Chairmen and Presidents."

41. Mayer, Martin, *Nightmare on Wall Street: Salomon Brothers and the Corruption of the Marketplace* (New York: Simon & Schuster, 1993). Quotation taken from book draft in Whalen, "Gone Fishing."

42. "Volcker Won the War against Inflation, but Dollar Again Weak," *Los Angeles Times,* June 7, 1987.

43. Einhorn, David, "Easy Money, Hard Truths," *New York Times,* May 26, 2010.

44. Reinhart, Carmen, "This Time Is Different Chartbook: Country Histories on Debt, Default, and Financial Crises," NBER Working Paper 18815 (March 2010), 119.

45. Whalen, Christopher, "So What About the Real Economy? Interview with Credit Risk Monitor," The Institutional Risk Analyst, October 26, 2009.

46. Warren, Elizabeth and Tyagi, Amelia, *The Two Income Trap* (New York: Basic Books, 2003).

47. Whalen, Christopher, "GSE Nation: Interview with Robert Feinberg," The Institutional Risk Analyst, March 17, 2008.

48. Interview with Josh Rosner, June 2010.

49. Interview with Josh Rosner.

50. White, Simon, "Dollar Has No Chance in Lender-of-First-Resort World: MacroScope," *Bloomberg,* August 15, 2024.

51. Woodward, 95.

Chapter 9

1. Interview: Robert Brusca on the Federal Open Market Committee, The Institutional Risk Analyst, June 10, 2024.

2. See Whalen, Riggi, and Scott, "Large & Small Bank Performance During the Financial Crisis," *Kroll Bond Rating Agency,* April 2015.

3. A policy termed "quantitative easing" (量的緩和, ryōteki kanwa, from 量的 "quantitative" + 緩和 "easing") was first used by the Bank of Japan to fight domestic deflation in the early 2000s.

4. Written comments to the author, July 2024.

5. Fisher, Irving, "The Debt Deflation Theory of Great Depressions," *Economica* (1933).

6. Bernanke, Ben and James, Harold, "The Gold Standard, Deflation, and Financial Crisis in the Great Depression: An International Comparison," NBER (1991).

7. Feldkamp, Fred and Whalen, Christopher, *Financial Stability: Fraud, Confidence & the Wealth of Nations* (Hoboken, NJ: John Wiley & Sons, 2017).

8. "Chronology of Fed's Quantitative Easing & Tightening," Yardeni Research.

9. Eisenbeis, Bob, "Seeking Normal at the Fed," The Institutional Risk Analyst, December 10, 2017.

10. Bernanke, Ben, "The Crisis and the Policy Response," Federal Reserve Board of Governors, January 13, 2009.

11. Selgin, George, "Frozen Money Markets & Competing with the Fed in Payments," The Institutional Risk Analyst, December 16, 2019.

12. Selgin, George, "Floored: How a Misguided Fed Experiment Deepened and Prolonged the Great Recession," Cato Institute, 2018, 7–10.

13. Boccia, Romina, "Book Review: The Menace of Fiscal QE," Cato Institute (2023).

14. Federal Reserve Bank of New York, "Large-Scale Asset Purchase," https:// www.newyorkfed.org/markets/programs-archive/large-scale-asset-purchases.

15. Siegle, Jeremy, "Janet Yellen: What the Fed Has Learned Since the Financial Crisis," Wharton School of Business, March 20, 2018.

16. Remarks by Claudio Borio, head of the Monetary and Economic Department of the BIS, at the Netherlands Bank Workshop, "Beyond Unconventional Policy: Implications for Central Banks' Operational Frameworks," March 10, 2023.

17. Interview with Jerome Powell, *PBS Newshour* with Judy Woodruff, October 3, 2018.

18. See Gorton, Gary B., Laarits, Toomas, and Metrick, Andrew, "The Run on Repo and the Fed's Response" Yale ICF Working Paper No. 2018-14 (June 2020).

19. Johnson, Simon, "Arrogance & Authority," Project Syndicate, April 26, 2011

20. Sri-Kumar, Komal, "Fed: Responsible or Play Cheerleader?," *Substack*, August 10, 2024.

21. Nelson, Bill, "The Fed is Stuck on the Floor: Here's How It Can Get Up," Bank Policy Institute, January 11, 2022.

22. See GNMA Mod Dur Index (LGNMMD Index), *Bloomberg Markets* (March 2023).

23. Palim, Mark and Zimmerman, Rachel, "'Lock-in Effect' Not the Only Reason for Housing Supply Woes," Fannie Mae, October 2023.

24. Alpert, Dan, "The Fed Has Put Our Housing Market in Jeopardy,' *New York Times*, November 14, 2023.

25. Malz, Allan M., Schaumburg, Ernst, Shimonov, Roman, et al., "Convexity Event Risks in a Rising Interest Rate Environment," Federal Reserve Bank of New York, March 24, 2014.

26. Salmon, Felix, "'Inflation' doesn't mean what it used to," *Axios*, May 24, 2024.

27. Patterson, Robert and Kearns Kevin, "The Twin Deficits Risk the American Way of Life," *The American Conservative*, March 16, 2024.

28. Tooze, Adam, "2020 Was Almost Worse Than 2008," *Atlantic*, September 6, 2021.

29. Menand, Lev and Younger, Joshua, "Money and the Public Debt: Treasury Market Liquidity as a Legal Phenomenon," Columbia Law School (2023).

30. Menand and Younger, 225.

31. Wachtel, Paul and Blejer, Mario, "A Fresh Look at Central Bank Independence," *CATO Journal* (Winter 2020).

32. Brusca interview (2024).

33. Tankus, Nathan, "Paul Volcker's Secret December 1973 Phone Call to Fed Chairman Arthur Burns Revealed," *Notes on the Crisis*, January 16, 2024.

34. Memo from Arthur L. Broida, Board of Governors, December 3, 1973.

35. Final Version of the Second Report on the Further Provision Necessary for Establishing Public Credit (Report on a National Bank), U.S. Treasury, December 1790.

36. Remarks by Secretary of the Treasury Janet L. Yellen on 2024 Filing Season Goals, "How Inflation Reduction Act Is Continuing to Deliver Improvements for Taxpayers," November 7, 2023.

37. Burke, Karen C. and McCouch, Grayson M.P., "Sham Partnerships and Equivocal Transactions," *American Lawyer*, 69 Tax Law, 625 (2016).

38. De, Nikhilesh, "The US Crypto Enforcement Framework Is a Warning to International Exchanges," *Coindesk*, September 14, 2021.

Chapter 10

1. Hoffer, Eric, "The Negro Revolution," in *The Temper of Our Time* (Cutchogue, NY: Buccaneer Books, 1967).

2. Editors of Encyclopaedia Britannica. "Herbert David Croly." *Encyclopedia Britannica*, May 13, 2024. https://www.britannica.com/biography/Herbert-David-Croly.

3. Croly, Herber "The Promise of American Life," *Cosimo, Inc* (2005), 400.

4. Siegle, Fred, *The Revolt Against the Masses* (New York: Encounter Books, 2013).

5. Pinto, Ed and Peter, Tobias, "Kamala Harris's Housing Plan Would Be Worse Than Doing Nothing," *Newsweek*, September 4, 2024.

6. Schrager, Allison, "Economic policy gets weird," *Substack*, September 16, 2024.

7. As a matter of geological history, Earth has been warming for about 11,000 years, when Maine was covered by a mile of ice.

8. Sherk, James, "F.D.R. Warned Us About Public Sector Unions," *The New York Times*, July 23, 2014.

9. Grant, James, *Money of the Mind* (New York: Macmillan, 1992), 5.

10. Conversation with William Dunkelberg, June 2010.

11. The Dollar Glut, International Monetary Fund, https://www.imf.org/external/np/exr/center/mm/eng/mm_sc_03.htm.

12. Davis, L.J., "Bad Money," *Signet*, 1982, 332.

13. Rickards, James, "The Treasury Should Buy Gold," The Institutional Risk Analyst, October 4, 2024.

14. Rickards, James, *Money GPT: AI and the Threat to the Global Economy* (New York: Portfolio Penguin. 2024).

15. "Talking the Economy: Alex Pollock, Bruce Bartlett and Josh Rosner," The Institutional Risk Analyst, June 21, 2010.

16. Evans-Pritchard, Ambrose, "Last Refuge Against Currency Current," *Sydney Morning Herald*, September 28, 2010.

17. Interview with David Kotok.

18. Interview with Vincent Reinhart, May 29, 2010.

19. Maidment, Paul, "R.I.P Long Bond," *Forbes*, June 6, 2013.

20. Remarks by Terrence J Checki, executive vice president of the Emerging Markets and International Affairs Group of the Federal Reserve Bank of New York, at the IIF Annual Meeting of Latin America Chief Executives, Santiago, Chile, March 6, 2013.

21. White, Simon, "Fed Rate Cuts Won't Move the Dial on Ballooning Fiscal Interest Bill," *Bloomberg*, August 29, 2024.

22. Cochrane, John, "Monetary Ignorance, Monetary Transmission, and a Great Time for Macroeconomics," *Substack*, September 7, 2024.

23. Cochrane.

24. Menand, Lev and Younger, Joshua, "Money and the Public Debt: Treasury Market Liquidity as a Legal Phenomenon," *Columbia Business Law Review*, Vol. 2023, No. 1 (2023).

25. Boocker, Sam and Wessel, David, "The Changing Role of the US Dollar," Brookings Institution, August 23, 2024.

26. Borio, Claudio, McCauley, Robert N., and McGuire, Patrick, "Dollar Debt in FX Swaps and Forwards: Huge, Missing and Growing" *BIS Quarterly Review*, December 2022.

27. Debt Intolerance Carmen M. Reinhart, Kenneth S. Rogoff, and Miguel A. Savastano NBER Working Paper No. 9908 August 2003.

28. Richter, Wolf, "Status of the US Dollar as Global Reserve Currency: Share Drops to Lowest since 1995. Central Banks Diversify to "Nontraditional" Currencies and Gold," Wolf Street, September 26, 2024.

29. Todd, Walker, "Triffin's Dilemma, Reserve Currencies, and Gold," American Institute for Economic Research (December 31, 2008).

30. Wood, Gordon S., "American Dream Money," *New York Review of Books*, November 10, 2011.

31. Setser, Brad, "'We hate you guys ... but there is nothing much we can do,' Follow the Money," Council on Foreign Relations (2009).

32. The author had the pleasure to meet Professor Dyson in 2013 as a member of the Princeton Astronomy Club.

33. Rickards, *Money GPT: AI and the Threat to the Global Economy*.

Selected References

Adams, J.T. (1932). *The Epic of America*. New York: Little Brown.

Barron, C.W. (1915). *The Audacious War*. New York: Houghton Mifflin Co.

Baruch, B. (1957). *The Public Years*. New York: Holt.

Bernard, H. (2002). *Independent Man: The Life of James Couzens*. Detroit, MI: Wayne State University Press.

Bernanke, Ben and James, Harold. "The Gold Standard, Deflation, and Financial Crisis in the Great Depression: An International Comparison," NBER (1991).

Brands, H.W. (2003). *The Age of Gold: The California Gold Rush and the New American dream*. New York: Anchor Books

Byrd, R.C. (1988). *The Senate, 1789–1989*. Washington, DC: U.S. Government Printing Office.

Calder, L. (1999). *Financing the American Dream: A Cultural History of Consumer Credit*. Princeton, NJ: Princeton University Press,

Catteral, R.C.H. (1903). *The Second Bank of the United States*. Chicago: The University of Chicago Press.

Chernow, R. (1990). *The House of Morgan: An American Banking Dynasty and the Rise of Modern Finance*. New York: Grove Press.

Chernow, R. (2004). *Alexander Hamilton*. New York: Penguin Books.

Clinton, G. (1933). *The Mirrors of Wall Street*. New York: Putnam & Sons.

Dubois, W.E.B. (1954). *The Suppression of the African Slave Trade in the United States of America, 1638–1870*. New York: Social Science Press.

Dunbar, W.F. and May, G. (1995) *Michigan: A History of the Wolverine State*. Grand Rapids, MI: Erdmans Publishing.

Federal Reserve Bank of San Francisco (1995). "1995 Annual Report: A Brief History of Our Nation's Paper Money."

Foulke, R.A. (1941). *The Sinews of American Commerce.* New York: Dunn & Bradstreet.

Friedman, M. and Schwartz, A. (1965). *A Monetary History of the United States, 1867–1960.* New York: National Bureau of Economic Research.

Galbraith, J.K. (1997). *The Great Crash 1929.* New York: Houghton Mifflin.

Goodwyn, L. (1978). *The Populist Moment: A Short History of the Agrarian Revolt in America.* London: Oxford University Press.

Graham, B. and Dodd, D. (1934). *Securities Analysis.* New York: McGraw Hill.

Grant, J. (1992). *Money on the Mind.* New York: Macmillan.

Grinath, A., Wallis, J., and Sylla, R. (March 1997). "Debt, Default and Revenue Structure: The American State Debt Crisis in the Early 1840s," Historical Paper 97, National Bureau of Economic Research.

Hayek, F.A. (1990). *Denationalisation of Money—The Argument Refined: An Analysis of the Theory and Practice of Concurrent Currencies.* 3rd ed. London: Institute of Economic Affairs.

Higgs, R. (February 1995). "How FDR Made the Depression Worse," *The Free Market,* Ludwig von Mises Institute.

Hixon, W.F., (1993). *Triumph of the Bankers: Money and Banking in the Eighteenth and Nineteenth Centuries.* Westport, CT: Praeger Publishers.

Homer, S. and Sylla, R. (1963). *A History of Interest Rates.* New Brunswick, NJ: Rutgers University Press.

Hoover, H. (1952). *The Great Depression.* New York: Macmillan.

Hornberger, J.G., (November 2000). "Legal Tender and the Civil War," *Freedom Daily,* Future of Freedom Foundation.

Jackson, A. (1832). "Veto Message Regarding the Bank of the United States," Yale Law School.

James, M. (1938). *The Life of Andrew Jackson.* Camden, NJ: Haddon Craftsmen.

Janeway, E. (1951). *The Struggle for Survival.* New York: Weybright & Talley.

Jones, J. and Angly, E. (1951). *Fifty Billion Dollars: My Thirteen Years at the RFC.* New York: Macmillan.

Josephson, M. (1934). *The Robber Barons.* New York: Harcourt Brace & Co.

Kamensky, J. (2008). *The Exchange Artist: A Tale of High-Flying Speculation and America's First Banking Collapse.* New York: Viking Penguin.

Keynes, J.M. (June 1933). "National Self-Sufficiency," *The Yale Review.*

Lippmann, W. (1937) *The Good Society.* Boston: Little Brown & Co.

McCullough, D. (2001) *John Adams.* New York: Simon & Schuster

McDill, K.M. and Sheehan, K.P. (2006). "Sources of Historical Banking Panics: A Markov Switching Approach." FDIC Working Paper 2006-01.

Meltzer, A.H. (2003). *A History of the Federal Reserve: 1913–1951.* Chicago: University of Chicago Press.

Menand, L. and Younger, J. (2023). "Money and the Public Debt: Treasury Market Liquidity as a Legal Phenomenon," *Columbia Business Law Review* Vol. 2023, No. 1. https://doi.org/10.52214/cblr.v2023i1.11900.

Minton, B. and Stuart, J. (1940). *The Fat Years and the Lean.* New York: International Publishers.

Miron, J.A. (February 1990). *The Founding of the Fed and the Destabilization of the Post-1914 Economy.* New York: National Bureau of Economic Research.

Myers, M.G. (1970). *A Financial History of the United States.* New York: Columbia University Press.

Nevins, A and Comanger, H.S. (1996) *A Short History of the United States.* New York: Knopf.

Phillips, K. (2009). *The Cousins' War.* New York: Basic Books.

Pollock, A. (2009). "Reprivatizing Credit: Remarks at a Federalist Society Conference on 'the Financial Services Bailout'." Washington, DC. March 19.

Pound, A. and Morse, S. (1930). *They Told Barron: The Notes of Clarence W. Barron.* New York: Harper Brothers.

Powell, J. (2003). *FDR's Folly: How Roosevelt and His New Deal Prolonged the Great Depression.* New York: Three Rivers Press.

Reinhart, C. and Rogoff, K. (2009). *This Time is Different: Eight Centuries of Financial Folly.* Princeton, NJ: Princeton University Press.

Roosevelt, T. (2008). *Autobiography of Theodore Roosevelt.* Blacksburg, VA: Wilder Publications.

Rothbard, M. (1994). *The Case Against the Fed.* Auburn, AL: The Ludwig von Mises Institute.

Rothbard, M. (2002). *A History of Money and Banking in the United States.* Auburn, AL: Ludwig von Mises Institute.

Safire, W. (1975). *Before the Fall.* New York: Doubleday.

Schlesinger, A. (2003). *The Politics of Upheaval, 1935–1936: The Age of Roosevelt.* New York: Houghton Mifflin Harcourt.

Schweikart, L. (1987). *Banking in the American South from the Age of Jackson to Reconstruction.* Baton Rouge, LA: Louisiana State University Press.

Smith, R., and Beasley, N. (1970). *Carter Glass.* New York: Ayer Publishing.

Sowell, T. (2007). *A Conflict of Visions: Ideological Origins of Political Struggles.* New York: Basic Books.

Sparling, E. (1930). *Mystery Men of Wall Street: The Power Behind the Market.* New York: Greenberg.

Steel, R. (1980). *Walter Lippmann and the American century.* New York: Little Brown.

Swanberg, W.A. (1960). *Jim Fisk: The Career of an Improbable Rascal.* New York: Longmans.

Tansil, C.C. (1938). *America Goes to War.* Boston: Little Brown and Co.

Taylor, G. (1949). *Jackson Versus Biddle: The Struggle over the Second Bank of the United States.* Boston: CD Heath.

The Unofficial Observer. (1934). *The New Dealers,* New York: Simon and Schuster.

Timberlake, R.H., (1978). *Monetary Policy in the United States: An Intellectual and Institutional History.* Chicago: University of Chicago Press.

Todd, W.F. (1991). "A History of International Lending." *Research in Financial Services, Private and Public Policy* Elsevier, ISSN 1052-7788, ZDB-ID 1048797-9. Vol. 3 (1991), 201–289.

Todd, W.F. (1993). "FDICIA's Emergency Liquidity Provisions." Federal Reserve Bank of Cleveland *Economic Review* (3rd quarter).

Todd, W.F. (1995). *The Federal Reserve Board and the Rise of the Corporate State, 1931–1934,*" *Economic Education Bulletin*, American Institute for Economic Research

Warburg, P.M. (1930). *The Federal Reserve System, Its Origins and Growth: Reflections and Recollections.* Vol. II. New York: The Macmillan Company.

Warren, E. (2004) *The Two Income Trap.* New York: Basic Books.

Whalen, R.J. (1964) *The Founding Father: The Story of Joseph P. Kennedy.* New York: New American Library.

Whalen, R.J. (1972). *Catch the Falling Flag: A Republican's Challenge to His Party.* New York: Houghton Mifflin.

Wilkeson, S. (1865). *How Our National Debt May Be a National Blessing.* Philadelphia: M'Laughlin Brothers Printers.

Woodward, B. (2000). *The Maestro: Greenspan's Fed and the American Boom.* New York: Simon & Schuster.

Acknowledgments

This book is the synthesis of several decades of conversations and research on the topic of politics and finance. The dialogue began with my parents, Richard and Joan Whalen, who taught their children to think and write independently. I especially want to thank my father and fellow writer Richard J. Whalen (1934–2023) for his suggestions regarding the first edition of this book, economics and politics, and about life over the past half century. And he taught me the most useful lesson for any writer, that the only free press is the one you own.

Many other friends and colleagues contributed to this book 15 years ago. In 2010, only two years after the collapse of the U.S. financial system, this book was written in some haste at the behest of my friend David Kotok. This second edition provides an opportunity to reconsider some of the judgments made during those hectic and frightening times even as Americans struggle with even greater challenges ahead.

As this second edition is finalized, Donald J. Trump has won a second term in the White House, the U.S. banking system and central bank have been rendered insolvent by the large increases in interest rates since 2021, and America arguably stands on the threshold of hyperinflation and fiscal crisis. Yet the lesson of history is that these ominous portends are nothing new. The means whereby America achieved global economic hegemony lies in benevolence and, yes, inflation rather than hard money and prudence. Lincoln financed the war to end slavery with Treasury debt known as "greenbacks." The fiat dollars borrowed and spent to win two World Wars and the Cold War led to the special role of the dollar as the world's preferred means of exchange.

F.A. Hayek is right about democracy being antithetical to hard money, but the American experience suggests that may not be such a bad thing. By living beyond our means, generations of Americans have accumulated debts and obligations that may seem daunting, but the economic benefit of the democratic free market system that is the foundation of American prosperity is greater and is shared by the world. Today President Donald Trump asks European nations to pay their fair share of defense costs. Will a future president ask the world to share the cost of operating the dollar as the primary reserve currency? As America progresses through the twenty-first century, the role of the dollar will evolve along with the global political economy, probably into a more equitable distribution of costs and benefits. Yet in the fullness of time and with a good bit of inflation, America's future earnings capacity dwarfs our current obligations and will provide a solution to all of today's seemingly insurmountable challenges.

Finally, let me thank the editorial and production staff of Wiley Global for helping me create this new and timely second edition of Inflated.

Christopher Whalen
February 2025
Ad majorem Dei gloriam

About the Author

Richard Christopher Whalen is an investment banker and author who lives in the Hudson Valley of New York. He founded Whalen Global Advisors LLC in 2017 and focuses on the banking, mortgage finance, and fintech sectors. Christopher is a contributing editor at National Mortgage News.

Chris has worked as an author, financial professional, and journalist in Washington, New York, and London for the past four decades. After graduating from Villanova University in 1981 with a BA in History, he worked for the House Republican Conference Committee under Rep. Jack Kemp (R-NY). In 1993, Chris was the first journalist to report on the discovery by Chairman Henry B. Gonzalez (D-TX) of the then-secret minutes of the Federal Open Market Committee concealed by Federal Reserve Board Chairman Alan Greenspan.

From 2014 through 2017, Christopher was Senior Managing Director and Head of Research at Kroll Bond Rating Agency, where he was responsible for ratings by the Financial Institutions and Corporate Ratings Groups. He was a principal of Institutional Risk Analytics from 2003–2013. Chris also worked at the Federal Reserve Bank of New York, Bear, Stearns & Co., Prudential Securities, Tangent Capital Partners, and Carrington Mortgage Holdings.

Christopher is the author of three other books, including *Ford Men: From Inspiration to Enterprise* (2017), a study of Ford Motor Co and the Ford family published by Laissez Faire Books; *Financial Stability: Fraud, Confidence & the Wealth of Nations* (2014), co-authored with Frederick Feldkamp and published by John Wiley & Sons; and *Inflated: How Money and Debt Built the American Dream* (2010), also published by John Wiley & Sons.

Christopher edits The Institutional Risk Analyst newsletter and contributes to other publications and forums. He has published a number of research papers, and has testified before Congress, the Securities and Exchange Commission, and Federal Deposit Insurance Corporation. Christopher is active on social media such as X and LinkedIn under "rcwhalen," and appears frequently in the media. Chris is a member of The Lotos Club of New York.

Index